CHANGING PLANES: A STRATEGIC MANAGEMENT PERSPECTIVE
ON AN INDUSTRY IN TRANSITION

VOLUME TWO: STRATEGIC CHOICE, IMPLEMENTATION, AND
           OUTCOME

In memory of Vera Holloway

Changing Planes: A Strategic Management Perspective on an Industry in Transition

Volume Two: Strategic Choice, Implementation, and Outcome

STEPHEN HOLLOWAY

Routledge
Taylor & Francis Group

LONDON AND NEW YORK

First published 1998 by Ashgate Publishing

Reissued 2018 by Routledge
2 Park Square, Milton Park, Abingdon, Oxon, OX14 4RN
711 Third Avenue, New York, NY 10017, USA

Routledge is an imprint of the Taylor & Francis Group, an informa business

Publisher's Note
The publisher has gone to great lengths to ensure the quality of this reprint but points out that some imperfections in the original copies may be apparent.

Disclaimer
The publisher has made every effort to trace copyright holders and welcomes correspondence from those they have been unable to contact.

A Library of Congress record exists under LC control number: 97044572

ISBN 13: 978-1-138-61582-3 (hbk)
ISBN 13: 978-1-138-61585-4 (pbk)
ISBN 13: 978-0-429-46280-1 (ebk)

Contents

Figures and tables

Acknowledgements

As was equally true of my last Ashgate publication - *Straight and Level: Practical Airline Economics* - this project has benefitted greatly from the helpful support of publisher John Hindley. Valerie Polding and the Ashgate editorial team also deserve my thanks, once again. Richard Hall's input into the graphics was invaluable and always timely. Finally, I am immeasurably grateful to my wife, whose optimism that the work would ultimately see the light of day was not something I always shared throughout its long gestation.

Abbreviations

ABC	advance booking charter
ACMI	aircraft, crew, maintenance, and insurance
AD	airworthiness directive
ADS	automatic dependent surveillance
AOG	aircraft on ground (i.e. unserviceable)
APALS	Autonomous Precision Approach and Landing System
APU	auxiliary power unit
ASA	air services agreement
ASK	available seat-kilometre
ASM	available seat-mile
ATAG	Air Transport Action Group
ATC	air traffic control
ATM	air traffic management
ATN	Aeronautical Telecommunications Network
BAR	board of airline representatives
CAA	Civil Aviation Authority (UK)
CAB	Civil Aeronautics Board (USA)
CAEP	Committee on Aviation Environmental Protection
CEO	chief executive officer
CNS	communications, navigation, and surveillance
CRS	computer(ized) reservations system
CSF	critical success factor
CVR	cockpit voice recorder
DGPS	differential GPS
DOJ	Department of Justice (USA)
DOT	Department of Transportation (USA)
EATCHIP	European Air Traffic Control Harmonization and Integration Programme
EC	European Commission
ECAC	European Civil Aviation Conference
EDI	electronic data interchange

EGPWS	enhanced ground proximity warning system
EIS	executive information system
ER	extended range
ERA	European Regions (formerly Regional) Airlines Association
ETOPS	extended-range twin-engined operations
EU	European Union
EUATMS	The European Unified ATM System
EVS	enhanced vision system
FAA	Federal Aviation Administration (USA)
FANS	Future Air Navigation System
FAR	Federal Aviation Regulations
FDR	flight data recorder
FFP	frequent flyer programme
FLIR	forward-looking infrared radar
GATS	General Agreement on Trade in Services
GATT	General Agreement on Tariffs and Trade
GDP	gross domestic product
GNP	gross national product
GPS	Global Positioning System
GSA	general sales agent
HDD	head-down display
HGS	head-up guidance system
HHI	Herfindahl-Hirschman Index
HRM	human resource management
HSCT	high-speed civil transport
HUD	head-up display
IASA	International Aviation Safety Assessment Program (USA)
IATA	International Air Transport Association
ICAO	International Civil Aviation Organization
IFE	inflight entertainment
ILS	instrument landing system
IMF	International Monetary Fund
INS	inertial navigation system
IO	industrial organization (school of economics)
IOS	inter-organization system
IS	information system(s)
IT	information technology
ITC	inclusive tour charter
JAA	Joint Aviation Authorities
LRU	line replaceable unit
MFN	most favoured nation
MIP	market investor principle
MLS	microwave landing system
MMWR	millimetre wave radar
MOU	memorandum of understanding
MRO	maintenance, repair, and overhaul

MTOW	maximum take-off weight
NAFTA	North American Free Trade Agreement
NLA	new large aircraft
NPRM	notice of proposed rule-making (USA)
OD	organization development
OECD	Organisation for Economic Co-operation and Development
OEM	original equipment manufacturer
PHARES	Programme for Harmonized Air Traffic Management Research in Eurocontrol
PNR	passenger name record
QFD	quality function deployment
RAA	Regional Airlines Association (USA)
RNAV	area navigation
RNP	required navigational performance
ROI	return on investment
RPK	revenue passenger-kilometre
RPM	revenue passenger-mile
RTK	revenue tonne-kilometre
SARATA	Southern African Regional Air Transport Authority
SSR	secondary surveillance radar
SST	supersonic transport
SVS	synthetic vision system
SWOT	strengths, weaknesses, opportunities, and threats
TACO	travel agency commission override
TCAS	traffic alert and collision avoidance system
TETN	Trans-European Transport Network
TGV	train à grande vitesse
TQM	total quality management
VFR	visiting friends and relations
VLCT	very large commercial transport
VMC	visual meteorological conditions
WTO	World Trade Organization
YMS	yield management system

Preface

Transition defined

The airline industry has always been dynamic, innovative, and challenging. Two things are now different, however. The first is that whereas the dynamism, innovations, and challenges have in the past tended to arise on the production side of the business, a torrent of change on the commercial side is being unleashed by regulatory liberalization. As a result, market and financial disciplines are gaining in importance relative to political disciplines. Second, the magnitude and rate of change are greater than anything previously encountered in the industry.[1]

This book is concerned with two distinct yet related transitions. The first is general, potentially affecting the strategic management of all types of company - notably, but not exclusively, in North America, Europe, Latin America, and parts of Asia. It is a transition to a new paradigm of strategic management.

According to the old paradigm, the task of strategic managers was to:

- predict what lay ahead;
- select strategies capable of 'fitting' the organization to its future environments;
- design organizational structures consistent with the chosen strategies and able as far as possible to harmonize human behaviour in support of those strategies;
- monitor and control outcomes, making adjustments in response to historical performance data fed upwards after distillation by middle management; and
- manage complexity, using the past as a guide to the future.

Watchwords were 'command' and 'control'.

The new paradigm sees the role of strategic managers as:

- channelling effort in support of generalized corporate purposes, guided by a unifying vision and sense of mission;
- releasing the creative energies of people close to the action, using corporate culture as an 'invisible hand';
- accepting that strategy is something which emerges from 'below' as well as being imposed from 'above';
- focusing on processes (e.g. **how** to sell effectively and efficiently to a targeted segment) rather than structures (e.g. **who** should be doing the selling), and on capabilities (e.g. network design and scheduling) rather than assets (e.g. aircraft ownership); and
- assembling the capabilities (i.e. skills and resources) required to respond flexibly and creatively to threats and opportunities emerging from complex and volatile environments that no longer support extrapolation or confident prediction.

Watchwords are 'culture' and 'nurture'.

This transition does not imply the redundancy of structures and controls. What it does entail is a shift in the emphasis of strategic management. Accumulation, release, and exploitation of knowledge are becoming the keys to success. People hold these keys; corporate culture and values are increasingly important determinants of how they are used.

The second transition with which this book concerns itself is the changing nature of strategic management in the growing number of airlines participating in liberalized and increasingly competitive markets.[2] The linkage between this and the more general changes discussed above is that the move from government tutelage to market disciplines is requiring affected airlines to adopt many of the new approaches to strategic management being pioneered in other industrial settings.

There was a time when environments were relatively benign, extrapolations were reasonably safe forecasting tools, quantum jumps in airframe and engine technology would come along regularly to drive down real unit costs, and the weight of government intervention offered little scope for commercial creativity. For perfectly rational reasons, strategic management in the airline industry therefore tended historically to involve little more than extrapolating demand into a relatively stable future and ensuring that resources - particularly aircraft - were available to meet that demand. Uncertainty, dynamism, and excitement affected the technological side of the business more than the commercial side. Strategic management and strategic planning were largely synonymous, and the process was primarily operations-led.

Chapter 1 of Volume One distinguished between strategic planning and other approaches to strategic management. It showed that the strategic planning appropriate to stable, predictable, government-controlled environments needs to make way for a more flexible approach to strategic management when environments become unstable, unpredictable, and more competitive. Airline activities now have to be managed rather than simply planned. This does not mean that the new realities exclude a need for planning: detailed operational planning is obviously essential in a business as inherently complex as the airline industry. What is happening is that turbulent environments make commercial activities less likely to yield planned outcomes. Operational activities now have to be planned as far as possible to fit flexibly with constantly changing commercial requirements rather than vice versa, and the two together must be managed as one. Successful airlines will be those able to design service-price offers that are more attractive to targeted customers than are competing offers, and able to deliver services as designed at a cost that allows profits to be made. This is the essence of the transition facing today's global airline industry.

An industry's attractiveness as a target for investment is largely dictated by the rules which govern its competitive environment. Strategy grows from a thorough understanding of these rules. Particularly where a company has to compete for investment, the ultimate aim of its strategies should be to cope with the rules and - if possible - change them to its own advantage.[3] Governments have historically been the rule-setters in most air transport markets, and in many they remain the fundamental players. Sometimes the rules have been to the advantage of individual airlines and sometimes they have not. Most airlines have over time developed 'coping' mechanisms which turn to their advantage the regulations imposed on them by government stakeholders. These coping mechanisms are not necessarily appropriate in competitive environments where rules are now being established to a greater extent by market forces than by regulators. Some airlines are much further advanced than others in adapting to the changing balance between regulatory and commercial imperatives which is shaping the industry's transition. Some are already too far behind to survive. In a few cases, newcomers from outside the industry will identify and seize emerging opportunities not recognized by existing players.

The two volumes of the book examine how the rules of the game are changing in many parts of the world, and how airlines are responding with new approaches to strategic management which draw on recent developments in the field. This is where the two transitions referred to above meet and merge.

Objectives and scope of the book

The present volume is the second in a two-volume book. The book as a whole has two primary objectives running through both volumes.

- To identify the most important changes currently taking place within and around the airline industry, to look at why they are happening, and to examine their impact on airline management. Not all the changes discussed affect every airline, but all affect some and some affect all.

• To set into a long-term, strategic context the day-to-day implementation issues which necessarily preoccupy airline managers and which can sometimes obscure broader perspectives on the industry's current transitional phase.

To achieve these objectives, and to help bring order to material drawn from a wide range of disciplines and sources, the book uses the classical strategic management process as a framework. **Chapter 1** in the first volume describes precisely what is meant by 'strategy' and 'strategic management', compares the classical (or 'rational') approach with alternative models, and justifies choice of the classical approach as a framework for the book. The main body of text is then divided into five parts, which broadly follow the stages of classical strategic management; Volume One contains the first two of these parts, and the other three are in the present volume.

At each stage, relevant aspects of strategic management and recent developments in the discipline are explained and then used as 'lenses' through which to examine changes taking place in and around the airline industry. Although the two volumes are best considered as constituent parts of a single work, they are nonetheless self-contained in order to allow them to be purchased separately. The first volume focuses on situation analysis (i.e. analysis of airlines' changing external and internal environments), whilst the second builds on this by looking at the choice, implementation, and outcome of strategy.

Volume One

Part One: External Analysis

The first part of Volume One examines changes in the key external environments within which airlines must function.

Chapter 2 defines the nature and scope of external analysis, introduces the concept of environmental scanning, and places into context the growing complexity and turbulence found in most airlines' external environments.

Chapters 3 to 5 examine the sociopolitical environment. Chapter 3 looks in depth at changes taking place in domestic and international regulatory regimes; in the international arena, air traffic freedoms and the development of bilateral air services agreements are considered, as are the emergence of open skies agreements and alternatives to the dominant regulatory regime such as multilateralism and plurilateralism. The focus of chapter 4 is the changing interpretation and use of competition laws, notably in the United States and the European Union, and the uncertainties these raise for airlines. Chapter 5 looks at how stakeholders impose on airlines certain of their expectations with regard to social responsibility; particular attention is given to safety, noise, and emissions.

Chapter 6 examines the impact on airlines of changes in the global economic environment.

Chapter 7 considers the rapidly evolving technological environment, looking in turn at marketing, production, integrative, and competing technologies. The section on production technologies is oriented primarily towards aircraft and their systems, and towards changes in communications, navigation, surveillance, and air traffic management.

Chapters 8 to 11 examine the competitive environment. Chapter 8 identifies changes affecting key airline suppliers, such as manufacturers of airframes, powerplants, and avionics equipment, suppliers of maintenance, finance, and labour, and suppliers of airport and air traffic services. Distribution channels for air transport products are the subject of chapter 9, whilst chapter 10 considers customers and markets. Chapter 11 reviews the changing impact of competitors, from both within and outside the airline industry.

Chapter 12 concludes Part One by taking a brief look at environmental forecasting, assessment, and influencing.

Part Two: Internal Analysis

The purpose of this part of Volume One is to provide a framework for the internal analysis of airlines which goes beyond the standard 'laundry-list' of strengths and weaknesses. The transition underway in the industry imposes a far wider range of demands than has historically been the case, and the chapters in Part Two draw on current strategic management theory and practice to exemplify how these demands are changing.

Chapter 13 explains the concepts of vision and mission, makes a case for their growing relevance to the industry, and discusses ways in which airline missions are changing.

Chapter 14 emphasizes the importance of corporate culture and values to the success of airlines moving from relatively stable into highly complex and turbulent environments, and it lays a foundation for the argument introduced at several points later in the book that these variables are becoming critical service differentiators in an increasingly competitive airline industry.

Chapter 15 considers the changing role of resources, skills, distinctive capabilities, and core competencies in the airline business.

Chapter 16 discusses the importance of internal stakeholders, and looks at how employees, managers, and shareholders can affect the ways in which different airlines adapt to changes arising from the industry's current restructuring.

Chapter 17 focuses on competitive advantage - the heart of any internal analysis. External and internal architecture, value chains, and the concept of the 'core business' are discussed.

Chapter 18 concludes Volume One with a brief discussion of momentum analysis, and a review of the changes in high-level ('strategic' as opposed to more 'tactical') objectives taking place at many airlines.

Volume Two

Part One: Strategic Alternatives and Choice

Following classical strategic management practice, external and internal analyses lead on to the formulation of strategic alternatives and the making of choices from amongst them. The purpose of this opening part of Volume Two is to examine the strategic alternatives becoming available to airlines as a result of changes in their external and internal environments, and to look at the ways in which choices amongst these alternatives are being reflected in strategies at the corporate, business, and functional levels.

Chapter 1 addresses corporate-level strategy. It first considers both growth and renewal, and then looks at the choices available and currently being made to determine airlines' industrial, vertical, product, and geographical scope.

Chapter 2 turns to business-level strategy, expanding on the earlier discussion of competitive advantage by examining alternative generic competitive strategies available to airlines.

Chapter 3 briefly reviews changes taking place at the functional level. Marketing, human resource management, information systems, financial management, and operations are considered.

Chapter 4 concludes the first part of Volume Two by looking at changes taking place in short- and medium-term objectives, operating goals, and critical success factors at many of the world's airlines.

Part Two: Implementation

The second part of Volume Two discusses new and evolving approaches to the implementation of airline strategies. It draws heavily on recent developments in the service management literature, many of which have yet to be widely reflected in airline practice but will become increasingly important as the industry's transition continues to unfold.

Chapter 5 considers the choices airlines are making about how to grow, looking first at internal/organic growth and at growth through acquisition, and then focusing in much greater depth on the forms, objectives, and ingredients of inter-airline alliances. Globalization is also considered in some detail.

Chapter 6 examines the nature of service, the component elements in an airline's service concept, and approaches to the management of the service-price offer.

Chapter 7 looks at service delivery as an interactive experience, examining the roles played by consumers, the service environment, service providers, and service delivery processes.

Chapter 8 considers the significance of corporate infrastructure to strategy implementation, with particular emphasis given to structures and to coordination and control processes.

Part Three: Outcome

Chapters 9 and 10 examine the outcome of implementation. The subjects of chapter 9 are service quality, service failure, and service recovery in the airline industry. Chapter 10 looks at changing approaches to customer loyalty, relationship marketing, and customer retention; frequent flyer programmes, corporate rebates, and branding are given particular attention. **Chapter 11** provides some brief overall conclusions.

Ricardo observed that profits arise from differential stupidity rather than differential cleverness. Neither volume contains checklists or infallible guides to action, the real value of which is anyway open to question if they become widely available: the efficient markets hypothesis can be applied as readily to books as to stock markets. The primary purpose is to provoke independent thought and analysis. The way in which it is hoped this can be accomplished is by using the strategic management process as a framework to help understand what is happening, and what is likely to happen, in the industry. The framework is rooted in the 'classical' approach to strategic management that has evolved over the last several decades. However, many recent developments in the discipline - including some that the passage of time might ultimately condemn as 'fads' - have also been incorporated. There is nothing wrong with fads if what is useful can be extracted from them and integrated into a company's managerial systems, leaving the rest to be discarded; indeed, they can make a valuable contribution to cumulative learning if handled with circumspection.

As well as using the strategic management process as a framework within which to analyze the transition that the airline industry is presently undergoing, the text also explains key strategic management concepts wherever these are relevant. This is intended to benefit readers unfamiliar with concepts which will in all likelihood gain considerably wider currency within the airline industry in the years ahead. Although - for reasons explained in the opening chapter of Volume One - the structure of the book is prescriptive, the solutions suggested or exemplified are not. The industry faces challenges too complex and, in many cases, too carrier-specific for all-embracing rules of 'best practice' to be meaningful.

Notwithstanding the cyclical upturn which followed, the airline industry went through a trauma so deep during the early 1990s that it had no alternative other than to consider all aspects of how it is regulated, organized, and managed. It is now widely, although perhaps not yet universally, recognized that everything to do with the industry must be opened up to scrutiny and questioning. Strategic management can provide some valuable tools and a comprehensive context to help achieve this.

Readership

Both volumes of the book are intended to be of interest to the following audiences:

- airline industry professionals needing a framework within which to set much of what is happening in the business as it evolves through the millennium;
- managers in industries which supply goods and services to airlines;
- those responsible for regulating various aspects of the airline business;
- practitioners of strategic management, who are well-served by a substantial number of books covering their subject in general but might benefit from a treatment which draws together many of the discipline's contemporary strands of thought within the context of a specific, currently volatile, and always exciting industry;
- students, of both management in its broadest sense and the airline industry in particular, pursuing courses in business policy, strategic management, or the strategic settings of functional activities; and
- anybody having an academic interest in the industry.

Conclusion

Deregulation, the need for tighter cost control, heightened market awareness, and many other symptoms of change have been on the agenda for so long that transition in the airline industry might be thought well on the way to having run its course. Yet in the mid-1990s a senior executive of a large North American airline was quoted as justifying the elimination of first class service on the grounds that although the front cabin was generally full, only 19 per cent of traffic was comprised of revenue passengers.[4] In few other industries would a producer have contemplated giving away 81 per cent of the output from its most prestigious product line to members of staff and to customers who had bought products from cheaper lines. The transition appears still to be very much underway. Boeing has described it as follows.

> The airline industry is currently in transition. It is evolving slowly but inexorably toward a more liberal environment that relies less on governmental control and more on market forces. More airlines will be privatized. New entrants will continue to enter and exit. Domestic airlines will add international services, and international airlines will initiate domestic feeder operations. Liberalization will also lead to changes in the ownership structure of the industry. More airlines will invest in greater shares of foreign airlines. This trend towards a more intensively competitive environment is irreversible, but it will force the airline industry to become more efficient and profitable than it has been in the past.[5]

Transition to being an industry like any other, judged by financial statements forged out of competition rather than inflated by public subsidy is inevitably painful. Labour, particularly organized labour, in many countries is adjusting only gradually to the emerging realities of increased competition. Some managements are infused with the wrong values and skills to compete aggressively in a liberalized, let alone a deregulated, environment. Where governments continue to protect their 'national champions' this might not matter to any great extent. Elsewhere, a paradigm shift - a fundamental change in the way airline managers perceive their environments and act in response to those perceptions - is placing responsibility on management teams to think strategically rather than plan mechanically. A corollary of this is the need to view their airlines as integrated systems of interlinked customer-serving processes, rather than to see the world from the perspectives of isolated functional units.

A principal focus of attention in a globalizing airline industry is its emerging consolidation. There is a tendency for this to obscure some of the deeper changes also taking place. These changes will lead not simply to a reduced cast of players, but to a far-reaching realignment of business practices and quite possibly of roles within the industry. The next few years will witness a continuing transition to new ways of doing business. The two volumes of the book use one particular model of the strategic management process to help chart that transition. It is to be hoped that the result will be a restructured industry capable of maintaining profitability throughout an entire economic cycle, in control of its capacity, on top of its cost structure, prudently leveraged, and attractive to customers, lenders, and equity investors alike.

Notes

1   This second point applies less in the United States than elsewhere, but even there - in the third decade after deregulation - important aspects of domestic operations are again being fundamentally restructured.
2   'Liberalization' is a word applied to relaxation of governmental controls over airlines' commercial decision-making in respect of route entry, capacity, and pricing. This relaxation varies widely between markets in degree and rate of change. 'Deregulation' implies a more comprehensive, and quite possibly more rapid, dismantling of marketplace controls.
3   Porter, M.E. (1985), *Competitive Advantage,* The Free Press.
4   *Aviation Week & Space Technology,* May 9, 1994, p. 33.
5   Boeing, *Current Market Outlook,* 1995, p. 24.

Part One
Strategic alternatives and choice

1 Corporate strategy: growth, renewal, and scope

Chapter 1 in the first volume of this book described the 'rational approach' to strategic management - still dominant despite being unfashionable - as a multi-stage process comprising analysis, formulation of alternatives, choice, implementation, feedback, and control. Whilst intellectually distinct, these stages are for practical purposes interrelated. Their interrelatedness is most in evidence during implementation and control, which will be covered in Part Two of the present volume. Prior to that, Part One will build on the analyses in the previous volume of changes taking place in the external and internal environments of many of the world's airlines. It will do this by looking at some of the strategic alternatives that environmental changes are creating. This chapter will consider the pursuit of growth, the significance of corporate renewal, and the choice of corporate scope. Chapter 2 will look at the alternative competitive strategies available pursuant to scope, growth, and renewal choices, whilst chapter 3 will briefly consider some key functional strategies and the importance of intra-organizational synergy.

Growth

Despite its pronounced cyclicality, commercial air transport as a whole is still growing at a more rapid pace than the general global accumulation of wealth. Strategies aimed at growth are therefore relatively easy to pursue in this industry. Compelling though growth is, however, we will see at several points later in the chapter that there are quite a few airlines that need to be thinking in terms of renewal, consolidation, and in some cases even downsizing strategies in order to secure their futures.

Some basic questions

Growth in what? Obvious possibilities include revenues and profitability. Market share has long been a favorite but, as will be discussed below, specifying exactly what is meant by 'market' requires care. Less fashionable these days are growth in output or fleet size - unless they generate incremental revenues and profits. Capacity expansion that is not paced by demand growth will place downward pressure on yields and load factors; new capacity comes with costs attached and so not only has to be sold, but sold at prices sufficient to more than cover those incremental costs. During the early 1990s, many airlines became more cautious about their demand forecasts and capacity planning than had been the case in the second half of the 1980s. Whether this caution will survive an entire economic cycle remains to be seen.

The answer to the question 'Growth in what?' will depend upon an airline's mission and high-level objectives. Upon this answer will in turn depend the choice of strategy. For example, an objective to increase return on capital employed could be achieved by boosting profits earned from an unchanged asset base and/or maintaining profits and reducing assets; profits could be boosted by growing revenues (driven by higher yields and/or increased traffic) and/or by lower costs; assets could be shrunk by cutting the fleet (perhaps through improved utilization or sale-and-leaseback, although the latter is largely cosmetic in its effect other than on cash-flow), by trimming other fixed assets (possibly by outsourcing noncore activities), or by squeezing working capital (which can be risky, notwithstanding that the fact scheduled airlines are paid in advance for their services - subject to some delays inherent in credit card and bank settlement plan payments - means that they can survive on lower current ratios than many other types of business).

What is meant by 'market'? It was noted in chapter 10 of Volume One that there are several levels of **geographical** market: city-pair, regional, national, international between countries in the same part of the world (e.g. intra-Asian), and intercontinental.[1] Airline markets are so fragmented that the city-pair is not a useful level of analysis when dealing with **corporate** (rather than **competitive**) strategy unless an airline holds such a small portfolio of routes that the addition of one or two would represent a significant augmentation in capacity, traffic, and revenue. Geographical markets are better considered in terms of 'route groups'; how these are defined will depend upon the nature of a particular carrier's network, but each group should generally be similar in terms of stage-length, region served (within a single country or in a wider sense), and aircraft types required.

As well as geographical markets there are **product** markets, which at their simplest level might be broken-down into first, business, and economy/coach on the passenger side and various levels of airport-to-airport and door-to-door service on the cargo side. In addition, we have already noted that some airlines or their holding companies sell products other than air transport services.

Why grow? This depends to some extent upon the answer to the preceding question. Whilst success often leads to size, there has long been a widespread assumption that causality runs more strongly in the opposite direction: growth is a prerequisite to success. Putting aside personal or corporate ego and the expectations of financial markets, there are several reasons why output growth in particular has been widely seen by airline managers as a worthwhile objective.

1   Growth provides the opportunity, at least in principle, to average down costs by adding incremental output at lower than average unit cost.

2   New routes or additional frequencies are often perceived as a way to stimulate demand.

3   Incremental output, deployed in the right way, can be used to subdue or eliminate competitors.

In practice, of course, incremental output does not always turn out to be as 'cheap' as anticipated, and neither is market share inevitably profitable - particularly when incremental output far in excess of market needs has to be sold at low yields to avoid 'spoilage'.[2] Nonetheless, growth does have some compelling merits for airlines: the learning effect can be a very real advantage in respect of both operational and marketing tasks, although the sustainability of this advantage is doubtful and it is certainly imitable; the industry can offer economies of scale in marketing, maintenance, data processing, and various central corporate functions (but not notably in flight operations beyond a relatively small 'minimum efficient scale'); and economies of scope and density are also available to be exploited, particularly by large, integrated hub-and-spoke networks.[3] Market share in a given catchment/delivery area is important for express package carriers because it affects the frequency of pick-ups and deliveries, and therefore both their economics and the quality of service being offered. More subjectively, growth can build a mission-oriented momentum which contributes towards the recruitment and retention of high-calibre staff and imbues stakeholders with a sense that the airline is guiding its own destiny.

Some years ago, IATA listed as follows the marketing benefits attainable by large airlines.[4]

1 Attractiveness to passengers of a large and widespread network.
2 Ability to dominate operations at a hub.

3 Control of distribution through access to large numbers of travel agents, especially when linked through a computer reservations system.
4 Ability to squeeze new entrants through selective pricing and/or frequency increases.
5 Ability to exercise price leadership.
6 Value of network size in 'loyalty' marketing schemes, such as 'frequent flyer' programmes.
7 Range of markets allowing cross-subsidizing of competitive pricing on particular routes.
8 Marketing power of large-scale advertising.

Doganis has exemplified the effect of these potential benefits on the strategies of some of Europe's larger airlines during the course of the liberalization process that began gathering pace in the late 1980s:[5]

- achievement of a dominant position within their own home markets through horizontal integration;
- cross-border share purchases in existing airlines to gain footholds in other major European markets; and
- establishment of a global presence through marketing alliances, which sometimes also involved share purchases.

Growth is frequently justified by pursuit of synergies - the exploitation of shared resources and skills across different product or geographical markets, and possibly also across industry boundaries - to save costs and/or add value. Synergies are the glue that should bind activities or businesses into coherent portfolios, and without synergy the rationale underlying such portfolios has to be questioned.

On the other hand, there are potential disadvantages to growth.

1   Diseconomies of scale can set in if bureaucracy and overheads increase disproportionately; improved IT capabilities, flatter hierarchies, and greater cost consciousness are now being more widely deployed than before to deal with these problems, however.

2   The larger an airline becomes, the more challenging it is to maintain consistently high standards of customer service.

3   Management structures and processes need to evolve as an airline grows, but often they are slow to adapt. People Express is a classic case study in adaptive failure.

4   Low operating margins have led historically to airline growth being financed more by debt and quasi-debt instruments (e.g. leases) than by internal cash-flow or fresh equity. This has tended to create

dangerously high financial leverage in what is anyway a cyclical industry prone to high operating leverage (i.e. a high ratio of fixed to total costs).[6]

5   Even when growth is profitable in financial accounting terms, it is not necessarily as advantageous when expressed in terms of the net present value of the future cash flows which it is expected to generate.

6   Synergies are sometimes easier to isolate in principle than in practice.

Size is becoming technically more manageable and its advantages more compelling for carriers with the vision to give direction to growth, the resources to expand without straining their balance sheets or their stakeholders' nerves, and the management capabilities to create and sustain a customer-focused, performance-oriented corporate culture. Nonetheless, size alone is unlikely ever to be a sustainable source of competitive advantage because, given the absence of other barriers to entry into key markets, it is replicable by competitors with sufficient resources. For example, global alliances are busy replicating each other's 'critical mass'. Within any particular strategic group, size is never more than an entry fee. And, as we shall see when discussing niche markets, there are several strategic groups within which raw size is not a critical success factor.

Where should growth be targeted?   The answer to this depends on an airline's mission and objectives. A profit-oriented carrier might judge market attractiveness in terms of revenue and profit potential, demand stability, and present or likely future levels of competitive intensity. The critical success factors required to serve a particular market need to be related to an airline's capabilities, and its competitive advantage or (preferably **and**) a source of synergy between existing activities and any new market to be entered should be identified. Finally, barriers to entry need to be considered. Those which are absolute - such as lack of route authority or slots - can be surmounted only by environmental influencing and/or regulatory liberalization and technological or procedural advances respectively (see Volume One, Part One); those which are commercial - such as a large incumbent's network, brand, or distribution strengths and its likely competitive reaction - have in the past often been overlooked in the enthusiasm of managements at new or small airlines to attain rapidly their own definitions of 'critical mass'.

Growing with the market(s) currently served

It is rarely possible to stand still for long in a competitive market other than during a recession. Consequently, the basic choices are to grow or to shrink. The growth option could involve growing **with** markets already served, or growing **into** existing and/or new markets. Growing **with** the air transport markets in which an airline currently operates is generally a viable option given that most are continuing to expand in terms of both traffic and, somewhat less consistently in some parts of the world than others, revenue. Iberia's approach to its domestic markets in the late 1990s, for example, was to mirror their annual growth rate of approximately 6 per cent; efforts to increase market share were instead focused on international routes.[7] This type of corporate-level strategy may or may not require a fresh competitive strategy.

Traffic growth can be accommodated by one or a combination of the following.

1   Higher load factors (i.e. selling more of the output of ASMs/ASKs produced).

2   Higher output (i.e. producing more ASMs/ASKs). Output can be raised by one or a combination of two strategies:
     • maintaining frequencies, but operating larger aircraft;
     • maintaining gauge, but boosting frequencies (either by adding aircraft or raising the utilization of the existing fleet).

Boeing has observed that although the manner in which individual airlines choose to accommodate growth will vary depending upon their specific competitive environments and business strategies, there has historically been a strong tendency to add frequencies and maintain or reduce airplane size whenever markets are liberalized.[8] The reason for this is that high-fare customers in particular value increased frequencies which allow departure and arrival times to be more precisely tailored to their own preferred travel schedules; this value appears, in general, to outweigh the higher expenses incurred by airlines operating smaller aircraft with higher seat-mile costs than would be the case were growth simply accommodated in larger aircraft.

The concept of measured growth became more acceptable to airline managements in the 1990s than it has been in the past, although the growth imperative has certainly not disappeared from the industry. It is instead focused less on rapid internal/organic growth than on expansion through alliances of various form. Growing **with** the markets currently served might anyway be all a particular airline is able to do given the regulatory or other barriers to market entry confronting it.

Nonetheless, there are pitfalls.

1   Unless the markets concerned are themselves expanding rapidly, as in parts of the Asia-Pacific region, this type of growth is the antithesis of 'strategic intent' insofar as it does not challenge the airline to 'stretch' and achieve.[9]

2   Anything which can be characterized as a 'do-nothing different' strategy could erode the positive, customer-focused corporate culture necessary to maintain high standards of service. It may also have a negative impact on stakeholders' perceptions of the carrier.

3   Once markets are liberalized or deregulated, it is a reasonable bet that any competitors choosing to swim along on the tide will find themselves being overtaken.

Growing into current and new markets

The essence of what is generally referred to as 'intensive growth' is exploitation of an airline's existing products and/or markets. The analysis below is based on the 'Ansoff Matrix', a four-cell construct which categorizes strategies on the basis of whether they involve new or existing products, or new or existing markets.[10] We will deal with three of the four cells - the 'intensive growth' options of market penetration, market development, and product development - in this part of the chapter; diversification, which is not an intensive growth strategy, is covered later.[11] The following categories are useful for analytical purposes, but it has to be borne in mind that definitions of both products and markets can be imprecise at their boundaries and also that a wide-market airline may simultaneously be pursuing several strategies in each category.

Market penetration   This involves increasing market share by selling more of an airline's existing products into markets and segments already served. There are three primary ways to achieve this.

1   Retain existing customers and get them to travel or ship more often. Frequent flyer programmes (FFPs), product differentiation, and branding are increasingly common tools used to help cement customer loyalty. We will be returning to this topic in chapter 10.

2   Attract competitors' customers. A current example would be efforts being made by some airlines to penetrate more deeply into the long-haul 'routine non-perishable' segment of heavy freight markets.

3   Draw on untapped customers. This is an approach exploited by low-fare/no-frills carriers which aim not only to draw traffic from other airlines and (in Europe and the United States) from surface modes, but also to stimulate travel that would not otherwise have taken place.

Market share has traditionally been considered important because of its correlation with low unit costs and high profitability in many volume manufacturing industries. Its direct relevance to airline profitability is empirically less clear, although the availability of economies of scope,

density, and to an extent scale are clearly not unimportant. It has been
suggested that a 10 per cent share of the global market is a minimum for
survival as a wide-market international carrier.[12] It is also commonly
believed that a high percentage share of any individual market is difficult
to reverse because of the 'S-curve' effect;[13] Emirates and Virgin Atlantic
amongst others have nonetheless proven that it can be done.

Generalizations are fraught, not least because the word 'market' can be
used to refer to so many different geographical and product categories
which - in a network industry - are never going to be quite as discrete as
analysts might like. Furthermore, as was pointed out in chapter 11 of
Volume One, the air transport industry serves some market segments
which can alternatively be served by other industries whose output is not
usually taken into account when computing market share.

And neither is the concept of an airline's 'position in its markets'
particularly helpful. Generally, market leaders (in share terms) are
supposed to have different strategies open to them compared with those
available to 'challengers' and 'followers', but any single carrier can be a
leader in some markets and a follower in others: British Airways is a
global leader, but for regulatory and/or commercial reasons is absent from
several important route-groups (e.g. North Pacific) and in certain of its
markets is locally a challenger rather than a leader (e.g. London-Dubai).
Southwest is a challenger rather than a leader in the US domestic market as
a whole, but in most of its city-pair markets it is a clear leader. The
industry's economics generally reward market share at most levels of
analysis, but the fragmentation of its markets and the particular economics
of flight operations make that reward potentially fragile in the face of a
challenger with the right competitive strategy for its targeted segment(s).
We will return to this in chapter 2.

Market penetration is normally considered a low-risk strategy because
product and customer knowledge are well-established. This could,
however, be outweighed if the share of a particularly aggressive
competitor is being attacked. A share gain driven by innovative
segmentation, clear positioning, more appropriate management of the
marketing mix, and development of a sustainable competitive advantage
can be particularly beneficial.[14] On the other hand, there will undoubtedly
be a cost involved somewhere in the marketing mix - possibly in terms of
price or marketing communications. Furthermore, believers in brand,
product, and market life cycles will want to ensure that by pursuing a
penetration strategy they are not overinvesting in yesterday's story.[15]

Penetrating further into a market in the mature stage of its life cycle can
be particularly challenging because it is likely that more of any growth
will have to come out of competitors' shares than if the market as a whole
were growing strongly. This fairly obvious fact belies a great deal of
controversy about how to define 'maturity' and, more particularly, which
air transport markets are in fact mature. Most forecasts of future traffic
growth place the US domestic market at the foot of the table and, as was

noted in chapter 15 of Volume One, several observers have claimed it to be either at or approaching maturity; yet in its 1995 *World Economic and Traffic Outlook,* McDonnell Douglas - relying primarily on an analysis of income elasticity of demand (traffic growth at a rate equivalent to GDP growth being taken as an indicator of maturity) - made a robust case for the US domestic market not only having yet to reach maturity, but in fact still being a growth market. In the United States only one-third of the adult population flies each year, fewer than half those who do fly take more than two trips, and only around 10 per cent of the population hold passports (thus limiting international travel). So even in what is undoubtedly the closest to maturity of the world's air transport regions, there is an argument that plenty of scope still exists for penetration strategies.

Market development This involves the selling of current or very similar products into new markets. It happens, for example, when an airline enters a new route or route-group, or when a widebodied aircraft replaces narrowbodies on an existing route and so allows its operator to tap into the cargo market. Market development is sometimes no more 'scientific' than deploying off-peak capacity into new markets in order to boost asset utilization. In this case products are looking for - rather than being designed for - customers, and price is likely to outweigh nonprice elements as a key marketing mix variable. Often, though, it is more innovative than this: airlines with established consultancy operations that have cutting-edge revenue management expertise, for example, are increasingly selling products outside the airline industry.

Market development can raise asset utilization and offer opportunities to leverage brand equity and corporate reputation. Success in the latter case will depend partly upon the relevance of attributes associated with the particular brand and reputation in the target market, and also upon the extent to which incumbents having their own strong reputations are already entrenched.

Product knowledge lowers one aspect of risk inherent in a market development strategy, but there is always the danger that a new market which appears similar to existing markets might be treated as though it is in fact the same. Questions also need to be asked about the competitive advantage being brought to the market and how any incumbent's competitive advantage is to be neutralized. In particular, if an airline is failing to 'get it right' in its current markets there ought to be a lot of soul-searching before it moves into unfamiliar territory. Even companies which are indeed 'getting it right' can stumble when they make a move, as FedEx did when expanding into Europe in the early 1990s for example.

Product development This originally encompassed the further development of current products for markets already served, but the concept has been expanded in usage to include the introduction of entirely new products into these markets. It might involve:

- addition of features to existing products (e.g. improved cabin configuration, better inflight entertainment, or a 'fast-track' through security and immigration);
- product relaunch (e.g. a major redesign of schedules and amenities to bring an established product more closely into line with evolving benefit requirements);
- product line expansion (e.g. the introduction of a business class into markets where previously just all-economy/coach or first and economy/coach were offered); or
- new products (e.g. interactive merchandising, the offering of inflight communications capabilities to existing passengers, or sale of fully integrated logistics management to established customers for express and traditional freight services).

The more closely a development resembles current products, the nearer it is in definition to market penetration and the lower will be the risk involved. Even so, similarity does not guarantee success - as airlines shifting from all-economy to mixed-class operations have proven on several occasions. Costs incurred launching or relaunching a product can be high. Finally, consideration needs to be given to the likely impact of product development on other products. For example, a new or upgraded business class might attract not only passengers currently paying full economy/coach fares but also some from first class.

Conclusion

Lovelock has summarized as follows the ways in which service businesses such as airlines can grow.

1 Attract new customers.
2 Encourage existing customers to purchase more units of service.
3 Encourage existing customers to purchase higher value services (for example, travel first class rather than economy).
4 Reduce the extent of turnover - or "churn" - resulting from desirable customers withdrawing their patronage.
5 Terminate unprofitable, stagnant, or otherwise unsatisfactory relationships and replace them by new customers who better match the firm's profit, growth, and positioning goals.[16]

Whilst the final point might have relatively limited application in a high fixed cost, volume-dependent industry such as the airline business, carriers worldwide are increasingly having to find innovative ways in which to achieve the other four imperatives. We will be discussing many of the approaches now being adopted as the book progresses.

Renewal strategies

In 1996, British Airways was the world's most profitable airline. The same year, it launched a $1.5 billion cost-cutting programme which within 12 months was contributing to mounting unrest amongst staff. Competitive environments in the airline industry are now so dynamic and turbulent that renewal strategies are no longer the sole domain of managements brought in to rescue carriers from the brink of collapse. Change on both the demand and supply sides has become almost constant with the result that, either incrementally or as part of a grand strategic reorientation, renewal strategies must be part of managers' armouries even in the most successful airlines. Emergent strategies and the organizational learning they embody have a particularly important role to play in support of ongoing strategic renewal.[17] The challenge is that whereas a single point of crisis can be dealt with by a single plan for corporate renewal agreeable to all stakeholder groups, ongoing renewal calls for continuous creativity in the generation of incremental revenues, the management of costs that have already undergone several rounds of paring, and the handling of staff morale (the impact of which on product quality and service consistency is always profound).

A period of extraordinary change began for the airline industry in the 1980s, and gathered real momentum in the 1990s. Boeing has summarized what happened in the following terms.

> Industry overcapacity characterized the early 1990s. So did the inability to raise prices sufficiently to cover costs and reach profitability. Many of the world's airlines have gone through a period of restructuring in response to these factors. Airline actions to reduce costs included privatizing, restructuring hubs, reducing labor costs, improving productivity, capping commissions, and introducing electronic ticketing. To build market strength, airlines focused on introducing better revenue management tools. They strengthened frequent flyer programs. Airlines also constructed alliances to gain access to global networks within the constraints of the current bilateral system. In many cases, they have entered into code-share agreements to maintain or expand network coverage.[18]

Cost control and refocusing on the core air transport business have been common throughout the industry. Perhaps the most difficult restructuring choices face medium-sized carriers which have neither the resources nor the market position needed as foundations for growth towards a leading global role, nor sufficiently competitive cost structures to shrink profitably into unassailable niches. SAS, for example, is a medium-sized carrier which tried first to grow and diversify out of its size constraint, and then retrenched and substituted its earlier leading position in a constellation of alliances for a secondary role in a global grouping; the geographical wide-market strategy formulated in the 1980s having proven flawed, it spent the first half of the 1990s rationalizing its intercontinental route structure and selling SAS Service Partner, SAS Leisure, and some of its hotel interests (although the Radisson SAS chain expanded during this period). Like Finnair, a neighbour on the northern extremities of Europe, SAS rationalized in order to survive commercially over the short and medium term. Its future at this point looks closely tied to that of alliance partner Lufthansa. Swissair is another good example of a medium-sized airline which is trying to transform itself within the context of an alliance structure.

In the United States, US Airways spent the mid-90s poised between a restructuring of its cost base that would permit the airline to grow, and downsizing into a 'super-regional' niche. The fundamental issue was disagreement between key internal stakeholders - management and pilots - about the nature of the unit cost problem confronting the airline and the solutions it called for. Whilst management portrayed downsizing (or 'rightsizing', to use their preferred term) as the only alternative to growth keyed-off a more competitive cost structure, they recognized that 'shrinking the carrier would not be a long-term solution; it only would eliminate the unprofitable routes and buy US Airways a little time...Ultimately, even a regional carrier must be cost competitive'.[19]

The need for almost constant change is being driven by pressures from both external and internal environments. External pressures include: the liberalization of route entry, capacity, and pricing regulations; rising consumer expectations, set within the context of burgeoning demand; increasingly innovative and aggressive competitive behaviour; and rapid change in the technological environment. Internal pressures vary depending on any given airline's precise circumstances, but many carriers face changing stakeholder expectations as governments and bureaucrats gradually make way for commercially driven managers; where this happens, vision, mission, and high-level corporate objectives must change.[20]

When an industry emerges from decades of regulatory protection, the appearance of start-ups together with a shake-out and consolidation amongst incumbents are inevitable. Start-ups come and go, but few survive over the long term; they might have a profound impact in certain markets, and it is possible that amongst the small number of survivors will be an even smaller number capable of changing the way certain segments of the industry do business.[21] Incumbents will almost inevitably have to adjust and transform themselves.

Corporate renewal can take many forms, but at its heart lie one or both of two thrusts.

1   Operational renewal: the attainment of significant improvements in the efficiency and effectiveness of organizational processes in general and of service delivery in particular.

2   Strategic renewal: the reassessment of decisions in respect of industrial, vertical, product, and geographical scope, and the creation or reharnessing of skills, resources, and capabilities in order to rebuild competitive advantage in whichever markets scope decisions require the airline to contest. Strategies have life cycles, just as do markets, products, and brands. Scope decisions are the subject of the remainder of this chapter. Competitive advantage, in the context of the competitive strategies that can be built upon it, is the subject of the following chapter.

Choice of scope

It was mentioned in the opening chapter of Volume One that corporate strategy answers the 'Where to compete?' question, whereas competitive strategy answers 'How to compete?' Although these two questions are of course closely linked in practice, it is nonetheless analytically useful to separate them. The scope of an airline's activities is an outcome of four fundamental choices made at the corporate level.

1   Industrial scope: the choice of industries in which an airline or its holding company is to participate. In addition to air transport, there might be involvement in other - related or, less commonly, unrelated - industries. Some related industries traditionally looked upon as being integral parts of an air transport operation are now beginning to be viewed as separate enterprises with their own industrial logic.

2   Vertical scope: the choices made with regard to which of the activities in each industry's value chain should be undertaken inhouse and which should be outsourced.

3   Geographical scope: the choice of geographical markets within which to compete.

4   Product scope: the choice of services to be offered into the selected geographical markets. Geographical and product scope are distinct but closely linked choices. The characteristics of demand in particular geographical markets clearly determine to a considerable degree the services required to satisfy needs underlying that demand.

Industrial scope

The essence of the industrial scope decision is whether and, if so, how far to diversify away from the core business. Because it involves products and markets that are both to some degree unfamiliar, diversification is usually seen as a high-risk strategy relative to staying with existing products and markets ('market penetration'), using existing products to develop new markets ('market development'), or developing new products to offer into markets that are already being served with other products ('product development'). It is a strategy that has fallen from grace since focusing on core competencies and core businesses became popular in the late 1980s. Furthermore, commercial air transport, particularly in scheduled markets, is a sufficiently cash-hungry enterprise in its own right to preclude all but the richest carriers from investing in substantial diversification.

Although more complex typologies have been developed, there are essentially two types of diversification: related and unrelated. The difference between related and unrelated diversification lies in the presence or absence of links between the value chains of the different activities or, perhaps more importantly, in whether or not a core competence is shared.[22]

Related diversification As will be noted in the next section of the chapter when vertical scope is discussed, many large airlines have internal suppliers of services such as engineering, maintenance, catering, and ground handling which - depending upon one's point of view and any particular airline's circumstances - do not inevitably have to be performed inhouse. These internal suppliers may or may not also do work for other carriers. When they do, there is an indistinct line that separates contracting-out, in order to utilize periodic excess capacity and spread fixed costs, from a deliberate programme of related diversification. The distinction is not always easy to draw, but often it is associated with managerial independence, and a set of missions, objectives, and strategies which make the affected units players in markets much wider than the airline's own internal market; their customers and competitors are clearly different from those of the airline's air transport operations.

When an airline or its subsidiaries invest heavily in capabilities well in excess of what is needed to support that particular carrier's air transport operations, it can be argued that a strategy of related diversification is being implemented. Such strategies are evident, for example, in AMR's Sabre Group, in the global CRS joint ventures, and in the catering operations of Lufthansa and Swissair subsidiaries. Clearly, there are some semantics here; there is no threshold percentage of business done with the parent as opposed to third parties which, once crossed, automatically turns a vertical scope decision (e.g. 'we will do our own airframe heavy maintenance') into an exercise in related diversification (e.g. 'we will actively bid for third party airframe heavy maintenance work and invest in sufficient capacity to ensure that this work accounts for a substantial proportion of activity relative to inhouse work'). The distinction is as much as anything a matter of intent - whether or not a strategy to diversify corporate revenue sources away from pure air transport business is being implemented.

Hotels and car hire are generally considered to be examples of related diversification. Their relatedness to air transport is in principle derived from the fact that all three industries serve 'travellers' and, to varying but sometimes relatively limited degrees, share similar distribution channels. Several airlines retain interests in hotels, but many have been actively withdrawing from this type of related diversification strategy since the late 1980s. Sometimes withdrawal has been precipitated by a financial need to divest assets and raise cash (e.g. Aer Lingus and Air France, both with some encouragement from the European Commission in return for approval of state aid); occasionally it has been a result of pressure from internal stakeholders preferring investment and management efforts to be concentrated on the core air transport business (e.g. United). Not infrequently, however, divestment has been a response to the fact that the returns from diversification into these activities have been disappointing, with anticipated benefits arising from value chain synergies and shared competencies proving elusive.[23]

As noted, the primary justification for related diversification has been to leverage core competencies or exploit economies of scale and scope - in other words, to share a capability or a cost. It saw its heyday in the mid-1980s, exemplified by United's abortive transformation into the Allegis travel conglomerate - which drained management attention and capital investment away from the airline and towards hotel chains and a car rental company. Similarly, the SAS 'Service Chain' concept tried unsuccessfully to appropriate more value from the total travel product by providing a wider range of services than air transport alone; the intention was not simply to provide air transport services, but also a global travel product distribution system, a hotel network, business centres, 24-hour hotlines, and a credit card company - a totally integrated travel concept for the business segment.

Refocusing on the 'core air transport business' is today very much in vogue, although the picture remains somewhat mixed - not least of all because different airlines have different opinions about what is 'core'. Whilst many airlines have neither sufficient funds nor appetite to launch major new diversification initiatives, several are continuing with established programmes. For example, through its subsidiaries SIA Engineering Company and SATS, Singapore Airlines is investing in engineering, line maintenance, cargo handling, and catering joint ventures outside Singapore. This policy of related diversification is designed to spread the Group's interests geographically, but without moving beyond existing areas of expertise.

Unrelated diversification Although sometimes intended to spread risk across industries with different cyclical or cash-flow profiles, a move into activities unrelated to existing products, customers, technologies or areas of expertise is inevitably going to carry its own set of risks. Frequently inconsistent with the 'core competence' concept, it is the home-field of portfolio analysis techniques, and - since strategists started reaching for their knitting needles in the mid-1980s - it has fallen on hard times. Few airlines have ever had sufficient resources to build significant portfolios of unrelated activities (unless the view is held that hotels and resorts are not sufficiently synergistic with air transport operations to be classified as 'related'). Unrelated diversification has never been a major factor in the airline industry. Neither philosophy nor finance seem likely to allow this to change in the near future.

As was noted in chapter 16 of Volume One, some airlines are themselves units of diversified industrial portfolios (e.g. EVA Air, Asiana, Cathay Pacific etc.). Others form parts of vertically integrated chains. Some of the clearest examples of airlines existing within a vertically integrated chain are provided by several of Europe's largest charter carriers, which are parts of groups comprising tour organizers and retail travel agencies. In Britain, various Thomson travel products are retailed through the Group's Lunn Poly agencies and use Britannia Airways for the air transport component; similarly, Airtours uses Airtours International to do most of its flying and retails through its Going Places agency chain (formed from the merger of Hogg Robinson and Pickfords). Some vertically integrated groups have cooperated to a degree across national boundaries, as exemplified by the link forged in the early 1990s between Air 2000 and First Choice on the one hand and LTU and Thomas Cook on the other. However, charter airlines do still vary widely in respect of the extent to which output is integrated with their parents' sales: as much as 75 per cent or more of Air 2000's flying is done for parent Owners Abroad, whereas under half of Monarch's is undertaken for parent Cosmos. In Canada, around half of the output from Air Transat - the country's largest charter airline since the demise of Nationair in 1993 - is tied to products wholesaled and/or retailed by other members of Groupe Transat.[24]

Conclusion The industrial scope decision may lead to a strategy of investing in a portfolio of related or unrelated activities or, as is much more common in the airline industry, it may leave the decision-making unit a single-business enterprise. Many airlines, particularly smaller carriers, are in essence single-business enterprises. Some airlines have diversified, but in most cases it is strategies of related diversification that have been pursued; even in these cases, considerably more caution is currently being exhibited when straying from the 'core business' (as variously defined) than was true in some instances during the 1980s.

Moving on from the choice of industrial scope, each company - whether a standalone single-business enterprise or part of a wider portfolio - must make decisions in respect of vertical scope, product scope, and geographical scope. These scope decisions are the subject of the rest of the chapter.

Vertical scope

'Integrative growth' is the pursuit of greater control over suppliers, distribution channels, or competitors in support of market penetration, market development, product development, or diversification strategies. There are two types of integrative growth.

1   Vertical integration, either by acquisition or internal growth, may be:
    • backward, if control over the supply of upstream products or services is acquired (e.g. catering or maintenance); or
    • forward if control over distribution channels is secured (e.g. the ownership of retail travel agencies by Ansett and Qantas, the purchase by Royal Air Maroc of several small European tour operators specializing in Morocco in order to protect its charter business, or the taking of stakes in small, specialized tour organizers by Lufthansa's charter subsidiary Condor in the mid-90s). Use of electronic distribution technology by airlines to encourage direct distribution is also a form of forward integration.

2   Horizontal integration involves acquisition of competitors or potential competitors or the formation of marketing alliances. Acquisition of regionals by larger airlines wanting to secure traffic feed into their hubs is arguably a form of vertical integration. Horizontal integration is better represented by the wave of mergers involving major carriers in the United States during the 1980s, and similar activity on a smaller scale in Canada (Canadian and Wardair), France (Air France, UTA, and Air Inter), and the United Kingdom (British Airways, BCal, and Dan-Air), and by the use of code-sharing and marketing alliances to extend horizontal scope without expanding the asset base.

Horizontal integration is essentially a means of broadening product scope and/or geographical scope, both of which will be considered shortly. The discussion here will focus on vertical integration and its fashionable alternative, outsourcing.

Vertical integration Many scheduled airlines are within themselves relatively highly integrated insofar as they are self-sufficient in a lot of the products and services required to run their businesses - relying on contractual rather than ownership relationships for major inputs such as capital equipment, infrastructural services, and fuel, and also for much of their distribution, but nonetheless still undertaking inhouse a large number of activities which could in principle be performed by outsiders. Sometimes the reason for this has been that the 'principle' does not work in practice, such that in some or all of the locations where a particular airline operates there is simply no alternative to self-sufficiency. In the case of many large carriers operating out of developed economies, however, their vertical architecture is often based as much on tradition, inertia, and the expectations of internal stakeholders as on commercial logic.

Arguments in favour of vertical integration, aside from necessity, have generally included the following:

- control is gained over performance and quality in more parts of the value chain, and the entire chain can be better integrated;
- the risk of being 'held to ransom' by a single-source supplier or by a supplier able to impose high switching costs on an airline buying its services is largely eliminated;
- access to information and organizational learning is enhanced;
- costs can be lowered through exploitation of synergies, economies of scale and scope can be exploited, supplier profit margins can be eliminated, and transaction costs will be reduced because the need for supplier search, negotiation, contracting, and monitoring is eliminated;[25]
- opportunities could arise to sell spare capacity to other carriers; and
- barriers to entry can be created where a potential competitor considering entry onto a particular route is faced by the prospect of having to rely on the airline in question as monopoly supplier of an important service at one end of that route.

Against these points might be arrayed the facts that:

- high airline costs are typically transferred into lower-wage industries such as catering, cleaning, and janitorial services;
- some non-location-specific services at offshore sites might offer cheaper rates;[26]
- smaller airlines are frequently unable to build critical mass sufficient to exploit the economies of scale available in industries such as maintenance, catering, and cleaning;
- unnecessary system complexity adds costs, particularly fixed costs;
- different, and often specialized, management skills are required;
- risk is being increased by investing more funds into the same value chain, but rewards are not being maximized because instead of the investment being focused on core activities it is directed towards activities from which no competitive advantage is ever likely to be gained;
- flexibility to respond to changes in markets and technologies is reduced, and there is potential exposure to overcapacity in the supplying industry during economic downturns;
- in the absence of strong corporate leadership, internal suppliers might offer no better quality and reliability than external sources, but at higher costs undisciplined by market forces; and

- entrepreneurial instincts are blunted by the existence of captive inhouse markets.

In the final analysis, many small carriers do not generate a 'critical mass' in certain of their activities (e.g. ground handling, catering etc.) sufficient to justify performing them inhouse, and the same can also be true even for relatively large carriers - particularly at outstations.

Because airlines in various parts of the globe function in supplier markets having very different levels of sophistication (distribution tending to be more uniform in nature) and also because each carrier has its own financial and emotional investment sunk into existing organizational architecture, there is little prescriptive that can be said about vertical integration in the industry. Each airline must ultimately come to its own conclusion on the costs and benefits of retaining activities in an inhouse portfolio rather than putting them out to the market - assuming there to be one in existence for the activities concerned; often, conclusions are shaped not just by the existence of external markets but by their structure - that is, by the numbers and relative market power of buyers and sellers. It is probably fair to say, however, that less is now being taken for granted in this respect than has historically been the case, and that where alternatives to vertical integration are present they are at least being considered by a greater number of airlines.

There is even an argument - perhaps extreme and certainly not yet widely accepted - that the core of the airline business lies in control over service conceptualization, network management (i.e. design and scheduling), revenue management, customer information, the management of brands and reputation, and mastery (not necessarily ownership) of distribution channels. As IT capabilities improve, market knowledge deepens, and attitudes become more flexible, there is therefore no necessary reason why the vertically-integrated template for corporate structures inherited from the 19th century should survive long into the 21st. Were market-driven - rather than ownership-driven - service chains to assert themselves in the industry, the task of airline managers would be to identify the true sources of economic rent, focus on these, and leave the rest to closely monitored subcontractors. Far-fetched though this picture undoubtedly is at present, one of its ingredients has been receiving widespread attention within parts of the airline industry in recent years: outsourcing.

Outsourcing Airlines often have no choice other than to contract-in services - monopoly ground handling being an obvious, but far from unique, example (and sometimes operations at a particular station are insufficient in scale to justify self-handling even were it permissible). Also, many airlines are based in, or operate to, locations in which there are few if any alternative suppliers of required products or services.

In principle, there might appear to be a distinction between simple support functions - either aviation-related (e.g. aircraft cleaning or maintenance) or unrelated (e.g. security or staff canteens) - which an airline chooses to perform inhouse and strategic business units which, although their businesses might be related in some way to air transport activities, are managed independently from those activities, have a distinct set of missions, objectives and strategies, and are substantially separate rather than simply being internal suppliers of services contracted-out to raise utilization and spread overheads. But, in fact, although the latter might be better candidates for 'spinning-off' or possibly 'joint venturing', both types of activity are susceptible to one form of outsourcing or another.

There is nothing new in airlines having the choice of whether to perform or subcontract for a service. Neither is there anything new in the fact that older and larger airlines tend to be relatively self-sufficient whilst newer and smaller airlines are less integrated and so rely on third parties to a greater extent. What is new about 'outsourcing' is the willingness of some older, larger airlines - notably in North America and Europe - to look more deeply into their operating systems for activities previously considered sacrosanct but now felt to be noncore and so appropriate for moving out of the 'inner organization' and into the wider network of external suppliers. The rationale is usually one or a combination of the following.

1   Strategy: there is no single airline that can be good at everything in the value chain, and competitive advantage which is both sustainable and not readily imitable is anyway more likely to stem from the core activities where real customer value is added. New-generation engines and avionics, for example, have become much more reliable and so need fewer shop visits, yet the infrastructure required to support them is considerably more expensive than in the past. Questions need to be asked about whether the investment in this infrastructure either provides or supports a real competitive advantage.[27]

2   Finance: overleveraged airlines can benefit from the infusion of cash generated by full or partial sale of support units (and those that do not already have such units can avoid the need to invest in them). More generally, the advantages of outsourcing frequently include transformation of fixed costs into variable costs and, importantly, both a reduction in total expenditure and greater cost transparency.

3   Efficiency: outsourced operations can benefit from more entrepreneurial and better motivated management than might be the case at an inhouse unit within a large airline, from faster decision-making, and from a greater willingness to benchmark performance

against the standards of their own industry and take responsibility for that performance.

4   Expertise: particularly in areas such as IT or maintenance, an airline might already have inhouse functions which it is fully prepared to retain for work on 'legacy' systems, but at the same time find it profitable to outsource specialized work on new systems in respect of which inhouse capabilities would otherwise have to be developed.

5   Control: it has been widely argued that management time is better spent focused on core activities than spread thinly over a multitude of peripheral functions. The logical extension of this is that 'core' activities could become the responsibility of a 'core' staff within the organization managed by traditional - if flatter - hierarchical relationships, while everything else will be outside the organization embodied in an equally, but differently, managed network of contractual relationships. One outcome would be improvement in clarity, flexibility, and accountability.

Within any given function, outsourcing might be either partial (e.g. just IT applications and development or just engine maintenance) or total (e.g. the entire IT or maintenance infrastructures). Examples of this 'internal decoupling' and parallel 'external coupling' have grown in number. Early in the 1990s, American spun-off Sky Chefs (25 per cent of which was bought by Lufthansa's LSG subsidiary in 1994) and entered into a long-term partnership deal, and United did something similar when it sold 15 flight kitchens to Dobbs International and committed to a 7-year catering contract; amongst US majors, only Continental and Southwest - the latter not renowned for its gourmet fare - had not outsourced flight catering by the mid-90s, and most European carriers also outsource their catering; British Airways sold its engine overhaul activities to General Electric in the early 1990s, disposed of its landing-gear overhaul operation several years later, and at the time of writing is rumoured to be a potential seller of its airframe maintenance and engineering business; Lufthansa has outsourced many of its property services functions, encompassing building maintenance and security; British Airways has outsourced management of its vehicle fleet; Canadian Airlines International outsources reservations, IT, passenger services planning, operational planning, yield management and a variety of other services from subsidiaries of its minority shareholder AMR Corporation; America West chose in the mid-90s to outsource substantial parts of its inhouse maintenance operations - and paid for selection of the lowest bidder (and for a lack of proper implementation planning) through the impact that unmet return-to-service commitments had on schedule integrity during the summer of 1996; Lufthansa CityLine has outsourced to Contact Air the operation of its F50 fleet, leaving the Lufthansa subsidiary to concentrate on jet operations; EDS manages

Aéromexico's reservations and inventory control systems. Amongst the most radical experiments in outsourcing witnessed to date - prototypical of the talked-about but rarely seen 'virtual airline' - have been in Venezuela, where Avensa essentially reinvented itself as Servivensa and began outsourcing practically every airline activity (including flight crew services, bought-in by the hour from an independent company formed from what remained of the carrier's pilots' union), and in Australia, where Qantas regional affiliate Airlink was functioning in the mid-90s with a core staff of just five people (aircraft being wet-leased and substantially all support services being outsourced[28]).

Outsourcing flight operations by wet-leasing aircraft and crews to meet specific needs for additional lift has been common industry practice for decades. The outsourcing of flight operations in their entirety has been relatively unusual. Several start-ups have chosen this route in recent years, however; one example is easyJet, a UK-based new entrant which began service in the mid-90s with a small fleet of B737s flying under Air Foyle's air operator's certificate. Separately but in similar vein, chapter 5 will be looking amongst other things at code-sharing and franchising - both of which can be characterized as forms of flight operations outsourcing (and have indeed been so characterized by several pilots' unions anxious to control their spread and protect jobs).

Distribution activities have long been substantially outsourced by airlines, and more are now giving consideration to the purchase of flight planning, maintenance planning and inventory control, load and departure control, revenue accounting, and other routine financial functions. In the United States, reservations services have at times been outsourced by a number of airlines, either on an overflow basis or - particularly in the case of start-ups - in their entirety. Globally, several airlines have decided to outsource their international offline sales and marketing activities to specialists such as AMR Services or Discover the World, which span multiple markets and offer market analysis, planning, and management services well beyond the scope of activities traditionally undertaken by general sales agencies.

The outsourcing of maintenance (heavy airframe, light airframe, line maintenance, powerplant, and/or avionics) has been common for decades and is becoming more so. The global market for heavy airframe work, engine and component overhaul, and for line maintenance is worth approximately $23 billion per annum; around 30 per cent is outsourced.[29] Although outsourcing by low-cost start-ups received a lot of adverse media coverage in the United States during the mid-90s, it is far from being solely a start-up strategy; around 25 per cent of total direct maintenance was being outsourced by nationals and majors at that time. Sometimes it is just peak loading or unanticipated work that goes outside the major airlines, but more carriers are now prepared to consider outsourcing entire lines; conversely, other well-established facilities are actively seeking third party work - current examples including those operated by Air France, American, and Northwest in airframe heavy maintenance.

Separately, a few airlines have been prepared to enter into 'total technical support contracts', under which another carrier manages fleet maintenance and overhaul in their entirety; for example, Lufthansa provides total technical support packages for Aeroflot's A310s and Uzbekistan Airways' A310s and B767-300ERs.

Although it is not uncommon to read about threshold figures, such as 100,000 flight-hours or 250 high-bypass turbofans, below which inhouse airframe or engine shops cannot be justified, decisions in respect of retention and outsourcing will depend upon a variety of factors. These include:

- an airline's cost structure;
- existing skills and resources;
- ability to win third-party work with which to make up any shortfall below minimum efficient scale;
- the strength of its unions;
- the cultural setting and specific expectations of stakeholders such as governments and employees; and
- the impact of network structure on the carrier's ability to undertake urgent work arising from AOG situations or airworthiness directives if inhouse facilities are lacking.

A growing trend amongst airlines that do not outsource all their maintenance is the outsourcing of parts inventories that support inhouse activities. In the mid-90s for example, British Airways Avionics Engineering entered into agreements with several original equipment manufacturers (OEMs) to hold inventory on its behalf, in some cases at convenient local distribution centres; any part required was to be made available within a day if held in the United Kingdom, three days if inventoried elsewhere in the world, or within seven days if it had to be manufactured.[30]

As cargo divisions are separated out and transformed into profit centres, it is possible that the large investments in development required to update their IT systems to something close to what has been achieved on the passenger side of the industry will lead them towards increased outsourcing. Relatively small carriers in particular often find it cost-effective to outsource the management of their entire cargo operations to a forwarder or specialized cargo services provider. A number of airlines outsource all-cargo flight operations in preference - or in addition - to operating their own freighters; British Airways, Emirates, and Swissair are just some of the carriers that have entered into fixed cost per block-hour wet leases of B747s with specialist Atlas Air, for example. Separately, some airlines are revenue-sharing with suppliers of interactive inflight entertainment equipment (IFE) who build, install, and maintain the systems at no cost to the carrier.

There is a view that the only reason outsourcing is not more common than it is in the airline industry - in other words, the only reason that internal monopolies persist - is the lingering operations-driven approach to business which in many carriers has yet to be fully exorcised by a commercial orientation. According to this view, outsourcing should lead to the creation of networks of suppliers and distributors clustered around the service conceptualization and management capabilities of the airline core, the whole being held together by information technology, culture, and a customer-focused sense of mission. The gap between the conceptualization of services and noncore aspects of their delivery becomes wider, asset ownership less relevant, and skills other than marketing more peripheral (insofar as they can as readily be managed through external as internal contracts). An airline becomes a system designer and integrator, in much the same manner as Boeing or Airbus design and integrate aircraft systems without necessarily manufacturing all the subsystems and components. Corporate boundaries blur as networks of internal and external service providers unite in support of a horizontal, customer-focused service chain.

One paradigm generally quoted in support of this argument is the hotel industry. A few globally franchised service concepts supplemented by a host of local competitors, some also franchised and others 'owner-operated'. Another is maritime transportation, an industry that commonly houses marketing, operations, maintenance, and ownership activities in quite separate and often unrelated companies. There are, however, some powerful brakes on this 'industrial unbundling'.

1   Risk: strategically important skills might be allowed to ebb away; customer service might suffer; the market awareness and shared information which pass through informal communication channels might be lost when the erstwhile receiver is no longer on 'the inside'; whereas the cost of retaining a function inhouse might be readily identifiable, the full costs of outsourcing might not - certain human resource management functions being a good example because of the need to have them embedded into the culture of a people-driven service industry such as the airline business; and opportunities for organizational learning will be strait-jacketed within the confines of performance-specific external contracts. Overall, there is a risk that the sine qua non of systems thinking - that the whole amounts to more than the sum of the parts - will be buried (doubtless to be 'rediscovered' by a new generation of management gurus).

2   Quality: in certain areas of airline operations, risks are such that there is a need for adherence to the highest possible quality standards. Maintenance, repair, and overhaul is one important example, and flight crew training is another. It is usual for start-ups to outsource their maintenance, engineering, purchasing, inventory management, and technical information activities, and the question was raised after

various incidents in the United States in the mid-90s whether low-cost start-ups in particular - some of which have been likened to 'virtual airlines' because of the extent of their outsourcing - are properly equipped to control the quality of outsourced work. No airline can outsource its ultimate responsibility for maintenance planning and control - for the airworthiness of its aircraft.

In fact, whatever the work being outsourced somebody, somewhere in the airline concerned has to be sufficiently qualified and knowledgeable to evaluate the quality of that work - something that is evidently easier in respect of aircraft cleaning and flight catering than, say, maintenance or IT. The close monitoring of quality is particularly vital when safety or key operational and business processes are involved, and also when corporate reputation and brand integrity are at risk.[31] More generally, airlines need to be extremely mindful of the component elements of customer satisfaction (discussed at length in Part Two), and cautious about outsourcing processes which contribute substantially to each of these elements.

3   Feasibility: some carriers are constrained from outsourcing by powerful labour unions, one example being the terms of United's employee buyout which leave management with relatively little room to manouevre in respect of asset sales disapproved of by employees. Many state-owned airlines are still expected by government stakeholders to provide jobs, and so would not want to consider significant outsourcing for this reason alone.[32] Airlines doing heavy maintenance on a progressive basis rather than in discrete blocks do not have the option to outsource this activity unless they share a maintenance base with a potential service provider. Finally, it has already been noted that in many countries outsourcing is simply not feasible because external suppliers capable of delivering on price and quality are unavailable.

4   Culture: whilst airlines globally might be able to benefit from some degree of outsourcing, the heartland of the concept has been the United States and the United Kingdom - where commitment to markets, internal as well as external - found its most ideologically extreme supplicants in the 1980s. Not every cultural setting is as welcoming. There are still many places in which preparing meals and fixing broken airplanes are considered as much the natural functions of an airline as designing and selling air transport services.

5   Strategy: one airline's periphery might be another's core. Several established carriers (e.g. American, Delta, and Northwest) have invested heavily in their airframe maintenance facilities in recent years, and in Asia and the Middle East EVA Air, Asiana, and Emirates have built theirs from the ground up.[33] In 1994, SAS sold its flight

catering operations to Swissair's Gate Gourmet, yet elsewhere in the flight catering industry Lufthansa seems intent on retaining a majority interest in Lufthansa Service Holding AG, and Singapore Airlines apparently regards SATS Catering and its various international joint ventures as core businesses.[34] The central point about outsourcing is not in fact whether it is good or bad, sensible or foolhardy in the abstract - but whether in the given circumstances of a particular airline it does or does not support a chosen strategy.

Conclusions on vertical integration and outsourcing We have seen that the dividing line between vertical integration and related diversification is ill-defined. The discussion in the last few pages does, nonetheless, help to identify several alternative strategies for securing the supply of services required to run an airline.

1   Inhouse supply by an internal department/cost centre. This has been the traditional approach in large, highly integrated airlines, and it is still widespread.

2   Inhouse supply by an internal profit centre. Some airlines that are prepared neither to spin-off internal service suppliers into separate subsidiaries nor to outsource the services they supply, have instead tried to introduce a more entrepreneurial and bottom-line oriented culture by enforcing greater cost transparency and expectations of profitability on what were previously accepted simply as necessary cost centres. Thus, whereas Lufthansa has transformed its cargo operation into a separately incorporated subsidiary, KLM and British Airways have to date retained theirs as internal profit centres.[35]

3   Inhouse supply by a subsidiary or a joint venture. Although it remains more unusual than the volume of press coverage might suggest, there has been a clear trend towards this solution amongst some of the world's larger airlines. The primary objectives have been to cut costs by removing the 'monopoly supplier' mentality and to earn incremental revenues by competing more aggressively for third party work;[36] in the case of joint ventures, motives can extend to the realization of cash from partial sale of existing assets or expertise, access to a 'captive' source of external skills, and the sharing of investment costs. In either case, such arrangements could be an interim step in the direction of divesting the operation entirely - a gradual approach being both more flexible from a strategic standpoint and, in some countries, more acceptable to organized labour and politically important external stakeholders.
    Going one step further than a joint venture with one or a small number of external parties, some airlines are considering public flotations of minority interests in certain of their subsidiaries. AMR

Corporation - American Airlines' parent - has taken this route with the Sabre Group. As well as the raising of cash, an additional motive for getting a subsidiary publicly listed might be to realize shareholder value in that subsidiary which is not reflected in the parent's balance sheet - that is, which the stock market does not presently recognize, but which would be recognized were the subsidiary evaluated as a standalone entity.

Some larger airlines have been concluding that what were once seen simply as support functions - possibly doing some contract work to spread fixed costs and perhaps generate incremental profit - are in fact capable of being active competitors in their own distinct markets. Frequently they are expected to compete for their parent's business as well as for third party work. Lufthansa, for example, has spun-off its maintenance and overhaul, cargo, information systems, and flight training operations into Lufthansa Technik (which does around half its work for third parties), Lufthansa Cargo, Lufthansa Systems (25 per cent owned by EDS), and Lufthansa Flight Training respectively. Lufthansa Consulting has been a separate subsidiary since 1988. The LSG/Sky Chefs joint venture appears at the time of writing to be a candidate for public flotation. Similarly, British Airways Avionics Engineering opened a 140,000 square feet, 400-employee facility in South Wales late in 1994 with the intention of throughputting 130,000 components per annum by 1998, approximately half of which would be from outside the parent airline. The operation is managerially and financially self-contained, with terms and conditions of employment different from those at British Airways Engineering (and, because it is a separate company, its own JAR-145 and FAR-145 certifications as a maintenance organization).

Despite their growing popularity, spin-offs do raise some potentially thorny issues - notably:

- the extent to which priority is in reality expected to be given to work being done for the parent airline when there is conflict with commitments to third parties;
- whether transfer pricing really is to be effected at market rates; and
- whether the parent does in practice have freedom to refer work to external suppliers.

Lufthansa, for example, gave its maintenance and engineering subsidiary three years to adjust both to the requirement to offer the parent company market-based prices, and to the reality of learning to live without guaranteed business volumes from the airline. For many carriers, this would still be a very difficult decision to take.

Neither do the cost transparency and market orientations anticipated as a result of spinning-off internal divisions or departments necessarily equate to cost competitiveness; Team Aer Lingus was spun-off into a separate subsidiary relatively early in the current round of restructurings, but failed to achieve anything close to cost parity with many of its competitors. Cost competitiveness is nonetheless vital for any true spin-off operating with its own income statement, because solicitation of third-party work can in this case no longer be looked upon as just a way of filling intermittent troughs in the parent airline's requirements (at marginal cost prices if necessary), but must instead be treated as an ongoing source of revenue and profits.

Another issue is just what should leave the core airline along with the spin-off. In other words, how much technical competence as a planner and buyer of services in the particular field of activities being spun off should be retained within the airline. Thus, Lufthansa's maintenance planning activities and its light and line maintenance have gone into the Lufthansa Technik subsidiary rather than staying within the airline, raising questions as to just how independent the carrier could ever really allow its affiliate to become.[37]

4   Outsourcing. The antithesis of integrative growth and diversification, this involves dispensing with inhouse suppliers of a particular service and turning instead to third parties - which may be other airlines, independent companies, or the former inhouse unit itself after having been sold. Cost savings and a desire to redirect investment into core activities in which sources of real competitive advantage can be found are the most frequently cited motivations for outsourcing.

The discussion of decisions currently being taken within the airline industry with respect to industrial scope and vertical scope makes it possible to identify several trends which, whilst by no means descriptive of every airline, reflect a broad strategic consensus - a consensus that inevitably comes under pressure during the course of any prolonged upswing in financial fortunes:

- widespread preference for measured growth focused on core activities, as variously defined;
- caution towards new diversification initiatives; and
- willingness to reassess the contribution to corporate goals and objectives being made by internal service providers.

There is thus a significant amount of analysis being undertaken in the industry with regard to how best to answer the 'Where to compete?' question inherent in corporate strategy. Turning more specifically to air transport services, there are two other sets of decisions in respect of corporate scope which also address 'Where to compete?' The next section will look at these alternatives, which together define product scope and geographical scope.

Product scope and geographical scope

A customer purchasing any good or service is simultaneously participating in both a product market and a geographical market. Although closely related, choices determining product scope and geographical scope are in many industries nonetheless quite distinct. In a network industry such as commercial air transportation, however, these scope decisions are fundamentally symbiotic. Indeed, every departure is in itself a product offered to one or more geographical markets, and different levels of ground and onboard amenities provided to consumers travelling in whatever separate classes are available on each departure can be characterized as product attributes offered to different segments of those markets. Thus, when discussing geographical scope choices, we are here referring to network management decisions that lead to the offering of departures on specific routes (which might serve intermediate and connecting markets as well as nonstop markets); when discussing product scope, we are referring to the range of alternative service offers being made - notably, but not uniquely, the classes available and the attributes associated with each. (We will be returning to this topic in considerably more detail in chapter 6, where the management of service-price offers is explored in some depth.)

Before proceeding further, it is necessary to define a number of descriptive terms in common usage: niche, start-up, new entrant, and low-cost carrier. According to ICAO:

- a *niche carrier* is an air carrier specializing on particular routes or in a particular segment of the market;
- a *start-up carrier* is a newly established air carrier;
- a *new entrant* means a carrier, newly established or not, that attempts to enter a market already served by other carriers;
- a *low-cost* carrier generally refers to an air carrier which has a relatively low cost structure in comparison with other comparable carriers and offers low fares or rates. Such a carrier may be independent, the subsidiary of a major carrier or, in some instances, the ex-charter arm of an airline group.[38]

A decision to enter a particular geographical market will very often either require or preclude the offering of particular products; similarly, decisions to focus on a particular type of product very often preclude entry into certain geographical markets. Thus, a decision to enter a long-haul market with high-frequency scheduled services almost inevitably requires the offering of a wide range of onboard products (i.e. first and/or business and economy/coach class) in order to exploit the economies of density likely to be needed to support a high level of frequencies;[39] similarly, a decision to offer a high-density, charter-type product with attributes designed primarily to appeal to short-haul leisure or VFR (visiting friends and relations) traffic is unlikely to have widespread appeal outside a fairly narrow spread of geographical markets. Although in many ways quite separate, airline product and geographical scope decisions are often so intimately related within the context of a particular network that they will here be treated together.

Geographical decisions might be constrained by government policies or by restrictive bilaterals, although - as was described in Volume One, chapter 3 - these constraints are being loosened in many parts of the world. Both geographical and product scope decisions might also be determined by the vision a carrier has for its future, the mission being pursued, and the strategic picture that it has of itself; both scope decisions will, at least in the short run, inevitably be affected by available resources and skills. Subject to these considerations, industry economics also have a powerful role to play in influencing managements faced with choices of product and geographical scope. Throughout most of the postwar era, the impact of industry economics has not been as powerful as would have been the case had air transport markets been free of commercial regulation; market forces were effectively blunted by the Chicago system described in chapter 3 of Volume One, as well as by the restrictive airline licensing and ownership policies adopted by most of the world's governments.

The defining feature of the airline industry's current transition is erosion of the regulatory 'sea-walls' that until the 1980s were keeping market forces at bay. Despite the immense progress that has been made towards liberalizing and even deregulating many important markets, however, the global airline industry as a whole remains far from being free of commercial regulation. Changes so far have nonetheless been sufficient to make it clear that choices regarding product scope and geographical scope will have to be made from what is in generic terms a fairly limited menu of alternatives. In future, it is likely to be industry economics that limit the menu more than the strait-jacket of commercial regulation.

Categorizing strategies is always going to be an exercise fraught with ambiguity and inconsistency, if only because no two airlines are ever in precisely the same situation or pursuing precisely the same strategy. Broad generalizations are nonetheless both possible and analytically helpful. The generalizations offered here will be based upon a distinction between 'wide-market' and 'niche' strategies popularized by Porter's work on competitive strategy in the 1980s (and already referred to when competitive advantage was discussed in Volume One, chapter 17). This chapter, being oriented towards the 'Where to compete?' question, will examine the fundamental choices between wide-market and niche product scope and geographical scope decisions; the next chapter will consider the 'How to compete?' question by looking at alternative competitive strategies available once product and geographical scope have been determined. Clearly, there is a close linkage between choices of scope and choices of competitive strategy, and often - although not invariably - the former will to a large extent determine the latter.

The following discussion will deal with air transport rather than any other type of enterprise in which an airline might be involved. It will look in turn at wide-market product scope and geographical scope alternatives, and then at geographical and segment niches.

Wide-market strategies: product scope The economics of the industry sometimes favour a wide-market product strategy, particularly on long-haul routes. Approximately 50-55 per cent of traffic at American, Delta, and United, for example, is comprised of business travellers, with the balance split amongst passengers travelling for leisure or VFR reasons. The advantages of simultaneously serving multiple segments - such as, say, business, leisure, VFR, and freight - can include:

- economies of scope, available from delivering multiple services into multiple markets and thereby raising the productivity of shared skills and resources;
- economies of density, available when by serving all segments of demand in a particular geographical market it is possible to operate at acceptable load factors larger aircraft (with lower seat-kilometre costs) than could be supported by one segment alone;
- marketing economies of scale;
- better accommodation of demand peaking; and/or
- a wider 'portfolio' of risks, some of which might be served by specialized units or subsidiaries.

Wide-market operations are expensive to mount. Furthermore, serving multiple segments requires the management of a range of different service-price offers, coordinating their delivery, and controlling different levels of service within the same service delivery systems. Maintaining a constant image across several segments and yet also making it appropriate to each can be challenging. For example, market research conducted by British Airways in the late 1980s identified that the airline's image of cool, somewhat detached professionalism, which was highly successful with the business segment, left many potential leisure travellers feeling its services 'must' be too expensive for them to use. Despite attempts to remedy this through marketing communications and through redesign of leisure products and the relaunching of leisure sub-brands, research was still showing the airline to have a somewhat 'impersonal' image in the mid-90s.

Wide-market carriers are also exposed to 'cherry-picking'. Low-cost airlines in the United States have done it to the point where the orchard's boundaries have been effectively redefined. Airlines such as Southwest and successive waves of low-cost/no-frills post-deregulation start-ups targeted the most price-sensitive subsegments of both leisure and (to a much lesser extent) business markets and tailored their network management, service concepts, and service delivery processes with the sole intent of delivering profitably the particular service-price offers demanded by the targeted segments and not yet being supplied by full-service incumbents. Aeropolitical liberalization has stimulated similar initiatives elsewhere during the 1990s (e.g. easyJet in the United Kingdom, Virgin Express in Western Europe, National Airlines in Chile, and LAPA in Argentina). Similarly, combination carriers essentially sat and watched while FedEx and the other integrators made the express/small package business their own in the 1980s - and this particular cherry has since grown into one of the airfreight industry's principal 'cash crops'.

Any airline committed to a high-frequency, scheduled, long-haul route network is, by virtue of the size of equipment required, also committed to a wide-market strategy - even though the degree of emphasis placed on each of the multiple segments served will vary between carriers (and also between routes). A focused strategy is more feasible over short-haul networks and this, for example, is what SAS set out to achieve when it targeted business travellers as part of its 1980s corporate turnaround. Even so, to maintain adequate resource utilization and productivity it is necessary to tap other segments during the middle of each weekday and at the weekend. Neither SAS nor any other scheduled European carrier has obvious competitive advantages in the short-haul mass leisure segment, but subsegments of leisure travel nonetheless have had to be tapped within their primarily business-oriented short-haul networks.

This hints at a generalization which is broad but nonetheless robust: there are strong, focused carriers in most market segments and some of these have become large by any standard (e.g. Britannia and UPS), but the majority of the world's airlines - certainly the bigger ones - pursue a wide-market product strategy. To a large extent they do this themselves but sometimes, for reasons of economics or brand image, subsidiaries are used. This has happened, for example, where European 'flag carriers' have chosen to serve the package tour subsegment of leisure demand through subsidiaries. A few are using the same approach to serve price-sensitive demand on scheduled routes. The use of affiliates in thin regional markets is another example. A further generalization - to which, inevitably, there will always be exceptions - is that the wider an airline's geographical scope, the more likely it is to follow a wide-market product strategy.

Wide-market strategies: geographical scope In domestic markets, airlines can become wide-market in a geographical sense. This is what several US majors tried to do after deregulation. Some failed because they spread their resources too thinly. The problem with applying the concept internationally is that the history of the industry's regulatory regime - based on sovereignty, reciprocity, and equal opportunity - has not left it with any truly global carriers; international airlines remain predominantly focused on routes from, to and - in the case of sixth freedom operations - through their home countries.

Many of the advantages of a wide-market approach to products carry over to wide-market geographical strategies. Economies of scope, together with marketing (primarily information) economies of scale, are particularly important. Furthermore, the wider the scope of its network - in terms of length of haul and types of destination - and the broader the range of market segments served, the better able an airline should be to raise resource utilization. Additional benefits include the preference for online connections amongst most consumers who are obliged to change planes en route, the attractions of a wide network offering a range of destinations for the redemption of frequent flyer awards (although joint programmes can reduce the impact of this), and the better ability to withstand competitive attack in one market by cross-subsidizing it from elsewhere in the network. On the basis of research into routes between the United Kingdom and Europe, for example, it has been estimated that British Airways' network coverage is capable of generating a fare premium of between four and five per cent.[40]

United is arguably closer to being a truly wide-market international airline than any others in its strategic group simply because it has a strong presence in more of the world's important route-groups than any other single carrier. Its alliance with Lufthansa, incorporating a growing band of other airlines (e.g. SAS, Thai, Air Canada, Varig, and several others), increases network scope even further. The largest European carriers are by themselves still a long way from being 'global', because they are precluded from participating directly in several geographical markets (e.g. the US domestic and transpacific markets) which together account for a significant proportion of the industry's traffic flows and revenues. This is one of the driving forces behind the alliance phenomenon that we will be looking at in chapter 5.

Wide-market strategies: the geographical scope decisions being made in practice Notwithstanding definitional imprecision inherent in trying to draw a boundary between wide-market and niche geographical scope decisions, it is possible to identify the emergence of a relatively limited choice of wide-market alternatives.

1 **Full-service global network carriers** As noted, no individual airline has - or is likely any time soon to develop - a truly global network of its own. A small number of the largest carriers have instead embarked upon geographical scope strategies intended to expand their networks and build global market share by using domestic and cross-border alliance relationships. Features common to this type of scope expansion include:
   - designing networks which tap O and D traffic in major nonstop markets and maximize access to flow traffic in connecting markets unable to support high-frequency nonstop service;
   - use of code-sharing, franchising, and similar techniques to extend network reach and, together with highly integrated scheduling, maximize city-pair connectivity with the objective of capturing and

retaining online a high proportion of end-to-end journeys made in targeted market segments;

- creating double-hub systems able both to dominate inter-hub markets and to capture flows of traffic originating in secondary points behind one hub and destined for secondary points beyond the other. For example, the Atlantic Excellence partnership established in 1997 by Delta, Austrian, Swissair, and Sabena connected at that time approximately 130 destinations in North America with a similar number in Europe, the Middle East, and Africa over interlinked - and therefore from the perspective of passengers originating behind and/or destined beyond - largely interchangeable hubs at New York JFK, Cincinnati, and Atlanta on one side of the Atlantic and Brussels, Zurich, and Vienna on the other side; and

- using separate operating units or, alternatively, ownership or contractual relationships with code-shared and/or franchised specialist carriers to extend network reach into specific niches unsuited to the 'mainline' full-service, wide-market product. Examples include: low-cost scheduled services in predominantly business-oriented markets exposed to attack by low-cost niche competitors (e.g. the United Shuttle); low-cost scheduled services in predominantly leisure-oriented markets (e.g. Delta Express); low-cost scheduled and nonscheduled services in leisure markets (e.g. Lufthansa's Condor subsidiary); high-frequency service on short, thin routes into or, less commonly in the United States than in Europe, bypassing the network carrier's hub(s); and services oriented to specific, point-to-point geographical niches (e.g. British Airways' franchised affiliate GB Airways, which has specialized in scheduled services to Mediterranean destinations).

2   **Other full-service, wide-market carriers operating outside the scope of a global network** Most remaining national 'flag carriers' (whether or not government-owned), as well as many 'independent' airlines, have made wide-market product and geographical scope decisions. They sometimes operate on a combination of short-, medium-, and long-haul routes, but none in this category come close to replicating the network reach being established by the world's largest carriers and their alliance partners. It is generally felt that, unable to grow into a global presence on their own, these airlines must either find that presence in the context of an alliance or carve for themselves distinctive niches within which each can survive entirely or largely alone. The long-run financial outcome of any other strategy, it is argued, will inevitably be unattractive. The scope choice therefore depends to a considerable degree upon the attractiveness - in geographical and service terms - of each such airline as a potential alliance partner, and the extent to which it has distinctive

and sustainable cost and/or service advantages upon which to build and defend a standalone niche.

Niche strategies: geographical niches What constitutes a geographical niche and what represents a geographical wide-market strategy is obvious at the extremes and very unclear in the middle-ground. Geographical niches can be served by carriers making wide-market product offers: Virgin Atlantic has targeted dense, long-haul routes out of London and at the same time initiated a redrawing of the parameters of wide-market product competition on the long-haul passenger side of the business.[41] Low-cost/no-frills challengers to wide-market incumbents in North America and Europe are in many cases constrained to serve short-haul, point-to-point markets that are sufficiently dense and airports that are sufficiently cheap and uncongested to support the competitive cost structures dictated by the particular service-price offers they are targeting at price-sensitive subsegments; to this extent, they can also often be characterized as geographical niche carriers (although Southwest in particular has expanded its 'niches' to the point where it is now the eighth largest US carrier). Ryanair's low-cost/low-fare product-market niche was originally founded on a geographical niche (connecting Britain and Ireland) - as, by definition, ethnic/VFR markets must be. Conversely, the nature of a chosen geographical niche might dictate the required product scope decision.

Regional airlines operate in distinct geographical niches, which might have one or more of several facets. They commonly feed network carriers at hubs, helping to build traffic flow by adding new points, increasing frequencies on their own routes, and possibly augmenting frequencies on the larger airlines' routes by adding low-gauge off-peak capacity. Regionals can also assist in sustaining a large carrier's brand presence in thin, short-haul markets which its cost structure is too high to allow it to serve profitably; they do this by taking over thin, short-haul routes and operating them for the network carrier. As well as boosting network flow traffic over major airlines' hubs, regionals serve thin O and D markets in and out of those same hubs and, particularly in Europe, operate hub bypass services; the latter could be standalone operations, or they might be designed to augment the network carrier's higher frequency connecting services over the hub and at the same time deter potential nonstop challengers.

Although US regionals remain heavily oriented towards hub-feed operations, several European regionals each simultaneously operate with a number of distinct network concepts. For example, Crossair:

- feeds Swissair at Zurich;
- operates its own mini-hub at Basle-Mulhouse;[42] and
- serves several point-to-point markets (e.g. in and out of Lugano).[43]

Technological developments are currently having a strong impact on regional airline niches. Perhaps the leading example is the introduction of regional jets, which allow carriers to:

- widen hub catchment areas by serving spoke outstations that turboprops cannot reach, so helping the hub to develop new markets and raid other hub hinterlands up to 1,000nm away;[44]
- replace either similar gauge or smaller turboprops on regional routes where greater passenger acceptance, and so potentially firmer yields, support the higher operating costs likely to be involved. The routes in question will usually be relatively long by regional airline standards, but Comair is just one of several carriers which has deployed regional jets on short hops of 100nm or less;
- replace larger aircraft operated by an affiliated major airline on long routes too thin to support high-frequency operations with 100-seaters, which are often the smallest aircraft in 'mainline' fleets;
- supplement majors' mainline fleets and improve their service offers by operating regional jets on trunk routes at off-peak hours;
- develop longer hub-bypass routes that have turboprop flying times greater than most consumers find acceptable; and
- compete in other niche markets.[45]

Growing out of a geographical niche can be dangerous: in the US domestic market Delta succeeded, albeit after stretching its balance sheet; Northwest and USAir both tried and then had second thoughts (although in the mid-90s USAir - by then reinvented as US Airways - had 'third thoughts', when a new senior management team started looking for opportunities to boost the carrier's average stage length by introducing more transcontinental and transatlantic services); Braniff tried and failed. Northwest, for example, has refocused domestically around network (as opposed to point-to-point) operations in the Upper Midwest.[46] On a smaller scale, start-up Western Pacific chose two years after its 1995 launch to take what some analysts at the time saw as a 'courageous' decision to shift substantial resources from its Colorado Springs hub and deploy them against United's high-cost 'fortress hub' at Denver;[47] in Europe, SAS has abandoned its global 'one-stop shop' ambitions, instead concentrating most effort on intra-European markets in partnership with Lufthansa. Intensive growth at larger international airlines tends to be very much more focused now than when 'everything to everybody' grabs for market share were in vogue, and alliances of various form have become the vehicles of choice for many expansion strategies.

Like all niches, a geographical niche can be eroded over time. An example of a market shifting away from a niche is Austrian Airlines' post-war strategy of feeding traffic between Western and Eastern Europe over its Vienna hub being overtaken by the opening of direct services following the end of the cold war.

A problem with small geographical niches in particular is that they expose those serving them to the economies of relatively few catchment areas (which could be regional or national in scale, depending upon how any particular niche is defined). Also, in deregulated or liberalized markets they can be the target of capacity - and price - dumping by larger airlines with a few spare block-hours available between peaks in their own primary markets. The failures encountered in the mid-90s by British Airways' affiliates TAT and Deutsche BA when attempting to establish profitable cross-border intra-EU routes out of Paris and Munich respectively illustrate the magnitude of the barriers faced even by strongly backed entrants taking on large incumbents at the heart of their networks. On the other hand, large airlines can be as capable of developing as they are of attacking geographical niches; sometimes this is done using specialized affiliates, such as Singapore Airlines' short-haul subsidiary SilkAir.

Niche strategies: segment niches Air transport markets can be segmented in many different ways, and leading airlines are now showing a considerable amount of imagination in this area of marketing. For the purpose of the present discussion, however, it is enough to rely on the traditional distinction between passengers travelling on business, for vacation, or to visit friends and relations and, in the airfreight market, between express packages and heavy freight.[48]

1 **Business passengers** The attraction of this segment is its generally higher yields and lower price elasticity than the leisure segment, the high number of trips per annum attributable to each traveller (which has implications for customer retention and loyalty, discussed in chapter 10), and the less pronounced seasonal peaking of demand.[49] On the other side of the ledger are the facts that strong intra-day and intra-week peaks can lower resource utilization unless addressed, the segment is growing more slowly than the leisure segment, and it is vulnerable to attack at the margins from the telecommunications industry. Another drawback counterbalancing the high revenues earned from business travellers is the greater delivery costs associated with many of the service attributes demanded. They generally require, for example:

- high frequencies, and therefore often smaller aircraft with higher seat-mile costs (and, incidentally, less freight capacity) than would be the case were larger aircraft flown at lower frequencies on the same route;
- high seat accessibility, which may lower load factors in the absence of finely tuned revenue management systems and so raises costs per unit of output sold; and

- higher standards in respect of ground handling (e.g. express check-in, airport lounges, and priority baggage reclaim) and the inflight product (e.g. pitch, width and recline angle of seats, cabin crew ratios, catering, amenities, carry-on storage, and access to washrooms).

Within the business segment it is often possible to identify subsegments at which specific offers can be targeted. Conferences and incentive travel are obvious examples. Several US ventures - Air Atlanta, MGM Grand Air, Regent Air, and Ultra Air for instance - have also tried various service-price combinations at the top end of the segment, but all failed. The Belgian carrier VLM entered the Antwerp-London City market in the early 1990s to exploit a niche serving the diamond trade, which had in fact first been identified several years before by a British start-up operating out of Gatwick; VLM later briefly used opportunities stemming from the European Union's Third Package of liberalization measures (see Volume One, chapter 3) to extend two of its four weekday services onto a consecutive cabotage sector from London City to Liverpool, exploiting shipping industry linkages between the three cities. In the United States, the Milwaukee-based former Kimberly-Clark subsidiary Midwest Express has been successful in pursuing a slow growth strategy, targeting high-quality service at business travellers in a small number of primarily O and D markets.[50] Midway Airlines - a reincarnation of a famous early post-deregulation name - was pursuing a similar high-cost/high-yield niche out of Raleigh-Durham in the mid-90s, but with uncertain results at the time of writing.

2 **Leisure and VFR passengers** Leisure travel in particular is the segment driving global air traffic growth. Both segments have relatively low delivery costs associated with them because product requirements in respect of schedule, frequency, accessibility, ground amenities, seating density, and inflight service are less demanding than those of the business segment. On the other hand, yields are low and both price and income elasticity are high; demand is cyclically volatile around the rising secular trend, and there is pronounced seasonal (and some weekend) peaking.

European charter carriers are amongst the purest examples of leisure segment niche focusers. That this is a large niche is evidenced by the size of airlines such as LTU and Britannia, the latter in particular being significantly bigger in terms of fleet and traffic than many 'wide-market' flag carriers. Operating strategies are not dissimilar to those which powered Southwest to success in the United States: high asset utilization, high-density point-to-point services, fairly basic amenity levels, no interlining facilities, and minimal CRS presence. The comparison should not be as closely drawn as it sometimes is, however: the European charter carriers wholesale much of their output in advance rather than retailing it direct - although this is changing slowly; most importantly, the nature of their networks and the low on-demand availability of their products keep output much more firmly focused on the leisure segment than is the case for Southwest, and also keep load factors very much higher. Furthermore, the charter carriers are intensely seasonal operations.

With their higher aircraft utilization, seating densities, and load factors, and their competitive staff and distribution costs, European charter airlines have significantly lower unit costs than that continent's scheduled carriers. The scheduled carriers cannot hope to compete head-on in point-to-point leisure markets other than through special purpose, low-cost subsidiaries - which are relatively few in number and limited in overall market impact.

Mixed business/leisure routes, however, present a more complex situation. Longer routes from Northern Europe to Mediterranean cities such as Athens, where summer peaking is marked, often do not provide much opportunity for scheduled carriers to penetrate the most price-sensitive segments other than with capacity-controlled fill-up fares. On shorter routes where the short- or weekend break segments represent significant components of leisure demand (e.g. London-Amsterdam), scheduled carriers are in a much stronger position; these routes are not suited to the operating profile of European charter airlines, but in the mid-90s started coming under attack from scheduled 'Southwest clones' such as easyJet and Virgin Express.

The Third Package of EU liberalization measures introduced in January 1993 eliminated the distinction between intra-European scheduled and nonscheduled services from a regulatory perspective, and the growth of seat-only sales on nonscheduled flights to leisure destinations - sales which now account for over one-third of the charter market - is gradually eliminating the distinction from a commercial perspective. The charter airlines carry only limited seat inventory risk because many seat-only sales are actually made by travel industry intermediaries that have bought space wholesale from the airlines; even when carriers do retail directly to the public, there is a significant difference between the risk involved in selling a few seats on an aircraft that has already been part-chartered to one or more tour operators, and the risk of running a scheduled, seat-only operation. Nonetheless, seat-only sales and the introduction of scheduled services into pure leisure markets previously served on a nonscheduled basis are growing, particularly in the latter case on long-haul routes out of Germany and the Netherlands.

A subject of widespread debate in recent years has been whether or not European nonscheduled carriers should exploit new commercial freedoms using the low cost structures that have allowed them to dominate their leisure niche by challenging high-cost full-service carriers in scheduled, predominantly business-oriented markets. Although in the mid-90s Spanish carriers Air Europa and Spanair had already begun attacking several of Iberia's scheduled routes (some of which do, in fact, benefit from quite strong demand from the leisure segment), this is not a scope strategy that has found much favour. There are a number of reasons underlying the reticence:

- many large European nonscheduled carriers are part of vertically integrated tour and travel organizations whose owners are firmly oriented towards the leisure segment and appear to have relatively little appetite for a battle with incumbents on scheduled, business-oriented routes;
- most of the larger independent charter airlines are based in the United Kingdom and Germany, whose scheduled network carriers are generally much stronger than many of those based elsewhere in the continent;
- not only would the nonscheduled carriers be fighting established brand names in their home countries, they would be virtually unknown at the other end of any scheduled routes they might enter to points which they do not currently serve;
- the aircraft operated by many European charter carriers are generally too large, and their seating configurations too dense, to meet the frequency and product requirements of scheduled markets having a significant business segment. The risk of unacceptably low load factors and yields would therefore be considerable; and
- lower load factors, lower aircraft utilization, and higher marketing and distribution costs would erode much of the unit cost advantage which makes the nonscheduled carriers such strong competitors in their own leisure niche.

Mention of Air Europe, AOM, and Dan-Air implies evidence enough of the difficulty inherent in moving out of a predominantly nonscheduled leisure niche into scheduled, primarily business-oriented markets.[51]

Again, the leisure market can be subsegmented. Special interest trips and sports events, for example, supplement 'pure' vacation travel.[52] Other approaches to subsegmentation are also possible. Around 60 per cent of the UK package tour market is controlled by four vertically integrated groups, with the balance in the hands of tour organizers too small to be able to justify having their own inhouse airlines. Excalibur Airways (which has since changed hands and ceased operations) was established in 1992 to exploit this market niche - a niche which has at times provoked warnings from industry strategists about the dangers that threaten an unaffiliated charter carrier without a steady source of demand from a tour-organizing parent. More recently, start-up Flying

Colours appears to have found a niche operating a small number of scheduled long-haul leisure routes 'outsourced' by British Airways.

Similar to the leisure niche in respect of many of its demand characteristics, but more specific in terms of geographical scope, are ethnic/VFR niches. In Mexico, for example, Taesa grew rapidly - in fact, too rapidly for its systems and resources - during the early 1990s in part by serving ethnic/VFR traffic flying between regional cities and the United States. Domestically, its strategy was to use a low cost structure to target traffic which would otherwise have travelled by bus. In Europe, Ryanair has targeted ethnic/VFR traffic between the United Kingdom and Ireland. Of course, there are also several wide-market scheduled flag carriers which rely heavily on this type of traffic, Air India being just one example.

3   **Express/small packages** The proportion of scheduled airfreight carried by pure freighters is generally expected to grow over the next two decades, but at present approximately two-thirds is shipped in the lower holds of passenger aircraft or on the main decks of combis. Of the ten largest producers of freight tonne-kilometres in recent years, only FedEx and UPS are all-freight carriers and one of the other eight - British Airways - has no freighters or combis in its fleet (although it does wet-lease the former). There is a numerically sizeable but shifting population of nonscheduled all-freight airlines in the global industry, but relatively few scheduled all-freight operators. The markets they serve can be segmented in many different ways, but at the highest level of abstraction they break down into express/small package and heavy freight (with the latter also including express freight).

The fastest growing segment in recent years has been express/small packages. What distinguishes this segment is its domination by a few fully-integrated carriers which have differentiated not just by offering door-to-door service but by simplifying tariffs and documentation compared with what was on offer from other airlines and freight forwarders, by branding their services, and by offering high levels of pick-up responsiveness, shipment tracking information, and ontime delivery. They have used heavy investments in technology to build customer switching costs and to automate service delivery. Barriers to entry are substantial, and opportunities to compete directly with FedEx, UPS, DHL, and TNT will not come cheaply.[53] Nonetheless, subsegments are exposed to specialized attack - as KLM has proven by being prepared to make the investment in warehousing and handling equipment necessary to build Schipol into a publications distribution centre.

4   **Heavy freight** This is much less commoditized in terms of its handling requirements but arguably more so in terms of the product

itself, and rather than retailing branded services most airlines wholesale their capacity through freight forwarders. Some, however, are investing heavily in technology and brand identity - British Airways World Cargo and Lufthansa Cargo being examples.[54] Since taking over Flying Tigers in 1989 (an acquisition aimed as much at widening geographical scope by securing Asian and Latin American traffic rights as at widening product scope), FedEx has also been a major player in this segment - thus, in effect, having adopted a 'wide-market' strategy within the freight niche. This piece of semantics underlines the dangers of getting carried away with text-book concepts such as 'niche' and 'wide-market'.

Multiple sourcing from different regions of a globalized economy, widespread adoption of just-in-time inventory management techniques, and the demand for faster time-to-market performance as product life cycles shorten are leading to rapid growth in the air shipment of goods which in the past might have been produced closer to their final assembly or sale points or, wherever produced, would have moved by surface modes. The primary benefit an all-freight airline can offer (and which is also offered by combination carriers with their own freighter fleets) is network design and scheduling attuned to the needs of shippers rather than passengers. It is also likely to offer a better 'flown as booked' rate because the temptation to offload freight in preference to bumping passengers when weather conditions limit payloads on long-haul routes does not arise. On the other hand, although passenger aircraft schedules are generally timed to meet the needs of passengers rather than freight shippers or forwarders, they do in most cases compensate at least in part by being operated at higher frequencies than could be sustained by freighters.

The yields earned by freight carriers suffer when competition in passenger markets leads as a byproduct to the dumping of large volumes of lower deck widebody freight capacity - particularly if, as often happens, this is priced at close to marginal cost. All-freight airlines also suffer proportionately more from the effects of directional imbalances than do combination carriers earning most of their revenues on the same routes from carriage of passengers - which, over time, flow equally in both directions.

There are relatively few all-cargo airlines offering heavy freight haulage on a scheduled basis; Cargolux, Nippon Cargo Airlines, and Air Hong Kong are three well-known examples. FedEx has also been active in this segment since its acquisition of Flying Tigers, and several other integrated express carriers are moving into it in at least some of their markets - often as part of strategies to provide 'one-stop shopping' to shippers having a range of document, light package, heavy package, and heavy freight requirements.

Subsegments have been exploited within the heavy freight segment. Polar Air Cargo, a joint venture founded in the early 1990s, set about targeting a niche for 'no-frills' line haul - reliable airport-to-airport transportation and delivery without real-time tracking capabilities - serving international freight forwarders.

Atlas Air provides long-haul, airport-to-airport services for airlines wanting to 'outsource' some or all of their cargo flight operations by wet-leasing B747 freighters on an ACMI (aircraft, crew, maintenance, and insurance) basis. These Atlas aircraft fly the lessees' schedules, using the lessees' own traffic rights, at a fixed cost per block-hour, with each lessee paying for fuel and handling. Contracts generally run for one to three years. Apart from its ambition to control a leading share of the burgeoning world fleet of B747-200 freighter conversions as these aircraft leave passenger service in growing numbers,[55] what distinguishes Atlas is the fact that unlike many other carriers that wet-lease freighters it does not sell any of its own capacity directly to forwarders or shippers - something which its airline customers might perceive as unwelcome competition.

AN-124 charters to carry outsize loads - arranged through vehicles such as the Air Foyle/Antonov joint venture - provide another example of subsegmentation. They became a particularly profitable business after the collapse of the Soviet Union. Airbus has also targeted the outsize cargo segment by setting-up Airbus Transport International to sell surplus time available on the A300-600ST fleet used to ship aircraft sub-assemblies to their final assembly points.

5 **Multi-niche strategies** Like so much else when strategies must be squeezed for the purpose of analysis into ill-fitting categories, the distinction between a multi-niche strategy and a wide-market strategy can get blurred at the edges. However, there are some airlines which could not be described as wide-market carriers, targeting instead a number of specific niches. For example, Martinair has targeted:

- three subsegments of the leisure segment - short-haul charters to the Mediterranean, long-haul charters, and scheduled service in a small number of leisure-oriented long-haul markets (frequently on behalf of its shareholder, KLM);
- long-haul cargo operations;[56] and
- wet-leasing to supplement the capacity of other airlines.

To serve these niches it built an operationally flexible fleet comprising B767s capable of flying both short- and long-haul sectors profitably, alongside convertible B747-200Cs and MD-11CFs.

Since the early 1990s, the larger European leisure airlines - still operating predominantly in charter mode, but in some cases also flying scheduled services on leisure routes - have rapidly expanded their cargo activities. This has been particularly true on long-haul routes and wherever twin-aisle aircraft are being flown, because cargo loading and off-loading is less likely to interfere with turnaround schedules on long- than short-haul routes. Management of much of their cargo operations is frequently outsourced by these airlines; an early example was Britannia Airways' arrangement with Pace Airline Services.

Reno Air provides an example of a relatively small low-cost carrier catering for distinct segments of the scheduled passenger market at its two hubs:

- Reno operations are targeted primarily at leisure travellers; whilst
- San Jose (a hub inherited from American) caters more for business traffic.

Each accounts for around 40 per cent of the airline's departures, with point-to-point services in non-hub markets responsible for the other 20 per cent.[57]

Niche strategies: low-cost/low-fare versus full-service There are very few long-haul (i.e. intercontinental) routes that will support leisure-oriented all-economy scheduled service. The majority of tourist arrivals are still intra-regional - within North America, within Europe, and within East and Southeast Asia. Any carrier choosing to operate in long-haul markets serving the leisure-product niche must have rock-bottom costs to compensate for the fact that its traffic will generate very low yields. In practice, the vast majority of long-haul scheduled services are in fact offered with both leisure- and/or VFR-oriented products and premium products; this is necessary in order to generate a traffic mix which includes at least some relatively high-yield passengers, and to stimulate traffic densities adequate to support reasonably high frequencies operated by large, long-range aircraft. Similarly, there are few long-haul routes on which business traffic is sufficiently dense to warrant service with just premium class offerings - at least, not service at the level of frequencies most business passengers will demand.

Whether operated by global network carriers, airlines well-established in a geographical niche, or mid-sized pseudo-network flag carriers, medium- and long-haul scheduled routes are generally served with a wide-market product offering that encompasses first and/or business classes and economy class; economy class is now commonly segmented into different fare classes on the basis of differential pricing and ticket conditionality.[58] There are very few exceptions. Widebodied aircraft offering only premium class service have been operated from time to time on long-haul routes out of Japan. In the leisure niche, some long-haul markets (e.g. Northern Europe-Florida) are sufficiently dense to support all-economy, quasi-scheduled service; even here, however, some type of business class product is frequently offered (e.g. by Martinair between Amsterdam, Miami, and Orlando). New York-based Tower Air has offered low-frequency, low-fare scheduled services for several years in a small number of transatlantic niche markets (e.g. Israel), and Belgian start-up CityBird began flying from Brussels to the United States and Mexico in 1997.

Although a low-cost/low-fare operation, CityBird did choose to offer a full-service - if not overgenerous - economy class product. This is unsurprising given the length of its hauls. More questionable in the eyes of some analysts at the time was the decision to offer a business class product as well; it was doubted whether low fares would compensate for low frequencies. On the other hand, business class cabins are not necessarily the sole preserve of business travellers. It could be that CityBird's management felt such a cabin might tap the 'premium end' of its low-fare leisure niche - people willing to pay for an upgrade, but neither needing nor willing to pay for the levels of service on offer from network carriers.[59] Several leisure-oriented long-haul niche carriers in fact offer upgraded service in the front cabin targeted at this sub-segment of demand.

A much wider range of product scope decisions is available in short-haul markets. There is, however, a growing polarization between full-service offers made available by network carriers and lower service/lower price offers made by low-cost carriers targeting the most price-elastic segments of demand - whether that demand comes from leisure, VFR, or cost-conscious business travellers.[60] Some of this demand - particularly from amongst business travellers - is drawn from competitors, but often it comes from people who either would not have travelled or would have used surface transport instead of flying but for the availability of low fares. Low-cost/low-fare carriers generally target point-to-point routes which have:

- little or no existing service but high growth potential; or
- existing service so high-priced that it is choking-off demand from the most price-elastic segments.

In both cases, especially the former, heavy reliance is placed on price elasticity to stimulate demand. This means in principle that the leisure and/or VFR components of targeted markets must be high, because these are the most price-elastic segments. However, the self-employed and people working for small- or medium-sized businesses are often also prepared to accept lower levels of service (in respect of amenities, if not frequency and reliability) provided the fare offered is substantially lower than full-service competitors are charging; during a recession, the likelihood increases that even large corporations will want their travelling executives to take cheaper options in short-haul markets - although the power of the network carriers' FFPs to influence consumer choice is certainly a consideration pressing in the opposite direction.

Generally, however, it is no longer a safe assumption in a growing number of short-haul markets that the entire business segment is going to be willing indefinitely to pay a significant price premium for brand image, upscale amenities, FFP awards, and other 'added value' features in order to support the higher costs of hub-based, full-service network carriers; particularly when low-fare alternatives offer reasonable frequencies, reliable schedules, and tolerable if not generous inflight product attributes, a proportion of business traveller demand in some markets - notably North American and European markets - will inevitably be drawn to limited-service/low-price offers and away from high-service/high-price offers. Some, although certainly not all, low-cost carriers do choose to offer high frequencies in the markets they serve: Southwest is the obvious example, and in the United Kingdom easyJet set out gradually to do the same as part of its initial operating strategy. Some also try to use corporate culture and service delivery style to build their own positive brand images and create the perception that they are offering a sensible, value-for-money alternative and a pleasant travel experience rather than just a 'knees-in-the-face, how soon will it be over' means of getting from A to B as cheaply as possible. Others just offer rock-bottom service experiences in return for rock-bottom prices.

However, there are several structural and behavioural reasons why low fares *by themselves* may not be a sufficient foundation upon which to build a strategy in the absence of other differentiating attributes:

- in liberalized markets, competitors tend to be strongly inclined towards matching fares in order to protect market share. When this happens, the competitive battle moves to service attributes such as frequency, FFPs, service style, and reputation, for example;
- within any given network, a volume-based pricing strategy is likely to be vital to viability. There are relatively few routes capable of sustaining high-frequency services on the basis of demand from full-fare passengers alone, with the result that any decision to build or retain a wide network of high-frequency services implies that discriminatory and promotional fares will have to be offered in order to stimulate the volume of traffic required to support such a strategy. 'Fill-up' fares may divert demand from any challenger competing on the basis of price alone. Whether or not this is serious on a particular route will depend upon the relative levels of capacity made available at such fares;
- a common cycle of events in the industry has seen the aggressive ordering of aircraft during economic upturns in pursuit of market share, followed by the outbreak of fare wars to help sell output left unsold as a result of capacity growth outstripping demand growth (particularly when, as has often happened, the new aircraft are delivered during an ensuing economic slowdown). If a significant number of carriers are dumping output at low prices, a low-fare strategy *by itself* might not be a sustainable option other than,

perhaps, for an extremely lean low-cost operation niching in carefully chosen markets.

The fates of many unsuccessful low-cost/low-fare ventures point to a need for entry into a carefully targeted segment to be followed by the building of defensible differentiation; low prices alone can too easily be matched by incumbents with deep pockets and greater capacity. Corporate culture and the emotional dimension of service delivery can be a source of defensible differentiation for carriers whose tangible product attributes are not sufficiently or favourably differentiated from those of full-service competitors. This is a subject we will be returning to in the next chapter and also in Part Two.

In a growing number of short-haul markets able to support the operation of aircraft with 100-seats or more, it is possible to move beyond the traditional business/leisure niche categorization and identify two broad types of product and geographical scope.

1   Network carriers, whose short-haul routes:
    • feed medium- and long-haul routes;
    • connect secondary short-haul points over a hub, where traffic densities between these points are insufficient to support nonstop service; and
    • provide nonstop service in O and D markets to and from a hub and on hub-bypass routes sufficiently dense to support point-to-point operations.

2   Non-network carriers, which generally concentrate on point-to-point service but in some cases do also flow traffic over their own mini-hubs.

The situation nonetheless varies in different parts of the world, in response to geography, patterns of demand, aeropolitics, and cultural influences on what represents an acceptable product. We will look briefly at what is happening in two regions that are presently experiencing the greatest rates of innovation in short-haul product scope strategies: the United States and Europe.

1   **The United States** For several years there has been a widening perception that the key consumer choice variables in short-haul markets are now frequency, convenience, reliability, and price. The implication is that **network carriers** have to find new, cheaper methods of competing in short-haul markets, and limit their domestic full-service products to medium-haul and transcontinental routes.[61] They have responded in broadly two ways:
    • by paring back standards of service on retained short-haul routes (in concert with more far-reaching cost management exercises). Whilst

products targeted at business travellers have in many cases been upgraded on longer routes, only USAir (as it then was) chose to make a substantial investment in cabin and service upgrades on short-haul routes during the early 1990s;[62]

- by starting their own low-cost operations. Although these operations appear to reflect similar product scope choices, there may in fact be some quite important distinctions between their specific orientations. For example, whilst both the United Shuttle and Delta Express offer seat assignment, FFP awards, and several other product attributes not offered by the majority of low-cost/no-frills carriers, the former is a two-class operation and the latter is single-class; the United Shuttle is heavily oriented towards feeding business travellers (over half its traffic) and FFP members (over 80 per cent of its traffic) into the mainline carrier's western hubs, whereas Delta Express largely operates point-to-point in Florida markets that are over 60 per cent leisure-oriented. Delta Express was started with the intention of leaving the mainline operation to serve the business market and so, as far as possible, tries not to undercut connecting flows over Atlanta. Both operations, however, were established to protect their parent carriers' presences in different parts of the United States which account for high percentages of the two majors' respective total revenues. One advantage that Delta Express and the United Shuttle had over Continental Lite is that they were formed as separate business units with their own dedicated fleets and flight crews, whereas the ill-fated Continental venture was a true 'airline-within-an-airline' and so faced severe operational and marketing communications challenges that were never overcome.

At the time of writing it remains to be seen whether low-cost operations can be succesfully melded with a full-service network. Optimists say that they can, and that as well as updating the short-haul service concept to meet evolving market requirements these units provide a laboratory in which to test new and more efficient service delivery processes. Pessimists warn of potential hub flow cannibalization (more a threat to Delta than to United, it would seem, given the different network strategies of their spin-offs at this time), image dilution, and incompatible service delivery systems wherever the spin-off and mainline networks meet.[63]

Moving away from the largest and relatively high-cost network carriers, several other types of airline are also actively participating in the reorientation of product scope decisions in US short-haul markets.

- A number of **reconstructed network carriers** emerged from Chapter 11 bankruptcy proceedings in the early 1990s with costs substantially lower than those of most other majors. Continental and America West are the primary examples, and Continental in particular made significant strides in upgrading its service concept and delivery.

- **Southwest** has steadily and profitably ploughed its own furrow since the 1970s, largely disavowing network operations and providing the low-cost, point-to-point paradigm for many post-deregulation start-ups. The mid- and late-90s saw it expanding steadily eastwards into Florida, the Mid-Atlantic states, and New England, and also inaugurating a small number of medium-haul routes.

- **Low-fare/no-frills** carriers are the archetypal US domestic start-up. Most have been designed primarily for point-to-point service, although some - such as ValuJet chose to do at Atlanta - connect a small proportion of their traffic over a mini-hub or 'focus city'. Operations and amenities are kept basic and cheap. Catering in principle to price-elastic customers whether travelling for leisure, VFR, or business purposes, many of these carriers tend to offer what in US markets are considered insufficient frequencies to attract significant numbers of business passengers; this was the case with ValuJet's initial operating plan, for example, compounded by a no-refund policy that many in the business segment would find unappealing. There is a marked contrast between this approach and Southwest's template operating strategy of building high frequencies, offering refundable fares, and ultimately dominating any market it enters.

- **Low-fare/full-service** and **same-fare/higher-service (and/or fewer conditions)** strategies targeted primarily at price-sensitive business travellers have met with limited success in the United States, where Kiwi International for instance struggled to establish itself throughout the four years between its 1992 launch and 1996 entry into Chapter 11 bankruptcy. On the other hand, Reno Air - which offers assigned seating, snacks or meals, interlining, participation in American Airlines' FFP, and a first class cabin - appears to have succeeded in establishing a low-fare/full-service niche in the Western United States; whether it would have sustained early losses and cash shortages long enough to do this had it not inherited American's business-oriented San Jose hub when the major pulled back from secondary hubbing in the mid-90s is an open question, however. As already mentioned, Midwest Express has been consistently successful in its high-yield/high-service niche out of Milwaukee. The fate of the new Pan Am, launched in 1996 to serve Florida and transcontinental markets from the northeast offering cheap, nonrefundable fares and a full-service product in coach, first class service for coach prices in the premium cabin, and a generous FFP remains open at the time of writing - as does the future of its particular service concept after the takeover of Carnival Air Lines. In general, though, there is a widespread body of opinion that in US domestic markets price rather than service differentiation is the best focus for start-ups with costs low enough to sustain the strategy.

There was a belief in the mid-90s that events had turned the tide against low-cost/low-fare strategies in US domestic markets:

- intensified FAA oversight of start-ups following the May 1996 ValuJet crash (referred to in Volume One, chapter 5) was expected to lead to higher operating costs and slower expansion than might previously have been the case;
- a mood-swing in Washington led, it was thought, to start-ups being afforded less informal antitrust protection against predatory actions by incumbents than some had received in the early 1990s (see Volume One, chapter 4); and
- several majors and their unions had apparently come to terms with the new competitive environment, and formulated more coherent strategic responses to the inroads into their traffic made by low-cost carriers than they were able to muster in the early-90s.

How real and how permanent these disabilities actually are remains to be seen.[64] The mid- and late-90s was anyway never going to be a halcyon period for most who follow this strategy, because carriers such as this tend very frequently to be 'children of recessions' - their cost advantages coming under pressure as labour and asset (particularly aircraft) markets tighten towards the peak of cyclical upturns. Much will depend upon whether low-cost carriers can keep themselves out of the headlines, and also how the majors behave; little more than a year after the ValuJet accident in 1996 had unleashed a torrent of adverse comments on low-cost start-ups, there were signs that the pricing behaviour and alleged predatory activities of the majors were helping public opinion refocus on the competitive merits of low-cost challengers.[65]

2   **Europe** Institutional and geographical circumstances are very different in Europe compared to the United States. One important difference is that a high percentage of intra-European leisure traffic is still carried on nonscheduled flights operated by specialized low-cost carriers which remain primarily charter-oriented. Another is that with the exception of some flows between the United Kingdom and Ireland and between several Northern European countries and the south of the continent, VFR traffic is considerably less important within Europe than within the United States; this reflects the fact that short-haul

demand arises within and between nation-states which are still some way from being socially integrated, even if supply is now being delivered within what is from a regulatory perspective a single market.

On the other hand, European business travellers and others needing to fly on scheduled services have for so long been subject to the egregiously high fares charged by protected monopolies and duopolies that plenty of scope exists in principle to attack incumbents' market shares and to target price-elastic incremental traffic that otherwise might not travel or would instead choose road or rail alternatives.

The following discussion again focuses on scope alternatives in respect of operations using aircraft with 100 or more seats.

- **Network carriers** fall into two main categories: those that are large in their own right and/or are at the core of emerging global alliances (e.g. British Airways, KLM, Lufthansa, and Swissair), and others which to varying degrees might suffer from geographically peripheral locations, process inefficiencies, weak shares of their business markets attributable to poor images and products, and weak shares of their leisure markets arising from uncompetitive costs (e.g. Alitalia, Iberia, and Olympic). Intercontinental traffic is more important than domestic or intra-European traffic for several European network carriers; some, however, operate primarily short- and medium-haul networks within which intercontinental routes - sometimes relics of national history rather than responses to commercial imperatives - play only peripheral roles. As in the United States, network carriers are in most cases endeavouring to lower their cost structures, and some are expanding separate low-cost units. Product upgrades have been more common in European than in US short-haul markets, reflecting the significance of high-yield business traffic - both connecting and point-to-point - as a proportion of traffic on intra-European scheduled networks.

- **Low-cost/no-frills carriers** have been present in the leisure niche for several decades; although some are based in destination countries around the Mediterranean, the largest are members of vertically integrated Northern European travel organizations that benefit from extensive presences in (and, in aggregate, control over) their respective origin markets. Low-cost entry into a niche VFR market was pioneered by Ireland's Ryanair in the mid-80s, offering relatively high frequencies and low fares. But it was not until a decade later that a wave of low-cost new entrants began - albeit in a small way - extending price competition to a wider range of domestic and intra-European markets. Examples include AirOne in Italy, easyJet out of the United Kingdom, and Brussels-based EuroBelgian (which in 1996 changed majority ownership and became Virgin Express). Ryanair also expanded onto a number of continental routes.

Because Europe's population is quite concentrated (compared with, say, the US population) and because so many flag carriers have histories of high costs and somnolent network strategies, there are opportunities to exploit unserved or underserved city-pairs as well as to take-on incumbents on their existing routes. Start-ups with low production costs have been adopting both approaches using a variety of no- or low-frills products, and with both low- and high-frequency schedules; the problem with low frequencies, of course, is that once a new entrant has successfully used price elasticity to develop a market, it is quite possible for a network carrier with sufficient spare capacity and deep pockets to move in, price and schedule in a predatory way, and drive competition from that market.

- **Low-cost/full-service concepts** were developed in the mid-90s, with mixed success, by several primarily business-oriented projects and actual start-ups such as AirJet, Azzurra Air, Debonair and World Airways. As already noted, Spain's Air Europa and Spanair were two relatively rare examples of pre-existing, predominantly charter airlines moving forcefully into scheduled markets in response to the opportunities created by market liberalization in the 1990s (although several had tried and failed just a few years earlier). Whilst both remained predominantly charter carriers, with the low cost bases which are mandatory in this part of the industry, neither Air Europa nor Spanair was offering a pure no-frills product. Spanair in particular built something of a reputation in Spanish domestic markets for the relatively high quality of its onboard service.

  Much more enduring has been British Midland's longstanding presence in this niche - although its cost base, whilst low by comparison with most European network carriers, is certainly not low when set against the new breed of start-ups. British Midland's costs nonetheless allow it to compete aggressively with network carriers on price whilst still offering high standards of service. These standards have facilitated the building up of extensive code-sharing arrangements with a relatively large number of long-haul carriers, boosting revenues, traffic, and the productivity of its valuable slot inventory at London Heathrow; they have allowed British Midland to develop 'virtual network' competition against British Airways for international passengers, as well as offering a high-quality point-to-point service for local O and D traffic.[66]

The last few subsections have discussed wide-market product scope and geographical scope alternatives, and then geographical and product niches.

They have looked in particular at alternative service concepts being developed in short-haul markets. The final section of the chapter will draw some conclusions on the effects that product scope and geographical scope decisions are having on the structure of the global airline industry.

Conclusions on product scope and geographical scope

Commenting on the US market, but equally applicable to developments that could emerge over time in Europe and perhaps elsewhere, Morrison and Winston have made the following observation.

> Carriers are likely to rely on two strategies for developing their networks: the Southwest model for shorter routes and the hub-and-spoke for longer domestic and international routes. The global American carriers are likely to focus on international and long-haul domestic operations, while regional carriers, new entrants, and possibly downsized major carriers or low-cost subsidiaries will compete on shorter domestic routes.[67]

Common wisdom holds that the global industry will ultimately be dominated by a small number of carriers operating within an even smaller number of alliances, and that in due course some of these alliances will coalesce into merged entities. They will be wide-market in both the product and geographical senses. Others will be able to prosper in product or geographical niches, particularly on point-to-point operations which do not require the network synergies offered exclusively by 'megacarriers'.

The days of nationally oriented 'mini-networks' intermediated by the various IATA functions which facilitate interlining are, we are told, drawing to a close. This middle ground is being eroded by economic fundamentals and commercial logic. The economic fundamentals and commercial logic favouring greater concentration within the industry are indeed compelling, but how far the political environment will permit them to go remains to be seen.

Notwithstanding the dangers inherent in trying to isolate a few neat pigeon-holes for filing what in practice are a plethora of strategies being followed by hundreds of different airlines around the world, each confronted by common industry trends but also having to cope with unique local circumstances, the next few subsections will look at the principal product scope and geographical scope strategies evident in the industry at the end of the 20th century.

Global network alliances These generally have one or more of the world's largest carriers at their core. Their geographical scope strategies aim to extend network reach into all major markets, establishing a presence in the most important nonstop O and D markets and maximizing connectivity between smaller points by constructing integrated, multi-hub systems. As well as attaining wide-market geographical scope, they also offer a wide range of products; full-service offerings on mainline routes are augmented by offers targeted at specific geographical markets or particular segments of demand, and delivered by specialized units or partners - such as low-cost subsidiaries, regional affiliates, franchisees, and code-share partners. In particular, global networks are battling for shares in long-haul business markets by enhancing service offers in respect of benefits valued by this segment. The ultimate objective of each alliance is to dominate as much inter-hub and flow traffic as network geographies, competitive circumstances, and competition authorities allow, and in so doing regain some of the influence over pricing that regulatory liberalization threatens to strip away.

As well as revenue gain, the global networks are also looking for benefits on the other side of the income statement through exploitation of the economies of scale, scope, and density available in the industry. The objective is both to raise profits and to allow room for selective competition with carriers following niche strategies or others whose lack of vision has left them 'stuck in the middle' in terms of geographical and/or product scope strategies.[68]

The mega-networks are positioning themselves to gain or consolidate dominant access to irreproducible strategic resources at key points in the global air transportation system - notably airport slots and gates. The attainment of 'critical mass' both in a specific market and across a large, integrated network of connecting services can also under many circumstances become a strategic asset that challengers lacking deep pockets and equal access to infrastructural resources find difficult to reproduce.

The fact that operating economies available from hub-based networks, particularly economies of scope, are only exhausted at relatively high output levels is frequently cited as one reason for the post-deregulation consolidation of a large percentage of the US domestic industry's output into the hands of a small number of networked majors. The same effect, it is argued, is in the process of making itself felt globally - the only difference being that until there is more dramatic change both in national sensibilities towards airline ownership and in the prevailing aeropolitical regime, cross-border consolidation will come about primarily through alliances rather than through outright mergers of the type that hallmarked US experience.

Particularly within Europe, it is probable that at least some flag carriers will establish joint ventures - quite likely within the larger structures of a global alliance system - and that in due course it will be felt appropriate for these ventures to pave the way for intra-European mergers. Opinions differ on what, precisely, is meant by 'in due course' and, as was noted in chapter 3 of Volume One, the feasibility of this development will depend upon how long national ownership clauses in bilaterals with non-EU states continue to be enforced. Cross-border mergers of alliance partners based outside North America, Latin America or Europe are likely to be a more distant prospect. We will return to this issue in chapter 5.

Product niche strategies There are a number of different product niches, such as all-cargo; there are also mixed product-geographical niches, such as high-frequency regional operations feeding predominantly business traffic down short-haul spokes into hubs. One product niche that is currently arousing a lot of interest is the delivery of low-fare/low- or no-frills service into short-haul, mostly point-to-point markets, by low-cost carriers. In US domestic markets, Southwest has been pursuing a short-haul, low-cost niche strategy so successfully and for so long that the niche is now large by any standards.

In some markets, the strategic assets underpinning hub-based networks do not support any particular competitive advantage. Thus, short-haul leisure travellers in Europe need neither connections at congested hubs to get them from secondary airports near their homes to Mediterranean resort destinations, nor the other benefits associated with full-service network operations; neither will they pay the fares necessary to underpin these operations. This is clearly a niche which network carriers can only access through specialized low-cost subsidiaries; some do (e.g. Lufthansa and Iberia), but others have refocused on their core scheduled networks by selling-off such operations (e.g. British Airways).

Whilst the low-cost European leisure niche has been exploited by charter airlines since the 1950s, what deregulation promises more generally is the prospect of low-cost/low-fare competition on previously protected scheduled routes. Successive waves of low-cost new entrants swept deregulated US domestic markets in the early 1980s and 1990s, and the first wave hit scheduled European routes in the mid-90s (following a limited number of abortive efforts around the turn of the decade). The history of low-cost entry into US domestic markets is not encouraging over the long run, although there are certainly one or two success stories. In principle, network carriers that have high costs relative to start-ups should be vulnerable to price competition, but in practice they have plenty of nonprice weapons in their armouries.[69]

Whether the arrival of a low-cost challenger provokes a feisty response from network incumbents or a willingness to 'live and let live' - provided network feed and strategically important O and D traffic are not threatened - will depend upon attitudes, circumstances, and the alertness of competition authorities. In chapter 11 of Volume One, reference was made to the suggestion by Barkin et al of an approach to low-cost entrants that full-service incumbents might take: understand the competitor's strengths; assess the threat to the core business; strengthen overall position; develop specific strategies tailored to each market; and seize any opportunities that arise to shape the industry's competitive environment.[70] These authors outline several alternative strategies that can be tailored for any particular route depending upon specific circumstances.

1   Route withdrawal by the network carrier. This could be acceptable if
the route concerned is unprofitable, generating little premium or
connecting traffic, if the carrier has other opportunities to deploy its
resources profitably, and if there is no substantial danger that
withdrawal would strengthen the low-cost carrier for a future assault
on another part of the network (as arguably happened when some of
the incumbent majors ceded their intra-California markets to
Southwest). On the other hand, many routes operated by network
carriers do indeed contribute valuable feed and so, quite frequently,
make a positive contribution to network profitability even if not
themselves profitable on a fully allocated basis. In extreme cases,
ceding such routes may risk undermining hub economics to the point
that a vicious circle of spoke-cutting is initiated to reestablish network
profitability - ultimately threatening viability of the hub itself. The
operational characteristics of a large hub-and-spoke operation make
downsizing in response to stagnant or declining revenues (whether
resulting from competition or from a recession) very difficult to
effect without causing a disproportionate further loss of traffic. Less
dramatic, although also potentially damaging, is the loss of FFP
members compelled to rely on other carriers in the vacated market(s).

2   Head-on competition with the low-cost entrant. This usually involves
matching fares - which might also be part of the fifth step referred to
above (shaping the competitive environment) if, instead of just waiting
for challengers to materialize and then matching them, a network
carrier moves to pre-empt their arrival either by signalling its
intention to match any entrant or by starting low-fare services of its
own. Other, nonprice, responses involving FFP awards, scheduling,
and marketing communications might be used to combat entry, but
fare matching - even if only on a capacity-controlled basis - is usually
the principal weapon in head-on competition of this sort. Ideally, the
incumbent should be working to get its costs down to a level that
supports such matching, either directly or by using a separate low-cost
operation, but just how essential this is - and how deep its pockets need
to be in the interim - will depend upon the challenger's staying power.
The network incumbent will also probably need to have sufficient
capacity available to boost frequencies in the market and so ensure that
the challenger does not benefit too greatly from whatever incremental
traffic is stimulated by any fare war(s).
If the challenger is attacked early and forcefully enough, it might
find profitability difficult to establish and therefore access to
additional capital with which to fund expansion less readily available -
unless it has the resources of a wealthy corporate or individual
shareholder behind it. What an incumbent can get away with in terms
of competitive response might depend upon the nature of competition
law in the jurisdiction concerned, the attitude of the authorities

charged with enforcing it, and the speed of due process. In the United States, for example, the authorities were keen to back low-cost entrants in the early 1990s and acted both formally and informally to protect them from potentially predatory responses by incumbents; after this sector of the industry came under the media spotlight following the 1996 loss of a ValuJet aircraft in Florida, overt support for low-cost start-ups became politically incorrect in some quarters. In the EU, on the other hand, there is a great deal of vocal support for the enforcement of competition law - in Brussels, if not in all the member states - but the processes can be so lengthy that a poorly resourced challenger may be dead and gone before meaningful action can be taken to protect it from predation.

Quite apart from whatever short-term body-blows fare matching may deliver to a full-service incumbent's income statement, this response also raises other issues. First, generalized efforts to lower costs can, if inadequately communicated and justified to staff and/or poorly implemented, lead to a downward spiral of falling staff morale and declining customer service. Equally threatening to brand equity for a full-service carrier under these circumstances can be the impact of unfocused marketing communications that leave customers and intermediaries confused as to just what is happening to the positioning of its overall service-price offer - as was the case with the Continental Lite low-cost airline-within-an-airline initiative.

3   Co-existence. This response would have the full-service incumbent cede most of the more price-sensitive segments of local traffic to the low-cost challenger, whilst continuing to serve both connecting passengers and higher yielding, predominantly business passengers in the O and D market. The incumbent might also retain a small slice of the most price-sensitive segment by offering capacity-controlled fill-up fares. Such has largely been American's approach to Southwest at Dallas, for example. This strategy is fine as long as there are sufficient volumes in each segment to keep both carriers content, and provided business traffic - particularly local rather than connecting business traffic - values the incumbent's service differentiation more highly than the challenger's price differentiation. The incumbent might have problems if these conditions do not hold and/or the challenger chooses to expand beyond its niche, as ValuJet was beginning to do at Atlanta just before the FAA acted to cut its fleet and rate of growth in 1996.

4   Joining forces. A full-service incumbent might decide to forgo bruising fare wars by withdrawing from a market in which it is challenged, whilst at the same time protecting its FFP membership base in that market and also its network coverage by entering into a marketing agreement with the challenger. Rare though this response is, it has been adopted in the past by American (with Reno Air at San

Jose and with Midway at Raleigh/Durham), by Alitalia (with Alpi Eagles in northern Italy), and by Sabena (with Virgin Express, initially between Brussels and London Heathrow, and with CityBird). Barkin et al have identified the following determinants of success for this particular strategic response:

- service levels offered by the airlines concerned should not be too far apart, which means that the challenger must in most cases be offering something more than rock-bottom service for rock-bottom prices; and
- both schedule integration and some degree of operational alignment should be feasible.

As with any route withdrawal, of course, the incumbent might later face a renewed challenge elsewhere in its network if the beneficiary continues to grow on the basis of what has been ceded to it, and at some point decides that the potential gains from a more aggressive posture outweigh the advantages of continued cooperation.

Many industry observers feel that there can be coexistence where network carriers interface with low-cost challengers, but that head-to-head competition is nonetheless likely to be fierce whenever a network carrier either moves to protect its flow traffic or initiates its own low-cost operations to defend, or pre-empt attacks on, point-to-point O and D traffic.

Geographical niche strategies It has already been mentioned that short-haul regional carriers occupy highly interrelated geographical and product niches. Airlines focusing largely or entirely on leisure or VFR segments also operate in interrelated geographical and product niches. Our interest here, however, is in carriers making a wide-market product offer into a relatively narrow range of geographical markets. Airlines in this category may include state-owned national airlines, privatized former flag carriers, or 'independents' operating networks which rely primarily on a mix of nonstop, one-stop or multi-stop point-to-point traffic in domestic, third, fourth, and fifth freedom markets; depending upon the location of their main centre of operations, some may also flow connecting traffic on a sixth freedom basis - but their volumes do not come close to rivalling those of the largest network carriers.[71] Many participate to some extent in alliance structures, although few could be said to constitute a core element in an emerging global network (Qantas and Austrian being current examples of two that do).

Like most niches, geographical niches are easier to identify than to define. In order to succeed financially, carriers occupying a geographical niche unprotected by commercial regulations or infrastructural constraints need strong customer loyalty founded both on a solid local image and on service-price positioning which is more relevant to the market(s) concerned than what is being offered by larger competitors. Relevant service-price positioning has to be built upon appropriate service conceptualization and delivery skills; we will be looking at these in Part Two of the book.

True of any niche strategy, the dangers are that the competitive advantages appearing to underpin it are illusory and that even if real they will be overreached by the pull of corporate or personal ambition during cyclical upturns.

Middle-of-the-road strategies Less a strategy than a symptom of inertia or even perhaps decline, the problem here arises from geographical and product scope decisions which lead neither to the building of 'critical mass' in global network terms nor to the attainment of inimitable service or price differentiation that is in some way relevant to an identifiable and defensible niche. This is a position in which many of the world's airlines, by number if not by the percentage of global air traffic for which they account, now find themselves. They make ill-defined wide-market product offerings into networks which are not sufficiently large to compete for 'reach' with the biggest carriers and the global alliances they are forming, nor sufficiently tightly designed to constitute identifiable niches.

The problem for medium-sized, wide-market carriers is that in many cases they bear the expense of operating networks which although substantial are not large enough by themselves to deliver the cost and revenue benefits available to megacarriers and their alliances. The excellence needed to mount a solo defence of a niche, on the other hand, will only come from major cultural and business process overhauls of which many are patently not capable. The future for any mid-sized middle-of-the-roader unable to offer something meaningful to potential alliance partners or to shrink into a defensible niche, and unprotected by a government which still sees it as a national policy tool worthy of either perennial or periodic subsidy, is financially bleak.

The middle ground has been eroding from under these carriers since the 1980s. Good and improving though some might be in certain respects, many are simply not good enough at what they do to survive unprotected in a polarizing world. They have neither the market presence, the customer loyalty nor the appropriate service-price positioning needed to outcompete global network carriers - or any niche operators they might face - on an equal basis in a liberalized competitive environment. Whether, and how long, they survive will be a political decision made by governments within the context of considerations described in Volume One, chapter 3.

Conclusion

This chapter has introduced and considered *corporate level* strategies, focusing first on growth and renewal in general, and then going on to consider the alternative choices that might be available to airline managers making industrial, vertical, geographical, and product scope decisions. Although this approach is analytically useful, it needs to be remembered that managers in a single-business enterprise may not distinguish between the 'Where to compete?' questions inherent in corporate strategy and the 'How to compete?' issues addressed by competitive strategy. Even in multi-business enterprises the two can never be entirely separated other than for analytical purposes, because the answer to 'Where to compete?' questions is almost inevitably framed by reference to markets - and reference to markets equally inevitably raises 'How to compete?' issues. It is to competitive strategy - 'How to compete?' - that we turn in the next chapter.

Notes

1   It was also noted that the words 'route' and 'market' may be synonymous but, particularly in hub-and-spoke networks, they very frequently are not. However, it is unnecessary to draw the distinction at this stage in the discussion.
2   See: Holloway, S. (1997), *Straight and Level: Practical Airline Economics,* Ashgate, chapters 1 and 3.
3   Ibid., chapter 1.
4   IATA (1985), *Deregulation Watch: Second Report,* cited in: Doganis, R. (1994), 'The Impact of Liberalization on European Airline Strategies', *Journal of Air Transport Management,* 1 (1).
5   Ibid.
6   In the absence of significant improvements in real yields or better productivity, higher revenues generally imply the addition of assets, and a growing balance sheet imposes a financing requirement. If it is assumed that the assets required to support the anticipated higher level of revenues remain an approximately constant proportion of sales (which, in fact, might not be the case if assets are managed more efficiently or if operating leases are increasingly relied upon and not capitalized onto the balance sheet), the assets required to support projected revenues in some future period 't' can be estimated as follows:
     Total assets / Revenues x Projected revenues at time t.
   Alternatively, the incremental investment in assets required to support the increase in sales from year t-1 to year t can be calculated:
     Total assets / Revenues x (Revenues at t - Revenues at t-1).
   Any investment in new assets has to be financed from some source, either internal or external. Thus, pro forma statements based on the investment decision inherent in forecast revenue growth must make assumptions about financing decisions, a corollary of which would be assumptions about additional interest or rental expenses.
   At zero or low rates of growth there is a tendency in profitable companies for the proportion of the balance sheet comprised of external liabilities to fall as retained earnings rise and supplant them in the financing of a stable or slowly growing asset base. At higher rates of growth the increase in assets is often greater than can be financed from retained profits, unless profitability is a lot higher than most of the airline industry has experienced even during cyclical upturns, and the dependency on external liabilities will accordingly rise. The rate at which an airline can generate

financial resources should dictate its maximum sustainable growth rate. However, over-indulgent government shareholders and insufficiently risk-averse financial markets can complicate the analysis.

7   Jones, L. (1997), 'A Red Flag to a Bull?', *Airline Business*, July.

8   Boeing (1997), *Current Market Outlook*, p. 21.

9   'Strategic intent' is a concept that is briefly discussed in chapter 15 of Volume One.

10 Ansoff, I. (1957), 'Strategies for Diversification', *Harvard Business Review*, September-October. See also: Johnson, S. and James, C. (1957), 'How to Organize for New Products', *Harvard Business Review*, May-June.

11 More sophisticated varieties of the model extend the matrix to nine cells by interposing 'new but related products' and 'new but related markets'. See, for example: Karlöf, B. (1993), *Key Business Concepts*, Routledge, pp. 196, 197. McDonald goes even further by extending the concept to a multi-cell matrix structured along the two continua of 'increasing market newness' and 'increasing technological newness': McDonald, M.H.B. (1989), *Marketing Plans* (2nd edition), Butterworth-Heinemann, p. 90.

12 As noted in chapter 18 of Volume One, KLM's global strategy launched in the late 1980s was predicated on the belief that a ten per cent share of the global market is the likely survival threshold for international 'mega-carriers'.

13 US Department of Transportation (1990), *Report of the Secretary's Task Force on Competition in the US Domestic Airline Industry*. For a brief explanation of the 'S-curve' effect, see: Holloway, op. cit.

14 Market segmentation is discussed at length in Holloway, op. cit., and more briefly in Volume One, chapter 10 of this book; competitive advantage is explained in chapter 17 of Volume One. Positioning and the marketing mix are considered in chapter 6 of the present volume.

15 Brand and product life cycles are discussed in Volume One, chapter 15.

16 Lovelock, C.H. (1996), *Services Marketing* (3rd edition), Prentice Hall, p. 186.

17 Emergent strategies - strategies which emerge unintended from the act of implementation rather than from formalized planning processes - are explained in the first chapter of Volume One.

18 Boeing (1996), *Current Market Outlook*, p. 5.

19 Rakesh Gingwal, President and CEO of US Airways, quoted in: Velocci, A.L. Jr. (1997), 'US Airways Edges Towards Massive Downsizing', *Aviation Week & Space Technology*, April 28, p. 34. The carrier eventually chose to grow.

20 The role of stakeholders, the importance of vision and mission, and the establishment of high-level corporate objectives are discussed in Volume One, chapters 2, 13, and 18 respectively.

21 Southwest is the obvious example, although having begun operations in 1971 as an intra-state carrier in Texas it is not strictly a post-deregulation start-up. It is now being imitated by start-ups in Europe and Latin America, as well as the United States.

22 The 'core competence' concept is explained in chapter 15 of Volume One, and value chains are discussed in chapter 17 of the same volume.

23 Hotel ownership has a long history in the airline industry, going back to the days when Imperial Airways and Pan Am needed somewhere to put their passengers during en route night stops and, more recently, when some US carriers - notably American, United, Pan Am, and TWA, but not Northwest or Delta - used hotel ownership at desired destinations to make cases to the CAB that they had sufficient 'historical interest' in those destinations to be allowed to serve them. More recently still, a number of airlines have helped develop resorts in order to stimulate traffic to new tourist destinations, as happened in Mauritius and the Seychelles for example. It was mentioned in chapter 13 of Volume One that Air Malta's founding charter requires it to develop tourism to the island, so justifying the ownership and operation of hotels and resorts. This type of strategy is something quite different from diversifying into hotels in large cities which are already well-served - as All Nippon has done, for example, with its policy of locating a hotel at every overseas station.

24   These percentages can vary widely from year to year. They are nevertheless indicative
      of different approaches to the sourcing of seats within the groups concerned.
25   Transaction cost analysis has become a popular tool for assessing alternative
      governance structures in a number of industries, although its use by most airlines
      appears to be more intuitive than explicit. See, for example: Jones, G.R. and Hill,
      C.W.L. (1988), 'Transaction Cost Analysis of Strategy-structure Choice', *Strategic
      Management Journal*, 9. In principle, all that distinguishes a 'firm' from a 'market' is
      relative costs. When it is cheaper to band together to produce output, firms are
      formed; when it is cheaper to let the invisible hand of the market take over,
      transactions should be externalized. In practice, politics, inertia, and strategic issues
      revolving around the unquantifiable costs of external dependency pollute this
      economic purity.
26   Take, for example, the three Chinese joint venture aircraft maintenance facilities
      (Ameco in Beijing, Gameco in Guangzhou, and Taikoo Aircraft Maintenance Co. in
      Xiamen). They will be preoccupied largely with China's own rapidly expanding fleet
      for a considerable time to come. But given that their costs for a widebody D-check are
      around half those in the United States - and considerably below half the cost in many
      European countries - there is a competitive advantage here waiting to be transformed
      into a globally relevant price differentiation strategy as the skills and resource base
      grow. Of course, activities do not have to be outsourced in order to move them
      offshore; several airlines based in high-cost countries have relocated data-intensive
      activities to cheaper offshore sites. See: Holloway, op. cit., chapter 7.
27   There can be no general, prescriptive argument - as is sometimes claimed - that
      outsourcing automatically lowers costs. For the case against maintenance outsourcing
      as a cost-saving technique, see the letter (name withheld) 'Outsourcing Not So
      Cheap', *Aviation Week & Space Technology*, May 26, 1997, p. 6. Separately, the
      following quotation hints at a similar story: 'Nearly 80 per cent of the light and heavy
      maintenance has been brought inhouse, saving millions of dollars for Continental and
      making Express more efficient operationally'. (Moorman, R.W. (1997), 'Expressly
      Different', *Air Transport World*, June, p. 122.)
          Furthermore, outsourcing strategies can change as an airline's maintenance
      requirements or fleet composition evolve. Whilst Continental, for example, has
      outsourced much of its heavy maintenance since the early 1990s, it has retained line
      maintenance. As retirements and acquisitions cycle out of and into its fleet over the
      next few years, the average age of that fleet will decline. One result will be that heavy
      maintenance will account for a much smaller proportion of total maintenance activity,
      and the overall percentage of outsourced maintenance will decline - a trend accelerated
      by the use on new aircraft of phased checks in a line maintenance environment.
      (*Aviation Week and Space Technology*, December 16, 1996, p. S30.)
28   *Commuter World*, April-May 1995.
29   This estimate comes from the Canaan Group (a US-based consultancy), and was
      cited in: McKenna, J.T. and Scott W.B. (1997), 'The MRO's Challenge: Quality vs.
      Cost', *Aviation Week & Space Technology*, April 14, p. 44.
30   *Aerospace*, October 1994.
31   Wherever customer-contact work is outsourced, for example, contracts should ideally
      build-in quality, performance, and staff training criteria. The problem is that whilst it
      might be possible to address contractually the mechanical aspects of service delivery,
      variables such as motivation, values, and identification with the airline's particular
      corporate culture are always going to be exceptionally difficult to incorporate into
      service-level agreements. Proactive steps, such as bringing suppliers' staff onto the
      airline's training programmes, might be necessary. See: Festa, P. (1997), 'Wheeling
      Out the Service', *Airline Business*, January. Clearly, the management, staff,
      facilities, work processes, and quality control systems of bidders for outsourced
      work need to be thoroughly evaluated and, once contracts have been awarded,
      carefully monitored.

32 It is interesting in this context that to develop local skills and provide a focus for industrial development (possibly even a future source of revenue as well), some airlines based in developing countries are demanding technology transfers in return for placing maintenance contracts with overseas suppliers.

33 Such investments, of course, do not prevent outsourcing: in the mid-1990s, UK third party shop FLS was doing 360,000 man-hours of work per annum for British Airways under a 5-year maintenance contract. A number of carriers see merit in mixing inhouse with outsourced work - a phenomenon known as 'tapered integration' - to avoid overcapacity in a downturn.

34 Noble, R. (1995), 'Catering for Profit', *Interavia,* February.

35 Of course, calling a unit a 'profit centre' and then shackling its ability to earn profits may in some circumstances raise questions about just what is being sought and achieved. For example, British Airways World Cargo is, at the time of writing, an internal profit centre which is obliged to buy the airline's entire belly-hold output - whether or not it wants that output and can make a profit from selling it on to shippers and forwarders at market rates.

36 For example, whilst in 1996 only DEM44 million out of Lufthansa Systems' total revenue of DEM535 million was earned from third parties, the subsidiary was nonetheless able to benefit its majority shareholder by establishing an arms-length customer-supplier relationship. Conversely, around one-third of Lufthansa Technik's 1996 revenue of just over DEM3 billion came from customers other than Lufthansa.

37 Smith, W. (1996), 'Shifting Spanners', *Airline Business,* October.

38 ICAO (1996), *Manual on the Regulation of International Air Transport,* p. 55.1-2.

39 See: Holloway, op. cit., chapter 1.

40 Cronshaw, M. and Thompson, D.J. (1991), 'Sources of Rent and Airline Deregulation in Europe', *Centre for Business Strategy Working Paper,* London Business School.

41 British Airways has in the past complained repeatedly about this 'cherry-picking', as though for some reason competitors are breaking the rules of the game by choosing to enter only markets in which they think they will be able to make money. British Airways' management is clearly not so naive as to believe this, leaving one to conclude that its public relations people must think that the travelling public is.

42 Some of the larger US regionals also have their own mini-hubs, of course, where they both feed their major airline partners and flow their own connecting traffic. Comair does this at Cincinnati, for example.

43 Whitaker, R. (1996), 'Hubbing Power', *Airline Business,* December.

44 Battles which are particularly interesting in this regard have developed between neighbouring regional jet hubs at Cincinnati, Cleveland, and Detroit - where affiliates of Delta, Continental, and Northwest respectively are scrapping for flow traffic. Regional jets help major carriers to access markets which their own cost structures and work practices do not allow them to serve with aircraft having fewer than 100 seats. In Europe, similar strategies have been pursued by Swissair (which has devolved operations with aircraft smaller than 100 seats to majority-owned subsidiary Crossair), Lufthansa (whose CityLine subsidiary flies regional jets and has itself outsourced turboprop operations), and British Airways (which has regional franchisees flying jets).

45 An interesting example is the bid by a newly established independent division of US regional Mesa to take-on parts of Southwest's Dallas Love Field network with a high-frequency regional jet operation based at Meacham Field in nearby Fort Worth. This iconoclastic initiative, launched in 1997, to deploy on short-haul, relatively high-density routes a type generally seen as best used either on longer, thin routes or as an off-peak supplement to mainline equipment on trunk routes pitched the regional jets' lower trip costs against Southwest's lower seat-mile costs.

46 Not that Northwest would readily be described by most observers as a geographical 'niche' carrier, but the point exemplified is valid in respect of its US domestic

network and serves to underline the definitional imprecision inherent in strategic categorization.

47   Western Pacific paralleled the move by trying to negotiate a merger with Denver-based Frontier - the objective being to mount a combined low-cost challenge to United. The merger never materialised; Western Pacific eventually filed for protection under Chapter 11, and became the target of an aborted takeover bid by Frontier.

48   Once again, it is important to make the point that concepts such as 'niche' are analytically useful, but in practice can be open to a fair amount of definitional imprecision. For example, how should a 'niche' be measured - by number of enplanements, RPKs flown, revenues earned, size of fleet, or market share? And if market share, how should 'the market' be defined in light of the definitional issues already raised when discussing growth at the beginning of the chapter?

49   Personal travel (i.e. private journeys for purposes other than vacation or visiting friends and relations) is not separately discussed. Particularly when personal travel is in response to an emergency (e.g. the unexpected illness of a family member) rather than a planned event (e.g. the start of a school or university year), it can share with business travel a tendency to be relatively price inelastic and insensitive to ticket conditionality. On the other hand, people travelling for personal reasons will rarely generate as many trips per annum as typical business travellers.

50   The airline's Skyway regional feeder (doing business as Midwest Express Connection) does fly some connecting traffic, but Midwest Express remains predominantly an O and D carrier. Its hallmark low seating densities and high standards of inflight cuisine contribute to unit costs which are at the upper end of US industry tables, but these are more than compensated for by industry-leading yields.

51   Lauda Air is one example of an airline which has successfully built a reputation for high-quality scheduled service alongside its original charter business.

52   An example of highly targeted niche marketing in the leisure segment is British Airways' decision in 1997 to offer safari departures dedicated to gay/lesbian vacationers as part of its Affordable Africa product line.

53   These carriers do not, of course, do all their own flying, with the result that as well as being competitors scheduled airlines often vie for their business (i.e. act as subcontractors in an important part of the service chain).

54   The future of British Airways World Cargo was, in fact, subject to intense debate during the mid-90s - not least because of difficulties faced in meeting service standards. In 1997, British Airways extracted pay and staffing concessions from the unit's employees in return for a commitment not to outsource cargo activities.

55   These are being supplemented by new B747-400s first ordered in 1997.

56   Cargo operations were augmented in 1997 by Martinair's acquisition of 40 per cent of Colombian cargo carrier Tampa.

57   Knibb, D. (1996), 'Desert Bloomer', *Airline Business,* October.

58   See: Holloway, op. cit., chapters 12 and 14 for full discussions of price discrimination and yield management.

59   The entrepreneur behind CityBird was the person who had built EuroBelgian and subsequently sold a majority stake in that carrier, which then became Virgin Express. Late in 1997, Sabena bought just over 10 per cent of CityBird and the two carriers announced plans to code-share on certain transatlantic routes.

60   Some discrimination between these segments is in fact maintained by the commonly imposed requirement for people travelling at short notice - often business travellers - to pay higher 'walk-up fares' than the, say, 7-day or 21-day fares that might be available to vacationers or others able to plan further in advance.

61   Bear in mind that we are talking here about routes able to support jets with 100 or more seats - not thin routes that could be, and in large numbers have been, devolved to regional affiliates.

62   The influence of British Airways at that time may have been a factor in USAir's approach. Continental subsequently upgraded its short-haul service.

63 It was, in fact, explicit in the initial Delta Express operating strategy that the unit would only serve stations already on the mainline carrier's network. The perspective here was that rather than generating problems from incompatible service delivery systems, the overlap would be positive insofar as it would reduce investment in facilities and marketing communications compared to what would have been required at greenfield sites.

On the other side of the Atlantic, British Airways - having considered and rejected the purchase of stakes in established low-cost carriers Ryanair and easyJet - turned its attention in late 1997 to the feasibility of establishing its own low-cost operation. Even though London's unfashionable third airport at Stansted was the preferred base, and this was not an airport at which British Airways had mainline operations, the broad reach of the short-haul mainline network made overlap of low-cost and full-service products at outstations inevitable.

64 The affected carriers themselves clearly saw them as very real when, in 1997, they established a trade association - the Air Carrier Association of America - to protect their particular interests. The association was founded to engage in common-issue environmental influencing on behalf of its members, with the initial points of concern being:

- predatory pricing and scheduling by majors, intended to drive small, low-cost carriers from their markets;
- safety and security proposals that bear more heavily on underresourced small airlines than on major carriers - an example being proposals to mandate passenger profiling, which would be easier to implement for large carriers possessing FFP databases than for small, low-cost carriers not having this type of resource;
- proposals to replace the ticket tax and other imposts with user charges as the mechanism for funding the FAA; and
- barriers to entry, such as long-term gate leasing and control of grandfathered slots by incumbents.

(Walker, K. (1997), 'When the Wolf's at Your Door', *Airline Business,* May.)

65 'Now, with the ValuJet crash receding into memory, the worm is turning and on Capitol Hill, last year's corner-cutting bottom-feeders may be becoming today's plucky underdogs'. (Flint, P. (1997), 'A Splendid First', *Air Transport World,* June, p. 135.) See also: Walker, K. (1997), 'US Targets Predators...', *Airline Business,* November; and, O'Toole, K. (1997), 'DOT Promises Action to Help Start-Ups', *Flight International,* 15-21 October.

66 At the time of writing, British Midland's role is widely believed likely to change, with a move closer to Lufthansa - alliance partner of 40 per cent shareholder SAS - considered probable. In 1997, the British carrier began operating a London-Cologne-Rome service as a Lufthansa code-share; this was felt by some observers to foreshadow further 'outsourcing' by Lufthansa of flights from Germany to other European points via 'fifth freedom' code-shares on British Midland flights, which offer both high-quality service and - relative to Lufthansa - low production costs.

67 Morrison, S.A. and Winston, C. (1995), *The Evolution of the Airline Industry,* Brookings, pp. 151, 152.

68 See: Holloway, op. cit., chapter 1 for a discussion of economies of scale, scope, and density in the airline industry.

69 Ibid., chapter 12.

70 Barkin, T.I., Hertzell, O.S., and Young, S.J. (1995), 'Facing Low-cost Competitors: Lessons for US Airlines', *The McKinsey Quarterly,* Number 4.

71 The air traffic freedoms are explained and discussed in Volume One, chapter 3.

2 Competitive strategy

We saw in chapter 1 that the scope of any airline's activities is an outcome of four fundamental choices made at the corporate level.

1   Industrial scope.

2   Vertical scope.

3   Geographical scope.

4   Product scope.

Of these four scope decisions, only industrial scope is a choice unique to the corporate level. The other three can also be relevant at the level of individual business units in a multi-business enterprise - which is what most large, and some smaller, airlines really are. Vision, mission, and high-level objectives should provide the unity of purpose linking all four dimensions.[1] Choices about which customers' needs to satisfy and which services to satisfy them with must be guided by overall mission and objectives, whilst at the same time these higher level considerations themselves have to be informed by environmental realities, particularly within the competitive environment.[2]

As already noted, many airlines either are or still consider themselves to be single-business enterprises. In these cases, the distinction between corporate and competitive strategies is not always immediately apparent. Nonetheless, there is merit in separating the 'Where to compete?' question - the arena of distinctive capabilities and core competencies - from 'How to compete?' - the arena in which distinctive capabilities and core competencies can be transformed into competitive advantage. It is to the 'How to compete?' question that we turn in this chapter.

Clearly, the answer to that question must depend very much on the outcome of internal analyses discussed in Part Two of Volume One -

particularly the analysis of potential sources of competitive advantage in chapter 17. A distinction was drawn in that chapter between the industrial organization (IO) theory of competitive advantage and the resource-based theory. Zou and Cavusgil have the following to say about how these different perspectives feed through into competitive strategy.

> Like IO-based theories, the resource-based theory sees above-normal returns as the firm's ultimate goal. Obtaining such returns requires either that the firm's product be distinctive in the eyes of buyers in comparison to competing products or that the firm sell a product identical to that of competitors at a lower cost. Thus, the critical problem is how to maintain product distinctiveness at low cost without making excessive investments. Unlike IO-based theory, which argues that competitive advantage can be sustained by the firm's conduct in response to industry structure, the resource-based theory contends that product distinctiveness or low cost are tied directly to the distinctiveness in the inputs (resources) used to make the product. In fact, it is hard-to-copy resources rather than monopoly power or market position which bring persistent, above-normal earnings to the firm. Moreover, the distinctiveness of those resources results from the firm's acumen or luck in acquiring, combining and deploying them, not from the forces related to industry structure, such as the number of sellers, barriers to entry, product differentiation or market growth.[3]

Answering the 'How to compete?' question requires selection of an overall competitive strategy. There can be as many of these as there are airlines, so for analytical purposes we will be looking at a small number of 'generic' strategies. The most influential categorization of generic competitive strategies in recent years was first suggested by Porter in 1980, and it is this that will form the basis for the discussion in the first sections of the present chapter. It largely follows the IO tradition referred to above; although resource-based theories have recently gained considerable popularity, Porter's approach to the analysis of competitive strategy remains highly influential. Furthermore, the two are anyway not mutually exclusive - as was pointed out in Volume One, chapter 17.

The chapter will then go on to characterize competitive strategy as being not so much a choice made from one of four distinct generic strategies as a choice of strategic positioning along a continuum of feasible service-price offers. In Part Two of the present volume we will consider implementation of strategies, focusing on the service concept, other marketing mix variables, and service delivery. This is the point of contact with actual customers and identifiable competitors, the point at which selection and execution of strategies will either prove to have created competitive advantage or not, and the point at which some intended strategies inevitably get dropped by the wayside and those that remain are augmented by emergent strategies - the result being 'realized strategy', as described in the opening chapter of Volume One. The discussion will focus primarily on scheduled passenger services, but some of what is said is equally relevant to cargo and nonscheduled passenger services and also to airline activities other than air transportation.

Generic competitive strategies

The most popular typology of competitive strategies has since the early 1980s been one put forward by Porter.[4] It presupposes that the purpose of competitive strategy is to outperform competitors in the marketplace and achieve an above average rate of return; although this is not yet a universal objective for airline managements, it is now more widely held than at any time in the industry's history.

Porter's analysis starts with consideration of industry attractiveness, which can be assessed using his 'five forces' model (i.e. supplier and buyer bargaining power, intensity of competitive rivalry, and threat of new entrants and substitutes).[5] He then moves on to investigate how a firm may deal with these forces and achieve above-average profitability given the structure of its particular industry. Efforts can be made to modify one or more of the forces: the intensity of internal rivalry might be reduced by building customers' switching costs (e.g. FFPs), supplier bargaining power might be reduced by pursuing tapered integration (referred to in chapter 1), buyer bargaining power might be reduced by sharpening yield management capabilities, and potential challenges might be curtailed by adopting entry-deterrence strategies. But it is possession of sustainable competitive advantage over specifically identifiable competitors that is the key.[6]

There are two generic methods for building competitive advantage and outperforming rivals - in other words, two fundamental positioning alternatives: differentiation and cost leadership. These can be pursued on a wide-market or niche basis. What is possible will depend upon market and industry structure, and upon the capabilities of individual competitors. Figure 2.1 illustrates the choice process - which will be influenced by the results of external analysis (Part One of Volume One), internal analysis (Part Two of Volume One), and strategic choices made at the corporate level (chapter 1 of the present volume). As was mentioned in chapter 1 and again at the beginning of this chapter, competitive scope in the air transport industry can be defined in terms of either or both geographical scope or product scope - the two being closely linked.

DEMAND SIDE

Market

Segmentation

Market targeting

Positioning

SUPPLY SIDE

Industry

Industry economics
and value chain

Airline choice of
value chain configuration

- - -▶ Detailed segmentation might be
considered unnecessary in some
markets

Choice of generic strategy

	Broad	Narrow
Lowest cost	WIDE-MARKET COST LEADERSHIP	SEGMENT COST FOCUS
Differentiation	WIDE-MARKET DIFFERENTIATION	SEGMENT DIFFERENTIATION FOCUS

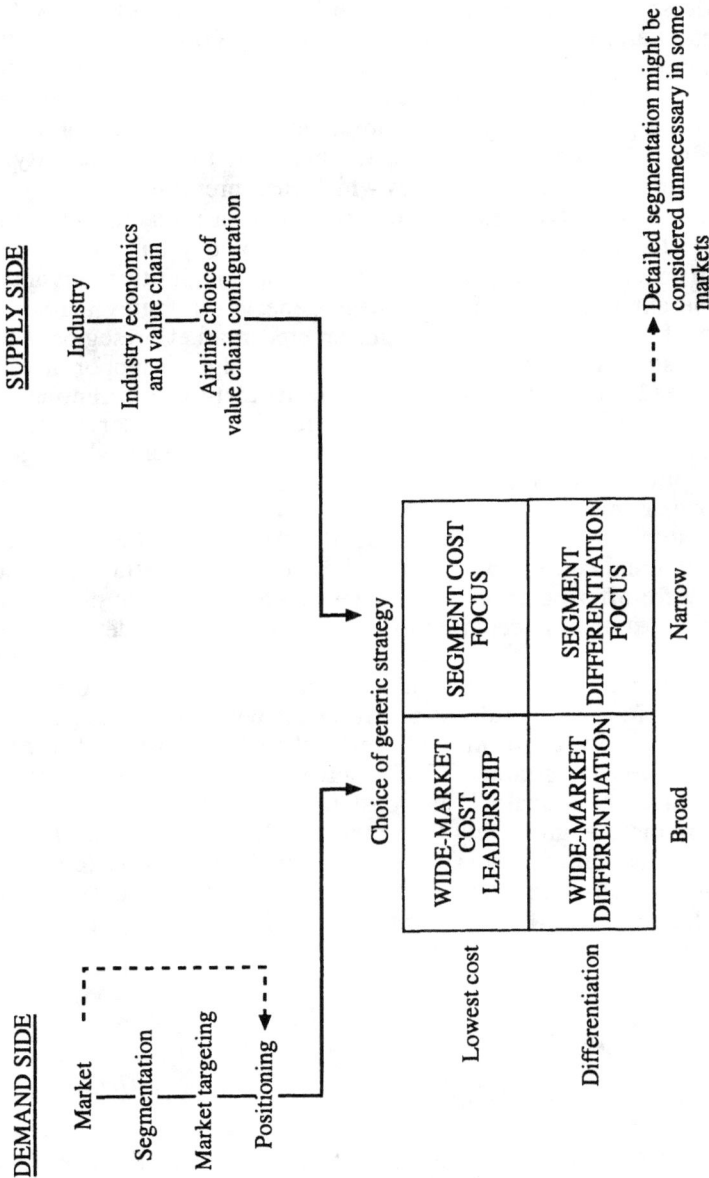

Figure 2.1 : Choice of generic competitive strategy

Source: Adapted from ideas proposed in Porter, M.E., *Competitive Strategy*, The Free Press, 1980

Cost leadership and differentiation, within either a wide-market or focused context are, with some exceptions noted by Porter, intended to be mutually exclusive - requiring clear decisions about how competitive advantage is to be sought in targeted markets and segments. A company choosing to adopt more than one should in principle house them in separate units to avoid possible clashes between the different styles, cultures, and service delivery processes which each presupposes.

The choices define **strategic groups** present in a market, and if they lead to competitive advantage being achieved mobility barriers between groups will be erected.[7] Failure to establish a competitive advantage through coherent pursuit of one of these generic strategies across the entire range of airline activities in each targeted market or segment will lead to being 'stuck in the middle' - with costs too high to support a wide-market cost leadership strategy, services insufficiently differentiated to support a wide-market differentiation strategy, and neither costs nor services appropriately focused on the specific needs of narrowly targeted segments or niches. This is the problem facing several European 'flag carriers', for example. Early 1990s Australian start-up Compass was also in a sense 'stuck in the middle', trapped between, on the one hand, marketing communications which touted higher service standards than incumbents were offering and, on the other, the almost manic discounting necessary to generate cash required to compensate for an undercapitalized launch.

Airlines might get 'stuck in the middle' either because they have emerged from the protection of a regulated environment without a strategy fit for the markets they now confront, or because they have lost control of an initially sound generic strategy.[8] Differentiators taking a hatchet to cost structures in need of a scalpel, and cost leaders with ambitions to start differentiating more aggressively than their capabilities allow can fall into the latter trap, as can focusers who widen their ambitions (e.g. post-deregulation low-cost US start-up Midway, with its business-oriented Metrolink concept, and People Express, which wandered far from its original short-haul, no-frills niche).

A closer look at the generic strategies

Wide-market cost leadership strategies

The objective here is to be **the** lowest cost producer, operating across a broad swathe of the market and aiming for the 'average' customer, differentiating no more than is necessary to achieve 'parity' and 'proximity' relative to competitors and certainly not enough to appeal to specific segments with highly individualized needs.[9] Failure to achieve parity or proximity often signifies heavy discounting, which edges the strategy away from cost leadership towards cost focus - the focus in this case being upon a segment constituted by the most highly price-sensitive consumers.

There are broadly two ways to achieve lower costs than competitors:

- understand and control cost drivers; and/or
- reconfigure the value chain.

A cost advantage can be sustained only by doing either or both of these in some way that cannot be replicated. Decisions made regarding the size and configuration of a fleet, the stage lengths dictated by network design, levels of service appropriate for targeted consumers, the calibre and productivity of staff, choice of distribution channels, and the nature of marketing communications, for example, all drive costs and have the power to influence configuration of the value chain. Because so little of the industry's knowledge or technology is proprietary to a single carrier, the shared understanding and the unique combination of skills and resources embedded in each airline - highlighted in chapter 15 of Volume One - can take on particular importance.

Although wide-market cost leaders are likely to offer relatively few 'frills' and are rarely innovators in terms of the service attributes they offer, their position is not simply built upon cutting out customer benefits; any competitor can do that. It has to be built on much deeper foundations. To be a wide-market cost leader according to the model, it is necessary not only to have the lowest costs but to be able to sell at or near average prices. 'Average price' is a fairly slippery concept in much of the airline business, of course, but the point is that cost leadership and rock-bottom prices do not necessarily go hand-in-hand. It was mentioned above that if a low-cost producer can **only** sell on price - perhaps because its product lacks parity - it has probably moved away from a wide-market strategy by implicitly segmenting the market and targeting the most cost-conscious consumers.

The experiences of Continental (during its periods in Chapter 11 bankruptcy) and Compass, two of several possible examples, illustrate that low costs are not necessarily enough to gain a cost leadership position, as defined by Porter's model, if there is trouble on the revenue side. That trouble could stem from lack of parity or from the industry's proven willingness to match prices irrespective of cost structures. Compass, for example, had unit operating costs three Australian cents per ASK below those of Ansett or Australian Airlines, attributable to a flexible workforce and favourable production economics inherent in operating a single-type fleet of high-capacity A300-600Rs over a predominantly medium-haul network.[10] The problem was that its yields were hit by the deep discounting necessary to fill these relatively large aircraft and to compensate business travellers for the lower frequencies which using them entailed.

Wide-market differentiation strategies

Wide-market differentiation implies greater efforts to segment the market than would be the case for a cost leadership strategy, but the intention would still be to have a broad appeal. To differentiate, an airline must offer something which is valued by customers and which is not offered (either at all or to the same standard) by other producers. The heart of any differentiation strategy is the building of preference out of customers' perceptions that some aspect of the airline's service-price offer is unique, thereby distancing it from alternative offers which might otherwise appear to be close substitutes.

Differentiation should be viewed from the customer's perspective - in terms of unmet needs for the benefits provided by service attributes, or for psychological satisfaction from brand association. The reward should be a sustainable price premium. In the same way that a cost leader must retain a certain level of service attributes in order not to be compelled to dilute its cost advantage by discounting below competitors' prices, so differentiators must have costs close to the industry average if their price premium is not to be eroded and the above-average rate of return whittled away.

In serving the business segment, a strong network offering high frequencies can be a critical source of differentiation. Generally, however, sustainable sources of differentiation are difficult to find in the airline industry because most innovations are easily replicable. This tends to make a positive brand image and corporate reputation backed by competent brand management skills particularly important, and the same is true of the corporate culture which frames service delivery activities. Differentiation in the airline industry is often - though not inevitably - associated with high customer-perceived quality and positive brand associations, and with a quality- and customer-focused corporate culture. These can offer psychological benefits to customers which are both unique and difficult for competitors to imitate.

Although most tangible aspects of the service delivery process are replicable, airlines able to institutionalize innovation can keep ahead of the pack. The problem - particularly widespread in this industry - is that their lead is likely to be only temporary, with the result that costs can be raised by doing something which will not necessarily contribute to *sustainably* higher revenues. On the other hand, the 'image' of being an innovator, of being at the cutting edge of what is best in airline service, may itself be a source of competitive advantage even though specific innovations are quickly copied. British Airways has benefitted from this type of image, for example.

Threats to differentiation strategies can arise if low-cost competitors are able to offer equally acceptable but lower-priced alternatives, if the chosen basis for differentiation either becomes less important to buyers or - as commonly happens - comes to be accepted as standard throughout the industry, or if a competitor 'leap-frogs' to higher levels of service. Focused differentiation might also pose a threat if the targeted segments are sufficiently important - as both British Midland and Virgin Atlantic have proven with their selective attacks on British Airways' densest short- and long-haul markets out of London Heathrow.

Focus strategies

Competitive advantage unavailable across a broad range of segments is here sought by focusing on the particular needs of customers in one or a small number of geographical and/or product markets.

Cost focus A cost focus strategy oriented towards provision of a no-frills service to the most price-sensitive segment of consumers is a common entry point for start-ups; this can be particularly appropriate on dense, linear routes which allow marketing communications to be carefully targeted in order to rapidly build brand recognition, which have favourable operating economics, and which do not require the network connectivity likely to be offered by wide-market incumbents. It might be defensible to the extent that full-service incumbents which are wide-market differentiators cannot risk weakening customer loyalty by drastically downgrading their service standards in pursuit of competitive costs, and to the extent that incumbents cannot easily 'reinvent' networks and service delivery processes that have been expensively created to provide a full-service product. On the other hand, this strategy is exposed to the willingness of incumbents to match prices in the short run irrespective of financial pain, to launch low-cost subsidiaries or units, or over time to get costs into closer proximity with those of the cost focuser. This is what has been happening in the US domestic industry throughout the 1990s. It is also a strategy easily replicated by other new entrants, and so needs to be supported by at least some differentiation - brand recognition or corporate culture, for example - as well as continuous attention to costs.

Differentiation focus This can provide better opportunities to build a defensible niche. Geographic and service segmentation can be used together to focus the strategy particularly strongly. The classic contrast here is between Laker and Virgin on transatlantic routes. Laker went after the most price-sensitive segments as a cost focuser, but incumbents proved ready to match prices. Despite its early backpacker image, Virgin Atlantic competes primarily on service by offering what is positioned as higher quality for essentially the same price as competitors are charging. In the mid-90s, AOM and Air Liberté also adopted differentiation focus strategies to enter French domestic markets against Air Inter's 'no-frills' service (although their ultimate fates suggest that both carriers 'got it wrong' in terms of either strategy formulation or implementation). Rapidly expanding Brazilian carrier TAM has carved a niche by offering service levels that allow it to charge a price premium in many of its markets. Indian start-up Jet Airways adopted the same strategy.

Another approach adopted in some markets has been to differentiate on ticket conditionality, offering similar levels of service at similar prices to those offered by competitors but without the same restrictive conditions on ticket purchase and usage. However, this strategy can be difficult to defend against an aggravated incumbent armed with a finely-tuned yield management system.

The downsides of differentiation focus are that the markets being entered might not be susceptible to clear segmentation, and that it can be expensive both to understand and monitor the bases for differentiation in targeted segments and then to provide that differentiation. Also, as MGM Grand Air and others have proven with their lack of success at the luxury end of the US domestic market, it is possible to over-differentiate. (Not that this stops people trying: at the time of writing, Dallas-based start-up Legend Airlines has plans to operate B737-200s or DC-9-30s configured with just 56 seats, and French start-up Fairlines is launching low-density MD-80 operations.)

The obvious weakness of any focus strategy is that the targeted segment(s) might be attacked by wide-market competitors; many niches grow over time and the larger they become, the more likely they are to attract attention. Narrow segments are also more open to attack by imitative start-ups, and there is always the danger that segment distinctiveness will gradually be eroded. Perhaps the most potent threat, however, is human nature: the deceptive lure of 'critical mass' seems to tempt focusers out of their niches with surprising regularity, and few succeed in making the transition to wide-market status. Delta is an example of a large differentiation focuser which managed to make it, but the corporate graveyard is littered with many more that did not. In future, this is probably a transition which, if it is to be attempted at all, is going to have to be made within the context of an alliance rather than through internal growth or acquisition.

Comments on the choice of competitive strategy

That Porter's contribution has been both analytically useful and extremely influential is beyond doubt. Inevitably, though, a body of literature critiquing the model has accumulated.[11] Of a long list of issues raised, many spurious but some well-founded, three are particularly noteworthy.

1 Efforts to become both the lowest cost producer and a high-quality differentiator are not necessarily incompatible: cost is a function not of quality alone but of how that quality is achieved. In manufacturing industries, flexible manufacturing systems have made pursuit of low-cost differentiation a feasible strategy. In the airline industry, for

example, IT provides a platform for both enhanced differentiation and lower unit costs. The challenge is perhaps better addressed as one involving a search for balance rather than as the resolution of an 'either/or' paradox.[12]

2   Wide-market cost leadership with differentiation and prices pitched at or near the average for the market might be a route to above-average returns, but it is arguably not a **competitive** strategy insofar as it offers customers no particular reason to buy; no unique proposition is being offered to the marketplace. Only if low relative costs are translated into low relative prices do they become the foundation of a competitive strategy - of an offer that is distinct from offers made by competitors. But in this case the strategy would become either one of wide-market 'price differentiation' or, if low costs were founded in particular on no-frills service, one of 'cost focus'. Either way, customers would then be offered a specific - price-related - reason to buy (although in practice both strategies are exposed to the industry's proven willingness to match prices).

3   It has been argued in recent years that Porter's analysis is too concerned with stable equilibrium in the context of given product-market structures, whereas what really matters in competitive terms is a company's ability to leverage resources and skills or, using Hamel and Prahalad's vocabulary, to 'stretch' itself in pursuit of some vision-driven 'strategic intent'.[13]

Marketing economies of scale and economies of scope and density will often allow airlines to profitably serve markets in which their generic competitive strategy gives them no particular competitive advantage. This is notably true of those wide-market differentiators whose distinctive capabilities are primarily oriented to the business segment - such as British Airways, with its premium brand image and relatively high-frequency Heathrow-based network - but which nonetheless need the added density of leisure segments in their existing geographical (particularly long-haul) markets and are able to serve them profitably.

Another question relevant to Porter's model which has been exercising a lot of minds in the airline industry is whether or not carriers are selling a 'commodity product'. This is significant because a commodity product is difficult to differentiate on a sustainable basis, brand loyalty is weak, and the most logical strategic response is to compete solely on price. Research undertaken by USAir in preparation for the launch of its ultimately abortive 'Project High Ground' low-cost airline-within-an-airline initiative in 1994 suggested that, in principle, certain categories of passenger were prepared to pay a premium for network connectivity and for amenities such as advance seat assignment. But how large this premium should be was always going to be difficult to judge and, in practice, whenever USAir came head-to-head against Southwest during that period the larger airline almost invariably matched prices. British Airways has explicitly targeted customers, particularly economy class customers, willing to pay a small (i.e. around 5 per cent) premium for 'superior service' (although a premium is clearly not attainable in all its markets). Whilst not charging price premia, Alaska Airlines pitches itself as a low-fare/high-quality airline - the message being that despite the cost-cutting that has been necessary to remain competitive and has eaten into its previously very high standards of service, it is still offering to its core West Coast O and D markets a product that differentiates it from low-cost/no-frills competitors. This is also a strategy that has been pursued, albeit with somewhat erratic results to date, by America West.

Travel behaviour and factors influencing customers' choices of airline inevitably differ between countries. The British tend to be less loyal to their own carriers than some continental Europeans, for example, and a distinction can also be drawn between behaviour in US markets and behaviour elsewhere. There is no denying the importance of price, particularly amongst coach/economy class passengers and in certain geographical regions. Branding, frequent flyer programmes, and - especially on long-haul routes - improved amenities are nonetheless a constant feature of the battle for consumer loyalty, and there is an argument that a service industry which captures and retains clients in contact-intensive service delivery systems for anything ranging from an hour to 24 hours is never going to be entirely commoditized. There will always be opportunities to differentiate not only what is done, but how it is done - that is, to differentiate both service concepts and service delivery; we will explore this point further in Part Two of the present volume.

If frozen chickens and household bleach can be differentiated to command price premia, it is difficult to see why airline seats should be treated as a pure commodity - notwithstanding that air transport has certainly been 'democratized' into a mass market industry since the 1970s. No matter how commonplace flying becomes, it will remain a unique enterprise in terms of its psychological impact on consumers. As long as this is so, characterization of an undeniably price-elastic business as one which has become 'commoditized' could lead to self-deception and missed marketing opportunities. It is today too often forgotten that profits are driven by revenues as well as by costs, and that overconcentration on just one side of the equation courts trouble. We will return to this point at the end of the next section of the chapter.

A proposition about competitive strategy[14]

1   Scheduled airlines provide a core benefit - safe air transport on specific routes at specific times.

2 Around this core benefit are bundled supplementary benefits, the nature of which varies across two dimensions:
  - over time: what was once supplementary tends over time to move closer to becoming 'core' as consumers' expectations rise and they take more for granted, and as innovators add attributes in search of sustainable bases for differentiation;
  - between geographical markets: different geographical markets are at different life cycle stages. Each has its own product history. The result is that the bundle of benefits acceptable as 'the norm' will vary; compare standards of service available in Chinese domestic markets with those offered on many intra-Asian trunk routes, for example. The different expectations of short- and long-haul passengers generate further distinctions between geographical markets.

3 Competitive strategy is a function of geographical scope and product scope decisions, both of which should be based on clearly identifiable sources of sustainable competitive advantage:
  - geographical scope can be wide-market or focused in orientation;
  - with regard to product scope:
    - air transport demand is highly susceptible to segmentation;
    - either selected geographical markets as a whole or one or more segments within them can be targeted with specific service-price offers (possible design variables being the subject of chapter 6);
    - differentiation on one or both sides of an airline's service-price offer to customers is the only true **competitive** strategy, because unless an airline differentiates in some way it is giving customers in a competitive market no particular reason to buy its services. Passengers in free markets do not choose an airline because its costs are low. They select on the basis of a service-price offer that appeals to them. This appeal can be based on one or both of service differentiation (i.e. offering higher levels of service than competitors) or price differentiation (i.e. offering lower prices, for either the same or lower levels of service);
    - service differentiation occurs when one or a number of supplementary attributes are added to what is generally accepted as the current 'norm' in the market concerned. One purpose of adding attributes is to be able to charge a premium price for the benefits they provide, but this can only be done if consumers value the benefits in question and they are not easily provided by competitors choosing not to charge a premium. Psychological benefits are less easily replicable than those attributable to more tangible service features, and brand image and the manner in which corporate culture affects service delivery are two of the least replicable sources of psychological benefit available in the industry. Taking away accepted benefits (either unbundling or

simply reducing quality) may require downward price differentiation. Conversely, a carrier with firm control over a competitive cost structure might be able to engage in downward price differentiation on a sustained basis without reducing or eliminating benefits.

4   Having low costs relative to others in the same strategic group or, indeed, to any potential challenger, is not so much a competitive strategy as a prerequisite (but not a guarantee) for survival.

5   Competitive strategy thus has twin pillars:
   • to sell, it is necessary to differentiate service and/or price in order to make the best service-price offer available to each targeted segment (however broad or narrow). This might not mean the best service or the lowest price - British Airways, for example offers neither of these in quite a few of its markets yet remains highly successful in part because of the attractive balance between service and price it manages to strike. Service and price are better characterized as scales which need to be balanced than as an 'either/or' choice;
   • to make a profit, expenditure has to be managed actively and with commitment to ensure that the level of service being delivered costs less than the price it can command in target segments.

6   Keeping the scales in balance requires detailed knowledge of targeted segments - their preferences and elasticities - and a constant monitoring of corporate skills and resources. Distinctive capabilities and competitive advantage have to be relevant to the type of service-price balance being offered.

There is a widespread belief in some quarters that price is becoming the only variable that matters. What is generally true is that consumers' expectations are pressing upwards on service levels and downwards on real yields, whilst in some (especially short-haul) markets a growing segment does appear readier than in the past to forgo certain amenities in return for significant price savings - particularly, if no longer exclusively, during economic downturns. There is evidence that this is happening in the US domestic market, for example.

But it is missing the point to assume that, say, Southwest sells on price alone. Southwest sells on value for money - on the right service-price offer. It has targeted consumers who prefer not to pay as much as other carriers wanted them to pay, and it gives them good value for what they do pay. Many of the 'hard' product attributes offered by full-service airlines, such as lounges, meals, seat assignment, and other amenities, are not a feature of Southwest's value proposition; but value is embodied in psychological benefits derived from using the brand and in the corporate culture underlying reliable standards of personal service, as well as in high frequencies and low prices. Were a new competitor to undercut Southwest's fares but in the process offer fully-depreciated Russian equipment (ignoring certification and operating cost issues for the purpose of the illustration), low frequencies, patchy schedule reliability, and surly service, it is doubtful that more than a very small percentage of demand would be attracted: the reason is that consumers are looking not just at price, but at the overall service-price offer.

Competitive strategy as the creation of value

When demand evaporated from low-cost entrants in the US domestic market during the summer of 1996, this was because the core benefit they were perceived to be offering in respect of safety was being reassessed by customers. Despite the low prices they continued to offer, the service-price positioning chosen by these carriers had been unbalanced by changing consumer perceptions of a key service attribute. Not even the leisure end of the US domestic market is driven entirely by price; customer-perceived value is the key issue.

Competitive strategy exists within a framework provided by the geographical scope (i.e. network management) and product scope (i.e. service-price positioning) choices discussed in chapter 1. It is in essence a number of interlinked decisions about what value is to be created and how this value should be appropriated.

> Strategy is the art of creating value. It provides the intellectual frameworks, conceptual models, and governing ideas that allow a company's managers to identify opportunities for bringing value to customers and for delivering that value at a profit.[15]

Value is a widely used but often loosely defined term. To put it into the context required here, consider the following propositions.[16]

1   A consumer's **perceived benefit** from using a service is equivalent to the gross benefits offered by that particular service (e.g. safety, schedule convenience, ontime performance, inflight comfort, enhanced self-image through brand association, frequent flyer miles etc.) minus nonmonetary costs (e.g. ticket conditionality, queues at various points in the service delivery system, elapsed journey time lengthened by having to connect over a hub, crowded airports and airplanes etc.).

2   **Value created** by a service is the perceived benefit as just defined, minus all the input costs that have been spent right along the value chain in order to create that service and deliver value to the consumer.

3   **Consumer surplus** is perceived benefit minus the monetary price
    paid by the consumer. In effect this is the portion of 'value created'
    that the consumer is capturing. In the absence of a consumer surplus
    (also widely referred to as 'customer-perceived value', although the
    two are not invariably treated as synonymous), there is no rational
    reason for the consumer to buy.

4   **Seller's profit** is the monetary price paid by the consumer minus the
    cost of inputs. This is the portion of 'value created' that the airline -
    the final seller of the service fashioned out of all the inputs that went
    into creating and delivering it - is capturing.

What airlines are, in principle, doing in the market is trying to win
business by giving away as little consumer surplus as possible whilst still
offering more than competitors are offering. They do this by manipulating
service-price offers - that is, by managing gross benefits, nonmonetary
costs, and price. The first objective is to pitch a better bid for the
consumer's business than competitors are pitching, by offering perceptibly
more consumer surplus; the ultimate objective, of course, should be to do
this and at the same time keep the price element of the service-price offer
above input costs in order to ensure profitability.

All this might seem vague and academic set against the cut-and-thrust of
an airline's real-time pricing environment in a highly competitive market.
It is nonetheless a sound model of the framework within which services
should be designed and priced. The more competitive a market becomes,
the greater the volatility of service-price offers and the more difficult is
the task of managing them without a framework. Increasing competition
frequently leads to greater customer-perceived value, as prices come under
downward pressure and/or the race to improve perceived benefits
intensifies; it is useful to have a framework within which to order these
developments if, indeed, they do occur.

Inherent in this proposition about what underpins competitive strategy
are two other sets of interlinked strategic choices: revenue strategy and
cost management strategy.

Revenue strategy

Some airlines bid for consumer surplus by offering relatively low levels of
perceived benefit, but compensating for this with low prices - prices that
are nonetheless profitable because of these carriers' low input costs; this is
the strategic path chosen by most low-cost/low-fare airlines. Others
concentrate on maximizing perceived benefits, particularly for those
segments of demand prepared to pay higher prices in return for improved
benefits; this approach underlies the continuous cycle of product upgrades
and relaunches in, for example, long-haul business and first class cabins -
although sometimes the battle here is less to boost prices than it is to

maintain them. The challenge in either approach (or any approach in between) lies in the fact that different consumers each have their own perceptions, and these perceptions are quite likely to change prior to, during, and after service delivery. Hence the need for careful management of consumers' perceptions and for close attention to service consistency.

Service-price positioning, of course, has to be supported by a cost structure capable of delivering costs per ASM that are low enough to allow profits to be earned given the revenues per ASM implied by that choice of strategic position.

Cost management strategy

One of management's most important tasks is therefore to decide on the level of service to be offered into targeted markets, and then provide it at a cost lower than the price that the market is prepared to pay.[17] If competitors can produce the same level of service more cheaply and choose to reflect this in their prices, or if competitors with a lower cost structure can profitably offer a higher level of service at the same price, the axe will fall - unless nonprice determinants of demand such as network scope, frequent flyer programmes, and better marketing communications can be brought into play.[18] A fundamental difference between this type of market-based pricing and the cost-plus approach is that the latter starts with costs and then turns to the market, whereas the former looks first to the market. In liberalized competitive environments it is to a considerable extent the market itself which determines the price that can be charged for a given level of service.

It has been widely argued in the past that one of the most fundamental problems facing many airlines is their inability to hold prices up in line with increasing costs. More recently, it has come to be realized that the real problem is an inability to keep costs down in line with prices that customers are willing to pay. The task is, accordingly, to design services for which customers are prepared to pay more than the cost of delivery. There are certainly markets which, especially during cyclical upturns, can sustain a hardening of yields in the premium classes and at times even down the back as well. But overall, yields are in secular decline; stripped of regulatory protection, airlines are therefore having to become much more innovative in respect of their cost management whilst at the same time adjusting service quality to constantly evolving consumer expectations.[19] Cost management efforts - whether aimed at lowering absolute input costs or raising input productivity - require a framework, and that framework is provided by the chosen service-price positioning.

'Cost management' frequently involves 'cost cutting', but the two are not necessarily synonymous. And neither is cost management, used in isolation, a strategy in itself; it is a fundamental management discipline which becomes a strategy only when linked to a defined revenue generation strategy within the context of a chosen competitive strategy which embodies the airline's overall strategic positioning.

What is 'competitive' about competitive strategies?

What transforms the strategic positioning implied by a choice of service-price offer into a competitive strategy is the manner in which the airline concerned combines its skills and resources, and deploys its capabilities. 'Competitive strategy is about being different. It means deliberately choosing a different set of activities to deliver a unique mix of value.'[20] Reference was made in Volume One to 'activity systems' as a source of sustainable, inimitable competitive advantage, and we will be meeting them again in Part Two of the present volume when implementation is discussed. Porter explains their significance as follows.

> Most managers describe strategic positioning in terms of their customers: "Southwest Airlines serves price- and convenience-sensitive travelers," for example. But the essence of strategy is in the activities - choosing to perform activities differently or to perform different activities than rivals. Otherwise, a strategy is nothing more than a marketing slogan that will not withstand competition.
>
> A full-service airline is configured to get passengers from almost any point A to any point B. To reach a large number of destinations and serve passengers with connecting flights, full-service airlines employ a hub-and-spoke system centered on major airports. To attract passengers who desire more comfort, they offer first-class or business-class service. To accommodate passengers who must change planes, they coordinate schedules and check and transfer baggage. Because some passengers will be traveling for many hours, full-service airlines serve meals.
>
> Southwest, in contrast, tailors all its activities to deliver low-cost, convenient service on its particular type of route. Through fast turnarounds at the gate of only 15 minutes, Southwest is able to keep planes flying longer hours than rivals and provide frequent departures with fewer aircraft. Southwest does not offer meals, assigned seats, interline baggage checking, or premium classes of service. Automated ticketing at the gate encourages customers to bypass travel agents, allowing Southwest to avoid their commissions. A standardized fleet of 737 aircraft boosts the efficiency of maintenance.
>
> Southwest has staked out a unique and valuable strategic position based on a tailored set of activities. On the routes served by Southwest, a full-service airline could never be as convenient or as low cost.[21]

As a whole, competitive interaction in the airline industry is now more dynamic across a wider spread of markets than in the past. What this means in practice is that competitive strategies are more varied and their outcome is more dependent on the reactions of both consumers and competitors.

The word 'competition' actually describes the manner in which airlines manage their competitive strategies in pursuit of competitive advantage. On a global level, if not in every individual market, the nature of competition is being altered by a number of trends affecting the competitive environment.

1   Liberalization is reducing the role of aeropolitics in deciding market shares and increasing the importance of competitive strategy.

2   Whilst air transport demand remains highly fragmented amongst a multitude of city-pair markets, a number of the industry's largest producers are moving singly or in partnership to consolidate the most important of these fragments into wider networks than have been seen before. **Inter**line connectivity, and the fare rigidity which tends to accompany it in the absence of specifically negotiated joint fares, is becoming less important than **intra**line connectivity. The result is that competition between larger and more highly integrated networks is intensifying. This introduces new players and allied combinations of players into local competitive environments.

3   Despite the fact that the industry is in different life cycle stages in various parts of the world, and both aeropolitical factors and market structures will allow a lot of small and medium-sized carriers to survive, on a global level the dynamics of competition are being shaped by the growing competitive interdependence of the leading networks.

The fact that we are dealing here with a network industry adds a further complication to consideration of competitive strategies, and one that can be particularly perplexing for proponents of the 'either/or' approach to differentiation, cost leadership, or focus. Consider, for example, Emirates' presence on the Dubai to London Heathrow route. Who are its competitors? What is it offering to customers? How should it price these offers? With regard to competitors, we noted in chapter 11 of Volume One that the situation in 1997 was as follows:

- 3rd/4th freedom, nonstop: British Airways - clearly a high-quality carrier with a strong network beyond Heathrow, competing against Emirates' higher frequencies and strong network behind Dubai;
- 5th freedom, nonstop: Royal Brunei, offering high service standards but with no network beyond Heathrow and both lower frequencies and a less well-established reputation amongst customers in the market concerned than either Emirates or British Airways. Biman, Malaysia

Airlines, and Pakistan International were also present on the route, but
at lower frequencies than Royal Brunei and with less clearly defined
service images;[22]
• 6th freedom: more than a dozen East and West European,
   Mediterranean, and Middle Eastern carriers whose frequencies,
   connections, and service standards ranged from excellent on
   downwards.

Complicating the situation further was the fact that for Emirates the
Dubai to Heathrow route is not only a market in its own right but part of
several other markets which it serves, on a sixth freedom basis, between a
number of Asian points and London. It was therefore carrying traffic ex-
Hong Kong in competition with nonstop services offered by British
Airways, Cathay Pacific, and Virgin Atlantic (shortly to be joined by Air
China); the same applied in respect of Bangkok, where nonstop
competitors were British Airways, Qantas, and Thai Airways
International, and also in respect of Singapore, Melbourne (served one-
stop by the third/fourth freedom carriers) and a number of other points.
In addition to competitors in the markets between these cities and
Heathrow which were offering nonstop or multi-stop service, several sixth
freedom routeings over intermediate 'hubs' were also available.
   There are three points that emerge from this summary.

1 To speak of a single service-price offer in general and outside the
   context of a specific market is meaningless. Emirates generally
   competes for Dubai-London traffic more on the basis of service
   differentiation than on price, but in its sixth freedom markets it relies
   quite heavily on price (and to a lesser extent stopover packages) in
   order to compensate for the inconvenience of having to make a
   connection.

2 The competitive dynamics of individual markets are potentially
   complex, are interdependent with those of other markets, and are
   bound to lead to an almost constant manipulation of service-price
   offers (bearing in mind that - as we will see in Part Two of the present
   volume - 'service' is a very broad concept, extending to much more
   than leg-room and smiles).

3 The merging of networks which is taking place as a result of the
   alliance-building trend, to be discussed in chapter 5, has the potential
   to complicate further an already complicated picture.

   It is quite clear that as markets are liberalized and their interdependence
becomes even more complex, differentiation and low costs are not
either/or strategies. Low costs are not a sustainable source of competitive
advantage by themselves. Service differentiation can be, but it has to be

deliverable at a cost which allows an airline both to be profitable and to price competitively in a range of different competitive environments against a range of different competitors. Ultimately, it is the **balance** between service and price that matters (rather than either the quality of the service or its price alone), the extent to which that balance reflects the wants and needs of the markets or segments targeted, and how it compares with competitors' service-price offers.[23]

The competitive strategy an airline chooses pursuant to its geographical and product scope decisions will guide operating strategies in the functional areas of the organization. It is to changes affecting strategies at the functional level that we turn in the next chapter.

Notes

1   These are discussed in Volume One, Part Two.
2   The competitive environment is discussed in chapters 8 to 11 of Volume One.
3   Zou, S. and Cavusgil, S.T. (1996), 'Global Strategy: A Review and an Integrated Conceptual Framework', *European Journal of Marketing*, Vol. 30, No. 1, pp. 59, 60.
4   Porter, M.E. (i) *Competitive Strategy*, The Free Press, 1980; (ii) *Competitive Advantage*, The Free Press, 1985. Porter's model of generic competitive strategies was first proposed in the 1980 book, then modified slightly in 1985.
5   Although he uses the word 'industry' (which, as explained in Volume One, is inherently a supply-side concept), Porter also refers in his model to demand side conditions which affect market attractiveness - notably the bargaining power of buyers.
6   Competitive advantage is not necessarily the same as 'market power', the latter being the ability to raise price or reduce the level of service without seriously damaging profitability or inviting a meaningful challenge from competitors: Alpert, E.I. (1984), 'Is Market Structure Proof of Market Power?', *Mergers and Acquisitions*, 47.
7   'Strategic mapping' can be used here, locating competitors in the 'strategic space' defined by the four-cell matrix in Figure 2.1.
8   In the last chapter, the expression 'stuck in the middle' was used in the context of scope decisions: a distinction was drawn between carriers in emerging global networks and others able to identify and defend geographical and/or product niches, with those fitting neither description being 'stuck in the middle' or 'middle-of-the-roaders'. Here the expression 'stuck in the middle' refers to a poorly chosen strategic position, which achieves neither high levels of product differentiation nor low costs relative to competitors. Thus, whilst clearly linked, the usages of the expression in the two chapters are somewhat different.
9   'Parity' implies that an airline is offering service attributes the same as or, if different, equally appealing to consumers as those offered by direct competitors. 'Proximity' means that any price discounting required to ensure an acceptable market share in the absence of parity is not enough to erode the contribution of the cost leader's cost advantage to its above-average returns.
10 Bureau of Transport and Communications Economics (1991), *A New Era in Australian Aviation*, Australian Government Publishing Service.
11 For a particularly erudite critique, see: Hendry, J. (1990), 'The Problem with Porter's Generic Strategies', *European Management Journal*, Vol. 8, No. 4, December.
12 For a more thorough exposition of this line of reasoning, see: Stacey, R. (1993), *Strategic Management and Organisational Dynamics*, Pitman, p. 92.

13   Hamel, G. and Prahalad, C.K. (1989), 'Strategic Intent', *Harvard Business Review*, May-June.

14   The ideas put forward in this section have in part been stimulated by, but cannot be blamed upon: Sharp, B. (1991), 'Competitive Marketing Strategy: Porter Revisited', *Marketing Intelligence & Planning*, Vol. 9, No. 1.

15   Normann, R. and Ramírez, R. (1993), 'From Value Chain to Value Constellation: Designing Interactive Strategy', *Harvard Business Review*, July-August.

16   Holloway, S. (1997), *Straight and Level: Practical Airline Economics*, Ashgate, chapter 12.

17   What the market will bear in terms of pricing is of course variable, not only between different segments but across a network and in response to daily, weekly, and seasonal demand peaks on the routes concerned.

18   A useful analysis in this context can be calculation of an airline's relative cost position (RCP). Most easily done on an airline-to-airline basis, this can also be applied to separate business units, products or functions if sufficient information on competitors is available. The technique involves dividing the subject's average costs by those of each of its competitors in turn: 1.0 implies cost parity, less than 1.0 suggests a cost advantage, and an index in excess of 1.0 a cost disadvantage. See: Karlöff, B. (1993), *Key Business Concepts*, Routledge, p. 122.

19   See: Holloway, op. cit., chapter 7 for a discussion of airline cost drivers and their management.

20   Porter, M.E. (1996), 'What is Strategy?', *Harvard Business Review*, November-December.

21   Ibid., pp. 64, 65.

22   Royal Nepal was serving Dubai-London Gatwick at the time, again on a low-frequency fifth freedom basis.

23   America West in the mid-90s provided an interesting example of this balance in action. The airline's low costs (7.43 cents per ASM in 1996) allowed it to compete on price with Southwest (7.5 cents per ASM) and to undercut larger, full-service network carriers; at the same time, its full-service product permitted it to out-differentiate Southwest on amenities and largely match the network carriers in this respect (although not in areas such as network scope, FFP coverage etc.).

3 Strategies at the functional level

This chapter will briefly examine changing approaches to strategy in a number of key functional areas: marketing, human resource management, information technology, finance, and operations.

Marketing

Kotler identifies a chain of core concepts which lie at the heart of marketing.[1]

1 **Needs** arise in people when deprivation is felt, **wants** are targeted at something capable of satisfying a need (preferences often being affected by the cultural setting), and **demand** materializes when a want is backed by the means and willingness to pay.

2 **Products** (including **services**) incorporate features which offer benefits capable of satisfying wants and needs (and it is the benefits which are actually being sold, rather than the features themselves).

3 Consumers having different **need sets** (e.g. safety, schedule, punctuality, inflight amenities etc.) are confronted by airlines offering different **product choice sets**. They assess the **value** of each by evaluating benefits being offered to satisfy their wants and needs against monetary and other forms of cost.

4 **Exchange** occurs when a customer accepts an offer and gives something (usually, but not necessarily, money) in return. Marketing has traditionally been seen as the process of eliciting this 'buying response' by correctly assessing wants and needs, designing benefits to satisfy them, communicating the availability and merits of these benefits, and offering them at a price acceptable to both consumer and

offeror. In recent years the emphasis in marketing literature has shifted from how to elicit single **transactional** responses to the ways in which multiple exchanges can be established within the context of an ongoing **relationship** founded on consumer loyalty.

5   A **market** is the sum of consumers who might potentially enter into an exchange in order to satisfy a want. Markets can be defined by need, want, geography, and/or various demographic criteria.

6   **Marketing management** is a series of processes intended to bring to specific markets offers which elicit desired buyer responses and at the same time help the airline attain its corporate objectives.

Marketing orientation

Marketing is a process of recognizing and stimulating the needs of consumers in target markets, orchestrating organizational resources and skills to design and deliver services capable of supplying the benefits required to satisfy those needs, and providing better value than competitors who have targeted the same customers. Airlines operating in increasingly competitive markets have to be marketing-oriented if they are to build consumer satisfaction and loyalty.[2] Some, however, have not yet absorbed the fact that they are in the business of competing to provide benefits to passengers and shippers rather than the business of flying airplanes. In other words, they remain 'process-driven' rather than 'customer-driven'; they, rather than their customers, set the agenda. In Part Two of this volume we will see how the two orientations ought to be combined.

Day has identified the principal features of a market orientation as:

- a set of beliefs that put the customer's interest first. Corporate culture and values are central in this respect;
- the ability of the organization to generate, disseminate, and use superior information about customers and competitors. This requires external focus and a marketing information system to keep in close contact with what is happening in the marketplace;
- the coordinated application of interfunctional resources to the creation of superior customer value. Frequently this will involve the matching of organizational capabilities with the requirements of targeted market segments, resulting in the formulation of positioning strategies capable of sustaining superior performance. Careful marketing planning is the requirement here although, as noted in the first chapter of Volume One, some scope must also be left for marketing strategies to 'emerge' from the implementation of 'intended' strategies.[3]

In any industry selling perishable services and as prone to overcapacity as the airline business, a 'sales orientation' is also likely to be widespread. This focuses less on identification of consumers' needs and the design of appropriate benefits than on the disposal of committed output. Since the early 1980s a growing number of airlines have become less production- and sales-oriented, turning instead to a marketing orientation and customer-focus. Some have made marketing the fabric of corporate culture, others have only paid lip-service to it. The former tend to treat it as an integrative activity rather than a functional department, coordinating efforts throughout the airline to satisfy consumers' needs and wants; the latter are more likely still to see it as one of several functional departments - sometimes primus inter pares, but often not.[4] Thus, for example, the head of marketing in one major airline is responsible for researching and communicating with markets but has no direct authority over schedules (flight operations), tariffs (finance), recruitment of customer-contact staff (personnel), the content and quality of inflight meals (catering), or cabin condition (maintenance). Whilst this state of affairs is becoming less common on the passenger side of the business, it remains relatively widespread on the cargo side; managers responsible for marketing cargo services very frequently have little or no control over their products.

The marketing **department** in a large, market-oriented and customer-focused carrier might house specialists in market research, marketing communications, distribution, brand management and so on, but marketing **management** itself will be a large element in the jobs of the airline's top management team, and marketing **responsibility** should be dispersed throughout the organization. Marketing ought to be seen as a capability, not a function; its foundation should be a shared understanding of the central role of the customer, not an organization chart. This insight is not 'leading edge'. As long ago as 1954, Drucker observed that:

> Marketing is not a specialized activity at all. It encompasses the entire business. It is the whole business seen from the point of view of its final result, that is from the customer's point of view. Concern and responsibility for marketing must therefore permeate all areas of the enterprise.[5]

Nonetheless, this is a model which is only slowly penetrating much of the global airline industry. As markets liberalize further and competition intensifies, it will become more widely accepted. Those carriers that have accepted it already have a clear head-start.

In a marketing-oriented airline responding to a largely commercial mandate from its stakeholders, marketing management and strategic management are - as we have seen - overlapping almost to the point of being synonymous. There are few sound arguments in favour of separating marketing (what the customer wants) from strategy (what the airline does).[6] At the very least there has to be a considerable amount of interaction between the two processes, with marketing responsible for both informing and responding to corporate objectives; it cannot be any other way if it is accepted that the primary purpose of strategic management is to create sustainable competitive advantage(s) amongst specific consumers in specific markets. The task of marketing is therefore to shape as well as implement corporate aspirations.

Marketing information systems

As airlines exploit liberalization by becoming active in a steadily growing number of markets, their marketing information requirements broaden: they need to know more about the shapes of demand curves in a greater number of marketplaces. As they rely increasingly on branding and on the targeted differentiation of service-price offers, their marketing information requirements deepen: they need to know more about the elasticities of the demand functions underlying these curves. The pressure is on for carriers to know what it is that customers and potential customers want, and the prices they are prepared to pay.

Detailed marketing information is required at a tactical level to initiate and react to constant changes in the competitive environment. It is also needed at the strategic level, where it can be input into external and internal analyses. As well as being a planning tool, marketing information is useful for control purposes - for identifying and explaining outcomes which are diverging from expectations.

Many airlines still have little in the way of formalized processes for the real-time capture of market data or for transforming data into actionable information. Particularly for small airlines, the resources and skills required to run an effective marketing information system that goes beyond the accumulation of skeletal statistics for plugging into the annual planning cycle constitute a considerable investment risk. This risk might well not be justified in specific cases. On the other hand, the globalization of networks being brought about by expansion of alliances is bringing a growing number of carriers into direct competition with airlines that are part of groups with access to sophisticated marketing support technologies. The risks involved in remaining underresourced when competing against carriers with well-developed marketing information systems are also potentially high.

Airlines operating in increasingly complex and turbulent competitive environments simply have to know whether or not their customers perceive them to be meeting expectations. This is what being 'close to the customer' actually means. It is preferable to spend some money on finding out whether the airline is getting things right or wrong in meeting constantly changing customer expectations than to wait and let traffic or unit revenue figures tell the story.[7]

Marketing information at large, well-resourced airlines is in a growing number of cases finding its way into customized executive information systems (EIS). For smaller, less resource-rich carriers there is an expanding selection of off-the-shelf packages available. One possible structure for an EIS is to organize marketing information into four stages corresponding to the customer activity cycle.[8]

1 Pre-booking stage: for example, information regarding accessible markets; customers' expectations; the design, distribution, and delivery of the airline's current service-price offers (i.e. the value it is offering to its target customers); the value being offered by competitors; customers' perceptions of the airline's offers and those of competitors; and the design and execution of marketing communications programmes intended to enhance awareness, change negative perceptions, or enhance positive perceptions of the airline's offers.

2 Booking stage: for example, information on forward bookings by market, service, and distribution channel; unaccommodated demand; and discernible linkages, if any, between the current marketing mix and forward bookings.

3 Travel stage: for example, information about which aspects of the airline's offers and its marketing communications programme triggered purchase decisions; whether or not customers' expectations were met and, if not, why not; what improvements or innovations in the airline's offers would be well-received.

4 Post-travel stage: for example, information regarding the marketplace performance of the airline in absolute terms and relative to competitors; reasons for the absolute and relative performances; whether there are any cross-selling opportunities that could be exploited.

Marketing planning

Short- (one year) and medium-term (one to three year) marketing plans might be prepared for each product, brand or route-group in a large airline, whilst for a small carrier a single plan per time period will suffice. Its primary purpose is to transform performance objectives into customer buying behaviour. Marketing planning shares the frames of reference and many of the tools used by strategic management. Payne,[9] drawing on the work of McDonald,[10] has suggested the following approach to marketing planning (which, although necessarily presented sequentially, involves interaction and iteration).

1 Strategic context: marketing activities have to be consistent with the overall corporate mission and contribute towards achievement of goals

and objectives. In a small airline, of course, it is possible that the marketing plan and the corporate plan will be the same.

2   Situation review: this involves a marketing audit of external and internal circumstances (focusing in particular on the competitive environments of specific markets and how the airline is serving them), a SWOT analysis which prescribes actions rather than simply recites circumstances, and a statement of key assumptions which will underlie the marketing strategy.

3   Marketing strategy formulation: marketing objectives and strategies are then formulated, expected results are estimated, alternative marketing mixes are sensitivity-tested, and contingency plans established in case key assumptions prove incorrect.

4   Resource allocation and monitoring: this is the stage at which marketing programmes are established and activated, after which their outcome is monitored, controlled, and reviewed.

Where marketing planning is adopted it should be more than a series of procedural steps, becoming instead part of the culture and value system of the airline. In reality, many small airlines do little or no formal marketing planning - and the same is true of a surprising number of relatively large carriers, particularly those accustomed to operating within managed competitive environments.[11] This will change.

Strategic human resource management

Successful customer relations start with successful employee relations. In any industry, but particularly in a labour-intensive service industry, the ultimate source of value is people. Recognition of this lay at the heart of the British Airways programmes referred to in Part Two of Volume One. Virgin's Richard Branson has been quoted as saying, 'I am convinced that companies should put their staff first, customers second and shareholders third - ultimately that's in the best interests of customers and shareholders'.[12] Strategic human resource management (HRM) is a set of processes which - through the recruitment, training, motivation, appraisal, reward, and development of individuals, and through the effective handling of industrial relations - translates strategy into action.[13] It is the function which ensures that an airline has the skills required to move it towards fulfillment of its mission and objectives; missions and objectives, in turn, provide a framework for managing the flow of people into, through, and out of the airline.

There is more to strategic HRM than conjuring manpower plans out of traffic forecasts and service quality decisions, however. Normann refers to successful service delivery systems 'mobilizing and focusing human energy'.[14] Strategic HRM is about accessing, developing, and releasing this energy.

> In times of discontinuity and accelerated change, survival depends on flexibility, on our ability to learn to adapt. Organizations which learn fast will survive. Management must take the lead. We must mobilize our greatest asset, our people, invest in their training and orchestrate their talents, skills and expertise. Their commitment, dedication, quality and care will build the competitive advantage of a winning team. Only they can provide our customers with the best product and service in the industry. The management of change takes tenacity, time, talent, and training.
> J.F.A. de Soet, President, KLM Royal Dutch Airlines.[15]

Strategic HRM in the airline industry faces a number of challenges, however.

1   Many skills used by the industry are exclusive to aviation, are costly and time-consuming to acquire, and need constant refinement in order to keep pace with regulatory, technological, and market developments. Added to this are the industry's pronounced cyclicality and the demand peaking characteristic of most transport systems, both of which can lead to periods of overcapacity in terms of expensive human skills as well as tangible resources.

2   Increasingly turbulent and complex competitive environments are generating a need for new or augmented skills. For example, whilst international carriers have in principle always required multilingual, culturally sensitive, and responsive customer-contact staff, this requirement has not invariably been given a high priority at some airlines; in intensely competitive international markets, these skills are now becoming a critical success factor.

3   Finding people with the right skills is no longer sufficient. To deliver high-quality service, attitudes and values are also important.

4   Industry practice has recently followed more generalized trends in the labour markets of some countries, notably the United States and the United Kingdom, towards the employment by scheduled airlines of increasing proportions of part-time and fixed-term contract staff (something most charter carriers have been doing for several decades). Whenever the traditional covenant between employer and employee[16] has been broken in this way, there is inevitably a challenge to mould acculturated, committed team-members out of 'contingent' or 'just in time' employees.[17] Given the now widespread recognition

of the importance of positive customer encounters in any service business, there is a surprising willingness amongst some managers within the Anglo-American business culture in particular to place 'nomads' in sensitive customer contact roles.

5   Encouragement of productivity growth through multi-skilling and more flexible working practices in what is a highly unionized and craft-oriented industry remains a major challenge, although the economic troubles of the early 1990s started to erode entrenched resistance to change and brought about a growing recognition in some quarters of the need for flexibility. At many, but not yet all, airlines the focus of discussion has moved on from 'Why?' to 'How?' and 'In return for what?'

6   How to control labour costs without detracting from service quality has become a significant challenge in an industry which remains broadly overstaffed and yet is having to compete in liberalized markets bounded by 'the rock' of soft yields and 'the hard place' of increasingly knowledgeable and demanding customers. Given the recognized linkage between satisfied staff and satisfied customers, there is a strong argument for placing greater reliance on productivity improvement than on salary and benefit cuts (although some 'downsizing' of lifestyles is clearly inevitable at a lot of state-owned carriers if they are to compete successfully on a purely commercial playing field).

7   The cross-utilization of human resources within global alliances - something which is at a very early stage and is seen mostly in the form of cabin crew exchanges - will prove a challenge given that variables relevant to the attraction, utilization, and motivation of talented employees differ widely between cultural settings. Furthermore, some unions perceive it to be a first step towards creation of a global labour pool and, as such, a long-term threat to their members' conditions of service and perhaps ultimately their jobs.[18]

8   Perhaps the least specific yet most significant challenge is to make human resource strategies as adaptive as corporate and competitive strategies have to be in the face of increasingly complex and turbulent environments.

Information technology and information systems

Information technology (IT) is any electronic means for storing, transmitting, processing, and retrieving words, numbers, images, and sounds.[19] Whereas IT encompasses hardware and software, information systems (IS) represent a broader concept. Information systems incorporate the people and procedures, as well as the technology, involved in collecting data and transforming it into information usable by decision-makers. Both the airline industry's value chain and the services it produces have long been recognized as being information-intensive.[20] What is changing is that information is now more widely seen as a critical organizational resource, and the capability to turn it into knowledge useful for the design of new products and the building of customer relationships as a critical skill.[21] Utilizing information and knowledge both effectively and efficiently is becoming recognized as a task that is at least as important as maximizing the productivity of other corporate resources, tangible or intangible.

The importance of IT/IS goes well beyond functional boundaries. Following a categorization developed by Ward et al, strategic IT/IS can contribute in four broad areas.[22]

1   Links to distributors, customers and suppliers: common examples of inter-organization systems (IOSs) are CRSs and cargo community systems; sites on the World Wide Web can also perform some of the functions of an IOS. IT/IS capabilities have evolved beyond electronic data interchange (EDI), now giving well-resourced airlines an opportunity to manage - within the context of organization-spanning strategic information systems - a much greater range of environmental inputs and external relationships.[23] Ultimately, those carriers building joint ventures, franchise operations, global alliances, and long-term supplier relationships will have to move beyond the exchange of **data between** organizations, to the use of **information** to **bind** them together. Redesign of business networks in this way will move the focus from transactions to knowledge.[24] As marketing, particularly to high-yield passengers, moves gradually from a transactional to a relationship format, the power of IT/IS to track purchase histories and responsiveness to targeted marketing communications on a 'segment of one' basis will become increasingly important for leading airlines. Customer information systems will help make comprehensive knowledge of customers and their dealings with the airline available at each point of contact - in other words, at the point of each service encounter.

2   Improved integration of internal processes: IT/IS capabilities are often an enabling factor in business process reengineering and the integration of processes. Although it is not yet happening widely in the airline industry (FedEx and a handful of others being notable exceptions), IT/IS capabilities also facilitate a move away from vertical hierarchies towards flatter, more horizontally oriented organizations. In the past, IT/IS has largely been used to channel upward flows of information in order to facilitate control. Some carriers are now transitioning to a situation in which employee

empowerment and the attendant need for shared access to information for all levels in the company challenge entrenched practices of knowledge 'gatekeeping' and 'husbandry'. It is as well to keep in mind that people - their behaviours, how they search for and use information, their politics, and their ingrained distaste for sharing what can be a potent source of power - are as much a part of any information system as microchips and ingenious software.[25] Changing this is a cultural as well as a technological challenge. On the other hand, in airlines that are not yet very far along the IT/IS 'flightpath', the problem is that 'islands of automation' in different functional departments often tend to live on in isolation, unintegrated and therefore largely underexploited - oriented towards departmental requirements rather than core processes of the airline as a whole.

3   Information-based products and services: a number of airlines - notably American, British Airways, and Lufthansa - have turned their airline-related IT/IS capabilities into saleable products. British Airways, for example, has sold packages based on its RTZ fare, reservations, ticketing, and departure control system, whilst American Airlines' affiliates in the Sabre Group sell off-the-shelf solutions for most automated airline management and operations processes. Sometimes products are developed and sold by airlines or their affiliates by themselves, but there is also now a considerable amount of 'partnering' with suppliers of applications and infrastructure from outside the industry.

4   Executive information/decision support systems: a large number of carriers still keep scattered around several departmental databases customer information which needs to be better integrated in order to guide service design and to assist with the management of other marketing mix variables. Well into the 1990s some large flag carriers were still unable to disaggregate revenues from overseas sales offices by class of travel, departure, or even destination. Whilst CRSs are providing reasonably sound front-end capabilities to those participants who want them and have access to the software required to use them (e.g. software to analyze CRS' marketing information data tapes), some airlines do not yet have a firm grip on departure control, revenue accounting, or management information generally. Strategic management needs timely information about service quality, the behaviour of cost drivers, revenue stream composition, and how competitors are performing. It is very difficult to manage a network without knowing how many people are buying, what they are buying, why they are buying, where they are going, how they are paying, where and when they are making reservations, or where they are being ticketed - yet relatively few airlines have rapid access to the disaggregated information they need in order to adjust pricing, hone

promotional efforts and fine-tune agency incentives in response to what is happening right now.

FedEx and British Airways each invest between three and five per cent of their annual revenues in IT/IS. It is this scale of commitment which has helped IT/IS capabilities move from their initial data processing and later decision support orientations to a point where they now have the power to shape the way in which businesses operate. En route, the benefits have moved from efficiency through effectiveness to competitive advantage. Sabre, for example, transitioned from being just a reservations system to providing yield management capabilities to American Airlines and then, more recently, to acting as the platform for a core competence of AMR Corporation subsidiaries in the development and sale of airline- and travel-related services. In doing this it has shown the potential of IT/IS to redefine business scope. FedEx has done much the same by leveraging its IT/IS capabilities to expand beyond integrated express delivery services and into total logistics management.

IT/IS provides two possible sources of competitive advantage.

1   Competitive advantage derived from IT/IS itself, attributable to:
    • the creation of new IT/IS-related businesses;
    • the building of customer switching costs and the deterrence of competitive market entry; and
    • the enhancement of cost or service differentiation advantages.[26]

2   Competitive advantage gained through effective integration of strategic management of IT/IS with strategic management of the airline as a whole. Effective and efficient IT/IS support for implementation of strategies developed to move the airline towards fulfillment of its mission and achievement of its objectives can be a source of competitive advantage if, for example, competitors are unable to integrate their own IT/IS efforts with corporate and competitive strategies.[27]

Airlines have a variety of different organizational 'hangars' for their IT/IS functions. Some have separate departments, whilst others 'park' them under finance, planning, management services or something similar. One implication in the latter case - not inevitably true, but frequently so - is that the corporate mindset has not yet transitioned from viewing IT/IS as a form of process automation to recognizing it as a tool for managing strategic information (from external as well as internal sources), turning information into knowledge, and using that knowledge quickly to gain competitive advantage.

Airlines are also pursuing different strategies with regard to IT/IS outsourcing. Some, as noted above, are keen not only to be self-sufficient but to sell their expertise; at the other end of the spectrum are carriers which outsource practically all their IT/IS requirements. Cathay Pacific's approach is an interesting example of a compromise:

- Migrate from "Build & Operate" to "Acquire and Manage".
- Assume a position of being a "quick follower" of industry practices.
- Adapt information technology, taking selective leadership only for clear and compelling strategic benefit.
- Give CX [Cathay Pacific] managers and staff the MIS [management information system] needed to better serve customers and manage the business.[28]

Strategic financial management

Taneja has identified financial management as the task of optimally combining three related decisions: the investment decision, the financing decision, and the dividend decision.[29] Lynch recognizes the finance function as comprising 'four main streams of activity': treasury, control, budgets, and internal audit.[30] More broadly, Ward and Grundy have identified the management of corporate value (not the same concept as 'customer-perceived value', which we discussed in chapter 2) as a responsibility that is increasingly being recognized by strategic managers.[31] They define corporate value as '...the present value of the expected returns from the combination of current business strategies and future investment programmes, based on the information available to management'.[32] They go on to explore three areas of the literature which have, to differing extents, sought to 'intermediate strategic management and corporate value'.

1   Corporate financial strategy: the process that relates external sources of finance to the financial needs created by corporate and competitive strategies.

2   Strategic management accounting: the process that gathers information on both internal performance and, importantly, marketplace performance.

3   Strategic value management: the key processes and programmes - investment decisions, strategic cost management initiatives, or change programmes (such as business process reengineering), for example - intended to create value for the company.

Ward and Grundy propose that the three should be brought together into a more coherent framework, which they refer to as 'strategic business finance'. This would be designed 'to explore the...boundaries between finance and strategy more effectively...'[33]

In the final analysis, a strong financial condition relative to competitors can in itself be a source of competitive advantage. Financial strength in the context of an industry already entering a downward spiral enabled Southwest to snap-up gates in California and Chicago and acquire the aircraft needed to expand in those markets as USAir pulled back and Midway collapsed in 1991. Financial strength relative to Continental left United alone, at least initially, to dominate the new (but high-cost) Denver International Airport.

Financial condition over time reflects, in large measure, the following factors.

1   An airline's choice of strategies.

2   The manner in which resources are allocated and utilized in pursuit of these strategies.

3   The methods chosen to finance resources and, in respect of external funding, the terms negotiated.

4   The extent to which cash-flows generated by the strategies are protected against foreign exchange, interest rate, fuel price, and other risks.[34]

It is the task of strategic financial management to ensure that an airline has sufficient cash, or a strong enough balance sheet to raise sufficient cash, to implement intended strategies, seize opportunities which emerge unexpectedly, and provide a buffer against unforeseen adversity. Although recovery got underway in 1994 and subsequent years saw record profits earned by several carriers, the global airline industry as a whole remains at the time of writing weakened by close to $20 billion in net losses incurred during the recession of the early 1990s; between 1990 and 1992, US carriers alone lost approximately $9 billion and yet at the same time took delivery of over 700 aircraft. It therefore seemed likely in the mid-90s that many of the US majors and European flag carriers responsible for the worst of the losses would be focusing on retrenchment, reconstructing balance sheets, reengineering business processes, building alliances, and seizing only carefully selected opportunities over the next few years rather than engaging in imperial grabs for market share. As the market began to peak several years later, this expectation of restraint was beginning to be considered too sanguine by some observers.

Common financial characteristics of airlines include the following:

•   revenue growth rates and absolute earnings are strongly cyclical. This is a fact of life, but more proactive airlines are setting about managing earnings volatility in particular by gaining better control over their cost structures;

- financial and operating leverage tend to be high;
- cash flows are more stable than earnings;
- conservative depreciation schedules can lead to 'hidden equity' in owned aircraft being available to offset high financial leverage to some extent, although continued growth in operating leasing has left many airlines with less fleet equity than superficial analysis might suggest; and
- profit margins are generally low compared to those earned in many of the other industries competing for capital and, combined with the asset intensity of the air transport business, this has led to airlines in aggregate being unable to fund more than around half their capital expenditures from internal sources at the best of times.

Some observers doubt that the industry will be able to sustain sufficient returns to attract funding adequate to finance expenditures on projected fleet reequipment and growth over the next decade.[35] Conversely, other observers see capital shortages as illusory insofar as there is almost always money available at a price - albeit not necessarily a price airlines are willing or able to pay.[36] According to this argument, when the price gets too high the rate of aircraft acquisition slows, as does capacity expansion; the result should be higher load factors, improved margins, and ultimately therefore the return of capital to the industry. This indeed is what appears to have happened at the end of the early-90s recession.

What is beyond doubt is that financial flexibility and access to finance on terms better than those available to competitors (whose 'hurdle' rates of return for proposed investments might therefore be expected to be higher) are critical success factors of growing importance. Fleet financing which allows an airline to grow flexibly - or to stop growing if market conditions make this the financially sensible strategy to pursue - can be particularly important in an industry capable of punishing overcapacity as harshly as the airline industry is prone to do.

Operations

There is rarely a single department called 'Operations'. More usually in an airline there will be a flight operations department, ground or ramp operations, passenger services or some similar structure. In modern management literature, however, the word 'operations' has a very much broader meaning, being concerned with all aspects of service delivery.

Like any business, an airline is a system within which processes (i.e. linked activities) take place, frequently across functional boundaries, in pursuit of mission and objectives. Processes have been defined as '...the procedures, tasks, schedules, mechanisms, activities and routines by which a product or service is delivered to the customer'.[37] These processes involve the management and maintenance of accounting systems, for example, as much as the management and maintenance of aircraft. Their immediate objective is to deliver benefits to customers. This requires achievement of a balance between effective customer service (expressed in terms of customer-perceived quality) and efficient resource utilization.[38] Where this balance is struck will depend upon the identified needs of customers in targeted segments and the resource management skills deployed in the serving of those needs.

At various points in the book we have referred to horizontal, cross-functional, customer-serving processes. One of the most popular frameworks within which to conceptualize these processes in recent years has been Porter's value chain (or its equivalent, the 'service chain'), introduced in Volume One, chapter 17. In chapters 7 and 8 of the present volume we will be looking at airline 'service delivery processes' and 'corporate infrastructure' in the context of strategy implementation. The underlying theme in all these cases is organizational processes crossing functional boundaries and being orchestrated with customer satisfaction as the ultimate objective.

One factor distinguishing service industries from manufacturing enterprises is that consumers are present throughout some of the most important service delivery processes, and indeed are expected to participate in many of them. They therefore evaluate these processes as part of the service itself. Process configuration accordingly involves choices which, because of their direct impact on consumers, are integral to the design of an airline's service concept (i.e. its product). Processes carried out with consumers present are widely referred to as the 'front-office' (or 'front-stage'), whilst those which consumers neither participate in nor witness are 'back-office' (or 'back-stage'); clearly, the two have to work tightly in unison.[39]

1 The 'front office' is where any mismatches between consumers' expectations and perceptions of service quality are likely to surface. It involves both active service encounters with staff and also passive experience of service environments, stretching throughout the customer activity cycle from first enquiry to the post-flight resolution of any outstanding problems. The configuration of front- and back-office processes, the trade-off between resource allocation and customer service which has been decided upon (particularly during periods of peak demand), the use of technology, and the attitudes and empowerment levels of staff will all affect perceived quality levels.

2 The 'back office' is where much of the effort takes place which ensures safe performance of published schedules and lays foundations for successful service encounters in the front office. Some airlines are now trying actively to ensure that back-office staff look upon those in the front office as 'internal customers' and stay focused on the impact their decisions and actions will have on the ultimate paying customer.

Clearly, as noted in the opening chapter of Volume One, the operations 'function' - the management of service delivery processes - is very difficult to separate from the management of marketing processes in a service industry. Operational and marketing strategies must be tightly coordinated. A production orientation - focused internally on airline requirements rather than externally on customers' wants and needs - is not the currency of competition in liberalized air transport markets, yet by the same token the best marketing capability will yield nothing sustainable if operational processes cannot deliver what customers in targeted segments have been led to expect. Whereas marketing delivers promises, operations delivers **on** promises.

Conclusion

This chapter has done no more than sample the ways in which some of the issues arising from the airline industry's current transition are impacting functional departments. The key conclusion to be drawn is that rather than a complex of isolated islands or fiefdoms, an airline should be seen as a unified system of processes, each defined by flows of materials, people, and/or information. Any one process is likely to be comprised of tasks or operations which, in many cases will be performed by employees based in different specialist departments. The processes should be integrated by a common purpose.

In service industries, there is a particularly close relationship between marketing, operations, and human resource functions.[40] The primary reason for this is the physical and emotional involvement of customers in service delivery processes - something we will return to at length in chapter 7. As the following quotation amply illustrates, cross-functional interrelationships run particularly deeply in the airline industry.

> Say you want to change...the seat pitch, which seems quite simple, it's not just a question of going to engineering and saying, 'Let's take a few seats out.' You start with engineering, but then you've got the safety implications - where are the over-wing exits and things like that? - then you've got things like what about the oxygen masks and the inflight entertainment plug-in points.
>
>   Then you've got the financial aspects - what it's going to cost you and how much business you're going to need to generate to pay back. Will more people fly with us because we're more comfortable now?
>
>   After that you've got people doing the schedules who work it out on required capacity and they say, 'If you're taking seats out that completely changes the capacity implications.' Then you've got catering saying, 'If you've got fewer people on board, that gives us more room in the galleys, which means we can do more in First Class or Club World because we've freed up some space in the ovens.' Then

you've got cabin crew who might say, 'How do we change our work routine and staffing because there are fewer people on board?' Then all the computer systems have to be changed to show where the seats now are, and all the check-in people have to be briefed because what was 'smoking' or 'extra leg-room' before maybe isn't any more, and then of course you've got to brief the sales force as well. Yet the only decision you made to start with was to add an inch or two on the seat pitch.[41]

An airline is a system which should be synergistic, meaning that its purpose is more readily achieved by combining processes and subsystems than by leaving them to function separately: this is the '2+2=5' effect. Synergies contributing to higher revenues and/or lower unit costs are frequently the justification for linkages between systems, whether by way of acquisition, merger, or horizontal alliance. Chapter 5 - which is the first of four dealing with strategy implementation issues - will consider these different forms of linkage. Prior to that, the next chapter will conclude Part One by considering the short- and medium-term objectives, operating goals, and critical success factors that might flow from choices of corporate, competitive, and functional strategies.

Notes

1   Kotler, P. (1991), *Marketing Management* (7th edition), Prentice-Hall.

2   Several authors have identified a three-stage process through which airlines pass, moving from a 'production orientation' where little effort is made to sell output (often because of overdemand and widespread lack of consumer choice), through a 'sales orientation' which refines sales techniques (probably in response to emerging overcapacity in the markets served), to a 'marketing orientation' which responds to increased competition by identifying consumers' needs, targeting those to be satisfied, and designing services capable of doing the job. Selling is treated only as the final predelivery act in a multi-stage process. See, for example: Wells, A. (1989), *Air Transport - A Management Perspective* (2nd edition), Wadsworth, p. 280.

     Airlines which have transitioned to a marketing orientation are relatively few in number, although more are having to do so as their markets are progressively liberalized. Many now use the appropriate vocabulary (e.g. quality, value, customer-orientation etc.) but have yet to put into action the concepts it describes. Sometimes this inertia can be attributed to markets that do not demand action. More frequently it can be attributed to hostile corporate cultures and/or corporate architecture which focuses inwards on production processes rather than outwards on customers' needs.

3   Day, G. (1990), *Market Driven Strategy: Processes for Creating Value*, The Free Press, cited in Meehan, S.A. (1996), 'Doctoral Research: What Do We Really Know About Market Orientation?', *London Business School Strategy Review*, Vol. 7, No. 1. Meehan's article provides a brief but useful summary of research perspectives in the field of market orientation, outlining in particular the 'far from conclusive' findings on linkages between market orientation and superior performance. (It should be noted that Meehan emphasizes the distinction between market- and marketing-orientation; this distinction is not drawn for the purposes of the present chapter.)

4   Taneja, N.K. (1981), *Airlines in Transition*, Lexington Books.

5   Drucker, P.F. (1954), *The Practice of Management*, Harper and Row.

6   Morris, M.H. and Pitt, L.F. (1994), 'The Organization of the Future: Unity of Marketing and Strategy', *Journal of Marketing Management,* 10.

7   Major sources of marketing information include internal company records, marketing intelligence activities, and marketing (as different from 'market') research. For a full explanation of the roles each could play in a marketing information system, see: Kotler, op. cit.

8   This example deals with passenger services, but a similar approach could be used in respect of other services sold by an airline.

9   Payne, A. (1993), *The Essence of Services Marketing,* Prentice Hall.

10   McDonald, M.H.B. (1989), *Marketing Plans* (2nd edition), Butterworth-Heinemann.

11   For comprehensive analyses of the reasons why marketing planning can fail to take root, see:
     • Leppard, J.W. and McDonald, M.H.B. (1991), 'Marketing Planning and Corporate Culture: A Conceptual Framework Which Examines Management Attitudes in the Context of Marketing Planning', *Journal of Marketing Management,* 7; and
     • McDonald, M.H.B. (1992), 'Strategic Marketing Planning: A State of the Art Review', *Marketing Intelligence & Planning,* Vol. 10. No. 4.
     Although the scales of expenditure clearly differ, it is nonetheless remarkable how little detailed financial analysis - as opposed to simple budgetting - tends to go into the planning of sizeable marketing investments, by comparison with the 'sophisticated' analytical tools deployed to assess fleet investments. Frequently, marketing expenditures are not looked upon as investments, and this attitude is reinforced by accounting principles in many countries. It is arguably rather strange that investments in aircraft are considered long-lived earning assets to be depreciated over a number of years, whereas investments in the brand image and many of the other reputation-related, intangible sources of competitive advantage which can sometimes be all that stands between the aircraft as a productive asset and the aircraft as mobile metalwork are in most cases considered expenses to be written off in the current year.

12   Sheff, D. (1995), 'The Virgin Billionaire', *Playboy,* February, cited in Hulbert, J.M. and Pitt, I. (1996), 'Exit Left Center Stage? The Future of Functional Marketing', *European Management Journal,* Vol. 14, No. 1.

13   Gratton, L. (1994), 'Implementing Strategic Intent: Human Resource Processes as a Force for Change', *Business Strategy,* Vol. 5, No. 1, Spring.

14   Normann, R. (1991), *Service Management: Strategy and Leadership in Service Business* (2nd edition), Wiley, p. 60.

15   Quoted in: Thompson, J.L (1993), *Strategic Management: Awareness and Change* (2nd edition), Chapman & Hall, p. 359.

16   Waterman, R.H. Jr., Waterman, J.A., and Collard, B.A. (1994), 'Toward a Career-resilient Workforce', *Harvard Business Review,* July-August.

17   Caudron, S. (1994), 'Contingent Workforce Spurs HR Planning', *Personnel Journal,* July.

18   See: Cameron, D. (1997), 'People Movers', *Airline Business,* March.

19   Bharadwaj, S.G., Varadarajan, P.R., and Fahy, J. (1993), 'Sustainable Competitive Advantage in Service Industries: A Conceptual Model and Research Propositions', *Journal of Marketing,* Vol. 57, October.

20   Porter, M.E. and Millar, V.E. (1985), 'How Information Gives You Competitive Advantage', *Harvard Business Review,* July-August.

21   Glazer, R. (1991), 'Marketing in an Information-intensive Environment: Strategic Implications of Knowledge as an Asset', *Journal of Marketing,* Vol. 55, October.

22   Ward, J., Griffiths, P., and Whitmore, P. (1990), *Strategic Planning for Information Systems,* Wiley, p. 22.

23   Huber, G.P. (1984), 'The Nature and Design of Post-industrial Organizations', *Management Science,* 30, 8.

24 Venkataraman, N. (1994), 'IT-enabled Business Transformation: From Automation to Business Scope Redefinition', *Sloan Management Review,* Winter.
25 Davenport, T.H. (1994), 'Saving IT's Soul: Human-centered Information Management', *Harvard Business Review,* March-April.
26 Bharadwaj et al., op. cit.
27 A particularly useful model for enabling integration is suggested in: Kovacevic, A. and Majluf, N. (1993), 'Six Stages of IT Strategic Management', *Sloan Management Review,* Summer.
28 Darroch, T. (1997), 'Smart-sourcing: Cathay's New Management and Acquisition Model for the Sourcing of IT Applications Development', presentation to IATA *Financial Management 97* conference, New York, 17th-19th March.
29 Taneja, N.K., op. cit., p. 186.
30 Lynch, J.J. (1984), *Airline Organization in the 1980s,* Globe Information Services, pp. 143, 144.
31 Ward, K. and Grundy, T. (1996), 'The Strategic Management of Corporate Value', *European Management Journal,* Vol. 14, No. 3.
32 This is therefore a wider concept than 'shareholder value' - defined as the financial value currently placed on the company by capital markets - because shareholder value is a figure necessarily based on imperfect knowledge. However, as Ward and Grundy note, it is management's responsibility 'to ensure that corporate value is properly represented in shareholder value'.
33 Op. cit.
34 The magnitude and nature of a particular airline's exposure to currency risk depend upon the structures of its revenue and expense streams. For example, an airline based in a country with a strong currency may suffer from labour costs which are high relative to those of competitors based in countries with weaker currencies - although this might be offset to some extent by a strong revenue base in its home market. Conversely, a carrier based in a country with a weak currency might be generating a high proportion of its revenues in that currency, whilst at the same time having to make payments in harder currencies for fuel and fleet financing; South African Airways, for instance, was earning around 65 per cent of its revenue in rand during the mid-90s, at a time when that currency was depreciating against the US dollar. These types of risk - along with interest and fuel price risks - can be hedged, but not always cheaply.
35 Despite now being somewhat dated, a succinct summary of the issues and numbers can be found in: *The Avmark Aviation Economist,* June/July 1993, p. 11.
36 See, for example: *The Airline Monitor,* November 1994.
37 Payne, op. cit., p. 168.
38 Wild, R. (1989), *Production and Operations Management* (4th edition), Cassell.
39 Wild (ibid.) calls these 'online' and 'offline' respectively. Whilst more evocative than 'front and back offices', his terms obviously convey their own very different meanings in an airline industry context.
40 A full explanation of the symbiotic nature of what he calls this 'service management trinity' can be found in: Lovelock, C.H. (1996), *Services Marketing,* (3rd edition), Prentice Hall, chapter 13.
41 Quotation from Mike Batt (who at the time was British Airways' head of products and brands), originally published in: Douglas, T. (1988), 'The Power of Branding', *Business Life,* April/May. Douglas' article was reproduced in: Lovelock, op. cit.

4 Conclusion to Part One

The analyses in Parts One and Two of Volume One were intended to establish what future courses of action are desirable and what is feasible. The outcome should be a set of long-term, high-level objectives to guide the selection of corporate, competitive, and functional strategies (the subject of Part One of this volume) and the implementation of those strategies (Part Two of this volume) over an extended period.

Strategic alternatives

These are clusters of activity intended to contribute to mission fulfillment and attainment of high-level objectives. They are formulated and chosen after external and internal analyses, and on the basis of the airline's current situation (see Volume One). It is with generic forms of strategic alternative that Part One of this volume has been concerned. Strategy-making is not a pre-flight checklist. The industry would not be as it is were there really just a handful of 'generic' strategies to choose from. Nonetheless, the only alternative to taking a liberty with reality is to admit that everything is contingent - which it is - and that there will always be as many strategies as there are airlines - which is broadly true. This, however, would contribute little to our understanding of what is currently happening in the industry.

Past success can be a deadweight at this stage of the process, closing the corporate mind to environmental changes which demand consideration of radical alternatives rather than extensions of a proven formula. Much depends upon what the success was based on and its relevance to prevailing and anticipated circumstances.[1]

Bearing in mind the distinction - drawn in the opening chapter of Volume One - between intended and emergent strategies, it is clear that alternatives do not just materialize out of a 'genie's lamp' called 'formulation'. They also arise or are created, and get pursued or rejected, in the cut-and-thrust of everyday activities. Of course, major strategic changes in direction will not 'emerge' every day - but the small causes which ultimately may lead to big effects often do. Inevitably, the manner and outcome of efforts to formulate alternatives - whether or not these efforts are themselves formalized - will depend on the individuals involved, their personal experiences and agendas, and the influence of intra-group, inter-group, and wider organizational dynamics. The same is equally true of the evaluation and choice stages in the process.

Strategic evaluation and choice

In principle, strategies are chosen after a 'rational' evaluation of alternatives. In practice, decision-making involves rational-analytical, intuitive-emotional, and political-behavioural elements.[2] Criteria include the following.

1 **Suitability** relative to the airline's vision, mission, and objectives. Several writers refer to 'strategic logic', which requires consideration of environmental fit as well as the relating of alternative strategies to corporate purpose. Environmental fit, itself a questionable concept in today's complex and turbulent environments, needs to be of two types:
    * internal: chosen strategies should be appropriate to organizational capabilities, culture, processes, and structures (or, alternatively, capabilities, culture, processes, and structures must be changed to accommodate the chosen strategies); and
    * external: they must also relate resources, skills, and capabilities to environmental, particularly market, requirements.

2 Closely related to the last point is **feasibility** - the requirement for a strategy to have a reasonable chance of success given internal and external circumstances.

3 What represents a 'reasonable chance' will be the subject of a **risk assessment**, which should relate possible downside outcomes to expected payoffs, and consider both the duration and scale of required commitments relative to the airline's resources. Allied to this would be consideration of the flexibility and the options allowed for within each alternative in the event that key assumptions prove incorrect.

4 **Timing** is, as with most things in life, a critical criterion.

5 **Acceptability** to key internal and external stakeholders. This can be the most important ingredient.

Arising from the selection of strategies, and intended to guide their implementation, are:

- short- and medium-term objectives;
- operating goals; and
- critical success factors.

Short- and medium-term objectives

These are specific targets to be attained within a given period of time, often three to five years, which can be used to guide the formulation and implementation of action plans. They are commonly framed in terms of financial measurements (e.g. revenues, costs, margins, profit, cash-flow, shareholder value, earnings per share, dividends, or return on capital), output, traffic, traffic mix, market share, productivity, service levels, and human resource development.

However, as airlines in increasingly competitive markets transition from being operators of aircraft to satisfiers of consumer needs, so their objectives are no longer as technically oriented as in the past. Increasingly, the list is being 'invaded' by targets relating to quality enhancement, customer satisfaction and value improvement, and to employee development - all keyed off choices of corporate and, more particularly, competitive strategy. It is arguable that these have far more long-term relevance than financial ratios or even absolute figures. For example, results could be massaged to meet a profitability target by lengthening depreciation periods on aircraft and other assets, or by capitalizing rather than expensing route development or fleet introduction costs. What arguably matters more than attaining that target is how the aircraft and routes concerned are being used to achieve the airline's necessarily more qualitative long-term goals.

Profits are vital because they impress financial markets, reward shareholders or relieve the burden on taxpayers to support state-owned carriers, and because they provide scope for future investment. But they are nothing more than a residual number derived from the application of arbitrary accounting principles and conventions to a set of records. In a well-managed airline, they should simply be what is left over once the right customer value has been designed for and delivered to its market(s). This is not to say that profits and profitability are anything other than important and legitimate metrics, but the fundamental means by which they are to be attained need to be seriously addressed rather than just the numbers alone.

Some airlines do specify qualitative 'lower order' objectives, particularly where they are to be circulated outside the company. However, most are quantified, and many observers feel that this must be the case if they are to be useful in charting progress towards fulfillment of the mission from which - presumably - they have been derived.

In 1988, for example, British Midland set the objective - which it subsequently achieved - of shifting what was an 85/15 domestic against international revenue split to 50/50. The underlying purpose was to move its relatively high-quality/low-fare service-price offer onto a greater number of high-density short-haul trunk routes (whilst at the same time extending network reach through a range of code-sharing partnerships). To give effect to the route expansion objective, it implemented a network strategy of opening one major European route each year. After five years, British Midland had succeeded in establishing itself on the five busiest cross-border intra-European scheduled routes.[3] All Nippon targeted international growth in the late 1990s for similar reasons. Unable to reach its 1.15 trillion yen per annum revenue target for 2001 by relying on slow-growing domestic markets which were being attacked by an expanding high-speed rail system and were under threat from low-fare start-ups, it turned instead to faster-growing markets elsewhere in Asia; the intention was to use expansion in these markets to help boost international revenues from 30 per cent of total revenues in 1996 to 50 per cent by 2001.[4]

If multiple, short- and medium-term objectives should be relatively small in number, readily communicable, mutually consistent, and ranked. They should be sufficiently challenging and feasible to be motivational, dynamic in the sense that they are reviewed and adjusted periodically in response to changing circumstances, and capable of guiding operational decisions.

An airline with a profit improvement objective might target one or both of revenue growth and higher productivity. Revenue growth could involve simply growing with its markets, taking a larger share of those existing markets, entering new markets, and/or developing new products. Productivity improvement could focus on reducing costs, improving resource utilization, and/or changing the company's asset base.

In the prevailing economic climate of the mid-1990s, many airlines set objectives aimed at attacking their unit costs. Delta launched 'Leadership 7.5' in 1994, a programme with the (ultimately unattained) objective of knocking two billion dollars off its cost base by 1997 and reducing unit costs to 7.5 cents per ASM. Beneath this lay a deeper objective of achieving a consistent operating margin. In 1996, when the 7.5 cent target was recognized as being beyond reach, Delta switched its medium-term objective to achievement of a 12 per cent operating margin within three years. Many Leadership 7.5 initiatives nonetheless remained in place.

Other US majors had similar cost-reduction objectives at around this time. Across the Atlantic, Lufthansa announced in mid-decade its 'Programme 15', one of the objectives of which was to cut costs per ASK from 17 to 15 pfennigs or better by the year 2001. More or less simultaneously, KLM's Focus 2000 project was being launched; it targeted a 20 per cent reduction in unit costs and DFl 1.5 billion improvement in operating performance over three years, and achievement of a 14 per cent return on equity. In Asia, All Nippon launched a three-year plan in 1995 to cut labour costs by 20 per cent and raise aircraft utilization by 10 per cent, whilst at the same time boosting revenues by 15 per cent.

Operating goals

These are specific, quantified targets to be attained within a short time-frame, often one financial year. Meshing closely with objectives, operating goals should be clearly and unambiguously measurable. Adherents to the classical/rational school of strategic management would see objectives as straddling the interface between strategy formulation and implementation, and operating goals as being firmly in the realm of implementation. Observers taking a more experiential or emergent view of strategy-making would be less inclined to draw this distinction.[5]

Whilst vision, mission, and high-level objectives should never be remote from environmental influences or from the realities of organizational potential, it is lower level objectives and operating goals which have to be linked to these influences and realities particularly closely. For example, revenue goals in an increasing number of markets can no longer be extrapolated from the past, but have instead to be keyed off competitive circumstances and an evaluation of what an airline's particular capabilities and advantages will let it achieve in terms of market share and yield.

Lower level objectives and operating goals, being relatively short-term, come and go. It is part of management's task to ensure that the next batch of targets is lined up as soon as the current ones have been hit.

Perhaps the most important point relevant both to objectives and operating goals is that considering them simply as targets to be hit is not sufficient. The processes used to attain them, the refinement of these processes, and the constant search for more efficient ways of 'doing' are now as important as what is actually 'done'. This is the essence of continuous improvement.

Critical success factors

Genuine critical success factors (CSFs), sometimes also called 'key success factors', are the pillars holding up the edifice of strategic management: start knocking them down and the edifice will become unstable until, ultimately, knocking away just one more induces collapse. Failure to achieve properly chosen CSFs will probably mean failure in fulfilling a mission and realizing a vision.

Some observers consider CSFs to be things which have to be done if given objectives and goals are to be met; each objective and goal has several CSFs underlying it. Others prefer to take a macro-view of the industry and their position within it, identify CSFs, and then derive objectives and goals. From this latter perspective, Rockart has suggested a three-step process.[6]

1   Generate success factors: 'What does it take to be successful in this business?'

2   Refine CSFs into objectives and goals: 'What should the organization's objectives be with respect to the critical success factors?'

3   Identify measures of performance: 'How will we know whether the organization has been successful?'

The best approach is to balance these two perspectives: use CSFs to chart progress towards objectives, but also think iteratively about CSFs relevant both to the airline industry in general and to chosen market segments in particular to ensure that selected objectives are pertinent. Having said this, it has to be recognized that some CSFs are so fundamental that they are not just milestones on a chosen strategy towards a stated objective. Instead, they actually dictate the strategy. Obvious examples are the need for most regional carriers in the United States and, increasingly, in Europe to be linked to a major airline with which they can exchange traffic,[7] the requirement in many competitive markets for a frequent flyer programme, and the need for most participants in scheduled international markets to distribute their products through a CRS.
This highlights the distinction between two types of CSF.

1   Common CSFs: these might be common to the industry as a whole or to a particular strategic group of airlines pursuing essentially the same market strategies. Achieving them is not likely to be enough to win, but failing to achieve them can put a player out of the game.

2   Unique CSFs: these should be the reporting points en route to sustainable competitive advantage(s) specific to the airline concerned.

What drives critical success factors?

Industry economics One of the most significant drivers of CSFs is industry economics. Given the high fixed costs of a relatively inflexible production infrastructure, high utilization of assets is essential in most sectors of the airline industry (one notable exception being the older aircraft operated by express carriers or integrators such as FedEx and UPS on many of their overnight spokes). High load factors are usually considered critical to success, but whether any given load factor is at or above break-even will depend on the yields being earned from the loads carried and the unit costs of producing output; asset utilization in general and load factor in particular are therefore not in themselves adequate yardsticks of criticality.[8] The service-price offers made to customers must not only generate utilization, they must generate utilization which produces yields in excess of the costs required to deliver the product.

Production economies of scale are an important CSF-driver in most capital intensive industries. In the airline industry, however, marketing economies of scale, economies of scope, and returns to network density appear to be more significant than economies of scale in flight operations.[9]

One of the most important advantages of considering CSF-drivers is that doing so provides an opportunity for a reality check. Whilst the inner core of any airline's CSFs should be driven by its concept of the business, by its vision, mission, goals and objectives, it is also necessary to ensure that the more general CSFs which flow from the economic structure of the industry have not been overlooked.

Vision and mission In addition to industry economics, a second major set of CSF-drivers is attributable to an airline's vision and mission - how it perceives the industry and decides to position itself, how it chooses to deploy resources so as to produce something the market will value more highly than whatever it is that competitors are producing, and how the airline intends developing a competitive advantage (always assuming, of course, that it operates in a competitive marketplace). A charter airline, a full-service network carrier, and a low-cost/no-frills scheduled operator will share some CSFs derived from industry economics, but each will have different concepts of the business which, in turn, will lead to a range of CSFs encompassing some that are common to other members of the same strategic groups and others that are unique.

The types of customer needs that are to be satisfied and the chosen method of satisfying them - the nature of the value being offered - will drive CSFs. Certainly, an airline will share CSFs with competitors and some might even be imposed by the activities of competitors, but to be a successful long-term player in a competitive market an airline must be able to derive from its service concept and the value being offered to its customers a number of CSFs which are unique to it alone.

Life-cycle stage A third CSF driver is the life-cycle stage of an airline's product(s) and, where appropriate, its separate business units. CSFs relevant to each stage will vary (as, incidentally, should the control measures derived from them).

Conclusion An airline as a whole should have CSFs, but in turn each business unit - possibly even every brand, product, or individual route - may also have its own subset. The most important point when considering what should be driving them is to ensure that effort is not being wasted trying to be good at things which do not matter to the vision, mission or objectives. This is something aircraft manufacturers are having to come to terms with by offering customers only what they need and are prepared to pay for: airlines are demanding cost-effective functionality rather than new, hi-tech 'bells and whistles' for their own sake. Similarly, airlines must look the other direction down the supply chain and make sure that they are only trying to be good at what matters to their own targeted customers. Although just another way of repeating the old admonition to be stakeholder-, especially customer-, driven rather than operations- and engineering-led, this is something which some airlines are only slowly taking on board.

Sample industry CSFs

The following is an indicative sample rather than a comprehensive list. Not all the listed CSFs will necessarily apply to every carrier. Furthermore, as already mentioned, each individual airline in a competitive market should have its own specific CSFs tied to vision and mission, in addition to those more widely applicable throughout the industry.

1   A capable management team able to take advantage of a rapidly evolving regulatory framework, to create and exploit competitive advantage, to deliver appropriate value to targeted markets and segments, to manage its cost structure in a manner consistent with the chosen value positioning, and to cope with rapid change in a turbulent competitive environment.

2   Financial management which focuses on ensuring a sound capital structure, conservative debt amortization profile, good liquidity, plenty of reserve borrowing capacity, and hedged foreign exchange and interest rate exposure. It is critical that:

  • the balance sheet and cash-flow are strong enough to support any strategic thrust launched to exploit opportunities or cope with threats which might materialize. Financial flexibility, implied by moderate leverage, a modern and largely unencumbered (i.e. unmortgaged) fleet and strong operating cash-flow, can be especially valuable during an economic downturn;
  • the cost structure is sufficiently low to support yields being earned, and is competitive relative both to carriers offering similar customer value in the same market(s) and to potential entrants; and
  • the covenants in any aircraft lease or debt documentation do not inhibit operational activities.

  Financial objectives (such as target profits, margins or returns on investment) are not CSFs in themselves. They may be vital but they are simply a quantification of what will happen if the real CSFs are identified and successfully pursued. For example, an airline might be able to meet a profitability goal by lengthening the period over which it charges depreciation on its aircraft, by cutting back on its marketing communications programme, or by delaying a product launch; however, the first will have no impact on the carrier's underlying business and the last two might - depending on market circumstances at the time - actually harm it in the long run. A CSF that could lead to harmful decisions being taken in order to attain it is not a true CSF.

3   Access to desirable markets - specifically, in the case of network rather than point-to-point carriers, freedom to build an integrated network based on defensible (where feasible, dominated) hubs with controlled traffic feed, probably incorporating code-share and possibly franchise partnerships to broaden network reach. This is one variety of the conventional wisdom which sees 'critical mass' and the economies of density and scope that it can generate as being essential to survival as a major player during the airline industry's transition.

4   Barriers to market entry by competitors, arising from grandfather rights to slots at congested hubs, product differentiation, branding, or network scope, for example.

5   Human resource management policies which lead to cooperative labour relations, and to the retention of well-trained, motivated, capable, suitably skilled, flexible, and knowledgeable staff who are committed to exceeding customers' expectations (in the context of the particular service-price offers - that is, in the context of the particular strategic positioning - chosen by the airline).

6   Participation in a global CRS (although this is not something that most low-cost/no-frills carriers consider a CSF).

7   Deployment of, or participation in, an attractive frequent flyer programme (which, again, is not necessarily a CSF for low-cost carriers).

8   A modern, fuel-efficient fleet standardized around as few aircraft types as the stage lengths and demand characteristics of the network to be served make desirable.

9   The ability to manage information technology to competitive advantage, especially with regard to revenue management, operational planning, and customer databases (i.e. automation of pricing, distribution, inventory control, and some aspects of marketing communications).

Benefits of establishing CSFs

The beauty of CSFs is that they can focus attention onto issues of which management might already be aware, but in a relatively unsystematic way. They do not occur naturally; they evolve from answers to the question, 'What must be accomplished in order for the airline to make progress towards its vision, achieve its mission, and attain its objectives and operating goals?' They can be used both to generate and to pace action plans. For example, a CSF specifying increased market share on a route as a requirement to reach a particular objective could:

- lead to one or more of a variety of marketing activities affecting product design, pricing, or the marketing communications mix;
- mandate the reengineering of operational activities, perhaps to improve ontime performance;
- initiate analysis of new feeder routes; and/or
- stimulate consideration of investment in, or partnership with, other carriers.

The point is that CSFs are things airlines have to go out and make happen in order for objectives and operating goals to be achieved.

Customer value is becoming the source of many of the CSFs that really matter in competitive markets. In the final analysis, though, what is going to be critical to the future of many airlines finding themselves for the first time facing relatively unconstrained competition in a newly liberalized environment will be the ability to cope with and, as far as possible, manage constant change. This will necessitate cultural reorientation and a shift in underlying values. But above all else, it will require leaders infused with a vision and a sense of mission.

Notes

1   Miller, D., (1994), 'What Happens after Success: the Perils of Excellence', *Journal of Management Studies*, 31: 3, May.
2   Glueck, W.F. and Jauch, L.R. (1985), *Business Policy and Strategic Management* (4th edition), McGraw-Hill.
3   London Heathrow to Amsterdam, Dublin, Paris, Brussels, and Frankfurt. By the end of 1995, 56 per cent of British Midland's traffic was international, and the carrier was in the process of establishing itself on Europe's sixth-busiest cross-border route: London Heathrow-Zurich. It subsequently moved onto other continental routes, some of which were operated as code-shares with Lufthansa.
4   Saunier, V. (1997), 'ANA Sees Growth in China Services', *Aviation Week & Space Technology*, May 26.
5   The difference between classical/rational and emergent strategy-making processes is explained in Volume One, chapter 1.
6   Rockart, J.F. (1979), 'Chief Executives Define Their Own Data Needs', *Harvard Business Review*, March-April.
7   Some regionals in both the United States and Europe feed more than one major each, e.g. Horizon Air and Eurowings.

8   For a discussion of yield, load factors, and other aspects of industry economics, see:
     Holloway, S. (1997), *Straight and Level: Practical Airline Economics,* Ashgate.
9   Ibid., chapter 1.

Part Two
Implementation

5 Growth, alliances, and globalization

Part Two of this volume will consider how corporate and competitive strategies might be implemented. Implementation is the stage in the strategic management process at which resources are allocated in pursuit of intended strategies, and diverted in response to others that emerge unintended. 'What, where, how, who, and when?' are the key questions.

In this chapter we will be extending the discussion in chapter 1 by looking at alternative modes of growth, beginning with internal or organic growth and then turning to acquisitions and alliances.[1] The discussion of alliances will first consider their forms and possible objectives, then look at equity linkages, code-sharing, block-spacing, joint services, and franchising; it will conclude with a review of their potential future role and the requirements for successful partnerships. The final section of the chapter will consider globalization - what it means, how it is being accomplished, what barriers it confronts, and its possible future course.

Extending the discussion in chapters 2 and 3, the next chapter will begin detailed consideration of what the industry's transition to new ways of doing business implies for the implementation of competitive strategies; it will look at changes in the management of airline service concepts and service-price offers. Chapter 7 will then discuss service delivery as an interactive experience, and in chapter 8 the evolving role of corporate infrastructure will be briefly outlined. Finally, Part Three of the book will look at the outcome of implementation; service quality, failure, and recovery will be the subjects of chapter 9, and customer retention and loyalty the focus of chapter 10.

Internal/organic growth

Given that the cross-border acquisition of airlines has been - subject to a handful of exceptions in Australasia and Latin America - largely impossible outside the European Union and that many countries do not have multi-airline air transport industries offering a wide range of domestic acquisition targets, internal/organic growth has historically been the primary mode for expansion. The relatively few exceptions to this generalization are, of course, highly significant because of their scale: horizontal integration has been an important feature of the post-deregulation US domestic industry, and there have been significant acquisitions within the United Kingdom, France, and a small number of other countries.[2] 'Vertical integration' of regional airlines into the systems of larger carriers has also been an outgrowth of the network restructuring brought about by deregulation in the United States and, on a somewhat smaller scale, by liberalization in Europe. Dramatic and important though some of these individual exceptions are, internal/organic growth was the most significant vehicle for expansion in the airline industry - certainly as far as air transport and related activities were concerned - until the alliance phenomenon took off in the late 1980s and early 1990s.

In favour of internal/organic growth as a medium for expansion is the fact that it is generally easier to control, and therefore less risky, than growth by acquisition. It is also more likely to leave in tact corporate culture, systems, and standards. On the other hand, it can be too slow once major competitors start consolidating rapidly and building commercial barriers to market entry. Lack of suitable aircraft may also be a constraint when manufacturers' production lines are booked and the secondary market is tight. Regulatory considerations often still limit direct access to desirable markets. In particular, organic growth does not yet offer rich opportunities to expand rapidly into fifth and seventh freedom or cabotage markets. The growth of many international airlines is constrained by the primarily national orientations of their historic business bases. Finally, infrastructural congestion and the non-availability of sufficient finance to fund expansion into untapped markets can also act as constraints on independent growth.[3]

Acquisition

Most acquisitions by airlines have taken the form of horizontal or vertical integration, the latter including the purchase of regional feeders; there has in the past been some concentric/related diversification away from air transport and even some unrelated diversification, but as has already been mentioned this type of growth is now largely out of favour. In heavily regulated environments the primary motivation for buying other airlines is frequently the need to rescue an ailing carrier. Broadly speaking, regulation tends to reduce the imperative or opportunity for either aggressive or defensive acquisitions. In environments which have been - or are about to be - liberalized, acquisitions within a single country's multi-airline industry have at a general level been motivated by 'the need to replace structures created in an environment of regulation with new organisations responding to market demands';[4] more specifically, they have been motivated by one or more of the following objectives.

1   To achieve a rapid increase in market share and revenues by expanding the network - ideally leading to future growth in return on investment (ROI), although in practice there is some doubt that this is where most acquisitions ultimately lead. In the EU, cross-border acquisitions are one way to gain rapid access to unserved corners of the 'single market'; however, British Airways' experiences with its French and German subsidiaries during the 1990s suggest that this can be an expensive strategy if not carefully implemented.

2   To eliminate actual or potential competitors (e.g. Air France and UTA), gain market power, and/or consolidate control over a hub (e.g. Northwest and Republic, and TWA and Ozark).

3   To gain quick access to economies of scope, density and, insofar as they exist, economies of scale.

4   To obtain slots or route rights which would otherwise be unavailable.[5]

5   To obtain other corporate resources or skills, possibly including aircraft and terminal capacity, or an established schedule pattern, sales force, operational infrastructure, and general market presence.

6   To acquire more direct financial benefits, such as undervalued assets, tax-loss carry-forwards, cash, or a better quality earnings stream.

7   To broaden the opportunities for exploiting distinctive capabilities.

Acquisitions - particularly large acquisitions - are seldom trouble-free. The first challenge is to minimize the premium paid in the acquisition price for control; due partly to the intervention of SAS, British Airways paid heavily for its purchase of British Caledonian, for example. Second, notwithstanding the relatedness of horizontal acquisitions, airlines have been no less immune to the problems of integrating their purchases than have companies in other industries. These include:

*   corporate cultures that prove difficult to blend (e.g. USAir and Piedmont, and Aéromexico and Mexicana);[6]
*   fleets incompatible in respect of type, specification or configuration, all of which raise training, maintenance, and other costs. Integrating maintenance programmes can be a major headache in itself, as Continental was still finding out several years after taking over the remnants of various carriers in the mid- and late-1980s;

- difficulties merging aircrew seniority lists (e.g. Northwest and Republic);
- tendencies for salaries and benefits to be levelled upwards (e.g. Delta and Western);[7]
- loss of loyalty amongst the acquiree's customers. USAir's takeover of PSA and, perhaps to a lesser extent, the same carrier's acquisition of Piedmont are examples of brand equity being paid for in the acquisition price and then largely squandered; and
- difficulties maintaining customer service standards if operations are only slowly integrated (e.g. Delta's purchase of Pan Am's Atlantic Division).

As will be discussed later in the chapter, there are now perceived to be intense pressures within the airline industry to gain 'critical mass' - however that might be defined - on a global scale. This imperative underlies most of the larger alliance structures discussed in the next section of the chapter and, notwithstanding the proven difficulties of implementing airline mergers, it motivated discussions during the mid-90s aimed at further consolidating the US airline industry (e.g. USAir/United, USAir/American, and Continental/Delta). On the other hand, implementing mergers necessarily takes up a lot of management time changing the power structure, melding work processes, and creating a new sense of identity - time during which the rethinking of precisely how the merged firm should compete tends to be sidelined.[8] The pace of change in the industry is now so rapid that this is time that might not be available if competitors continue relentlessly to sharpen the management of their service concepts and service delivery systems while the newly merged airline is focusing primarily on internal issues.

With regard to diversification away from air transport activities, acquisitions often either do not give rise to the synergies anticipated or if synergies really do exist they are not properly exploited. Hotels and car rental companies, once again, provide obvious examples.

Acquisitions of airlines by other carriers - along with the closure of failing competitors - tends to accelerate industry **consolidation**. As was pointed out in chapter 3 of Volume One, however, the steadily growing concentration of global market share that is currently underway is constrained from running its course because of aeropolitical barriers to cross-border mergers and acquisitions. Even where cross-border mergers and acquisitions are possible, as within the EU, their development has been slowed by entrenched attachments - amongst politicians, some airline managers, and public opinion - to the concept of a national airline industry, certainly insofar as the leading 'flag carriers' are concerned. Pending their erosion by market forces as the industry continues to liberalize, a route around these obstacles which has become increasingly popular is the use of alliances.

Alliances

Precluded by both aeropolitics and economics from each serving every market, airlines have for decades cooperated both multilaterally and bilaterally to facilitate the movement of passengers and cargo between their respective networks. Interlining, joint tariffs, and the pro-ration of fares have been around for years, as has cooperation in the international distribution of what have largely remained nationally oriented services. The qualitative change from past practice is that these established operating procedures are now being repackaged and broadened in scope; preferential relationships between carriers are being forged and, on the revenue side, marketed to customers as either 'seamless' products or (often more realistically) different products of consistent quality.

Alliances are the airline industry's response to three influences in particular:

- strong customer preference for single-carrier service;
- economies of scope, density, and scale available from multi-hub operating systems; and
- restrictions placed both by the Chicago regulatory regime and by most bodies of domestic law on the cross-border ownership of airlines.[9]

Alliances, which now number around 400 globally, should be looked upon only as vehicles with which to implement one or more defined strategies oriented towards clearly identified goals and objectives. There has, however, been a tendency amongst some airline strategists and outside observers to treat them as ends rather than means.

Forms of alliance

Alliances come in many different forms and can incorporate anything selected from an extensive menu of possible ingredients. Nonetheless, whereas talk of alliances in other industries conjures images of joint ventures and possibly mergers, in the airline industry cross-border alliances remain for the most part largely commercial agreements. It is certainly possible in some markets, aided as we will see by antitrust immunity, to forge fairly deep relationships; but the industry's track record to date shows arrangements to be surprisingly disposable, and the rapidly evolving but still relatively restrictive international regulatory environment leaves cross-border airline alliances in most cases substantially more unstable and shallow than those in many other globalizing industries.

Perhaps the most useful distinction that can be drawn in order to categorize inter-airline relationships is between what we will call here 'focused' alliances and 'comprehensive' alliances.[10]

Focused alliances

These can be quite short-term in duration, but this need not necessarily be so - as the longevity of the Atlas and KSSU maintenance consortia and the multi-shareholder CRS ventures illustrate. They frequently address perceived needs to access or share specific passenger or cargo markets but, as is shown by the examples just cited, focus can instead be turned on some aspect of product distribution or the service delivery process.

It is not uncommon for carriers to have multiple focused alliances with different collaborators in different markets or separate areas of the value chain. Thus, Air Canada has an alliance with United that is becoming gradually more comprehensive, and yet still cooperates with former investment target Continental in specific markets such as Newark and Houston. South African Airways code-shares with American, but at the same time is becoming more deeply involved with the comprehensive alliance being formed around the United-Lufthansa axis.

British Midland has been an accomplished practitioner of focused alliances. By the mid-90s it had entered into over a dozen code-sharing agreements with long-haul carriers serving London Heathrow - some of which were direct competitors of each other, such as United and American. These deals appear to have been driven more by network synergies than by any desire for wider strategic relationships; some were little more than 'supercharged' interline agreements intended to exploit the very real marketing advantages arising from the appearance of offering online connections. The British carrier for many years resisted pressure to resolve conflicts arising from its non-exclusive approach by choosing between partners, arguing the need to maximize feed in order to keep slot productivity high.

American Airlines, long a denigrator of code-sharing, limited itself largely to route-specific relationships until a wide-ranging partnership with British Airways was proposed in 1996.[11] The following quotation exemplifies well the ad hoc approach to alliances.

> ANA's pact [referring to a code-sharing and limited blocked-space agreement entered into by All Nippon Airways in conjunction with Air Canada's Osaka-Vancouver service] is typical of the Japanese carrier in that it does not fit into its broader scheme of alliances. Air Canada is a partner of United Airlines, while ANA's US partner is Delta Air Lines. Air Canada's rival Canadian has a limited code-share with British Airways on some routes, yet ANA's frequent flyer programme is linked to the UK carrier's. 'Alliances are still relatively new in our industry,' says Kuzuhisa Shin, ANA's senior director for network management. 'We don't worry about the global picture. Our policy is to pick partners in individual markets.'[12]

Comprehensive alliances

Instead of or, more usually, as well as focused cooperation, a relatively small but rapidly growing number of carriers have entered into comprehensive alliances. These are normally comprehensive in the sense that the airlines concerned intend to integrate and cross-sell each other's products across their respective networks rather than in just one or a handful of markets, and there is frequently also an intention to maximize cooperation through a wide range of revenue-enhancing and cost-containing activities. There is normally one or a pair of large carriers at their core and, as discussed in chapter 1, the alliance is in each case seen as a vehicle for extending network reach into as many as possible of the world's major point-to-point markets and - importantly - to gain access to literally tens of thousands of connecting city-pair markets. Although O and D passengers still account for a majority of international traffic, connecting passengers are believed to generate around half of international revenues;[13] any device capable of expanding the number of connecting markets covered by a network without requiring concomitant investment in assets - as code-sharing can - is therefore a potentially revenue-rich option.

One of the earliest examples of a comprehensive partnership was the Global Excellence Alliance, linking Delta, Singapore Airlines, and Swissair and involving limited exchanges of equity. Despite several positive developments, however, Singapore Airlines remained on the periphery whilst Delta and Swissair (together with the Swiss carrier's partners, Sabena and Austrian) tightened their transatlantic cooperation. In June 1997, Singapore Airlines, Ansett Australia, and Ansett's 50 per cent shareholder Air New Zealand signed a memorandum of understanding which covered 'worldwide policy regarding code-sharing, networks, scheduling and ticketing integration, capacity planning, joint purchasing, product development, marketing, and common cargo and information technologies'.[14] Cross-shareholdings were not part of the arrangement, but analysts were predicting at the time that Singapore Airlines would ultimately become a shareholder in Ansett Australia - and possibly also in Air New Zealand. The fact that the Australasian carriers were already allied with members of the recently formed Star Alliance (see below), together with Singapore Airlines' apparently limited gains from Global Excellence, made it seem likely that the Singaporean carrier would eventually switch from one comprehensive alliance to the other. In late 1997, Singapore Airlines announced a bilateral deal with Lufthansa (a core member of Star) and withdrew from Global Excellence.

In the mid-90s, Delta's transatlantic grouping was further expanded by an extensive code-sharing deal with Air France, raising the prospect of a larger bloc emerging in due course and possibly including Continental (also an Air France code-share partner). A major hurdle, however, was the slow pace of Franco-US bilateral negotiations at the time. Although both sides accepted an open skies regime as the objective, the United States was pressing for immediate implementation whilst France wanted it phased-in over nine years. Without a new bilateral in some acceptable form, US approval of the code-sharing deals was unlikely, and without an open skies agreement any alliance between Air France and its US partner(s) would not receive antitrust immunity.

Separately, Continental had in 1996 approached Delta about a possible merger, but discussions did not progress. Continental then set about creating what it billed as an 'alliance of equals'. At the time of writing this amounts to a patchwork of relationships with several European carriers, and limited deals with EVA Air (Taiwan) and Aces (Colombia). What will ultimately emerge is difficult to predict - but the strategic intent of Continental's management to leverage their recently transformed airline into a global network partnership is apparent.

The KLM-Northwest alliance was a pioneer in being the first to obtain antitrust immunity.[15] We will see in chapter 10 that this partnership also went much further and faster than others in terms of joint branding and operational integration; its harmony was nonetheless disturbed in the mid-90s by a board-room squabble. This was resolved in 1997 when KLM agreed to sell back its 19 per cent equity stake in Northwest, and the two carriers entered into a ten-year cooperation pact. Meanwhile, KLM set about building a comprehensive alliance in Europe by acquiring control of Air UK, buying into Braathens SAFE, code-sharing with French and German regionals, and pursuing talks with Alitalia; links with Japan Air System, already a code-sharing partner of Northwest, were also explored.

British Airways has had a chequered history of alliance-building since the late 1980s, marked by failures with KLM, Sabena, and in Russia. Its first attempt at transatlantic partnership - with United - faltered early, after which it turned to building a network based to a larger degree than other alliances on the concept of central direction: control was effected over a variety of subsidiaries and affiliates in the United Kingdom and Europe, whilst a fair degree of influence was extended through substantial minority shareholdings in USAir and Qantas. In the mid-90s, the British carrier's transatlantic alliance strategy went through its third metamorphosis when a link-up with American Airlines was proposed; the objective was that this should lead to operational integration over the North Atlantic and code-sharing elsewhere on their respective networks. Whether expected or otherwise, it provoked termination of the relationship with USAir. Quite how the corporate cultures of American and British Airways - both addicted to control and neither notably humble - were to accommodate each other was an issue left open at the time the partnership was proposed.[16]

One of the largest 'comprehensive' groupings yet to emerge has evolved out of the United-Lufthansa relationship, and now incorporates SAS alongside these two and their affiliates as well as - to varying degrees - Thai, Air Canada, South African, Varig, Ansett, and Air New Zealand. In

1997, five of these carriers - Air Canada, Lufthansa, SAS, Thai, and United - extended their bilateral relationships into the multilateral 'Star Alliance'; Varig became the sixth member shortly afterwards, and others - including Singapore Airlines, as already noted - were also on the candidate list. The primary objective of the alliance is to integrate networks and make the experiences of connecting passengers as seamless as possible; a secondary objective is to attack costs through joint purchasing and shared utilization of assets. Despite its scope, however,[17] the Star Alliance is loosely structured and does not, at least initially, appear to be as ambitious in terms of operational and service integration as some of the other comprehensive alliances in existence or proposed.

'Focused' and 'comprehensive' alliances are not necessarily an either/or proposition. Austrian Airlines, for example, has since the early 1970s been gradually developing what is an increasingly comprehensive relationship with its minority shareholder Swissair, whilst at the same time entering into a considerable number of market-specific arrangements with other carriers. Similarly, United has a comprehensive alliance with its partners in Star, as well as more focused code-sharing and franchising agreements with several other carriers in various parts of the world. British Airways, generally considered an adherent to the 'grand strategy' approach, has since the mid-90s been actively entering into focused agreements (e.g. for feed at Phoenix from America West).

It is from the global **traffic systems** created by comprehensive alliances that many observers expect tomorrow's truly global **airlines** to emerge; we will return to this topic shortly. These collaborative arrangements in particular are the most publicly visible evidence of the blurring boundaries between some cooperating firms to which reference was made in Volume One. Neither truly internal nor external to the participating airlines, comprehensive alliances need to be managed with techniques different from the command-and-control formulations traditionally employed internally, or the legalistic, win-lose postures still typical of many external relationships.

Alliance objectives

Why the enthusiasm for alliances? On a general level, the answer should be to leverage skills and resources in an effort to attain strategic objectives, and/or to compensate for a missing critical success factor which it is impossible or too expensive to deal with internally or through acquisition. On an even more general level, there is a widespread belief that survival as a major international player in a globalizing industry will be predicated on having sufficient 'critical mass' - a certain minimum market share. The survival of many smaller carriers, notably but not exclusively regionals, is now seen as dependent on their ability to forge links with major airlines. On a practical level, motivations can encompass improved positioning, organizational learning, risk reduction, or an intent to reshape the competitive environment, but they all lie ultimately in revenue enhancement and/or cost containment.

Revenue enhancement

A scheduled airline's core product is the schedule of departures within its network. If that network can be broadened and/or the schedule can be increased by incorporating the departures of an alliance partner, the airline has more to offer its customers. Alliances might be the only way into these new markets for aeropolitical reasons (e.g. the airline has no traffic rights and is precluded from controlling a foreign carrier which does), for economic reasons (e.g. its fleet and/or cost structure are unsuitable for the markets concerned or those markets will not support competing services), for infrastructural reasons (e.g. slots are unavailable at a desired destination), or for financial reasons (e.g. the airline has insufficient resources to develop new markets on its own). In other words, alliances can be a relatively low-cost (and therefore potentially high-ROI) method for airlines to get their brands into a wider spread of markets than they are able to serve directly. Alliances can also be effective devices for pre-empting competitors, either in existing or new markets. In the mid-1990s, United's code-sharing arrangements were adding approximately 550 daily departures - or around 25 per cent - to its own 2,200 flights. This was being achieved without investing in the aircraft and other resources required to mount incremental operations on such a scale.

Alliances might therefore enhance revenue by:

•   feeding traffic from aeropolitically inaccessible and/or relatively low-demand cities into an airline's existing network (e.g. alliances between regional and major airlines or between international and domestic airlines);
•   allowing a carrier to establish itself in previously untapped markets or segments (as British Airways is doing domestically in several countries); or
•   giving the airline access to growth opportunities away from its own congested hubs (a problem which British Airways faces at London Heathrow and - to a lesser extent - at Gatwick, for example).

Network integration can generate distribution benefits which flow directly through to the revenue stream. Most notable amongst these is the appearance of online (and therefore superior quality) connecting service presented to customers by some forms of code-sharing; in many countries, code-shared connections gain higher CRS display positions than ordinary interline connections, so further enhancing their potential for generating incremental revenue.

Although there seems to be a growing consensus that comprehensive alliances in particular can deliver significant revenue enhancement through the creation of an integrated global network, separation of rhetoric from reality remains difficult. One of the earliest reliable studies of transatlantic alliances estimated that the KLM/Northwest relationship boosted revenues for the Dutch carrier in 1994 by around $100 million ($45 million from code-sharing and $55 million from increased non-code-share interlining) and for its US partner by between $125 million and $175 million; traffic gain was reckoned to be around 350,000 passengers. In the same year, British Airways is thought to have enhanced its revenues by $100 million and USAir by $20 million as a result of their alliance;[18] traffic gain for British Airways on code-shared routes in the mid-1990s was estimated to be around 150,000 passengers per annum. British Airways and USAir together were at that time serving over 17,000 city-pair markets, whilst United and Lufthansa together served over 18,000.[19] Market access on this scale gained through creation of a joint traffic system can obviously have a profound impact on revenues.

Cost savings

One benefit of alliances is that incremental traffic and revenue might be generated at lower unit production and marketing costs than would follow from internal expansion. This can happen where the resources of one of the parties are better utilized than would otherwise be the case and where the partners' respective presences at different ends of shared routes lower marketing communication costs below what would be necessary were either to establish 'greenfield' operations. In addition to economies of scale in respect of marketing activities and station facilities, economies of scope and density might be available - particularly where networks can be combined by means of integrated alliance hubbing. Benefits may also be reaped from joint purchasing and other shared activities.[20]

There are few forms of endeavour in which synergy is more likely to be present than in a network industry. Interest in the British Airways investment in Qantas has been concentrated on the potential for anticompetitive practices in the UK-Australia market, and on the British carrier's Pacific Rim ambitions. Less attention has been given to the long-term revenue enhancement and cost saving opportunities available from network interfaces at multiple Asian stations, at several in North America and Europe, and at two in Africa. Not all alliances are blessed with such obvious geographical synergies. Whoever decided to 'exploit' Alitalia's purchase of 30 per cent of Málev by routeing the Hungarian carrier's Budapest-New York service over Rome must have had a very personalized sense of spatial awareness.[21]

Alliance ingredients

There are as many potential ingredients in airline alliances as their architects are capable of extracting from each specific set of circumstances. The following paragraphs look at only the most common elements. They are not mutually exclusive and, indeed, are often complementary.

Equity linkages

Perhaps the most vexed question surrounds the issue of whether shareholdings are necessary. Equity investments are an element in relatively few alliances - around 15 per cent in 1997.[22] Most airlines holding equity stakes in one or more of their partners in a comprehensive alliance have also entered into separate, often but not inevitably more focused, relationships with other carriers. Much clearly depends upon the objectives and circumstances of each relationship.

When an airline has embarked on an alliance strategy as the forerunner to outright acquisition once regulatory conditions permit, equity stakes are more likely to be seen as imperative. Similarly, if two carriers are on track to merging their identities it is not surprising that they should mark the betrothal, as KLM and Northwest appeared at one time to have done. The 'trade sale' to a 'strategic investor' of a tranche of equity in a state-owned carrier undergoing privatization has been another source of shareholding linkages (e.g. British Airways/Qantas, KLM/Kenya Airways, and several examples in Latin America). Sometimes, of course, the target companies are in need of external funds; marketing alliances would not therefore be sufficient in themselves without the injection of fresh equity.

Smaller, token investments made as a symbol of commitment to pursuit of the cost and/or revenue benefits that motivate nearly all alliances are more open to question, and some airlines are on record as doubting their relevance - Cathay Pacific being one notable example. The argument is that a good agreement should stand on its own feet commercially, without needing the artificial prop of an investment or exchange of shares. There is also a question as to whether the best return open to a particularly successful carrier is likely to come from investing in a partner or reinvesting in itself. A counter-argument might be that even a token investment could pre-empt a competitor from establishing a position with the partner, although the logic underlying this view is very much open to question given actual events in the airline industry as well as in other industries.

Despite fine words and notwithstanding tangible financial benefits, even a substantial minority equity stake will not be enough to save an alliance if the management of the target airline decides to take action, either in its own interests or in the interests of the majority of shareholders, that is incompatible with the preferences of the investing partner. This was made abundantly clear in 1995 when USAir put itself on the auction block and stimulated a wave of merger speculation in the US industry that led Northwest's board to take measures alleged to have been prejudicial to the interests of KLM. These measures were widely interpreted as being intended to fend-off hostile takeovers whilst making friendly takeovers more straightforward, so raising questions about whether Northwest's executive directors were really in the airline business - and therefore the airline alliance business - for the long term, or were instead purely financial investors.

It remains to be seen whether Lufthansa will get any less out of its 'non-equity alliance' with United than KLM or British Airways, both of which paid so handsomely to buy into their relationships with Northwest and USAir respectively. United could of course dump Lufthansa if regulatory circumstances change and it prefers to fly solo into newly opened markets - much as happened when the same carrier left British Airways standing at the altar in the late-80s; but this seems improbable given the investment that would now be required, and it is anyway highly unlikely that a minority shareholding would make much difference were the 'urge to diverge' to become sufficiently strong.

A desire to change partners is perhaps these days a more credible motive for ending a comprehensive alliance but, once again, a token equity investment is not going to be allowed to get in the way. It is interesting that the British Airways-American Airlines partnership proposal provided for a significant amount of operational integration, but no immediate exchange of equity. (On the other hand, both carriers were in late 1997 considering 'symbolic' investments in Iberia to cement planned marketing agreements, and American had also by then already bought 10 per cent of Aerolines Argentinas' majority shareholder, Interinvest S.A.)

Control Clearly, control is potentially a key issue in deciding whether and how much to invest in another carrier's shares. There are broadly two ways to achieve it.

1   Through the creation of a dependency relationship founded on exploitation of the stronger partner's strategic resources and skills - its brand, reputation, sales organization, production capabilities, and management skills, for example.

2   By taking a 'controlling stake'. Majority ownership of airlines by foreign carriers or other overseas interests is still very much the exception rather than the rule, but barriers have come down within the EU and to some extent in Latin America. How large a stake of less than 51 per cent must be before it constitutes 'control' is a debatable point, but 25 per cent of Qantas - for example - offers its holder more control when the balance is held by thousands of individual investors than when it was held by the Australian government. Conversely, a 40

per cent stake in British Midland's privately owned holding company appears to have given SAS a 'right to contribute their views', but 'no right to contribute to strategic decisions'.[23]

A strong argument in favour of control rather than a balanced partnership is that a shared vision might only be as long-lasting as the management teams which share it. Once one goes, so could the vision. It is also arguable that the more closely integrated partners become, the greater is the need for at least some centralized decision-making.

Joint ventures Alliances using separately incorporated and branded joint ventures as a vehicle for cooperation between existing airlines in the delivery of air transport services are relatively rare. SAS is the oldest current example, although it has become so well-established over the last half-century that its origin as a joint venture between three national carriers is frequently overlooked. Shorouk Air, formed by Egyptair and Kuwait Airways, is another - more recent - example.

In 1993, the Alcazar joint venture linking Austrian, KLM, SAS, and Swissair narrowly failed to get off the ground. Time will tell whether this was just one of many blind alleys down which alliance-building carriers have travelled, or a valid response to the emerging European competitive environment that was simply ahead of its time.

Air transport joint ventures have been established in greater numbers between airlines and non-airline interests - for example, the clutch of charter carriers created in the late 1980s and early 1990s by North European airlines and various travel interests to serve Mediterranean vacation markets. More common still has been the sight of airlines entering into joint ventures to pursue strategies of related diversification. We saw in chapter 1 that units of Singapore Airlines have been actively pursuing joint ventures in flight catering and engineering; Cathay Pacific is using them in similar fields to position itself in China's aviation industry. An example from Europe is the Shannon Aerospace joint venture between Swissair and Lufthansa (originally including GPA as well), which offers maintenance capacity at costs up to 25 per cent lower than can be achieved by either airline partner in its home country.

Conclusion Equity stakes do not lead inevitably to blissful cooperation. The discord between Northwest and KLM has already been noted. Whilst 19.4 per cent owned by Qantas, Air New Zealand competed with its shareholder on fifth freedom routes out of Australia to Asia, secured a 50 per cent stake in the Australian carrier's primary domestic rival, and (until the appointment by Qantas of two independent directors to replace its own executives sitting on the Air New Zealand board) excluded Qantas nominees from board discussions of commercially sensitive topics. Air New Zealand also joined forces with United in 1997, rather than with

Qantas, British Airways or American (the latter already a Qantas code-sharing partner).[24]

Minority equity stakes appear to offer little benefit unless the spread of other shareholdings, and the attitudes of the target's executive management, are such that what is in absolute terms a minority position nonetheless brings with it disproportionate influence and the ability to exclude potential competitors. This appears to be the case in respect of British Airways' stake in Qantas, for example, but a slightly smaller stake in USAir did not stop that carrier putting itself into play as a potential acquisition candidate in the mid-90s or suing the British airline when its proposed linkage with American came to light.

As barriers to cross-border majority ownership come down and national sensibilities soften, carriers that see themselves in a lead role within their alliances will probably move to take majority holdings in some of their partners. However, many of the emerging comprehensive alliances have two or more relatively large carriers at their core, and in these cases who should take a majority holding in whom is likely to be a knotty problem with complex financial and political implications. It is also worth remembering the potential problems accompanying acquisitions and mergers that were mentioned earlier in the chapter.

Code-sharing

Code-sharing is the most widespread, and in revenue terms the most important, element in the majority of airline alliances - whether focused or comprehensive. It involves an aircraft operator using another airline's designator code on a flight either as well as or instead of its own; the flight numbers following each designator may be identical or different. There will usually be at least some degree of schedule alignment between partners, and in many cases this alignment is close. Code-sharing can involve passenger and/or cargo sales on a given flight.[25] The carrier whose airplane operates the flight is generally known as the 'operating partner', whilst others which simply apply their designators (and possibly contribute some cabin crew) are 'code-sharing partners'.[26] The overwhelming majority of code-sharing agreements involve just one partner in each category, but there are also a few tripartite arrangements on intercontinental routes (e.g. Austrian, Delta, and Swissair on the Vienna-Zurich-Washington route).

The most visible effect of many code-sharing arrangements is to present customers at the time of booking with the appearance of an online connection when in fact what they will be getting in most such cases is a refined version of the traditional interline connection (franchising and common branding being exceptions to this latter generalization which we will discuss shortly). Not all code-sharing involves connections, however. Three principal types of code-sharing can be identified - any one or more of which might appear in a particular code-sharing agreement, depending upon the requirements and the negotiating strengths of the airlines concerned.[27]

1   US domestic code-sharing, typified by regionals feeding majors under the larger airlines' designator codes and often not offering service under their own codes or corporate identities.[28] This type of arrangement has also spread to Europe.

2   International connection code-sharing, which involves a carrier operating flights that are sold in the local market under its own designator code and are also sold under the code of another airline with whose services they are timed to connect. Two types can be identified:
   • reciprocal: in this case, alliance partners place their respective codes on services connecting beyond one of their hubs. For example, Sabena's Brussels-Cincinnati service is code-shared with Delta and connects with US domestic flights operated by Delta which carry both the DL and SN codes. Similarly, Delta's Atlanta-Zurich service is code-shared with Swissair and connects with Swissair flights to Eastern Europe and the Middle East which carry both the DL and SR codes;
   • non-reciprocal: it is sometimes the case that whereas domestic or short-haul international connections carry the codes of both the operating partner and the long-haul code-sharing partner, the connecting long-haul flight carries only its operator's code. This is particularly likely where the alliance relationship is focused rather than comprehensive. Thus, many domestic trunk services operated by British Midland also carry the codes of long-haul carriers with whose flights they connect, but the BD code does not in general appear on those long-haul flights. Non-reciprocal code-sharing can also arise where a wider, more comprehensive alliance is balanced in favour of one of the 'partners'; during much of the period of their relationship, for example, the BA code appeared on a large number of USAir flights whilst the US code did not appear on British Airways' flights.

3   International parallel code-sharing, where two (and very occasionally three) airlines sell under their own designators space on a single flight operated by just one of them. This arrangement often, although not inevitably, involves a blocked space agreement (see below). Three types can be identified:
   • sole-service: the partners consolidate their services on a route, with only one of them operating flights. This often happens on thin routes unable to support more than one operator at frequencies satisfactory to business travellers (e.g. Delta withdrew from the

direct Budapest-New York route and replaced its presence with a Málev code-share);
- dual service: both partners operate their own flights on a route, but each code-shares on the other's services. The objective here might be to increase the number of frequencies each has available to offer for sale without physically increasing the number of flights (e.g. Malaysia Airlines and Lauda Air code-share on each others' flights between Kuala Lumpur and Vienna); and
- reciprocal parallel: the partners each operate sequential sectors on a route, but code-share over the entire route (e.g. Qantas and Canadian code-share from Sydney to Vancouver, with the former flying only Sydney-Honolulu, and the latter flying only Honolulu-Vancouver).[29]

Delta's code-sharing in mid-1997 provided examples of each type:

- US domestic: The Delta Connection, encompassing Atlantic Southeast Airlines, Business Express, Comair, and Skywest Airlines;
- international connection and/or parallel: Aer Lingus, Aéromexico, Air France, All Nippon, Austrian Airlines, China Southern, Finnair, Korean Air, Málev, Sabena, Singapore Airlines, Swissair, TAP Air Portugal, and Transbrasil.[30]

It is difficult to argue that the international partners in particular share much in the way of corporate culture or service delivery style. At the very least this example raises tricky questions about the importance of carefully managing corporate reputation and brand image, relative to the importance of simply being shown on a CRS screen to be present in a market. Whilst Delta argues that it carefully audits potential partners' operational and service standards, maintains an ongoing quality assurance programme to monitor those with which it enters into code-sharing agreements, and places at least one of its own flight attendants on partners' flights bearing the DL code, it remains a fact of life that travel experiences on each of these carriers can - for reasons attributable to both corporate and national culture, as well as service conceptualization and delivery - be very different. This is not, of course, a problem unique to Delta's code-sharing alliances.

Code-sharing agreements can either be route-specific, 'one-off' arrangements or part of a wider marketing relationship which in its most developed form aims to offer a shared service concept and brand image; de Groot refers to these as 'naked code-sharing' and 'common product code-sharing' respectively.[31] They might be constrained by antitrust/competition laws in some markets, compelling 'partners' to compete on pricing and promotion in order to sell separately space on the same flight and run their own individual risks of profit or loss. Several transatlantic alliances have been granted substantial immunity from US antitrust laws, however. The practical effect of immunity is that the partners are able to cooperate closely on capacity fixing, scheduling, marketing communications, pricing, commission levels, net fares, and frequent flyer mileage awards, for example; in other words, they are able to sell jointly out of a shared inventory. Delta, Austrian, Sabena, and Swissair, for instance, have established - under the name 'Atlantic Excellence' - a revenue pool and commonly managed seat inventory (as opposed to fixed quotas) on their code-shared transatlantic routes; the four essentially act as one in the pricing and selling of transatlantic space (subject to 'carve-outs' in respect of time-sensitive local traffic on certain inter-hub routes, which are not immunized from antitrust restrictions). The advantage as far as pricing is concerned, for example, is that joint fares can be introduced quickly in response to market dynamics, rather than having to be formally negotiated as arms-length pro-rate agreements.

Four primary motivations behind code-sharing have been identified, with incremental profits the ultimate goal:[32]

- to increase traffic (and, hopefully, revenues) by expanding onto new routes and/or deepening service on existing routes;
- to contain capacity growth, thereby holding down production costs and supporting load factors;
- to safeguard traffic rights, as when a strong international carrier is compelled to code-share with a weaker national airline which either does not want, or is unable, to participate in a particular 3rd/4th freedom market; and
- to remain competitive, by drawing into the partners' combined networks traffic which would otherwise flow through competing networks, and by improving the quality of service (e.g. by offering through check-ins, shared terminals and lounges, and access to wider FFP benefits).[33]

There are downsides, however. In US domestic and some international connection code-sharing arrangements it is possible for partners - particularly those operating short-haul routes - to have their yields put under pressure both by pro-rate deals balanced in favour of the partner competing in lower yielding (but perhaps more profitable) long-haul markets and by the periodic fare wars which tend to erupt between larger airlines in competitive markets.[34]

Code-sharing deals contain many standard elements, but each is nonetheless unique; where the balance of benefits lies will depend in large measure upon the partners' relative strengths and negotiating skills. Thus, in return for a $400 million investment in cash-strapped USAir in 1993, British Airways was able to negotiate a highly favourable deal which gave it a preponderance of the benefits accruing out of the arrangement.[35]

Something else that needs to be borne in mind is projection of the code-sharing partner's corporate identity. This might require the presence of that partner's staff and/or signage at different points in the service delivery process and be reflected in the phrasing (possibly also the language) of terminal and inflight announcements. Code-sharing partners sometimes place one or two of their own cabin staff onto flights either to establish a visible presence in the aircraft generally, or to identify and serve their own premium passengers in particular. This practice raises issues in respect of:

- labour relations (e.g. duty-times, inflight rest procedures on long-haul sectors, and whether the staff should fly in addition to or instead of the operating partner's cabin attendants will have to be agreed);
- service standards (e.g. service levels and procedures are likely to differ between partners until such time as they have a common product to offer consumers);
- safety standards (e.g. the operating partner's national authorities may mandate safety procedures in respect of aircraft on their registries which differ from those applied to the same type by the code-sharing partner's authorities); and
- costs (e.g. additional training is required for the code-sharing partner's staff in respect of service and safety procedures on the operating partner's aircraft).

Code-sharing: the aeropolitical and competition issues

International regulatory issues Whilst some governments take a relatively relaxed view on airlines' freedom to enter into code-sharing agreements, others insist that code-sharing partners must either have existing traffic rights in markets where their codes are displayed for sale or obtain explicit authorization. The United States takes the latter position. Thus, the path-breaking KLM/Northwest code-sharing arrangement was made possible by the 1992 United States-Netherlands open skies bilateral; when the United States enters into an open skies agreement, carriers from the other country are given authority to serve any US city and so are free to enter wide-ranging code-shares with US airlines. British Airways/USAir code-sharing in the US domestic market, on the other hand, was allowable because of a limited quid pro quo already negotiated by the United Kingdom in return for granting American and United access to Heathrow in 1991. Neither British Airways nor KLM was exploiting generally available rights. The European Union has yet to adopt a formal position on intra-EU code-sharing (external code-sharing still in principle being within the authority of individual member states unless it affects the internal market), but it does have the power to review agreements within the context of competition laws.

Elsewhere in the world the regulatory position remains variable and ill-defined. What is generally true, however, is that having initially been considered primarily a marketing device, code-sharing has in recent years moved onto the agenda for bilateral negotiations. It has been put there in particular by US disputes with both the United Kingdom and Germany in the early-90s, and by the objections of some third countries (initially including Germany) to Northwest's designator code appearing on KLM services beyond Amsterdam to points in Europe and the Middle East.

A minority of governments now see code-sharing as a quasi-traffic right, arguing that it can provide to designated carriers market access in excess of agreed bilateral limitations and to undesignated carriers access into markets which they have no current right to enter. Future bargaining positions could be eroded, according to this view, were foreign carriers to obtain market access through code-sharing without their governments first having to come to the negotiating table and offer something in return. The counter-argument is that the only flights physically operated are those which have been bilaterally agreed, and all code-sharing does is channel traffic onto certain of those flights.

What matters in practice, however, is less the merit of either argument than the reality that potential bargaining chips are difficult to resist. Thus, fifth freedom transatlantic rights beyond the United Kingdom for Singapore Airlines became inextricably bound-up in negotiations between Australia and Singapore in 1996 and 1997 because the Australian government wanted, amongst other objectives, to secure code-sharing rights for British Airways and Qantas over Singapore.[36]

The trouble is - as two major US research reports pointed out in the mid-90s[37] - that the people doing the bargaining often do not know precisely what the chip is worth in terms of revenues gained by code-sharers and lost by their competitors. Benefits can become particularly obscure when code-sharing is only one part of a wider menu of cooperative arrangements set within the context of a comprehensive alliance. But benefits are certainly available. For example, relaxation of the UK-Australia bilateral in 1996 permitted a wider variety of routeings between the two via third countries (subject to the terms of bilaterals with those countries) and allowed Australian carriers to code-share through the United States; whilst the British Airways/Qantas alliance benefitted as well, the agreement marked a major breakthrough for Ansett's ambitions to extend its small international network.[38] Similarly, Delta's efforts to inaugurate code-sharing with All Nippon beyond Japan and into Asia during the mid-90s was an important attempt to gain indirect fifth freedom rights, so circumventing the problem it faced as an 'MOU carrier' not holding these rights under the prevailing US-Japan bilateral.[39]

Competition issues Code-sharing can add competition to a market in which otherwise only a traditional interline agreement would be competing against one or more established nonstop, direct or online connecting services. This can be extended from competition in an individual market to encompass network competition; British Midland, for example, is on record as wanting to create through its code-sharing partnerships 'a clear alternative to the British Airways network'. Code-sharing can also permit flights to be operated, or frequencies to be increased, in a market which otherwise would not support the same level of service; indeed, the additional supply of output might even stimulate traffic and, perhaps, lead to the eventual entry of new competitors.

Code-sharing can improve other aspects of service quality by facilitating or encouraging, for example:

- integrated scheduling, ideally leading to more connections and/or reduced layovers;
- through-check-in and baggage interlining;
- connections to proximate gates within the same terminal buildings at hubs or interchange points;
- shared lounges;
- joint tour products;
- reciprocity between frequent flyer programmes; and
- lower joint fares resulting from competition to serve individual city-pair markets over alternative network routeings.

Of course, most of the benefits just listed are - or could be - made available through commercial arrangements or interline agreements without the inclusion of code-sharing. But code-sharing is open to more far-reaching criticisms, the most important of which are its anticompetitive potential and the possible deception of consumers.

1 Anticompetitive potential. There are two principal issues.
- International parallel code-sharing in particular can remove competition or the prospect of competition from a market if two or more established or potential competitors decide to combine their offers onto a single code-shared service. Even dual-service parallel code-sharing can be anticompetitive. Competition laws are used by the authorities in some countries to ensure that the 'partners' continue to compete across those dimensions of the marketing mix which still remain open to competition, but the effect of such measures has to be doubted. Service design competition in respect of attributes such as schedule, frequency, and inflight amenities is removed by definition. Whilst competition in pricing and marketing communications should still be present, it stretches credulity to believe that airlines which have entered into agreements specifically casting each other as 'partners' will - other than in exceptional circumstances - go to war in order to unload seats on a shared airplane.[40]
  In principle, much might depend upon the terms of the bilateral between the countries concerned. A liberal or open skies bilateral permitting new competitors to enter a market against two former competitors which decide to code-share raises less of a prima facie

competition issue than would be the case were the two code-sharers each the sole carrier designated by their respective governments under a highly restrictive, protectionist bilateral. In reality, the fact that a market is contestable from a regulatory perspective might not make it economically contestable if, for example, one end is slot-constrained (e.g. London Heathrow) or if the origin and destination are hubs dominated by the code-sharers, with both carriers having sufficient network strength at their respective hubs to make market entry a sporty prospect (e.g. Brussels and Atlanta).

It is, of course, arguable that this is a problem that largely concerns local O and D traffic on code-shared nonstops between the partners' hubs rather than through-traffic, because the latter often benefits from the presence of alternative routeings over competing hubs. Where local traffic between two hubs is insignificant (e.g. Zurich and Cincinnati) the problem may indeed not be particularly acute because most inter-hub passengers are flow-traffic that could in many cases readily use competing connections offered by other networks; but competition issues loom larger where local inter-hub traffic density is very much greater (e.g. Frankfurt and Copenhagen) and there is no alternative that offers a similar level of service (i.e. nonstop) between the two hubs.[41]

It can also sometimes happen that a small carrier flying into a large airline's 'fortress hub' and in need of both onward connections to offer arriving passengers and feed to boost outbound traffic has little practical alternative other than to code-share with the dominant carrier - which is the only one able to offer the required range of connections over that hub. Several Latin American carriers serving Miami, for example, have been obliged by circumstances such as these to come to terms with American Airlines' dominance there by code-sharing with what would otherwise have been their primary competitor on the international sector in and out of the gateway.

- Code-shared flights can distort distribution channels. Some CRSs have algorithms which treat code-shared connections as being online, and so give them display preference over interline connections irrespective of elapsed journey time. (In Europe both the EU and ECAC CRS codes of conduct - the former mandatory, the latter only discretionary - prohibit the favouring of online or code-shared connections; in the United States major CRSs also follow this neutral practice in respect of international - but not necessarily domestic - markets. The situation elsewhere in the world varies.) Another problem is that multiple listings of the same code-shared flights under their different designators can be used to push competing services away from the top of the first CRS display screen - which is where most travel agency bookings come from.

(Again, limits have been placed on such 'screen padding' in Europe.)

2   Deception of consumers. An airline's designator code on a flight tells a customer what to expect in terms of service quality. Leading airlines spend hundreds of millions of dollars each year designing, branding, and promoting their services to ensure that this is the case. When a customer buys service based on that designator but finds herself exposed to a different standard offered by another service provider, without being made aware this would happen, she has been deceived. Problems most frequently arise when the operating partner offers standards below those marketed by the code-sharing partner. But even where this is not the case, there is still an important matter of principle at stake. A not insignificant additional source of problems is the confusion that can arise when passengers holding tickets bearing the designator of a code-sharing partner do not appreciate that they should be checking-in at the terminal and desks used by the operating partner. Finally, there is scope for confusion in respect of which carrier is liable to consumers should there be an accident or some lesser incident.

Airlines in general voice the opinion that code-sharing seems not to be an issue that greatly troubles consumers and, if it were, the marketplace would impose its own sanctions on carriers choosing to enter partnerships with airlines that are significantly weaker in terms of service or safety.[42] They might also argue by analogy that somebody buying bottles of Coca-Cola in different countries receives essentially the same product irrespective of the fact that each is produced and bottled locally.[43] This analogy could be defensible in the case of common product code-sharing, but such arrangements remain a small minority of total code-sharing deals. Air transport consumers have a right to be concerned with the not inconsiderable chance in many other cases of finding 'tap-water' in the bottle. The particular nature of what is an image-sensitive industry makes this promiscuity with their reputations potentially dangerous for airlines.

In the mid-1990s the problem of consumer deception was addressed in the United States by a notice of proposed rule-making on code-sharing (designed to strengthen rules first introduced in 1985), and in Europe by a ten-point code of conduct proposed by British Midland and a code of conduct drafted under the auspices of ECAC. At the heart of each was an imperative to inform customers in advance of travel about the identities of airlines actually operating each sector of their journeys. The British Midland proposal went further by addressing possible incompatibilities in service delivery standards.

Conclusions With regard to its anticompetitive consequences, the impact of code-sharing will clearly depend upon who would have been in the market without it, who is left there because of it, and how intensely the remaining competitors set about competing. There appears to be insufficient data available with which to reliably assess either the effect of code-sharing upon fares in the short term, or whether in the long term such arrangements reduce or increase competition (thereby leading in principle to higher or lower fares).[44]

However, there is certainly no proven case that global network alliances using extensive code-sharing to compete in open skies environments will inevitably be conducive to the interests of consumers. The effect of each of these alliances needs to be considered not within the generalized context often presented by their proponents, who picture competitive battles being waged between network carriers across some imprecisely defined global marketplace, but in the context of specific individual markets - assessed in terms of their size, whether real opportunities exist for other network airlines or for niche carriers to enter, and the availability of viable alternative routeings. It is in this latter context that opponents objected so sharply to the likely outcome of American Airlines' massive effort in 1996 and 1997 to establish dominance in certain transatlantic and Latin American markets in concert with potential partners as diverse as British Airways, the Taca group,[45] BWIA, Air Aruba, Avianca, TAM, LanChile and Aerolineas Argentinas. The presence of American and each of its partners on key routes between the United States and their respective countries (specifically, routes from New York to London in the British Airways case and from Miami in the other cases) would be so dominant, it was argued, that notwithstanding the existence of open skies agreements (which in some cases had yet to be negotiated) the markets would be too concentrated to allow significant challengers to develop meaningful presences.

As far as the potential for consumer deception is concerned, the case is much clearer. Consumers are exposed to deception unless the partners to a code-sharing arrangement have essentially merged their products, and even then an overall level of service associated with a large airline operating jets might not easily be carried over onto thin, short-haul routes flown by turboprops. Point-of-sale disclosure is one possible answer, but few observers consider it at this time to be better than inconsistent in practice. In fairness, the problem appears more often to lie with distributors than airlines themselves. 'Disclosure' might anyway not always disclose very much - as in the United States, where some reservations media list regionals not as separately identifiable airlines but under the generic network name of their associated major (e.g. Northwest Airlink).

Code-sharing is not inevitably to a consumer's disadvantage; few people booking on Delta and finding themselves travelling on Swissair would feel mightily aggrieved by differential service levels. The issue here is whether somebody buying 'Coke' from an airline has a right to find 'Coke' in the bottle - irrespective of how good the '7-Up' actually in it might be.[46] In other cases, consumers could have much more specific cause for complaint. Some Japanese passengers, for example, have booked on All Nippon and found themselves instead on foreign airlines carrying only a token number of Japanese-speaking cabin crew - partly a reflection of All Nippon's strategy in the early 1990s of code-sharing its way into international markets, in response to Japan's sluggish economy and Narita's slot shortage.

Airlines clearly see significant potential benefits in code-sharing. Such benefits are likely to be at their most attractive when code-sharing takes place within the framework of a wider marketing alliance which - unfettered by competition laws - facilitates a 'virtual operational merger', creating a fully integrated multi-hub system. As far as consumers are concerned, the benefits will depend on circumstances in individual markets and the risk of deception is always present. In approving various applications for code-sharing between US and foreign carriers, the US Department of Transportation has found the arrangements in question to be in the interests of consumers. However questionable some of these judgements might have been in individual cases, consumers' interests were at least ostensibly a major point of reference in the evaluations. Several other governments, in contrast, appear to be more concerned about code-sharing partners posing as holders of traffic rights they have not been awarded than about them posing as the providers of services they do not in fact provide.

Block-spacing

Code-sharing is often effected on a 'free-sale' basis, under which the code-sharing partner pays a price for each seat taken from the operating partner's inventory - a price that will vary depending upon the negotiated rate for the booking class concerned. There would be no commitment to take a specific number of seats on each flight. An important point whenever yield management remains the sole responsibility of the operating partner is agreement on the overbooking policy, mismanagement of which could have negative consequences for the code-sharing partner's reputation.

Alternatively, code-sharing agreements might involve block-spacing. In a blocked-space arrangement, the code-sharing partner buys an agreed number of seats on the operating partner's flights (at a price below free sale) and sells them under its own designator from a separate inventory. Arrangements might cover every available class on the flight to provide the purchaser with its required traffic mix, and they might also allow the purchaser to take more than its minimum commitment whenever demand merits or possibly even to give back some unused seats (a 'modified blocked space' arrangement). An interesting example is the 1996 agreement through which Sabena wet-leased Virgin Express B737-300s to operate services between Brussels and London Heathrow; under this agreement, not only did Sabena have the right to take its seat allocation over 50 per cent if required, but it alone was to sell business class space on the aircraft - Virgin Express preferring to remain focused on its low-fare/no-frills competitive strategy.[47]

The advantage to the seller is that it has a proportion of its capacity 'underwritten' by guaranteed sales to the partner; this might be sufficient to justify an increase in frequency, which in turn might lead ultimately to a larger market share. Against this is the fact that the sale will be at 'wholesale' prices, which implies that the seller may lose revenue if any of its own traffic gets displaced into the partner's block. This could occur where the partners continue to compete on price and promotion, and also because their respective networks behind the origin and beyond the destination of the code-shared flight might offer different benefits to consumers. It can therefore sometimes be the case that there are fewer potential sources of conflict between the partners in a variable price free-sale agreement than in a fixed price blocked-space deal.

Cargo output can also be sold under blocked-space arrangements. A relatively extreme example is Sabena's decision in 1997 to sell its entire cargo output that year to Swissair.

Blocked-space agreements are a relatively common feature of code-sharing, and can be particularly useful where partners do not have the necessary immunity from competition laws (where applicable) to allow them to manage their seat inventories jointly. (Block-spacing can also arise outside the context of alliance arrangements and code-sharing, of course; for example, a European airline with a service terminating in Singapore might want to secure space for its interline passengers travelling to and from Australia on another carrier's heavily booked flights by entering into blocked-space agreements with that carrier between Singapore and points in Australia and vice-versa.)

Joint services

Whereas under a blocked-space arrangement each carrier independently manages its own allocated space, yield management for a joint service is undertaken by one carrier acting for both or by both acting together. Inventories on joint services can be jointly priced and promoted, in which case the partners are not competing against each other. Joint services generally require either a revenue-sharing agreement (based on some level of assumed costs attributed to the operating partner) or a cost- and revenue-sharing agreement. Some states consider them to be essentially the same as code-sharing agreements, whereas others maintain a distinction founded on the existence of cost- and revenue-sharing. They are frequently frowned upon by competition laws, which is one reason why antitrust immunity has had to be sought for the transatlantic alliances mentioned above. As was discussed in chapter 4 of Volume One, the European Commission is in the process of trying to wrest from member governments the authority required to give it competence to act in respect of routes outside the EU; its current position as far as intra-EU joint services are concerned is embodied in a block exemption granted in 1993, which permits them only in the case of new, thin routes operated by 'small or medium-sized' airlines.

Franchising

Franchising is an alliance strategy which can be pursued in conjunction with an airline's own operations, those of its subsidiaries, and also in tandem with looser code-sharing agreements. It involves a substantial carrier with a strong brand (the 'franchisor') licensing to a franchisee the use of that brand, the associated service concept, and aspects of the service delivery process. The franchisee will be a separate corporate entity in which the franchisor may or may not hold an equity interest.[48] The franchisee typically pays a front-end licensing fee and an ongoing royalty for use of the brand, the sizes of which will to some extent depend on the balance of benefits each party anticipates from the relationship. Franchisees might also either choose or be obliged to use various services provided by the franchisor for which they make separate payments - including possibly brand advertising, training, traffic handling, reservations, sales, inventory control, yield management, revenue accounting, and management services.

The use of reservations and revenue accounting support is frequently compulsory. These and other services are sometimes provided at a level of sophistication in excess of what is needed by a regional airline and, despite usually being sold 'at cost' and perhaps benefitting from economies of scale, the price could be well in excess of what it would cost the franchisee were it to undertake the same work inhouse. Distribution costs will also tend to be relatively high because most major airlines (i.e. franchisors) require a presence in all the largest CRSs at the highest levels of functionality available. Finally, it is quite likely that the major will have product standards that impose additional service delivery costs on the franchisee.

Most commonly to date it is corporate brand identities which have been franchised into sub-brands - such as British Airways into British Airways Express, Lufthansa into Team Lufthansa (inaugurated with franchisee Augsburg Airways in 1996) or Delta into The Delta Connection. Franchising does not always involve creation of a sub-brand, however; late in 1996, for example, Air France franchised Jersey European to operate two BAe 146-100s in Air France logo from London Heathrow to Toulouse and Lyons.[49] Similarly, British Airways franchisees Maersk Air, British Mediterranean Airways, and GB Airways operate under the corporate master-brand because they offer the same levels of service (i.e. the Club Europe and Euro Traveller sub-brands) as does the mainline operation on short- and medium-haul flights; in contrast, the regional carriers doing business as British Airways Express each offer only a single class, and so are separately identified using the 'Express' sub-brand. An early example of a sub-brand itself being franchised was the licensing by British Airways of its Club World and World Traveller identities for use by USAir on transatlantic flights to Paris and Frankfurt.

Benefits and risks for franchisors In return for little or no up-front investment, a franchisor will generate revenue from the licensing of its brand. Depending upon the extent of network complementarity, the franchisor might also gain incremental revenue from traffic feed. Indeed, this is often one of the franchisor's primary objectives. British Airways estimated that in 1996-7 its franchise operations were already generating approximately £75 million in incremental revenue. Franchisors are in addition able to extend awareness of their brand identities into markets where either they have no traffic rights or - more usually to date - no ability to offer service given their cost and fleet structures relative to the demand characteristics of the markets concerned; this is typically the case with franchised feeder services, for example. Franchising to a non-controlled franchisee may offer a way around structural cost problems which, because of labour agreements, the major airline would face were it to control the operation. United, for example, has been limited by agreements with its pilots requiring the airline's wage rates be applied to flight crew at controlled affiliates. In practice, the balance of franchisor benefits as between traffic feed (i.e. using a franchisee to operate what would otherwise be uneconomic routes) and simple fee generation will vary from situation to situation; much will depend on potential network synergies.

Awareness of a major's brand created by a franchised operation in an area where the major is not strongly represented might translate into brand loyalty when customers from that regional airline's catchment area face a choice between the major and a competitor on medium- or long-haul journeys. This is particularly likely if the regional and major share a frequent flyer programme. Franchisors can in this way leverage their systemwide resources and skills to create revenue-generating intangible assets. Nonetheless, brands should in general only be franchised into regions where there is at least a basic pre-existing level of brand equity, and franchising should always be part of a coherent regional strategy.

It is also possible that franchising on a significant scale could generate sufficient incremental business for some of the franchisor's functional units that their retention inhouse can be justified as an alternative to outsourcing - assuming that outsourcing is under consideration.

Apart from the dangers of poor franchisee service quality (which includes operating standards as well as customer service) or clashes between geographically contiguous franchisees, both of which can be addressed contractually, there are few downside risks for franchisors. One risk is the implication for the major's reputation were a franchisee to collapse financially. Less dramatic but still potentially damaging is the possibility that franchisors might face labour relations problems were franchises to be perceived by their unions as a form of low-cost flight operations outsourcing.[50] Finally, wherever a franchisee represents a corporate master-brand but offers a diluted product, as opposed to separately branding that product as a distinct sub-brand, the risk of failing to meet consumers' expectations with regard to brand consistency is very real.

Benefits and risks for franchisees Franchisees expect to gain revenue from the marketing communications and distribution power of their partner, from network synergies, a strengthened image, and from customer loyalty built on stronger branding and participation in an attractive frequent flyer programme. Cost savings could be available through joint purchasing and certain economies of scale, and technical assistance can also be valuable. In light of globalization and industry concentration, cynics might argue that the outstanding benefit of a franchise from the franchisee's perspective is likely to be survival. Even carriers for which survival is not in doubt can benefit enormously from association with a strong, well-managed brand; for example, London Gatwick-based CityFlyer Express doubled its annual boardings (to 500,000) within a year of becoming the first franchisee to operate with the British Airways Express brand identity.[51]

Against these benefits and aside from any financial costs attributable to fees, services, and management reporting requirements, franchisees - particularly when they are existing carriers rather than start-ups - must weigh several disadvantages. Most notable is the loss of an independent identity in their markets, which might be irrecoverable were the franchise agreement to be terminated.[52] Another challenge can be the loss of traffic feed from other carriers. This is not a serious problem for most branded regionals in the United States (not all of which can strictly be considered franchisees anyway, being in some cases wholly-owned subsidiaries), because they typically interchange as much as 70 or 80 per cent of their traffic with the major airlines whose brands they use.[53] In Europe and elsewhere, franchisees often depend on a more balanced mix of local O and D traffic, intraline connections (with the franchisor), and interline connections - and it is the latter that can be threatened. Furthermore, 'intraline' traffic feeding the franchisor will probably be subject to a negotiated pro-rate agreement, and so will generate lower yields than O and D traffic and perhaps even than ordinary interline traffic - depending, in the latter case, on the terms of any interline agreements with other carriers outside the alliance. Conversely, there might be times when the franchisee wants to cut fares but is constrained from doing so; at least one European major has been known to apply pressure in this respect.

Because franchisors are generally large airlines with slower decision-making processes than are customary at smaller franchisees, gaining approval for initiatives that bear on the product (including network planning) or the brand identity can sometimes be frustrating for a franchisee. Finally, some franchisees might be pressured by their staff for pay and benefits closer to those available from the franchisor - which could undermine the cost advantages offered by most smaller airlines in the thin markets they are franchised to serve.

Benefits and risks for consumers   When a franchisor franchises and carefully monitors the use of a strong brand image, franchising has the potential to offer consumers standards close to those offered by the franchisor in its own operations - subject always to limitations imposed by equipment type. By offering a fully-branded and quality-controlled product, franchising is likely to be better able to meet consumer expectations than is naked code-sharing.

Often, though, the consumer pays handsomely for the benefits offered by high-cost/high-fare branded products, especially in uncontested point-to-point markets. Particularly on thin regional routes, the danger that small, independent carriers will be overwhelmed by the network strengths of franchised competitors is a very real threat to competition. It is a threat which crystallized in the United States during the 1980s, is in the process of crystallizing in the United Kingdom where British Airways has used franchising effectively to extend its dominant position in domestic markets, and which is likely to spread throughout Europe as the objections of politicians and organized labour are gradually overcome. There has, however, been little outward sign of concern from regulators.

The counter-argument might be that such markets would anyway support no more than one operator or, alternatively, that without network synergies available as a result of the franchise relationship no service at all would be economically feasible. On the other hand, were a market in fact able to support competition it is quite possible that entry would be deterred where the sole incumbent is a franchisee of a major brand. Thus, an aspiring UK regional start-up will likely be less inclined to launch service head-to-head against CityFlyer doing business as British Airways Express than against CityFlyer selling under its own name.

The future of airline franchising   Franchising could have a big future ahead of it in the airline industry. Providing control issues can be resolved, locally owned and licensed franchisees might be a route into domestic markets for carriers denied cabotage rights (e.g. British Airways' franchising of long-established South African carrier Comair); it can also be a way for a global carrier (or alliance) to generate short- and medium-haul feed for its various hubs and interchange points around the world and to serve larger O and D markets that are untenable given its mainline cost structure. Indeed, some combination of equity ownership and brand franchising might turn out to be the best means for emerging megacarriers to 'think globally and act locally' as the industry transitions to the next stage of its development.

On the other hand, we will discuss in chapters 7 and 8 the problems of ensuring service consistency in a delivery system which although technology-intensive can involve multiple and prolonged social interactions between customers and staff. Given the difficulty some airlines have maintaining consistency of service within their existing operations and national cultural settings, it remains to be seen whether air transport really will lend itself as readily as hamburgers to the cross-border selling of systematized service delivery systems.

Conclusion on revenue-side initiatives

In looking at common elements in airline alliances we have so far concentrated on the issue of equity investment and on techniques intended to enhance revenues, such as code-sharing, blocked-space agreements, joint operations, and franchising. Revenue enhancement can come from gaining access to markets closed by bilateral and other restrictions to either direct operations or to investment in a local airline, or closed by virtue of fleet or cost structures inappropriate to the density and characteristics of the demand being accessed; it can also come from the deeper penetration into existing markets facilitated by dual-service parallel code-sharing. Common to these techniques - particularly in the context of a comprehensive alliance - are the needs to integrate network and revenue management, as far as is legally permissible, and to ensure that both the network being marketed and the capacity provider generating the output benefit whenever the two are different entities.

Cooperation on the revenue side can, in fact, encompass the full range of marketing activities - subject to whatever limitations are imposed by local antitrust/competition laws. Even where fully integrated network management is not achieved, a properly functioning alliance may nonetheless lead to substantially increased interline traffic flows between the partners on routes that are not code-shared.

Cost management initiatives

Benefits from some of these joint activities are also felt on the cost side, particularly where marketing economies of scale and economies of scope are available. By feeding traffic into an existing network, code-sharing can help to raise densities and reduce unit production costs. Furthermore, a marketing and code-sharing alliance might allow the code-sharing partner to stop flying inefficient tag-end sectors; United has been able to cut costs in this way by replacing services out of London to Germany with a Lufthansa code-share, and intra-Hawaiian legs beyond Honolulu with an Aloha code-share. Network management through code-sharing can therefore lead to new and more efficient forms of service to existing points as well as to the addition of new points. An alliance may also enable a carrier to benefit, in respect of marketing and sales effectiveness, from the 'reach' of a partner that is stronger in a particular regional or national market.

Cooperation could in principle be targeted at any area of functional or geographical overlap, although industrial relations can be an issue where jobs are threatened. Branding might also be an issue. For example, when long-haul aircraft have extended turnarounds at outbound destinations where two partners' networks meet (e.g. the US West Coast in respect of Qantas and British Airways), it might be possible for utilization to be raised by interchanging them (e.g. using a Qantas aircraft to continue beyond the West Coast by flying a British Airways route to London, or using a British Airways aircraft to continue beyond the West Coast in the other direction by flying a Qantas route to Australia). (At the time of writing, British Airways already has an application pending with the UK CAA to use Qantas aircraft during their layovers at London Heathrow.) Local traffic on the respective airlines would, however, be exposed to an inflight service environment incompatible with the brand it had bought into - although the incompatibility would be no worse, and could be somewhat less, than is the case in respect of naked code-sharing. The obvious answer is common service environments, which may require changes in certain aspects of one or both parties' corporate images as communicated inside their airplanes.

Efforts oriented specifically towards cost savings are a feature of most comprehensive alliances. They include **shared activities** (both marketing and operational) intended to increase resource and skill utilization and reduce duplication, and also **joint purchasing** of significant inputs such as insurance, fuel, catering, aircraft spares, and in some cases even aircraft themselves. For example, Delta, Singapore Airlines, and Swissair established a joint purchasing operation; within the context of its 'Focus 2000' cost-cutting and revenue enhancement project launched in 1996 and already mentioned in chapter 4, KLM established a joint purchasing programme along with some of its partners under the name 'Mercurious'; Swissair, Sabena, and Austrian have jointly ordered A330-200s. To help move material out of rather than into their respective maintenance organizations, SAS and Lufthansa have formed SAS/Lufthansa Technik Surplus Sales Alliance. SAS and Lufthansa have also been cooperating closely in pursuit of greater efficiencies in the marketing and delivery of their respective cargo products, and overall cooperation between the two airlines was expected to have saved Lufthansa $60 million in 1997.[54]

Again, it is worth noting that formal alliances are not an essential ingredient of cooperative cost saving efforts. Rotables, high-value aircraft components which are overhauled rather than consumed in use or discarded after use, are frequently pooled; competitors often pool ground-handling equipment at outstations where they are permitted to self-handle, as Air France, British Airways, and KLM have done for many years at Bangkok. There is nothing particularly significant about alliances in this respect; to be significant their contributions to cost saving have to be wide-ranging and systematized.

The potential for alliances

Alliances offer many potential advantages, but there must be synergies there to exploit in the first place - whether in terms of geography, vision and corporate culture, or operations. Sometimes clear and specific objectives are missing, and competitive advantage is nowhere on the screen; this was the case when Air France bought into CSA and Alitalia invested in Málev, both strategies motivated more by a combination of national foreign policy objectives and the momentum of the industry's alliance 'bandwagon' than by clear assessments of who was offering what to whom. On other occasions an alliance might not be relevant to the particular challenges facing one of its partners at a given point in time. In 1993, Chile's two leading passenger carriers were each aligned with separate high-profile European partners, SAS in the case of LanChile and Iberia in the case of Ladeco. The European airlines had their own fairly acute difficulties, and neither could anyway do much to deal with the common problem threatening the future of the Chilean airlines: deployment by US carriers (notably American) of large amounts of additional capacity into markets which accounted for 40 per cent and 25 per cent of LanChile's and Ladeco's respective system revenues at the time.

Furthermore, alliances may not always be able to fulfill their entire economic potential. Although they can be used to sidestep the nationality clauses in bilateral air services agreements, which are amongst the most important limiting factor in respect of cross-border mergers and acquisitions, they cannot necessarily sidestep competition laws. Thus, depending upon the jurisdictions involved and the extent to which the partners would otherwise be competitors, there might be constraints on the freedom of those partners to engage in coordinated network planning, joint pricing and yield management, or integrated marketing. This is the case in both the United States and the EU for example, albeit subject to possible exemptions as we have seen.

Choosing the right partner can be difficult. It requires at least the following steps.

1   Definition of alliance objectives. For example, one carrier might rate the ability of a potential partner to inject additional capital into its balance sheet as a key criterion, whereas another might be more concerned about network synergies, improved access to distribution channels, or the opportunity to gain management expertise; potential partners will usually have their own specific objectives, and these need to be mutually compatible.

2   Evaluation and ranking of feasible candidates on the basis of general
     compatibility, prospective benefits, and likelihood of success.

3   Detailed analysis and ranking of shortlisted candidates in respect of:
     • their business profiles (e.g. financials, output, tangible and
       intangible resources, skills, and management); and
     • the gains to be anticipated from an alliance involving each (e.g.
       traffic, revenue, yields, costs).[55]

Once the selection hurdle has been cleared and an agreement has been
structured, the management skills - particularly the attitudes towards
control and decision-making - necessary to develop the relationship may or
may not be available. Focus is likely to turn inwards as systems and
procedures are interfaced and, at least in part, integrated. Disputes are
inevitable - in respect of scheduling, cost allocations, and fees for services
sold by one partner to another, for example. Different corporate and
national cultures can raise barriers to cooperation, as can a lack of
harmony in compensation schemes, career aspirations, and motivational
frames of reference amongst the people who have to make alliances work
in practice. Uncertainties regarding where job losses brought about by
rationalization of activities will fall may also create mistrust. This all takes
expensive management time to sort out. Furthermore, alliance
partnerships, perhaps even more than mergers, may involve an ongoing
and potentially open-ended commitment to negotiate even relatively minor
details.

When an alliance is narrow and focused, failure to fulfill expectations
might not matter greatly. For example, American and Cathay Pacific went
their separate ways after a code-sharing deal over Los Angeles to Hong
Kong failed to meet the US carrier's expectations. A tie-up between Asiana
and Lauda Air was also abandoned in the mid-90s, and there have been
many other possible examples.

The breakdown of arrangements which are or are intended to be
comprehensive can be more damaging, at least in the short term. British
Airways found out only from media reports that its partner in an extensive
marketing alliance was shortly to become its biggest transatlantic
competitor; United's strategic circumstances changed when it decided to
seize an opportunity to buy Pan Am's routes into London Heathrow and
the alliance with British Airways (which had already participated in a
failed buy-out of United) became irrelevant. Any joint venturer in any
industry can potentially be at risk from giving up knowledge of its markets
to, or basing future marketing plans on, a partner who later becomes a
competitor. The closer an alliance and the higher each party's switching
costs are raised by integration, the less likely this is to happen.

Alliances remain potentially transitory in the absence of corporate
integration, yet a great deal of trust is required to forgo independence,

combine service delivery processes and, particularly, commit core competencies to a common endeavour. Where such an endeavour is a cross-border partnership, the Chicago system anyway remains a blocking factor standing in the way of total integration. This blockage will eventually be removed from many markets, but how soon, how extensively, and with what outcome is not yet clear. In the meantime, alliances will continue to grow in importance as the industry restructures and, in due course, they will become more stable than was the case during the early waves of relationship-building in the late 1980s and the first half of the 1990s. As comprehensive alliances stabilize, attention will broaden from network management to encompass process integration and, on the revenue side, franchising and co-branding.

Whether or not alliances are indeed waypoints en route to widespread cross-border mergers once the Chicago system has evolved to accommodate such developments, the bandwagon is not one that will roll smoothly. Anybody doubting this need only consider the national rivalries which still permeate SAS - by far the industry's most successful alliance - and which periodically surface in the politicization of issues such as where to perform maintenance work (as when B737-600s were introduced into the fleet, for example).

Requirements for successful comprehensive alliances

Whether the airline industry is to see a shifting kaleidoscope of focused alliances, a small number of comprehensive alliances formed as precursors to eventual merger, or a combination of forms, it is clear that the phenomenon will remain an important structural feature for several years to come. As far as long-term comprehensive (as opposed to possibly shorter-term, focused) alliances are concerned, most if not all of the following must be present for there to be any real chance of success.

1   Strategic symmetry: partners should have the same broad types of vision, mission, and high-level objectives. This symmetry should feed through into mutually compatible service concepts and brand images. Symmetry has been lacking in a number of airline alliances, some of which appear to have been built less upon the exploitation of capabilities than the overcoming of shared weaknesses in cost structure or market position.

2   Complementary capabilities: strengths should offset weaknesses and synergies, both geographical and functional, should be available to build upon. This involves minimizing network overlap and 'hub clutter', for example.[56] It may also involve getting the partners' cost structures sufficiently into line that they can support a shared strategic position and the service-price offers to go with that position.

3   Plausible, shared expectations: these need to be built around a win-win agreement that is moderated by patience and realism and is sufficiently flexible to allow the partners to react to unforeseen developments. Expectations should be actively managed.

4   Sustained imperatives: the factors which first brought the parties together must either be sustained or be replaced by an equally compelling commercial logic. Alliances are an inherently unstable form of architecture, needing either (preferably both) sustained or new benefits for each partner in order to retain their appeal relative to the alternatives that will undoubtedly materialize over time.

5   Operational fit: a common platform for as many different service delivery processes as possible should be shared amongst the partners, with room nonetheless remaining to add local 'flavour' wherever necessary.

6   Cultural compatibility: organizational cultures must blend, because it is the ability of individuals to share information and work together that will determine what is achieved.

7   Commitment throughout both organizations: appropriate resources and skills have to be committed to negotiating, contracting, and managing the relationship. But arguably the most important form of commitment is in the minds of people up and down (or, these days, right across) each hierarchy - a commitment to open communication, to make cooperation happen, and to avoid the arrogance of the 'not invented here' syndrome. Vision and commitment must come from the top, and action and commitment from throughout each partner.

Commitment can be difficult to establish and sustain. Any British Airways employee who has worked for the airline since the late 1980s will have been asked to invest enthusiasm in three successive transatlantic partners. Yet that employee will know that the first partner (United) disengaged from the relationship via the media, and that the second (USAir) filed suit against British Airways without any contact apparently taking place between the respective chief executives immediately before or after the filing.[57] A well-informed employee will also be aware that KLM has met Northwest's controlling directors in court, that both SAS and Iberia have seen alliance structures crumble around them, and that their own carrier's third transatlantic partner (American) spent over a decade avoiding comprehensive alliances and vilifying code-sharing as consumer fraud. Against this background, commitment to yet another partnership might be expected to take a fair amount of nurturing in some quarters.

8   Appropriate organizational architecture: steering committees and task forces guide most alliances on a day-to-day basis, but as they mature these partnerships between what are highly complex organizations will in most cases need to adopt more permanent forms of architecture. The assigning and discharging of responsibilities will almost inevitably run up against fear and information 'gate-keeping', which will need to be anticipated and openly faced.

9   Shared (or at least compatible) metrics by which to assess achievements: the precise balance of benefits will generally depend upon the value-creation logic underlying the alliance, the particular structure of the agreement, and how efficiently intentions are implemented.

10   The ability to develop common branding: this is a contentious area, but some observers believe that without a commitment to common branding by two or more ostensibly equal partners entering into a comprehensive (as opposed to a focused) alliance, it is likely either that the partnership will ultimately fail or that the weaker brand identity(ies) will be lost. Most alliances have yet to go this far; integrated network management, joint customer loyalty programmes, and the sharing of airport and city-centre facilities can only be a first step, however. We will return to this issue in chapter 10, where branding is discussed in greater detail.

11   Trust.

The airlines - relatively few in number but significant in terms of their market presence - that have to date formed comprehensive alliances have drawn on the full menu of techniques, involving in many cases focused, market-specific arrangements with other carriers alongside the more comprehensive linkages created with their primary partners. The common denominator is network management and the broadening of geographic scope, but there are other cost and revenue motivations as well. A tangle of relationships has been created which in some cases invite conflicts of interest and in most cases absorb considerable management time. These relationships are an inevitable, albeit perhaps temporary, byproduct of the industry's attempt to globalize within the constraints of the Chicago regulatory regime. What is meant by 'globalization' is the topic to which we turn next.

Globalization

A key issue defining the international airline industry's present transitional phase, globalization is a topic which raises several questions.

Globalization of what?

Revenue sources 'Globalization' is a catch-all description of the trend towards economic interdependence amongst countries. One result of the globalization of economies has been that demand for international air transportation has grown rapidly; in particular, demand - albeit from just a handful of passengers each day in some cases - now exists in city-pair markets which 10 or 20 years ago were generating no demand at all. This last fact in particular is helping drive the expansion of international double-hub systems capable of capturing traffic behind, say, Zurich and distributing it beyond, say, Cincinnati. It is flows such as this that most sharply throw into relief the commercially anachronistic nature of bilateral air services agreements.

No airline is yet present in all of the world's top 100, 30 or even 10 city-pair markets, and neither does any single carrier have a strong presence in all six of the most important intra- and inter-regional traffic flows.[58] Globalization entails greater freedom for airlines to serve demand in markets from which they have previously been excluded by commercial regulation - particularly markets which do not touch the home country. However, this does not mean that it is markets (defined by demand) which are being globalized; what is slowly being globalized is the industry (defined by supply).[59]

Because the air transport industry services demand which is fragmented into tens of thousands of separate markets, individual airlines neither access all the different sources of demand nor face the same competitors in each of the markets where they are present.[60] Globalization at this point in time is most evident in the use of alliances to extend network coverage beyond what is economically and/or politically feasible for individual airlines. One result of this is that a few geographically wide-market comprehensive alliances (supplemented in most cases by more focused arrangements with other carriers separately entered into by the alliance partners) are increasingly competing across markets in which many of the airlines involved would not previously have expected to confront each other.

An important metric of globalization on the revenue side is the extent to which particular brands and service concepts are recognized in all the world's major markets. Few airlines are yet near to becoming 'global' in this sense either. For example, even an airline as significant as Delta struggled for several years after inheriting Pan Am's Atlantic Division to get its highly regarded brand established in Europe. (Ironically, it is arguable that Pan Am in its heyday was as close to building a global brand identity as the industry has yet seen.)

Cost structures As an industry globalizes, its major producers find themselves competing with less protection against input cost disadvantages. Competitors are freed to enter markets from which they were previously excluded, and new benchmarks for process efficiency are established. Pressure to produce output at globally competitive cost levels can lead to the location of some business processes in low-cost countries, as has already happened on a small scale in respect of revenue accounting, data processing, software development, and several other support activities, for example. It may lead to outsourcing as one means for escaping the overheads associated with vertically integrated organizations, and to the reengineering of retained processes. Globalization also brings with it economies of network scope and, particularly where networks can be interfaced over hubs, economies of density; indeed, this is one of its primary motivations.

Distribution channels Although the structures of travel agency and freight forwarding industries vary between countries, the technology that automated travel agencies in particular use to distribute airline products is increasingly global in scope - hence the larger CRSs are now widely referred to as 'global' distribution systems. The Internet - which will gradually become a more significant distribution channel than is presently the case - is, of course, truly global.

Markets for airline capital Markets for airline debt obligations are in many cases closer to being global than are markets in airline equity.[61] This is because quite a few carriers continue to be state-owned, and those that are not in most cases have limitations placed on foreign ownership by either or both foreign investment regulations and the national ownership clauses incorporated into bilateral air services agreements subject to which they fly international routes.

Ancillary industries Some ancillary industries, notably flight catering, are in the early stages of extending their own geographic scope. Aircraft maintenance is also moving towards becoming a truly global industry and, as was just mentioned, the leading reservations systems are already close to globalization (although levels of travel agency automation do still vary between countries).

Why globalize?

Of many plausible motivations, the following are likely to be fundamental:

- to extend as far as possible the reach of a common brand, at the same time exploiting what is believed to be a widespread preference - amongst business travellers in particular - for airlines with extensive networks (and also extensive FFPs);
- to seize opportunities in markets offering better growth prospects than are available in the relatively mature domestic and international markets where many of the industry's largest producers still generate

the bulk of their output. This might ultimately be expected to involve use of a single brand or of several geographically or functionally specialized sub-brands, but at this still early stage in the industry's restructuring neither is yet a common medium for uniting partners from different countries;

• to leverage core competencies and to benefit from economies of scope, density, and (where they exist) scale; or

• to spread systemic risk into a wider portfolio of markets.

What particularly matters in liberalized environments are, first, the revenue-generating capability of an airline's brand, which in turn is closely tied to the structure and yield potential of the network it can create either directly or in cooperation with alliance partners and, second, the cost of serving that network. Size in itself is not important, but its impact on these variables can be. On one side of the argument are 'globalists' who believe size vital to survival as a top-ranking international carrier and see considerable first-mover advantages to be gained by 'getting out of the blocks' as quickly as possible. On the other side are those who see globalization as another fad; nimbleness and flexibility, focused on clearly defined geographical or product strengths are the keys to survival according to this view.

Clearly, scheduled airline networks are volume-driven structures requiring, wherever possible, high levels of throughput over which to spread fixed costs. The larger a network, the greater is likely to be its aggregate traffic flow and the more opportunity there is to channel that flow in a way that exploits economies of density and scope.[62] There is, however, an argument that size is less important to profitability than how it is managed - than how distinctive capabilities are developed and deployed - and that this applies equally to large and small enterprises.

How is globalization being accomplished?

Under the prevailing international regulatory regime, internally generated network expansion is usually limited to exploiting fully whatever domestic or third, fourth, fifth, and sixth freedom markets a particular airline might have available to it. Other than EU carriers operating within the single market, airlines generally do not have access to seventh freedom or cabotage (i.e. eighth or ninth freedom) markets.[63] Furthermore, few carriers have sufficient resources to grow internally to a size which would qualify them as truly global. External growth through acquisition has taken place within some countries that have multi-airline industries, but cross-border investment flows have been constrained by aeropolitical factors.

At the present time, therefore, external growth through alliances offers the most suitable vehicle for today's larger and better resourced carriers to move closer to becoming global airlines. Pending a significant aeropolitical regime change, alliances provide the only way to reach the critical mass many observers now feel is essential for international airlines wanting to survive as geographical wide-market competitors.[64]

What are the barriers to globalization?

The prevailing aeropolitical regime leads the list, with foreign investment limitations, incompatible corporate cultures, inadequate branding skills, lack of financial and managerial resources, alternative ambitions, or no ambition at all being in close contention for runner-up.

The imperatives of globalization are largely commercial, driven by industry economics and competitive pressures. Despite in many cases being more commercially aware than has been true in the past, there are still many governments which have public policy agendas for their air transport industries driven by non-commercial criteria. This continues to slow industry restructuring and the globalization process.

Some years ago, Wheatcroft and Lipman identified four barriers to be overcome before multinational airlines could be formed.[65]

1   The concept of national ownership and control: this was expected to fade gradually in some countries but barely at all in others.

2   Human nature: the desire to control one's own destiny, together with nationalistic instincts, was expected to hinder trans-border acquisitions. It was anticipated that these attitudes would eventually be changed by the combination of particular necessities with a more general evolution of the airline industry as a whole towards being perceived by the public, policy-makers, and managers as the same as other industries.

3   Conservatism: the 'not invented here' syndrome was thought likely to stand in the path of commitment to other people's ideas and could hinder the adoption of common branding, for example.

4   Competition laws.

Wheatcroft and Lipman's conclusion was that these barriers would slow but not stop the evolution of leading airlines into multinational enterprises. Without splitting hairs over possible distinctions between 'multinationalism' and 'globalization', the analysis was broadly correct and yet remains equally sound today notwithstanding progress allowed by changes in the aeropolitical postures of some countries and impelled by the mind-focusing consequences of the early-1990s recession.

Well into the industry's globalization process alliances and partnerships are likely to remain the primary vehicle for expansion. Whether or not they prove to be just a passing phase will depend in part upon how comprehensively the barriers referred to above can be overcome. There are many countries which simply will not countenance the disappearance of their airlines, either as independent corporate entities or separately identifiable brands. This is widely appreciated, but too often it is an observation applied only to weak national airlines; in fact, there are many high-growth Asian countries with strong or potentially strong carriers in which minority foreign shareholdings are or might be tolerated but in respect of which loss of control or identity would be politically unacceptable.

One challenge frequently overlooked in the enthusiasm for globalization is the distinctly 'national' images retained by many airlines. Not all of these images are as globally saleable as those so well exploited by a number of Southeast Asian carriers. Few airlines have yet managed to 'de-nationalize' their brands, although KLM and Northwest have come close with their World Business Class. It is generally much easier for manufacturers of tangible goods to do this than for service industries, particularly contact-intensive service industries such as airlines. This has been compounded by the legacy of the airline industry's regulatory history, which has made most producers profoundly 'national' in geographical scope and general orientation.

British Airways provides an interesting case in point, as the following quotation shows.

> BA has always operated worldwide and probably has the widest global route network of any airline. However, it is essentially a very British company with its product being quintessentially British. This provides the greatest challenge to its management and staff: how to act globally but retain its essential character.[66]

The issue which has yet to be resolved is whether 'quintessential Britishness' is a significant brand attribute for passengers travelling between Pittsburgh and Cleveland, Dallas and Tucson, Sydney and Osaka, or Paris and Munich. If not, airlines are going to have to 'de-nationalize' their identities in order to globalize; there is arguably an acknowledgement of this in British Airways' 'citizen of the world' image make-over launched in mid-1997.[67] It is not yet clear whether global airlines and alliances will be able to sell a single corporate brand (e.g. British Airways) and closely linked product sub-brands (e.g. Club World) into all their markets, or whether globalization will turn out to be better accomplished by retaining separately identifiable regional sub-brands (e.g. Deutsche BA and Qantas[68]), possibly in conjunction with common product sub-brands. At the time of writing, British Airways' publicly stated ambition is still to create a global **network**, not a global **airline** - in other words, a global service delivery system rather than a global corporation. Shortly after his appointment in 1996, British Airways' chief executive was widely quoted as expressing the 'view that BA should be more like a McDonald's style franchise and less like a body which runs planes from London to the rest of the world'.[69]

What future for globalization?

Global open skies and the freedom of airlines to enter markets at will irrespective of national origin will not come about in the foreseeable future. An open skies regime on routes between Western Europe and North America is clearly on the way to materializing, however, and this is important because transatlantic routes account for around 25 per cent of global RPKs (only around half that percentage if expressed in terms of passenger enplanements); exchanges of cabotage rights between these or any other regional blocs still seem some way off, however, although US fifth freedom rights within the EU might be argued to equate to cabotage in substance if not legal form. Whilst several large US and European carriers are edging towards increasingly close cooperation within alliance structures, others have yet to find their partners and the constitution of alliances generally is still unstable.

Given that Asian markets will be accounting for the highest rates of growth and increasingly important shares of global traffic and revenues, the aeropolitical stances of governments in that region are going to take on more importance. Some are now embracing the philosophy underlying open skies. For cultural and political reasons, however, it is not possible to foresee most of these countries acceding to the merger of their airlines into transnational entities - particularly if control is to be exercised elsewhere.

The most likely outcome of the structural transition now underway in the international airline industry is that **cooperation** - cemented in some cases by equity investments - will continue to bring carriers from different regions closer together, but that partners in Asia and the Middle East in particular are generally going to be less inclined to accept the emergence of a single locus of **control** than those in Europe or North America. Even in the latter case the prospect of, say, Swissair being controlled from Atlanta or Lufthansa from Chicago still seems very distant. In the absence of control, what will probably evolve is more sophisticated forms of the comprehensive alliances that have been developing since the late 1980s. The most intense and committed of these will see closer system integration and take on substantial permanence, but there are still too many unknowns to predict precisely where this evolutionary process will lead.

Whilst a significant number of niche producers will survive - some in product niches but many making wide-market product offers into geographical niches - output on a global level will almost certainly become more concentrated in the hands of fewer competitors. This does not necessarily imply less competition in individual markets. Despite the growing interdependence of markets incorporated into global networks, it is between individual city-pairs that competition - if there is any - takes place. Opportunities will continue to exist for small, flexible carriers able to identify new markets and segments, or able to challenge those parts of their networks that traditional flag carriers are no longer able to defend.[70]

Much will depend upon the height of remaining barriers to entry and the intensity with which alliances and any niche carriers which might also be present choose to compete. Individual air transport markets have historically in many cases been monopolistic or oligopolistic. Concentration of output at a global level will not necessarily worsen this situation. It will ultimately change the cast of players in particular markets. However, it could possibly improve the situation in some medium- and long-haul markets unconstrained by infrastructural barriers, especially if competition intensifies across different alliances' international hubs and if well-resourced carriers use new generation aircraft to augment this competition with hub-bypass services to secondary points.

After initially falling in the years immediately following deregulation, the concentration of output in the US domestic industry as a whole has been rising again since the mid-1980s. However, the consolidation of the industry which has caused this has not led to increased concentration in every individual market - in fact, quite the contrary.[71] What matters there - and what will matter globally as the industry continues liberalizing - is how effectively different networks are managed in order to seize opportunities to compete in individual city-pair markets, whether infrastructural and other barriers to entry inhibit competition, and how actively those present choose to compete in practice.

Prevailing wisdom supports the following summary.

1   Single company global 'megacarriers' will be a long time coming because of both regulatory intransigence and the sheer diseconomies of scale likely to be encountered. 'Companies have become very wary of seeking economies of scale through merger (because in many cases they turned out to be diseconomies). Companies or units of companies have to be small and flexible enough to deal with local conditions while benefitting from global expertise in technology.'[72]

2   Comprehensive alliances will grow in importance and a small number of global network alliances will come to dominate world air transport output by offering high levels of connectivity in tens of thousands of city-pair markets, in addition to nonstop and direct service in high-volume O and D markets. 'They will operate from a range of strategic hubs located primarily in the major market areas: Europe, North America, and Asia-Pacific...[and these]...global systems will be underpinned by fast developing regional networks, providing opportunity for existing airlines and new entrants alike.'[73] Their structures and approaches to common branding, however, will not be uniform.

As in the hotel industry, it is highly likely that once any given carrier grouping has established a global system of sufficient size and diversity to enable it to compete effectively in an adequate proportion of all markets, management's focus will shift rapidly towards first developing a loyal, stable customer base through distinctive branding, product differentiation and frequent flier programmes, etc. and, second, towards reducing costs by the optimum use of franchising and contracting techniques. In an industry where the only demonstrable economies of scale are in marketing and capital acquisitions, and where there are significant diseconomies of scale in most operational areas, the key to success will be achieving the optimum combination of global marketing and local production.[74]

One important symptom of airline industry restructuring will be an evolving focus away from vertical integration and towards horizontal control.[75]

3   Some carriers will prefer to continue relying on focused alliances.

4   Start-ups will decline in number and none will grow independently to challenge today's established carriers for leading roles in global partnerships. They can nonetheless be expected to have an impact on distinct niches - although opportunities to identify and exploit these niches may decrease over time as wide-market network carriers use franchising to further extend their reach.

5   Some (but by no means all) of the smaller existing airlines will be able to survive, even flourish, in geographical and product niches - differentiating by service or price. Some will feed larger carriers - in which case they might ultimately be absorbed into alliance structures, depending on the strength of political and cultural sensitivities. Others will compete within their chosen segments against those larger airlines and alliances, and the lucky (or astute) ones will have niches to themselves.[76] 'Middle-of-the-roaders' able to find neither a global network to feed nor a niche to exploit will be in danger of disappearing, absent the support of a state shareholder.

6   Concentration of traffic will increase at the aggregate level, but what will matter more in individual city-pair markets is what has always mattered:
    • how many competitors are present *in that particular market;*
    • their corporate missions and objectives, and the impact these have on the manner in which they choose to compete;
    • the availability of capacity relative to demand; and

- the role of governments, particularly the extent to which they are prepared to move from the enforcement of aeropolitical barriers to market entry towards the enforcement of competition rules in order to control the erection of alternative, commercial barriers.

One unresolved issue is how the few major globe-spanning alliances in the process of formation will deal with the branding conundrum - whether they will go global, with all that implies for control and the dominance of the master-brand, or whether a multi-domestic/multi-regional approach will be preferred. The question is whether:

- management of one partner's - presumably the dominant partner's - brand and sub-brands is a core competence to be leveraged across an alliance comprised of subsidiaries, affiliates, and franchisees;
- new alliance master-brands should be created, with existing master-brands retained as alliance sub-brands; or
- new alliance master-brands and sub-brands should be created.

Implicit in this decision is the issue of how readily service concepts and delivery processes are transferable in this type of contact-intensive service business.[77]

In a global network industry comprised of thousands of different markets, size can offer undoubted advantages - notably economies of scope and density, and marketing economies of scale. However, the issue of how to combine global reach and central coordination with local focus, how to become a major supplier of air transport services in all the domestic and international markets that matter, has yet to be resolved. Indeed, the industry's aeropolitical regime has been such that until recently there has been no particular urgency about addressing the issue in detail. The growth of alliances and the widely felt imperative amongst the largest dozen or so airlines to 'go global' are now investing it with considerably more urgency.

A global airline in the truest sense of the expression - that is to say, a **global** airline rather than a **globe-spanning** airline - will be one which is free to enter markets more or less at will irrespective of national origin, and to choose where to perform its non-location-specific business processes so as to serve those markets both effectively and at the lowest possible cost. Clearly, such entities remain a distant prospect.

Notes

1   Growth is not the only option open to strategic managers and, as noted in chapter 1, there are often sound reasons to moderate, curtail or reverse growth strategies. It was also noted, however, that there can be convincing economic justifications for expanding an airline. Furthermore, growth can also be motivational; one senior airline executive put the case succinctly when observing that, 'We have to grow in order to

achieve'. (Quotation from Peter Henning Thöle, executive board member of Lauda Air, cited in: Hill, L. (1997), 'Grand Prix Airline', *Air Transport World,* July, p. 165.)

2   On a more modest scale, Austrian Airlines has consolidated its national industry by taking control of Tyrolean and acquiring a substantial minority shareholding in Lauda Air (together with an option to acquire control). Separate brand identities and distinct corporate cultures have been retained, however.

3   Gialloreto, L. (1994), 'No Space for the Middle-of-the-Roader', *The Avmark Aviation Economist,* September. Organic growth does not bring automatic access to sufficient additional slots or gates at congested airports, whereas acquisitions or alliances involving carriers already possessing these resources do provide access.

4   OECD (1997), *The Future of International Air Transport Policy: Responding to Global Change,* p. 90.

5   In the United States it has been possible to buy either individual foreign routes or route-groups without acquiring the seller in its entirety. For example, since the mid-1980s United has purchased Pan Am's Pacific Division, London Heathrow routes, and Latin American routes; American has bought Heathrow routes from TWA and Latin American routes from Eastern; and Delta has acquired Pan Am's remaining Atlantic routes, including its Frankfurt hub (which has since been 'dehubbed').

6   Aéromexico and Mexicana are commonly owned, but have been kept apart - at least as far as domestic cooperation is concerned - by Mexican antitrust law as well as by corporate incompatibility.

7   This is not inevitable, as former Dan-Air staff retained in British Airways' London Gatwick operation can attest. In 1997, British Airways tried the same formula again when it acquired a majority holding in bankrupt French carrier Air Liberté, began merging the acquisition with its existing French subsidiary TAT, and set about imposing the less generous employment conditions of Air Liberté on TAT staff; not surprisingly, resistance was encountered.

8   Blumenthal, B. and Haspeslagh, P. (1994), 'Toward a Definition of Corporate Transformation', *Sloan Management Review,* Spring.

9   Rabinovitz, B.H. (1997), 'Airline Strategic Alliances', presentation to the IATA *Legal Symposium 97,* Miami, 3rd-4th February.

10   More commonly used terms would be 'tactical' and 'strategic'. However, these are neither sufficiently descriptive nor, given the difficulty inherent in deciding until after the event what is strategic and what is tactical (referred to in Volume One, chapter 1), clear as to meaning. It should also be noted that the word 'alliance' is used here in its broadest sense. This is in line with practice in the industry and its trade press, but not necessarily with the academic literature. Some academic studies limit use of the word to inter-firm collaborations that are tightly defined at their outset as to both economic space and time. See, for example: Buckley, P.J., (1992), 'Alliances, Technology and Markets: A Continuing Tale', in Buckley, P.J., *Studies in International Business,* Macmillan.

A final point to be borne in mind is that alliances, as the word is being used in this chapter, are generally relationships between airlines (i.e. relationships between producers of similar products). They are therefore different from the vertical relationships encountered in long-term 'partnerships' with suppliers, distributors, or providers of complementary travel products (e.g. hotels, car hire, or charge cards).

11   American's parent corporation did already hold an influential minority stake in Canadian by this time, but the scale of this relationship was not in the same league as the British Airways alliance proposal. Separately, rumours surfaced in 1997 linking All Nippon with United and other members of the Star Alliance.

12   Knibb, D. (1996), 'ANA Alliances Mix N' Match', *Airline Business,* September. The code-sharing arrangement between British Airways and Canadian which is referred to in the quotation as 'limited' has since been considerably widened.

13   Cameron, D. (1996), 'Deciphering Codes', *Airline Business,* September.

14   Thomas, G. (1997), 'Ansett Turns to SIA for Help With Expansion', *Aviation Week & Space Technology*, June 30, p. 33. Later in 1997, Singapore and Air New Zealand signed an open skies agreement.

15   The significance of antitrust immunity for alliances is discussed in Volume One, chapter 4.

16   The news in mid-1997 that American and British Airways were considering buying up to ten per cent each in Iberia raised further questions in the minds of some observers as to whether corporate cultures could be successfully blended in order to exploit the geographical synergies apparently being sought. Twelve per cent of the Spanish carrier's equity had several months earlier been sold to employees.

17   Over 200,000 staff and 1,300 aircraft serving close to 600 destinations in more than 100 countries.

18   GAO estimate cited in *The Avmark Aviation Economist,* April 1995, p. 7. It is also worth noting, however, that when in 1996 USAir announced its intention to end code-sharing and other forms of cooperation with British Airways, some analysts were estimating the benefit to the US carrier to be as low as $12 million per annum (*Airline Business,* December 1996.)

19   These markets were not necessarily all served on a code-share basis. The figures are highly tentative, and during position-taking over the American Airlines-British Airways linkage first proposed in 1996 far higher numbers were aired. The following quotation gives an idea of the sort of numbers potentially involved.
       Speaking to the *Airline Business / ASM* Routes 97 forum in Abu Dhabi, de Graauw [Henk de Graauw, KLM's director of strategy and commercial cooperation] said that KLM and its partners now serve 90,000 city-pairs...In the last six years, KLM's own city-pair count has risen from 10,000 to 15,000. Its European code-share partners account for a further 5,000, but the bulk of the increase - 70,000 - arises from the Northwest alliance. (Whitaker, R. (1996), 'Hubbing Power', *Airline Business,* December.)
       For a discussion of network connectivity issues and the unreliability of city-pair figures, see: Holloway, S. (1997), *Straight and Level: Practical Airline Economics,* Ashgate, chapter 8.

20   However, 'junior' partners in particular need to be careful to ensure that they do not get hit by rapidly rising reservations, frequent flyer programme administration, or traffic-handling costs.

21   Málev subsequently began serving Budapest-New York nonstop (as the operating partner on a code-share with Delta). At the time of writing, sale of Alitalia's stake in Málev to Hungarian interests ahead of a wider privatization of the carrier is believed to be imminent.

22   The *Airline Business* alliance survey published in June 1997 identified 54 out of 363 alliances as involving equity stakes; at 14.9 per cent, both the percentage and the absolute figure were down slightly on previous years.

23   Feldman, J.M. (1997), 'Code-sharing Promiscuity Pays', *Air Transport World,* February, p. 39.

24   Qantas disposed of its investment in Air New Zealand in 1997.

25   Several airlines (e.g. Korean Air and Lufthansa) have been discussing formation of global cargo alliances. (*Air Transport World,* July 1997, p. 189.)

26   de Groot, J.E.C. (1994), 'Code-sharing', *Air & Space Law,* Vol. XIX, No. 2.

27   Shenton, H. (1994), 'Is Airlines' Gain Consumers' Loss?', *The Avmark Aviation Economist,* October. Note that the distinction drawn between reciprocal and non-reciprocal international connection code-sharing is not Shenton's.

28   Some US regionals do manage to preserve an element of their own identity - one notable case being Horizon Air, a subsidiary of Alaska Airlines which has a well-defined service image. Horizon flies a lot of point-to-point passengers and so carries what, by US regional airline standards, is a relatively small 20 per cent of connecting traffic for its parent (and an even smaller percentage for Northwest, another code-share partner). Several carriers in fact continue to offer service under their own brand

identities in some markets whilst operating code-shares for one (or occasionally more than one) major in others (e.g. Mesa). It is also worth noting that one of the largest US domestic code-sharing deals in revenue terms in the mid-90s actually involved two majors, America West and Continental (the latter being an indirect minority shareholder in the former).

29 Clearly, the distinction between reciprocal international connection code-sharing and reciprocal parallel code-sharing can get rather semantic. It arguably lies in the fact that the connection occurs at one of the partner's hubs in its home country in the former case, but not in the latter. The relevance of this will probably become progressively less significant as networks are 'de-nationalized' and globalized.

30 Several of these deals (e.g. All Nippon and Air France) were at the time in abeyance pending government approval - itself dependent on renegotiation of the relevant bilaterals. An agreement with Varig was dropped in 1997 when the Brazilian carrier - which was already code-sharing with Lufthansa on European routes - switched to United; an agreement with Virgin Atlantic ended the same year, when the British airline switched to Continental.

31 de Groot, op. cit. Naked code-sharing can occur in either focused or comprehensive alliances. Common product code-sharing is more likely to be part of a comprehensive alliance, although few comprehensive alliances have yet moved close to the merging of services and images implied by the 'common product' label.

32 Shenton, op. cit.

33 In a separate article, Shenton makes two further points relevant to the items in this list. First, he observes, notably in respect of US-Europe code-sharing, that the device is primarily useful for market share protection and that its utility diminishes as competitors enter into their own separate code-sharing arrangements. This observation concurs with the findings of several studies that on many transatlantic routes code-sharing seems more likely to redistribute than to stimulate traffic. Second, in the absence of the type of cooperation rights provided by extensive antitrust immunity, the primary *social* benefits of the device probably lie in its potential for saving costs. (Shenton, H. (1994), 'GRA Report Sanctifies DOT Policy', *The Avmark Aviation Economist*, December.) Any cost savings might or might not be passed through to consumers.

34 Short-haul carriers do frequently negotiate pro-rate deals that take account of these problems. As far as carriers flying the longer sectors are concerned, international connection code-sharing arrangements are nonetheless often more favourable than standard interline pro-rates. For example, referring to Aéromexico/Delta and Mexicana/United code-sharing arrangements, the chief executive of Mexicana 'explains that the main problem for Mexican airlines is that interline agreements for connections on to US domestic sectors often require the Mexican airlines to pay higher prorates to their US counterparts than the US airlines flying to Mexico charge their own passengers for on-line connections. The difference makes interline connections uncompetitive - hence code-shares'. (Knibb, D. (1997), 'No Unity Over Rio Grande', *Airline Business*, February, p. 9.)

35 United States General Accounting Office (1995), *International Aviation: Airline Alliances Produce Benefits, But Effect on Competition is Uncertain*, GAO/REED-95-99. See also : ICAO (1997) *Implications of Airline Codesharing*, Circular 269-AT/110. It should be noted that all of these studies cover periods during which today's most important transatlantic alliances either did not exist or were at formative stages; their data were therefore necessarily limited.

36 Ballantyne, T. (1997), 'United Allies Down Under', *Airline Business*, January.

37 Gellman Research Associates (1994), *A Study of International Airline Code-sharing*, Report to the US Department of Transportation; and, United States General Accounting Office, op. cit.

38 Ballantyne, op. cit.

39   See Volume One, chapter 3 for an explanation of the position of carriers operating
      US-Japan services under MOUs (memoranda of understanding) rather than under the
      terms of the two countries' 1952 bilateral.
40   Code-sharing is not, of course, a prerequisite for collusion. The airline industry
      remains rife with nominal competitors who collude either openly - as in the 'yield
      improvement committees' still operating (albeit not always very effectively) in some
      international markets - or covertly. See, for example: CAA (1994), *Airline
      Competition on European Long Haul Routes,* CAP 639.
41   It is for this reason that 'carve-outs' were imposed in respect of the antitrust
      immunities granted to Delta, Sabena, and Swissair in the mid-90s. Their effect was to
      remove from joint revenue management certain traffic on flights from Zurich to
      Atlanta and Cincinnati (and vice versa) and between Brussels and Atlanta (and vice
      versa). What was affected was local, inter-hub traffic in time-sensitive segments;
      neither local discounted-fare traffic nor flow traffic of any sort was de-immunized.
42   Cameron, op. cit.
43   de Groot, op. cit.
44   GAO, op. cit.
45   The Taca group is headed by Taca International (El Salvador), which has
      shareholdings in Aviateca (Guatemala), Lacsa (Costa Rica), and Nica (Nicaragua),
      and a management contract with Copa (Panama). Separately, it should be noted that
      American Airlines was not seeking antitrust immunity for all the listed alliances -
      although this was certainly on the agenda as far as the largest of them, the one with
      British Airways, was concerned.
46   There is no implication here that Delta sets out deliberately to deceive consumers or
      that it is lax in trying to convey information about which partner actually operates a
      code-shared flight. Because its North Atlantic market strategy in particular is so
      heavily dependent upon exploiting network synergies with alliance partners, Delta has
      actually spent a lot of money on marketing communications which focus specifically
      on its code-sharing partnerships. Information flows are rarely perfect, however, and
      it is largely because of this choice of strategy that Delta provides so many sound
      examples of the potential pitfalls - as well as the potential benefits - of code-sharing;
      neither can marketing communications be expected to overcome the very real
      contrasts in corporate and national cultures which shape the different service delivery
      styles that distinguish partners in any cross-border alliance.
47   The arrangement was subsequently extended to other intra-European trunk routes
      from Brussels. It is very unusual for a 'flag carrier' to hand over key-routes to a
      separately branded and unaffiliated entrant in this manner, with all that is implied for
      brand presence and possible service incompatibility in the markets being ceded. There
      is some doubt at the time of writing whether this arrangement represents a long-term
      strategy, or a short-term expedient in reaction to Sabena's mid-90s cost crisis.
48   The franchising concept has another, much less widespread, meaning in the airline
      industry. There has been talk in recent years of governments 'franchising' airlines to
      operate routes subject to competitive renewal bids every few years. See, for example:
      Lucking, T. (1993), 'Airline Competition Isn't Working', *Aerospace,* May.
49   Air France subsequently entered into a much wider franchise arrangement with
      French regional Brit Air, which flies under the Air France Express sub-brand.
      Proteus Airlines is another regional currently operating under the same sub-brand.
50   Axelsson, R. (1993), 'Cloning a Winner?', *Airline Business,* September.
51   *Air Transport World,* November, 1994.
52   CityFlyer had previously done business as Air Europe Express (and before that had
      been trading under its original name, Connectair) prior to rebranding as British
      Airways Express - so the challenge is clearly not insurmountable. On the other hand,
      several US regionals have followed their failing partners into oblivion, and Irish
      carrier CityJet ran into difficulties after ceasing to be a Virgin franchisee in the
      summer of 1996.

53   These figures are not representative of all franchised regionals in the United States. Atlantic Coast Airlines, for example, is a United franchisee which feeds only around one-third of its traffic into the major's system at their shared Washington Dulles hub.

54   Taverna, M.A. (1997), 'Five Airlines Form Worldwide Alliance', *Aviation Week & Space Technology*, May 19. Lufthansa was quoted in the same article as having saved $120 million in 1996 as a result of cost-saving activities across all of its alliance partnerships.

55   Lowden, I. (1997), 'A Rational Approach to Partner Selection', presentation to SMi conference *Managing & Rationalising Market-led Airline Alliances*, London, 27th-28th January.

56   'Hub clutter' refers to having hubs too close to each other. For example, although British Airways and KLM may yet get together, Amsterdam is too close to London to satisfy the British carrier's requirement for a centrally located intra-European hub to mediate connecting flows to which it does not yet have access. (Deutsche BA's Munich operation might ultimately grow to satisfy this requirement, of course.) Similarly, London Heathrow and Gatwick offer very little to KLM in network terms. Globally, an important aspect of network synergy for any alliance is to have partners with well-located hubs and strong networks in each of the major traffic-generating regions - primarily Europe, North America, and Asia.

57   Jennings, M. (1996), 'USAir Smells Conspiracy', *Airline Business*, September.

58   Within and between North America, Europe, and Asia.

59   Kay, J. (1995), *Foundations of Corporate Success*, Oxford University Press, p. 31. Apart from a small number of commodities which have prices in relatively close alignment or almost entirely equalized across the globe (e.g. crude oil, certain types of financial instrument, and foreign exchange), goods are not traded in global *markets*. An air journey between two cities cannot be traded at all; to say it exists in a global market is meaningless. It is the industry supplying the service which is becoming - but is still a long way short of actually being - global. This point is expanded upon later in the text.

60   According to *Air Transport World* (August, 1994, p. 67) 'the combined databases of ABC World Airways Guide and Official Airline Guides, now both owned by Reed Elsevier, list 130,000 flight numbers offered by 790 airlines connecting 3,900 locations'.

61   Which is not the same as saying that these debt markets are necessarily *liquid* as well.

62   See: Holloway, op. cit., chapter 1.

63   These terms are defined and discussed in Volume One, chapter 3.

64   'Critical mass' is commonly, and unhelpfully, used as a synonym for 'big'. It is a concept driven by recognition of the economic benefits potentially accruing to size. The critical mass required to 'make it' as a global carrier is open to debate but, as has been mentioned already, at least a 10 per cent share of the international scheduled passenger market is what KLM decided upon some years ago. (At the time of writing, KLM also has an intra-European market share goal of 15 per cent.)

65   Wheatcroft, S. and Lipman, G. (1990), *European Liberalisation and World Air Transport - Towards a Transnational Industry*, Economist Intelligence Unit.

66   Lauermann, E. (1992), 'British Airways in Europe: A Human Resources View of Development', *European Management Journal*, Vol. 10, No. 1, March. Ms. Lauermann was in a good position to make this observation, being the airline's General Manager, Human Resources. More recently, others have argued that British Airways' high spending on brand marketing has successfully enabled it to reposition itself from a 'national brand' to a 'ubiquitous global brand' (Jones, L. (1996), 'Keeping Up Appearances', *Airline Business*, October.)

67   Key features of what was a wide-ranging image change included replacement of the stylized British flag on aircraft tail-fins with artwork from a wide range of global cultures, and elimination of the 'We fly to serve' crest.

The changes met with mixed reviews. Inevitably, British Airways' de-emphasis of its Britishness led to a riposte from Virgin Atlantic, which cloaked the 'Scarlet Lady' images on the nose sections of its own aircraft fuselages with the Union Jack. The role of national identity in this globalizing industry has clearly yet to be settled.

68   Retention of the Qantas brand-name was in fact stipulated at the time the first 25 per cent of the Australian carrier's equity was privatized in the trade-sale to British Airways.
69   Brummer, A. (1997), 'Global Traders Will Win Economic War', *Airline Business,* January.
70   McMullan, K. (1995), 'Europe's New Wave: The Global Paradox', *The Avmark Aviation Economist,* December.
71   See, for example: Belobaba, P.P. and Van Acker, J. (1994), 'Airline Market Concentration: An Analysis of US Origin-Destination Markets', *Journal of Air Transport Management,* Vol. 1, No. 1; and Morrison, S.A. and Winston, C. (1995), *The Evolution of the Airline Industry,* Brookings, pp. 7-11.
72   McMullan, op. cit.
73   Marshall, Sir Colin (1996), 'Britain's Role in the Future of Air Transport', *Aerospace,* February. Similar conclusions can be found in: Oum, T.H., Taylor, A.J., and Zhang, A. (1993), 'Strategic Airline Policy in the Globalizing Networks', *Transportation Journal,* Vol. 32 (3); Debbage, K.G. (1994), 'The International Airline Industry: Globalization, Regulation and Strategic Alliances', *Journal of Transport Geography,* Vol. 2 (3); and in Oum, T.H. and Taylor, A.J. (1995), 'Emerging Patterns in Intercontinental Air Linkages and Implications for International Route Allocation Policy', *Transportation Journal,* Summer.
74   Holden, K.J. (1993), 'Aircraft Requirements and Financing in the 1990s', *Airfinance Annual 1993/94,* Euromoney Publications, p. 6.
75   Axelsson, op. cit.
76   Some of these segments are large. It is often overlooked, for example, that more than half the cross-border intra-European RPKs generated each year are produced by nonscheduled carriers largely independent of the handful of increasingly dominant - but much higher cost - major airlines which are expected to control between them most of the continent's scheduled traffic.
77   Master-brands and sub-brands are further discussed in chapter 10.

6 Managing service-price offers

Chapters 1 to 3 considered some of the changes taking place in airline corporate, competitive, and functional strategies; chapter 4 briefly reviewed lower-level objectives, operating goals, and critical success factors. We began consideration of strategy implementation in chapter 5 by discussing growth alternatives, focusing first on internal growth and then on acquisitions and alliances.

The next three chapters will consider how to create customer value consistent with the competitive strategy that has been chosen and the specific competitive advantages being exploited. The basic elements of any value proposition are:

- concept: the service-price offer;
- context: the service delivery system; and
- corporate infrastructure: enabling factors.[1]

In Volume One, chapter 13 the concept of a 'strategic service vision' was introduced; this helps focus the picture an airline has of its fundamental purpose, and also clarify the position it is trying to establish for itself in customers' perceptions. The strategic service vision both incorporates and integrates the management of an airline's service concept and the system of processes and human interactions used to deliver the level of service embodied in that concept. Nonetheless, it is useful for analytical purposes to separate concept from delivery, and this we will do by considering them in different chapters. This chapter will look at the nature of service, service positioning, the airline service concept, and then at management of the overall service-price offer. Chapter 7 will discuss changes taking place in service delivery, and chapter 8 will consider evolving approaches to corporate infrastructure.[2]

In liberalized competitive environments, unwavering attention has to be given to 'the three Cs' - customers, costs, and competitors. Specifically, close attention must be focused on:

- what it is that customers need, want, and expect;
- what it costs to deliver what they need, want, and expect; and
- what competitors are doing to meet, exceed, or change customers' wants and expectations.

This is the point in the strategic management process at which intended strategies succeed or fail, and emergent strategies materialize unanticipated from the heat of competition. Intended strategies can fail for two primary reasons: either because they are inappropriate or because, although soundly formulated, they are badly implemented.[3]

The nature of service

Most airlines offer several distinct air transport services into a number of different passenger and cargo markets, and the larger of them also offer other types of service as well - such as reservations, maintenance and engineering, catering, traffic handling, decision support software, and consultancy. Competitive strategies for each type of service will obviously vary, because their competitive environments are different, and so therefore will implementation. Here we will be concentrating on the implementation of strategies in respect of scheduled passenger services, with some reference also to nonscheduled passenger services and to cargo operations.

The first question is, 'What is meant by service?' The core service on the scheduled passenger side of the business is clearly safe air transportation on chosen routes, consistent with a published schedule. But in addition to this what is being sold is a bundle of supplementary benefits, some of which are tangible (e.g. seat design or inflight meals) but many of which are purely experiential (e.g. service encounters with individual members of staff). Service therefore comprises both locational transformation and a range of additional benefits. It is either perceived to live up to customers' expectations, or it is not. It is either perceived to offer acceptable value given the price and other sacrifices incurred in using it - a balanced service-price offer - or it is not.

The meaning of 'service-price offer'

In chapter 2, when discussing alternative competitive strategies, we defined four constructs.

1   A consumer's **perceived benefit**: gross benefits gained by a consumer from use of a service (e.g. schedule convenience, ontime performance, inflight comfort, enhanced self-image etc.) less nonmonetary costs (e.g. ticket conditionality or the need to spend time connecting at a hub).

2   **Value created**: perceived benefit less all the input costs that went into creating that service.

3   **Consumer surplus**: often treated as synonymous with **customer value**, this is perceived benefit minus the monetary price paid by the consumer. In other words, it is the portion of 'value created' that is being captured by the consumer.

4   **Seller's profit**: the monetary price paid by the consumer less the cost of inputs. This represents the portion of 'value created' that the airline, the final seller of the service, is capturing.

We saw that what in principle airlines are doing in the marketplace is 'bidding' for business by managing gross benefits, nonmonetary costs, and price - in other words, by managing the service-price offer. Two other comments were made which are relevant to the discussion in this chapter:

• the more competitive a market becomes, the greater the volatility of service-price offers and the more difficult it is to manage them without the sort of framework created by a clearly defined competitive strategy; and

• whereas some airlines create customer value by offering relatively low levels of perceived benefit and compensating for this with low prices, others concentrate on maximizing perceived benefit and, where possible, charging a premium price for the benefits offered. We will return to this shortly.

The characteristics of a service

Now well-established in the marketing literature is the view that there are four characteristics of services which distinguish them from tangible goods and so affect how they are marketed and delivered.[4]

1   Intangibility: a service offer is an offer to perform a process rather than to transfer ownership of a tangible good. This creates 'purchase risk' because the consumer cannot generally experience a service in advance. It also creates a differentiation challenge for service providers. It is the reason why reputation, branding, and the introduction of tangible elements to cue positive consumer reactions (e.g. staff uniforms and attractive physical surroundings) have become important means for providing reassurance about quality amongst airlines, some of which have in the past produced output more or less on a 'take-it-or-leave-it' basis. A long-running example of positioning based on a theme designed to give tangibility to the essentially intangible attribute of high-quality service is 'Singapore Girl'; this has

been used to convey 'warmth, friendliness, efficiency, and professionalism'.[5]

2   Inseparability of production and consumption: whereas the majority of consumer goods are produced and then sold, scheduled air transport is committed, sold, then produced - and the consumers have to be present for the most important of the production activities. There is no separation in either space or time between consumption on the one hand and many of the production processes on the other. This should bring marketing and operations into close proximity - something which is happening at a growing number of airlines as they face increasingly liberal markets and have to move away from an operations orientation towards a customer focus.

3   Heterogeneity: by being present during 'production', consumers experience multiple **service encounters**. However, it is not straightforward for service companies such as airlines to ensure consistent standards across all of these 'moments of truth'.[6] Service inconsistencies can arise because any individual service provider performs differently over time, because different service providers deliver the same service on different occasions, or because the presence of different consumers may evoke different interactions between one particular consumer and a particular service provider.[7]
     This is where staff skills and motivation interact with customers' expectations and behaviours. An airline averaging, say, eight service encounters per passenger and carrying 30 million passengers a year has close to a quarter of a billion 'moments of truth' to get right (and this ignores potential passengers who have not yet made a decision to purchase from the airline but nonetheless come into contact with its staff). In the case of an international airline, many of these encounters cross cultural boundaries; furthermore, staff from different cultural backgrounds might have contrasting views of their role in the service delivery system and distinct styles of delivery, whilst consumers from different cultural settings are very likely to have separate, culturally influenced expectations. A final point to bear in mind is that a single service transaction in the airline business may require a passenger to interface with an airline's people for up to 24 hours. Reducing heterogeneity to an acceptable level is a major service management challenge. Code-sharing and alliance-building do not make it any more simple.

4   Perishability: services clearly cannot be produced and then inventoried ahead of sale, and are equally clearly lost if not consumed when produced. Service delivery systems have a tendency towards either overcapacity or overdemand, something which is particularly acute when the markets being served are as prone to peaking as most air

transport markets, and efficient capacity management is therefore vital.

In the remainder of this chapter we will look at the conceptualization and management of service-price offers: this is the process of getting people into the system. In chapter 7 we will turn to service delivery, the concern of which is getting consumers through the system and ensuring a satisfactory outcome; outcome is the subject of chapters 9 and 10.

Positioning and the service concept

Figure 6.1 illustrates a framework for service conceptualization and management. This section of the chapter looks at positioning, customer value and the service concept (i.e. product design), and the next will briefly consider management of the service-price offer. (Action plans and associated expenditures are not dealt with in this text.)

Positioning

'Differentiation' is the act of designing and pricing attributes capable of providing distinctive, important, and communicable benefits that are desired by targeted consumers and which distinguish some aspect of the service-price offer from offers being made by competitors. It defines the value being offered to customers.[8] 'Positioning' is the act which unites differentiation, service delivery, and marketing communications to locate the offer at a chosen place in consumers' perceptions relative to the position held by competitors. Either an airline as a whole, a line of related services, or a single service can be 'positioned'; it is the latter to which we are largely referring here. Together, differentiation and positioning are intended to give customers a reason to buy.

There are two aspects to service positioning, both of which are now occupying more airline management time than in the past.

1   The use of marketing communications to locate (or relocate) a service at a chosen place in consumers' minds relative to other offers competing in the same segment, and to make it distinguishable along some dimension which consumers value. The challenge here is to choose an appropriate battleground for the airline's service-price offer.[9] This choice process is intimately linked to the choice of competitive strategy discussed in chapter 2. Many airlines' positioning has evolved unplanned over time; these days, a growing number of carriers are planning actively in order to establish explicit, clearly differentiated positions for the particular value inherent in their specific service-price offer(s).

Capability to serve segment

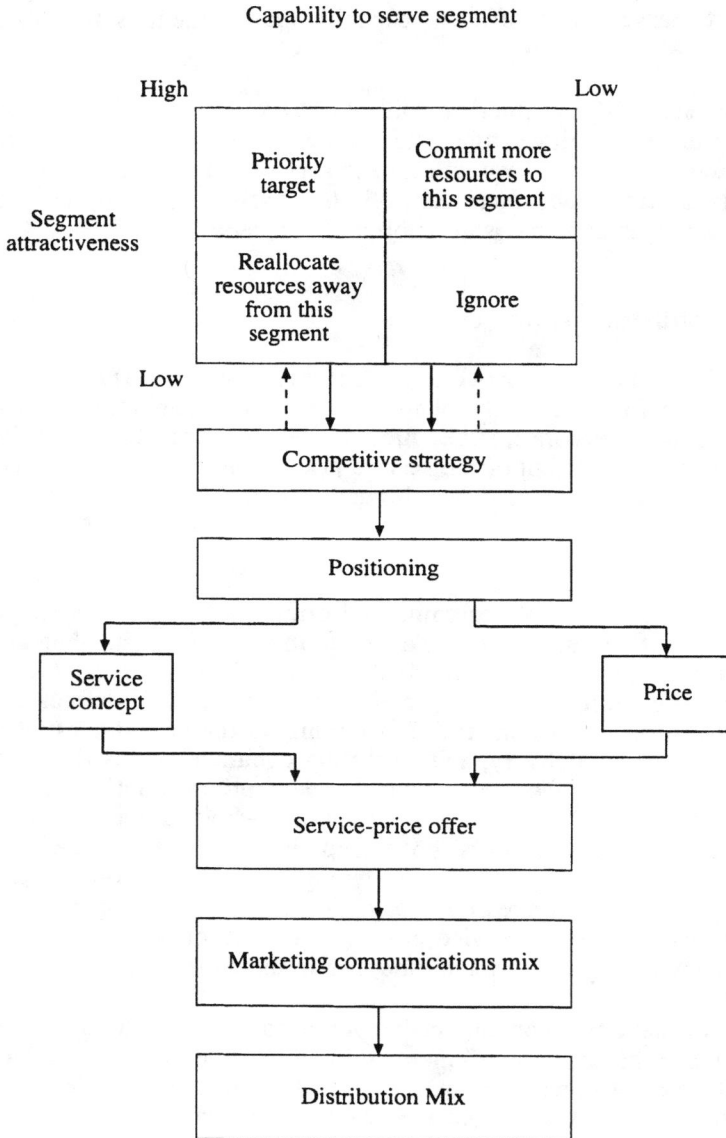

Figure 6.1: A framework for service conceptualization and management

2 The reality of where service design, the service-price offer as a whole, and the functioning of the service delivery system actually places a particular service in consumers' minds.

The linkage between the two is provided by consumers' expectations and their experiences, both of which we will be discussing in greater detail later in the present volume.

To achieve positioning objectives, marketing-oriented airlines are increasingly searching for ways to differentiate their service-price offers, using distinctive capabilities to create sustainable competitive advantage. This is not easy. It can be done by:

- conceptualizing the service and/or configuring its delivery processes in a manner which caters distinctly and uniquely to the needs of targeted consumers. Safe locational transformation is the core benefit, as we have seen, but most differentiation actually focuses around supplementary benefits such as reliability and comfort; and by
- manipulating the prices paid by consumers.[10]

Positioning should reflect the 'price/performance' combination chosen by an airline for its service(s). It links external analysis (what customers want, governments are allowing, and competitors are doing) with internal analysis (what the airline wants to be and the capabilities it has available to achieve this). Positioning should reflect competitive advantage. Market position is not proprietary, so if imitating successful positioning were itself the key to replicating success, returns to position would rapidly be equalized. Positioning does not **create** competitive advantage, it **exploits** it; positioning can only lead to success over the long run if it is sustained by some competitive advantage which makes it correct for the airline concerned.

In practice, the positioning achieved by an airline is a result of the following.

1 Its intended positioning strategy.

2 The perceptions of customers and potential customers, which might not always develop in the manner intended by the airline.

3 The activities of competitors.

A complicating factor for airlines is that the larger of them are competing in so many discrete geographical markets, each with its own cast of competitors and each with its own particular service-price offers (in respect of schedules and routeings for example), that the best they can achieve is to fix a position in these markets which is relatively consistent across their networks.

Customer value

Customer value was defined earlier in this chapter as 'perceived benefit minus the monetary price paid by the consumer'. Value is in this sense a matter of offering customers what they want, when they want it, at a price they consider acceptable given the level of service provided. If service is improved in some meaningful way or price is lowered in respect of an unchanged level of service, value increases. Low price and low service standards ('low' meaning that attributes are not offered or are offered at a relatively low level of quality) do not necessarily equate to poor value; they could mean simply that the customer is receiving a different value proposition from that offered by a higher service, higher priced competitor. A problem faced by airlines in a lot of international markets is that they are chasing each other up the 'differentiation ladder', offering supplementary attributes which are soon replicated by competitors, which become embedded into customers' expectations of baseline service at a given price, and which therefore enhance customer value without doing much for airline revenues or market shares.

There is a clear link between customer value and positioning. Value in this sense is a subjective, customer-defined point in competitive space. Figure 6.2 illustrates one possible approach to the mapping of this space.

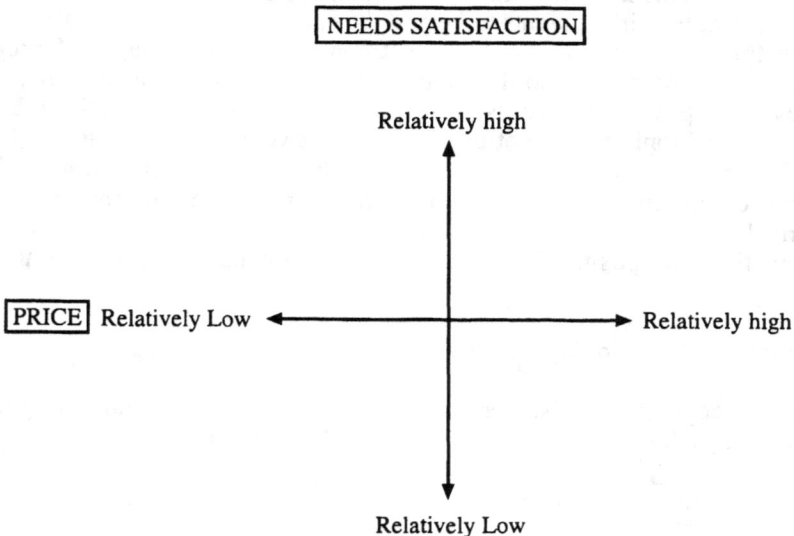

NEEDS SATISFACTION

Relatively high

PRICE Relatively Low ← → Relatively high

Relatively Low

Figure 6.2 : A customer value framework

The southeast quadrant represents 'bad' value (e.g. some intra-European business class service-price offers), whilst the northwest quadrant is 'good' value. Positioning in the southeast quadrant is unlikely to remain a sustainable strategy in truly open competitive markets. The other three quadrants are legitimate positioning targets, with the choice dependent upon characteristics of demand in targeted markets and given effect by the airline's selected competitive strategy.

Performance value and esteem value It can be useful to distinguish between 'performance value' and 'esteem value'. In any strategic group (assuming there to be no regulatory, infrastructural or other barriers that significantly constrain market entry or service delivery), performance value - which depends upon the delivery of non-psychological benefits to customers - tends broadly to equalize over time because so many airline service attributes are easily replicable. This makes esteem value - based on the psychological benefits gained from association with an esteemed brand, reputation, image or corporate culture - a potentially important source of differentiation and non-replicable value.

Customer value as outcome rather than output Customer value is a measure of what customers perceive themselves to be getting out of an airline's service-price offer, not what the airline itself is putting into it. Whereas passenger-kilometres or enplanements are common measures of an airline's sold **output**, customer value is a less commonly measured **outcome**. Airlines in competitive markets now have to be less concerned about raw outputs and more focused on outcomes. This is what the much-used expression 'customer focus' is all about.

Clearly then, before designing a service it is necessary to understand what contributes to target customers' perceptions of value. Axiomatic though this is, surprisingly few airlines - even in highly competitive markets - make any serious attempt at customer value analysis (i.e. the listing and ranking of attributes which customers say contribute to value, and the rating of how each airline and its competitors perform in respect of these attributes).

Service concept

Research is necessary to identify customer needs in targeted segments and to evaluate the extent to which particular service attributes are perceived by customers to offer benefits which satisfy these needs. One of the several problems that brought down Australian start-up Compass in the early 1990s was its management's cavalier attitude towards market research.[11] Whilst it is necessary to know what customers want and need, finding out what if anything they are prepared to pay for specific benefits - in other words, finding out the relationship between the cost of providing attributes and their impact on revenue - is not easy, particularly when these attributes are supplementary to the core service. This can be seen clearly in the debate currently surrounding the merits of highly complex and expensive (to acquire and maintain) interactive inflight entertainment systems.

From this research should stem a service (or benefits) concept which encapsulates all the benefits offered to consumers. A service is in essence a bundle of benefits. If a service attribute cannot logically be linked to an identified customer need by using the phrase '...which means that...', it is probably worthwhile reanalyzing what it contributes to customer value. Being a service, air transport generally offers benefits in the form of experiences and outcomes. It is these at which all the corporate and competitive strategizing discussed in the preceding chapters should ultimately be aimed. Thus, Southwest never set out to be a wide-market carrier, focusing instead on customers travelling on short-haul, point-to-point itineraries; it chose to differentiate itself on the basis of price, corporate culture, and image; its service concept is defined by high-frequency point-to-point flights spread relatively evenly throughout the day, predominantly short-haul routes, very limited hubbing, no interlining, and few amenities relative to full-service competitors. We will see in the next chapter how this service concept has been married to service delivery to create a self-reinforcing 'activity system' - self-reinforcing in the sense that service concept and delivery are consistent and are supportive of the airline's chosen competitive strategy.

As was noted above, the scheduled airline service concept offers a core benefit augmented by supplementary benefits.

1   Core benefit: safe, rapid, convenient transportation offered at or close to the required time. In fact, though, it is not always as simple as this. Because air travel demand is derived from the demand to satisfy deeper, underlying wants and needs, it can sometimes be difficult to separate locational transformation from other core elements of what it is that the customer is buying. For example, some airlines sell air transport as part of vacation packages which they themselves assemble, offering a discount on the package - air travel, accommodation, car hire, cruise, and so on - compared to the aggregate cost of each complementary service sold separately. In cases such as this the question arises as to whether air transportation is any 'more core' than the other elements, without which there would be no need for air travel in the first place.[12]

2   Supplementary benefits: these are the focus of many of the more highly visible differentiation, positioning, and value-building activities in which airlines now engage. Supplementary benefits stem from attributes that are part of a bundled offering, which overall might take one of three forms:[13]

- consistent with the accepted norm: what is accepted as the norm, of course, varies between geographical markets and also with length of haul. Most US domestic passengers paying full fare have to accept a norm which is very different from what is expected by customers in this segment on intra-European and intra-Asian flights of similar length, for example;
- below the accepted norm: by limiting service attributes (e.g. seat assignment, inflight meals, seat pitch, FFP benefits, airport lounges etc.), an airline targeting price-sensitive segments can build the basis for price differentiation (although there is a lot more to this strategy than simply cutting customer benefits which, as already observed in chapter 2, is not a difficult challenge for any competitor);
- above the accepted norm: this is the basis for attribute differentiation which, along with branding, is at the front-line in the battle against commoditization of air transport. It is particularly strongly fought in long-haul markets. Again, the problems here are the ease of replication and the difficulty often encountered getting customers to part with sufficient additional money to cover the cost of the incremental attributes.

A common core augmented by different levels of supplementary service can be the basis for a deep product line comprised of differentiated offers - such as first, business, and economy/coach class. On the other hand, carriers operating in product niches (e.g. low-fare/no-frills) will not generally build complex product lines.

In the final analysis, service is - as FedEx put it as long ago as the mid-1970s - 'all activities and reactions that customers perceive they have purchased'.[14] These perceptions drive customer expectations, which we will be looking at in chapters 9 and 10.

Common elements in the airline service concept

The objective of service conceptualization should be to meet customers' needs effectively and efficiently. It is necessary to spend money in order to understand the needs of customers in targeted segments before designing or redesigning a service concept. In general, the easier and cheaper it is to change a service attribute, the more replicable this attribute is likely to be and the shorter the span of time over which it can remain a meaningful source of differentiation.

Different attributes matter to different people. The primary requirements vary with purpose of travel and length of haul.

- **Leisure travellers**: most have relatively few product requirements beyond the provision of capacity to meet seasonal or perhaps weekend peaks, together with a basic level of ground and inflight service -

although what constitutes 'basic' is changing in some long-haul markets as the expectations of increasingly knowledgeable consumers continue to rise. Nonetheless, their requirements do not contribute anything like as much to production costs as those of business travellers.

• **Business travellers**: this segment tends to want expensive attributes such as high seat accessibility even at peak departure times, convenient schedules with high frequencies (what is meant by 'high' depending in part on length of haul), a wide network that offers integrated connections for those not travelling nonstop, good punctuality, and high standards of ground and inflight service. Having said this, there are some markets in which a growing proportion of people travelling on business, particularly those not on large corporate expense accounts, are willing to trade ground and inflight service for lower priced short- and medium-haul flights provided timings, frequencies, and punctuality are acceptable.[15]

• **Length of haul**: the longer the haul, the more important onboard comfort and service become relative to other attributes.

When considering elements of the service concept listed below, it should be borne in mind that in most cases it is not just the design of the attributes that is important but also the manner in which they are delivered. Service delivery is the subject of the next chapter. It is concept and delivery together that result in a particular outcome - ideally, a satisfied and loyal customer.

Safety and security Information search costs are too high for most consumers unless there has been a recent newsworthy incident, with the result that governments are relied upon to oversee this aspect of service. Safety and security have, in most well-established markets, been 'commoditized' to the extent that although they represent (along with schedule) the core product offered by any airline, much of the battle to differentiate service concepts and influence customer choice takes place in respect of supplementary attributes.[16] The longer the battle rages, of course, the more of these supplementary attributes themselves become 'commoditized'; this is one of the reasons why the growing importance of inimitable soft-side variables affecting style of delivery - variables such as corporate culture and values, for example - has been repeatedly stressed throughout both volumes of the book.

Network and schedule Given a forecast level of demand in a particular market, an airline's most basic service decision is whether to serve it with a nonstop, multi-stop, online connecting, interline connecting, or code-shared product (or possibly some combination of these), and whether service should be offered at a high frequency - perhaps implying a relatively high unit cost operation with smaller aircraft than might otherwise be used - or at a low frequency, possibly implying a larger aircraft and lower unit costs. The choice made will in part reflect the need to balance basic airline economics with the product design requirements that arise from the traffic mix in the market concerned; the airline's cost structure and market strategy must be weighed against the preferences of target customers and their willingness to pay for different levels of service quality. Fleet mix and, in the case of international routes, the terms of relevant bilaterals will also influence the choices that are made.

1   **Network.** A scheduled airline's network is evidently the foundation underpinning its service-price offer(s). What represents a 'strong' network will depend upon the competitive strategy and product positioning of the airline concerned. Full-service network airlines require the sort of hub strengths described in chapter 15 of Volume One as well as extensive network reach, whereas low-cost/no-frills carriers will generally be content tapping the most price-sensitive segments in a relatively small number of nonstop or one-stop O and D markets. Network strategy is closely linked - through the service-price offer it implies - to both revenue and cost management strategies. We saw this in chapter 2 when discussing strategic positioning, and we will return to the same point in chapter 7 when further exploring the concept of 'activity systems'.

Because airlines operate networks, an individual city-pair market may not be the same as a route; similarly, many of the passengers on a particular route are likely each to be travelling in separate city-pair markets. In any international market, for example, there could be a choice available between nonstop, direct, or indirect routeings. The level of competition in an international market is therefore not simply a reflection of whether it is dominated by a monopolist or bilaterally sanctioned duopolists operating third and fourth freedom services. It will depend as well upon the access, permitted capacity, traffic rights, and pricing flexibility available to fifth and sixth freedom carriers flying routes which serve the same market. As discussed in chapter 5, many airlines now extend their marketable networks by entering into code-sharing, blocked space, or franchising agreements.

Domestically, most notably in the United States, the same principle holds true insofar as long-haul markets (which means in this case from around 2,000 kilometres out to transcontinental) might be served indirectly over competing hubs as well as by direct and nonstop flights. When a market is characterized by a short distance between origin and destination, the level of competition faced by a nonstop monopolist or by duopolists is more likely to depend on the availability and price of competing surface modes. It is in medium-haul markets around 1,000 kilometres or perhaps beyond, where surface transport (assuming it to be an option) tends to be less competitive and geography does not favour competition over an intervening hub, that nonstop monopolists and duopolists are often in the strongest position. On the other hand, where an existing service is in fact over a hub there might be scope for a competing hub-bypass route.

Passengers prefer, in order, nonstop, direct, online connecting, and lastly interline routeings; many markets, of course, do not have the density or mix of traffic to support nonstop service - or at least not the high-frequency nonstop service demanded by the business segment. Airlines nonetheless have to bear these preferences in mind when designing their networks - as well as bearing in mind what competitors are doing. The result of this is that the world's larger carriers, alone or with alliance partners, are now more focused than ever before on their customers' complete journeys - wanting to design networks capable of carrying as many customers as possible all the way, to achieve this 'seamlessly', and to capture the entire revenue stream from customer itineraries.

2   **Frequency**. High frequencies are expensive to produce relative to lower frequencies with larger aircraft, but in business-oriented markets in particular they can contribute greatly to the capture of market share. Indeed, frequency is one of the primary forms of nonprice competition. The more frequently an airline serves a given route, the more likely it is that it will be able to match travellers' desired departure times, or at least minimize the implicit costs of not matching them.

The 'S-curve theory' holds that the carrier with most frequencies on a route will attract a greater proportion of traffic than the proportion of total frequencies contributed by its services, until the point is reached at which no further value attaches to time savings. This 'theory' is not universally accepted. Intuitively, it seems likely that a dominant carrier might benefit from a higher profile than airlines offering lower frequencies, but if the difference is only small it is unlikely that it would register in the minds of consumers. On the other hand, offering more frequencies tends to lead to a better presence high on the first screen of CRS displays, which is where most of the bookings come from in automated agencies. It is also worth bearing in mind a little mathematics: if an airline offers three return flights on a route each day it is providing nine return products (not necessarily all day-return products, of course), whereas a competitor with only two return flights has just four products available; by having one extra return flight, the first airline is therefore able to provide nine of the 13 single-carrier products on offer.

Deregulation, liberalization and the attendant evolution of hub-and-spoke systems have contributed to a tendency to meet growing demand by increasing frequencies rather than using larger aircraft, although infrastructural congestion places limits on this trend in some markets. Looked at on a route-by-route basis, increased frequencies have generally accounted for a significantly higher percentage of additional capacity supplied to meet demand growth than has the introduction of larger aircraft.[17] High frequencies are especially important for short-haul carriers, which must operate at least twice daily in the early morning and late afternoon/early evening in order to offer a day-return product for business travellers. More generally, on flights of 2-2^1/$_2$ hours, frequency has been found to have a very strong influence on demand from the business segment.[18] Regionals, particularly in the United States, also have the added incentive that in most cases a significant part of their service offer is connectivity to the network of the major carrier with which they are affiliated, and connectivity clearly improves as frequencies rise.

Frequency is a fundamental point of competition in business markets because these consumers generally value their time more highly in an economic sense than do most leisure travellers. The demand for business travel has historically been sufficiently price-inelastic to permit airlines to build into their tariffs a charge to compensate for the smaller aircraft, higher accessibility, and lower load factors which high frequencies imply on all but the most dense routes.

3 **Departure timings.** There are two complicating factors:

- first, as in the case of any transport system, airlines have the cost burden of accommodating peak demand - the pattern of which will vary depending upon the market or segment being targeted; and
- second, timings are not always under direct airline control if one end of a route is slot-constrained.

Generally, the first outbound and the last inbound service are strongly competitive on short-haul routes serving the business segment,[19] whilst on long-haul routes the effect of time zones tends to provide fairly narrow departure windows within which most competitors cluster if they are to schedule feasible and/or desirable arrival times.

Scheduling strategies determine frequencies, routeings and, particularly over hub-based networks, the extent of connectivity between points served by an airline. They are accordingly a major driver of product quality, especially insofar as the business segment - which generally wants the convenience offered by high frequencies, minimum elapsed journey times, and maximum network connectivity - is concerned.[20]

4 **Punctuality**. Despatch reliability (on departure) and ontime performance (on arrival) are usually judged on the basis of delays in excess of 15 minutes. This is an important service attribute for most segments, but particularly so for business travellers. Weather and traffic congestion take it outside complete airline control, but investment in technology (as described in Volume One, chapter 7) may be able to reduce weather delays. Although technical delays tend to be associated with ageing aircraft, new types often bring with them teething troubles for launch customers. Other factors affecting punctuality include the efficiency of passenger-handling and aircraft turnaround processes, line maintenance capacity, policies in respect of the holding of spares, and scheduling policy. With regard to scheduling, tight turnarounds and aggressive timetabled block times increase aircraft utilization but threaten both punctuality and schedule integrity unless carefully managed. Clearly, any airline operating a high-activity hub-and-spoke system can face congestion and heavy resource loading during peaks of activity at the hub, and yet its product to a large extent stands or falls on achieving good punctuality.

5 **Ticket conditionality**. Anything other than a full-fare on-demand ticket might have imposed upon it restrictions in respect of schedule and itinerary. Restrictions are commonly applied to rescheduling (which might be disallowed or subjected to an administration fee), stopovers, rerouteing, endorsement, interlining, period of stay, cancellation or refund.

Image Image and positioning are closely related. Image provides information, which can have a positive, neutral, or negative effect on buying behaviour (as well as on stakeholders other than customers, internal and external). It is affected not only by receipt or non-receipt of benefits, but by everybody and everything in an airline which is visible to the consumer or potential consumer. The effect of a good image is to attract potential consumers and to impose on existing consumers a 'psychological switching cost'. Image and reality are rarely congruent, but the further apart they are the less sustainable the gap over a protracted period.[21]

Reservations Ease of access to distribution channels and ready availability of information are the key criteria. Airlines have to ensure that any intermediaries used are informed about, and where necessary trained to sell, their services in addition to having easy access to seat and cargo space inventories. From the perspective of passengers there are several other important service attributes which might be required at this point.

1 **Seat accessibility**. This is a measure of the probability that a reservation can be made in the preferred class on a chosen flight, with

high accessibility being indicative of a good probability of success even close to departure. Different market segments have different requirements, with business travellers in particular demanding high levels of accessibility to facilitate late bookings, rescheduling, or rerouteing. This is an expensive product feature to provide because it often leads to lower load factors than might otherwise have been achieved; on the other hand, it is a feature which attracts higher yielding traffic. An airline's accessibility policy should to a large extent be dictated by the segments it has chosen to serve; it will also be a function of aircraft type, frequency, and cabin configurations deployed on a route, and of the capabilities of the yield management system used to monitor booking profiles against historical patterns.

2   **Overbooking.** Intended to combat 'no-shows', overbooking (often more delicately referred to as 'oversales') could be argued to provide a hidden service to late-booking passengers by 'creating' accessibility. Passengers who are subjected to involuntary denied boarding doubtless have other views. Generally, the lower a carrier's break-even load factor the easier it is to adopt a conservative overbooking policy. Airlines experiencing low yields and high break-even load factors, on the other hand, have more incentive to overbook aggressively.[22] Minimum denied boarding compensation is mandated in the United States and the EU, but this aspect of airline service recovery varies widely elsewhere in the world.[23]

3   **Ticket conditionality.** Advance booking requirements are commonly applied to discounted tickets to prevent yield dilution. This is a trade-off likely to be acceptable to passengers with low accessibility requirements.

Ground experience Airlines are judged by a wide range of ground service attributes which, depending on the carrier and the class of travel, might include any of the following:

- convenience of the airport, where there is more than one airport serving an origin or destination point;
- limousine service to and from the airport (possibly including in-car check-in for departing premium passengers);
- valet parking;
- airport facilities, including access, parking, common user facilities, walking distances, ability to cope with passengers having special needs, quality and availability of information, availability of baggage carts and porters, and the quality of shops, bars and restaurants (most of which are outside the direct control of airlines, other than carriers owning or leasing terminals);[24]

- check-in style (e.g. positive-name check-in), procedures and facilities, including advance check-in, telephone or Internet check-in, remote check-in (e.g. at hotels, or in the terminal but away from check-in desks), through-check-in for connecting (including code-shared) flights, round-trip check-in for day-return passengers with hand-baggage only, automated check-in for regular travellers, number of desks and nature of queueing (single-line queueing still being surprisingly uncommon outside the United States), and priority check-in for first and business class passengers or those with only carry-on luggage;
- nature/size of baggage allowance, and degree of flexibility in respect of excess baggage charges;
- 'fast-track' channels through security and immigration;
- lounges;
- response to delays. Research has proven that waits accompanied by ignorance are perceived to be longer - and are therefore likely to be more frustrating - than waits of the same duration accompanied by an explanation and, if possible, a forecast. To the extent that one school of thought on the nature of service encounters characterizes them as a battle for control between provider and consumer, information also helps those consumers who need to do so to feel more in control of the encounter. A related product quality factor is whether or not the airline assumes responsibility for delayed passengers;
- priority embarkation and disembarkation of first and business class passengers;
- general availability of assistance when required;
- facilities for first and business class passengers to freshen up on arrival off long-haul flights, either in an airline arrivals lounge or a day-room at an airport hotel (which can be particularly valuable when flights arrive in the early hours of the morning);
- speed and accuracy of baggage handling (together with priority for first and business class passengers); and
- the manner in which any post-flight problems or complaints are dealt with.

Inflight experience There are several service attributes to consider here, notably relating to the aircraft itself, the cabin, and to amenities and processes.

1   **Aircraft-related.** Age of equipment may or may not be an issue; some airlines consider a young fleet to be a strong marketing advantage, whilst others hold the view that provided an aircraft has modern and well-maintained external and internal appearances few passengers either know or much care how old it is (within limits, of course). A more heated debate has raged in recent years around the 'jet versus high-speed turboprop' choice on longer regional routes.

Despite strides made in suppressing the cabin noise and vibration levels of turboprops, the tolerance for them amongst passengers with a choice rarely exceeds two hours - and is considerably less in many parts of the world. In some markets, 'turboprop avoidance' amongst customers is becoming an important service design issue.

A minor issue which might grow in importance over time is cabin air quality. Airlines operating modern equipment have considerable control over air recirculation and exchange rates and fresh air supply. Some opt for standards lower than would be permissible for public buildings in many countries.[25] Finally, the size of the cabin cross-section can vary significantly between aircraft types sharing broadly the same mission performance capabilities, and could affect consumers' perceptions; certainly, there is often a preference for twin-aisle over single-aisle equipment where the choice exists.

2 **Cabin-related.** Some segments of demand are served with separate cabins, notably those being offered first and business class products but also including - in just a few cases - passengers travelling on full economy fares in long-haul markets.

Whereas some airlines still present their cabins to customers as capsules in which to be transported, others take a more proactive approach to the marketing of aircraft as places in which to rest, work, be pampered, be entertained, be informed, and/or shop. Cabin-related attributes which shape the inflight experience can include:
- the ability to select a preferred seat at check-in or, in premium classes, at the time of reservation (which can affect a passenger's perception of the cabin environment once on board);
- presence of an adjacent empty seat. This can be a significant influence on consumers' satisfaction. Airlines can do more than many yet do to help themselves in this regard by allocating centre seats last (especially on single-aisle aircraft), for example, or by choosing widebody seating configurations that raise the load factor threshold up to which all passengers can in principle be placed next to an empty seat - a threshold which varies through the 50 and 60 per cent ranges in respect of a nine-abreast aircraft, depending upon whether the chosen configuration is 3-3-3, 2-5-2, 2-4-3 etc.;
- availability of smoking sections or, conversely, the imposition of either flight-specific or systemwide smoking bans;
- availability of 'quiet zones' on long-haul flights;[26]
- amount of space for carry-on items in closets and overhead bins;
- seating density, which is a reflection of seat pitch, seat width, and the width of aisles, and is to a large extent dependent on class of travel;[27]
- maximum angle of seat recline;
- seating quality, which on long-haul flights could be augmented by sleeper seats, footrests, adjustable headrests, and lumbar support

(again, dependent on service conceptualization within the context of class of travel). Long-haul first class accommodation on many of those airlines retaining it appears to be moving to a 'modular' concept, with full 180-degree recline and considerable privacy being available within each seating module;
- ratios of passengers to lavatories in each cabin and the cleanliness of lavatories;[28] and
- decor, appearance, and cleanliness of the cabin interior and condition of the windows.[29]

3   **Amenities and processes.** As well as polite and efficient service, the battle for attribute differentiation includes:
- cabin crew ratios in each class, which might be set at the regulatory minimum, varied in relation to numbers of boarded passengers, or set permanently high in search of a service advantage;
- visibility and responsiveness of cabin crew throughout the flight, not just during meal or beverage service (research having shown that high visibility enhances consumer satisfaction, even when no specific attention is required);
- inflight entertainment, which is becoming an increasingly important (if short-lived and not invariably successful) source of differentiation efforts amongst long-haul carriers, with the emphasis being on in-seat videos (or, in a few cases, Video Walkmen for premium class passengers) offering both more options and greater flexibility as to when and how they can be used. Pre-ordering of movies or video-games will soon become feasible;
- inflight communications, including telephone, fax, and eventually e-mail facilities;
- inflight retailing, which currently runs in most cases to duty-free and mail-order catalogue shopping but will eventually include widespread adoption of interactive systems on medium- and long-haul flights;
- food and beverages. Expectations vary widely between geographical regions, particularly on short-haul flights. Food service has been curtailed on many short-haul US flights, for example (Continental and one or two niche carriers being the primary exceptions). On some German domestic services Lufthansa introduced a popular 'Gate Buffet' to offer carry-on selections as part of the Lufthansa Express service concept, but subsequently dropped it when the concept as a whole was abolished; at the time of writing, SAS has recently begun experimenting with a similar approach on some trunk routes within Scandinavia. On long-haul flights, light meals and meals on demand are available in several first and business classes, and a few airlines serve meals to first class passengers on the ground prior to evening departures;[30]

- journals and newspapers, amenity kits, pillows, blankets (or duvets on a very small number of carriers), and giveaways;
- special programmes on a few long-haul services, such as British Airways' 'Well-being in the Air' diet, exercise, and aromatherapy offering, and Virgin's manicure and massage service; and
- more prosaically, clear and helpful information in the event of delays.

Emotional factors By virtue of its nature, provision of a service has both functional/tangible and emotional/intangible dimensions. It is very easy to focus on functional attributes when designing a service concept and ignore the mood, atmosphere, and tone of the service experience. Emotional - particularly interpersonal - aspects of the experience can often be a primary source of differentiation leading, if positive, to customer satisfaction and loyalty. This is why an airline's corporate culture and the attitudes and values of employees - notably, but not only, those in the 'front office' - are so important. It is these that underlie the tenor of the human interactions which help shape the emotional attributes of a particular service concept.

Cargo services Depending upon the manner in which a specific service concept is designed, attributes could include:

- convenient schedules over a high-frequency network with good market coverage;
- rapid response times, together with willingness to handle late pick-ups and short close-outs prior to departure;
- high 'flown as booked' rates (which are not always easy to achieve when weight and volume are not precisely known in advance of a shipment's arrival for loading);
- straightforward documentation;
- real-time tracking capabilities (now being offered on the World Wide Web by some carriers);
- efficient ground handling (more readily automated for parcels than for bulk shipments);
- good security, and responsive claims service when things go wrong;
- ontime performance and rapid confirmation of delivery;
- responsive tracing services; and
- accurate and timely billing.

What is quite apparent is that it is not just physical goods that are being processed, but information as well. Integrated carriers have raised service standards by offering all these attributes within the context of a reliable, one-stop, door-to-door service which has segmented the market with a range of time-definite products from overnight through seven or more days.

With the advent of lean production methods, economising on time and inventory holding is often more important than direct cost savings. Time precision will, therefore, become increasingly important for international trade, in particular for intermediate goods - which form part of just-in-time production chains - and for spare parts.[31]

Integrated carriers have also raised the competitive stakes, and customers' switching costs, by placing hardware and software for booking and administering shipments right onto consignors' desks. More recently they have been moving into logistics management for their larger clients (e.g. collection, storage, stock control, customs/administration, international shipment, and delivery); this responds to the needs of some customers for frequent and direct distribution to their markets rather than for the bulk shipments typical in the past.[32] It also reflects the needs these carriers have to generate greater profits from the heavy investments they have made, and to lock major accounts into customized, long-term relationships.[33]

As we saw in chapter 2, however, there are many different ways in which to approach strategic positioning in cargo markets. Carriers that look upon their output of cargo space largely as a commoditized byproduct of passenger services will be making very different offers to the marketplace compared with those made by airlines trying to position themselves as reliable members of their major customers' logistics chains. In reality, many airlines have yet to approach the conceptualization of cargo services in a manner that reflects full understanding of customer requirements; outside the top tier, widespread inattention to quality concerns and a lack of clearly articulated strategic positioning are not uncommon. These problems reflect the fact that much of the airfreight industry has in the past been more attentive to revenue targets than service standards. Furthermore, despite the significant revenue contribution it is able to make in many air transport markets, airfreight has tended historically to be marginalized in some airlines, receiving disproportionately less senior management attention than the more glamorous passenger side of the business.

Circumstances are nonetheless changing, driven by rising customer expectations which have themselves been partly stimulated by the innovative service offers emanating in particular from integrated carriers. Delta, for example, developed the following domestic cargo products in the mid-90s:

- Delta Air Cargo Special Handling (DASH): express service for packages under 70lbs.;
- Priority First Freight: express service for packages too large to qualify for DASH; and
- Priority Second Day and Priority Third Day: non-premium services for general freight.

A few of the larger airlines, either independently or in partnership with forwarders, are making available the easy-to-use, guaranteed, time-definite, door-to-door services which a rapidly growing segment of the customer base has been 'trained' by the integrators to demand. Having said this, it remains true that there is still a healthy demand for efficient, reliable, competitively priced airport-to-airport haulage. We saw this in chapter 2 when cargo market niches were discussed. Many small and medium-sized airlines are never realistically going to be in a position to offer a comprehensive range of integrated products. There is an argument that carriers such as these should concentrate their efforts on line haulage, and leave creation and marketing of integrated products to those forwarders prepared to take on the fight.

Nonscheduled services ICAO has defined several different types of nonscheduled products, which have evolved in response both to changing market demands and to the constraints imposed by various regulatory circumstances at different times and in different parts of the world.[34]

1 Passenger charter flights.
   • Those open to the general public: advance booking charters (ABCs); inclusive tour charters (ITCs); public charters.
   • Those open only to eligible segments of the public: affinity group charters; common purpose charters; special event charters; student charters; single-entity or own-use charters.

2 Cargo charter flights include the following.
   • Charters for resale by forwarders, consolidators, shippers' associations and similar entities.
   • Single entity or own-use charters.

3 Combinations or variants of the above categories.
   • Mixed passenger/cargo charters.
   • Split charters, where the capacity of the chartered aircraft is shared by two or more charterers.
   • 'Co-mingling' of different types of charter traffic on the same flight (e.g. ABC and ITC).
   • 'Intermingling' of outbound and return charter traffic on the same flights.

4 Nonscheduled, non-charter flights. Capacity is sold to individually ticketed or waybilled members of the public on flights which serve authorized routes, but not according to a published schedule.

Notwithstanding the existence of these alternatives within the nonscheduled product range, it is the case that in recent years there has been considerable blurring of the distinction between nonscheduled and scheduled products in some markets. In several popular leisure markets, for example, 'schedulized charters' open to the public are now available with such regularity that they are difficult to categorize as 'nonscheduled'; similarly, some scheduled airlines offer deeply discounted products to leisure segments which are so heavily conditioned that they are practically indistinguishable from publicly available charter products. In the EU, as was noted in chapter 3 of Volume One, the regulatory distinction between scheduled and nonscheduled services has now been essentially eliminated.

Other points regarding service conceptualization

There are several further points which need to be made in respect of service conceptualization.

1   Not all product attributes are under direct airline control; airport authorities, monopoly handling agents, traffic congestion, the weather, and other passengers can all influence a consumer's perception of her experience on a carrier.

2   Whereas service conceptualization is about what **should** be done, service delivery is about what **is** done and **how** it is done; clearly, though, because consumers are active participants in service delivery processes they themselves can drive a wedge between 'should' on the one hand and 'is' and 'how' on the other. We will return to this point in chapter 7.

3   Airlines' approaches to the outcome of market segmentation exercises vary. In most US domestic markets, for example, business and leisure segments are offered services differentiated from each other largely on the basis of price and ticket conditionality, with ground and inflight benefits common to all segments of what is increasingly being treated in this respect as a 'mass market'. (There are separate business classes on some flights, but these as well as first class have tended in recent years to be populated as much by frequent flyer upgrades as by members of a defined segment at which a specific service-price offer has been targeted.) In other parts of the world, where segment price elasticities are different, the same exercise yields a range of service attributes offering benefits to the business segment, most notably in the form of priority check-in and baggage handling arrangements, airport lounges, and higher standards of inflight care and comfort; again, ticket conditionality to minimize revenue dilution is a feature of offers made to more price-elastic segments of demand.

The vigour of price and service competition between carriers on any given route depends not only on the number of airlines competing but also on whether all are providing the same type of service, how those offering lower frequencies or lower standards in respect of other service attributes choose to price their offers, and how 'full-service' competitors respond. As markets liberalize, it is becoming increasingly important for airline managements to understand and, if possible, anticipate customers' needs, wants, and expectations. Pressures created by deregulation and liberalization are also requiring airline managers to devote larger proportions of their time to the pursuit of innovation and to the tactical manipulation of the marketing mix within the context of chosen competitive strategies. It is to the marketing mix that we turn next.

Managing the service-price offer

Using market share as the criterion, the literature recognizes market leaders, challengers, and followers. Each might pursue a different set of objectives, which may be conflicting or compatible. What makes the airline business particularly interesting is that because it is a network industry serving increasingly interdependent but nonetheless still highly fragmented markets, these three roles are interchanged amongst a variable cast of competitors across thousands of individual city-pairs. One effect of alliances and globalization is to expand the scope of competition between a small number of emerging integrated networks, each spanning more of these individual markets than any single player has previously covered.

As competitive environments liberalize, they are opened to previously excluded airlines or - on a much smaller scale - to start-ups. Market leaders and comfortably balanced oligopolists are challenged. The tactical weapons used on both sides of this battle are found in the '4Ps' of the marketing mix: product (i.e. the service concept), price, promotion (i.e. marketing communications), and place (i.e. distribution). Although primarily tactical, the marketing mix also embodies an airline's strategic approach to its customers. In particular, it is the means by which positioning strategies are implemented.[35]

Sometimes, management of the marketing mix gives rise to service-price offers that satisfy some segments of demand whilst dissatisfying others. This has happened in large parts of the US domestic market, for example. A growing number of customers have been demanding a service-price balance different from what the full-service network carriers have in most cases been offering: lower fares are being demanded in return for less inflight service. Full-fare (primarily business) passengers travelling in coach are on the receiving end of the 'less inflight service' part of the revised offer, but are seldom able to benefit from the lower fares (which generally require advance booking). This underlines the point made in Volume One, chapter 10 with regard to segmentation: no matter how many ways are found to segment any given market, there is a limit to the number of ways an aluminium tube can be sliced. It does, nonetheless, show a lack of imagination on the part of several US network carriers which have, in the opinions of some observers, seemed quite willing to exploit rather than satisfy their higher yielding domestic passengers.[36]

The impact of marketing mix initiatives will vary between markets and segments depending upon where they sit on a continuum bounded by 'expansible' and 'inexpansible' extremes.

1   Expansible markets are sensitive to industry-wide marketing efforts, and within the industry individual market shares will be sensitive to particular airlines' efforts. In this case, a carrier's revenue forecast will to a considerable extent depend not only on more obvious demand determinants such as price and the state of the economy, but also on how much effort and cash it is prepared to invest in nonprice elements of the marketing mix. Forecast traffic and revenue are therefore as much an outgrowth of the marketing plan as an input into that plan.

2   At the other end of the continuum, an inexpansible market offers little more than the opportunity to push on the proverbial 'piece of string': levels of marketing expenditure will have only limited direct bearing on demand.

The reality of most airline markets is some way from either end of this continuum. One of management's primary tasks is to identify approximately where - that is, to identify the marketing elasticities it faces - and invest accordingly. Figure 6.3 provides a simple conceptualization of the issues.

Proactive management of the marketing mix needs to be guided not only by an airline's mission and objectives; it must also be responsive to changing conditions in the competitive environment, to economic cycles, and to the evolution of markets, products, and brands through their own life cycles. Quite a few airlines are only just beginning to think in these terms. The following paragraphs make brief reference to each of the four marketing mix variables. Greater detail can be found in specialized texts.[37]

Managing the service concept

We looked earlier at various attributes that can be designed into the service concept. Distinctions are drawn in the literature between 'qualifying' and 'determinant' attributes:

*   **qualifying attributes** are those that a service concept must possess just in order to get into a potential customer's 'consideration set';
*   **determinant attributes** are those that determine choice, either because they are uniquely available from the airline concerned or because the chosen carrier delivers them to a higher standard than its competitors.[38]

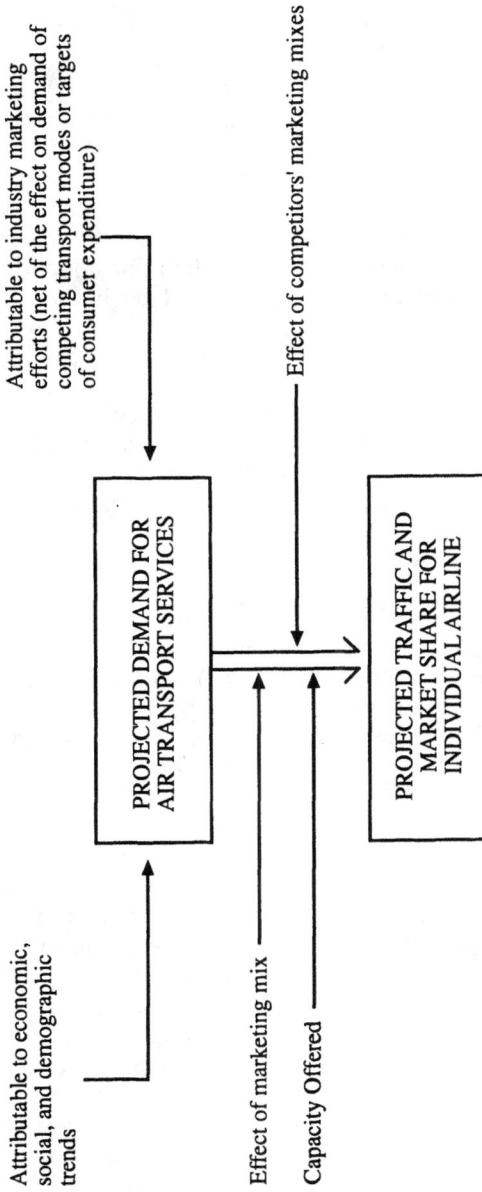

Attributable to industry marketing
efforts (net of the effect on demand of
competing transport modes or targets
of consumer expenditure)

Effect of competitors' marketing mixes

Attributable to economic,
social, and demographic
trends

Effect of marketing mix

Capacity Offered

PROJECTED DEMAND FOR
AIR TRANSPORT SERVICES

PROJECTED TRAFFIC AND
MARKET SHARE FOR
INDIVIDUAL AIRLINE

Figure 6.3 : The role of industry and individual airline marketing mix management in determining demand and market share

Just as is the case with tangible goods, services have life cycles. As markets become more competitive, so airlines need to extend their skills at developing new service-price offers, launching them cost-effectively, and understanding the impact their progress through the life cycle has on other marketing mix variables.[39] The service development process involves a search for and screening of ideas, followed by market research and cost analysis, and then development and testing, concluding with a final decision on whether or not to go with a commercial launch. A few airlines are constantly iterating through this process, some do so intermittently, whilst many just react to new ideas after their introduction by others - either replicating them quickly or waiting until later in their life cycles.

Innovation Innovation can stem from a number of sources:

- more airlines are now willing to listen to feedback from their most important customers - in other words, to accept the 'knowledge capital' these customers are prepared to invest in their relationships with the airline - and to turn the knowledge gained into innovative services;
- airlines are also spending more time trying to anticipate customers' needs;
- finally, there are times when competitive advantage can be gained by proactively leading customer requirements. Without wasting money on giving people attributes they do not want and/or are unwilling to pay for, there can sometimes be merit in taking initiatives to change their perceptions of what is both possible and desirable. Virgin Atlantic did this when it chose to introduce its innovative and successful Upper Class airport lounges, for example, despite survey evidence suggesting that customers were not notably excited by libraries, train sets, putting greens or ski simulators.

Whereas vision is a mental picture of the future, innovation is a step along the path towards creation of that future. Innovation involves finding new and better ways of competing in an industry (e.g. Southwest) or possibly even the building of an entirely new industry (e.g. FedEx). Service innovation can be rooted in changes to either a service concept or to the processes used to deliver it. Clearly, though, most forms of service innovation cannot be commercialized in order to allow the innovators to appropriate all the benefits derived from them. (Having said this, it is true that some airlines have copyrighted or patented certain computer software and cabin seating innovations, for example, but this is relatively rare when the industry is taken as a whole.) The ease with which most service innovations can be imitated is one reason why barriers to market entry - which physically exclude competitors - and the particularity of individual corporate cultures - which powerfully shape a carrier's service delivery style - can be such important sources of competitive advantage.

In a service industry, it is vital that the knowledge and insight of front-line staff are used in the development of new service concepts. The simultaneity of service production and consumption mean that they are receiving almost constant feedback from consumers of existing services. Furthermore, they are also the people who will have to deliver any innovation into the marketplace. The most important requirement of service innovation, however, is to focus the development of new or revised service concepts firmly on customer needs and expectations.

Several tools used in other industries are gradually finding their way into the airline business to assist in the service development process; one of these is quality function deployment (QFD). QFD is a sequential approach which starts by identifying customer requirements and expectations, and then links each to one or more specific design elements in the service concept, allowing evaluation of whether and how well requirements can be met by the design under review; after this has been accomplished, various metrics can be established so that performance in respect of each element can be tracked. It is sometimes necessary to arrive at trade-offs between what is desirable and what is feasible, but QFD helps to make this type of decision rational by allowing customer requirements - now clearly defined and linked to specific elements within the service concept - to be ranked, weighted, and prioritized, and by permitting analysis of the linkages between multiple requirements and multiple design elements. Finally, QFD can be used to bring focus to analyses of competitors' service-price offers. In essence, then, by linking 'What?' to 'How?' and 'How well?', QFD provides a framework for customer-oriented service innovation. It encourages the breaking-down of services into their design and delivery elements, enabling each to be analyzed and tested in the market so that any change in the service concept is capable of satisfying specific, identified physical and emotional needs of targeted customers.

Doing all this is relatively straightforward when the competitive environment is stable. When it becomes as turbulent and complex as it is now becoming for most airlines, assessment of how consumers will perceive particular service attributes two or three years into the future and judgement of what competitors might get up to over a similar time-span is a very real challenge. Continuous experimentation, the almost constant testing of new ideas, and the evaluation of new service attributes in the context of the value they offer to customers and the costs they impose on the airline is one response to such environments. This is not inexpensive, and it requires a leadership committed to the fostering of change and learning - leaders who are as receptive to the emergence of unplanned new approaches to the serving of target customers as they are to the results of deliberately planned initiatives. Even when an existing service concept is successful, continuous experimentation around the core of the concept and its delivery processes is necessary to keep it updated in the face of constantly changing customer expectations and competitor offerings. Away from the flight-line, 'if it ain't broke, don't fix it' is no longer an attitude likely to breed long-term commercial success.

One of the 'spaces to be watched' in respect of airline service concept and delivery process innovation is the incipient trend amongst some leading international carriers away from the treatment of consumers as captive, dominated objects to be passed through the system and provided with one-size-fits-all, take-it-or-leave-it service attributes. Particularly in the premium classes, there is a growing emphasis on the recognition of individuality and the need for greater consumer choice regarding whether and when to use supplementary attributes such as inflight meals and entertainment, for example. Greater spontaneity in both scripted and unscripted service encounters is also being stressed by these carriers.

In the final analysis, however, product upgrades and relaunches are investments which need to be evaluated in terms of the returns anticipated from them relative to costs incurred - much as though they were tangible assets. What can make the mathematics rather difficult is the fact that upgrading 'hard' product features, such as the inflight service environment or the range of amenities offered, may have an unquantifiable but nonetheless positive effect on 'soft' variables, such as employee morale, motivation, and attitudes. This effect broadens the dimensions across which consumers' experiences are being improved and contributes, through enhanced consumer satisfaction, to higher levels of customer retention.

For several reasons, business class is perhaps the major battleground for long-haul network carriers in particular.

1   It is a major revenue generator in its own right: British Airways earns approximately half its revenues from the premium cabins (including first class).

2   Loyal business travellers might be expected to choose their preferred carrier for vacation travel, assuming it offers service (itself or in conjunction with an alliance partner) to the desired destination.

3   There is a possibility that a business traveller impressed with what he or she sees of an airline might prefer the same carrier for freight shipments.

These and similar reasons underlie the regular cycle of business class product upgrades and relaunches in which leading international network carriers are now engaged.

Institutionalization of innovation   'Change' is no longer just a discrete event, but a continuous process of reassessment and innovation. Almost as important as service innovation itself are the institutionalization of a corporate architecture and a corporate culture supportive of innovation, and the building of a marketplace reputation as an industry leader. In service industries, what appears to be a competitive advantage founded on innovation is often actually an advantage founded on the capability to innovate continuously; this is particularly true in the airline business, where individual innovations are difficult to appropriate because of rapid imitation and so are rarely the source of sustainable competitive advantage in themselves.

If an architecture supportive of innovation can be more important than any particular innovation itself, it is also true that reputation can be as significant as reality. Provided an airline's service offers do not visibly fall behind those of its competitors and it has the capability to absorb and adapt the best of others' innovations, a reputation as an innovator can - once established - become a source of competitive advantage even if the carrier concerned is not invariably at the cutting edge of new developments. Such a reputation is a form of marketing communications. It can be a relatively inexpensive form if in its absence every new service initiative would have to be explicitly and expensively communicated to a marketplace which, unless told otherwise, does not link the carrier concerned to meaningful service innovation.

Service mix/range An airline with a portfolio of several service-price offers pitched at different markets and market segments will have a service mix/service range which can be measured along several dimensions:

- breadth: the number of product lines offered (e.g. scheduled passenger, scheduled freight, charter, third-party engineering and maintenance, reservations etc.);
- depth: the number of variations within a single line (e.g. scheduled passenger: different service-price offers in first, business, and coach/economy classes and perhaps different levels or types of service offered through low-cost units, franchised regionals etc.; scheduled freight: express parcels, heavy freight, door-to-door, airport-to-airport, time-definite over a range of periods);
- length: the total number of service-price offers embodied in all the lines;
- consistency: the relationship between lines. Such relationships often exist in respect of shared distribution channels and service delivery subsystems, for example. The presence of core competencies, discussed in chapter 15 of Volume One, can be a significant factor here.

A service mix is managed by adding to or deleting from breadth and depth, which in turn will affect overall length and perhaps also consistency. As noted in chapter 15 of Volume One, some long-haul carriers, for example, have in recent years dropped first class service and upgraded aspects of their business class products to something close to old first class service.

Because the demand for airline seats is a derived demand, potential complementary products abound. We saw earlier that some airlines tempted to broaden their product lines into industries such as hotels and car rental have met with only limited success, and many have recently shrunk lines to focus on redefined 'core businesses'. It was also noted that the opinions of airline managements still vary somewhat with regard to which lines are 'core' and which are not.

The more complex an airline's service mix, the greater the variety likely to be found in other marketing mix elements - price, promotion, and place.

Managing price [40]

Price is one of the most important threads binding the service concept (i.e. product design), marketing communications, and distribution strategy into a single, coherent, strategically positioned offer to the marketplace. As such, it is a significant strategic variable. It is also a tactical variable in the daily cut-and-thrust of liberalized competitive environments, used to manage fluctuations in demand on individual routes. Pricing influences demand, supply, costs, profits, market share, cash-flow, and product positioning. For example, a price reduction may:

- stimulate demand, thereby expanding the total market. The net effect on revenues might be positive, negative, or neutral depending upon the market's price elasticity of demand;
- divert demand, thereby shifting revenue from one competitor to another or from one of the initiating airline's products to another of the same airline's products; or
- be demand-neutral, and therefore dilute yields.

Airlines, of course, do not inevitably have total freedom to manage prices at will. It was explained in Volume One, chapter 3 that although several significant domestic and international markets are now either deregulated or sufficiently liberal to permit wide latitude in pricing decisions, many more are still subject to direct or indirect regulation. Nonetheless, as liberalization spreads, pricing moves from being a largely administrative function conducted in a relatively predictable competitive environment to a critical skill practised in a highly volatile competitive environment.

Value-based pricing Amongst factors other than airline collusion backed by regulatory 'fiat' that are generally assumed to drive prices, two of the most pervasive are cost and value. We have already seen that a fundamental difference between value-based pricing and the cost-plus approach is that the latter starts with costs and then turns to the market, whereas the former looks first to the market. By bringing value and consumer surplus into the picture the question being asked is no longer simply, 'What will the market bear?' Instead, we are asking 'What will the market pay for the service being offered given its quality and the offers being made by competitors, and will this cover our costs of production?' The service is likely to offer both core and supplementary benefits. Core benefits, such as basic levels of safety, comfort, and schedule convenience, can often be 'commoditized' in markets where there are few barriers to entry. Particularly when this happens, attributes that cannot easily be replicated - such as brand image or the impact of corporate culture on service delivery - might be an important source of customer value, notably in the less price-sensitive segments.

The clever trick, of course, is to assess market needs correctly, design a service which satisfies those needs and which the airline concerned is both capable of offering and able to produce at a competitive cost, and then pitch the price correctly in the context of other marketing mix variables and rather imprecisely estimated elasticities. Nonetheless, there is strong appeal in value-based pricing insofar as it is keyed off demand, price elasticity, and product positioning rather than costs - and the closer an airline can get to charging a fare (in excess of costs) that equates to the maximum that target customers would be willing to pay, the more of the added value in the air transport service it is capturing for itself.[41]

The importance of market structure Market structure is clearly an important determinant of price. Despite all the talk about airline consolidation and globalization, the air transport industry as a whole remains highly fragmented. Irrespective of the scope of its overall network, every airline is operating in a number of separate city-pair markets which, because of hubbing and multi-stop services, might involve multiple flight segments. Pricing in each market will be differently affected by competition and by the varying demand elasticities of the particular types of traffic that predominate. An airline's pricing behaviour will therefore not necessarily be consistent between a market dominated by business traffic in which it faces little or no competition, and a highly competitive leisure route.

An airline offering high-frequency, nonstop schedules on a route dominated by business travellers, having an attractive inflight product, a comprehensive frequent flyer loyalty scheme, and a strong brand image will be offering a different set of benefits and sacrifices than a competitor with a low-frequency, indirect service and other generally less desirable product features. To compensate for the sacrifices inherent in longer journey time, less flexible rescheduling opportunities and lower levels of other benefits being offered, the latter carrier may want to set its price below that of the better-placed competitor. Elsewhere in its network, however, the second carrier in this example might be offering the best schedules and service available on a particular route, and therefore need not price below competitors in order to generate traffic.

Price as part of a service-price offer Pricing affects customer value both directly and also through its effect on the image of an airline and its services. In deregulated or liberalized markets fares are driven by competitive pressures and become largely delinked from costs except, perhaps, to the extent that they are sometimes dictated by the cost structure of the lowest cost airline in a particular market. This has happened most clearly in the United States. The only ways an unsubsidized airline which is not the lowest cost producer can compete in a fully competitive, liberalized environment is by lowering its costs so that it can more profitably match fares and/or by offering a more competitive package of nonprice benefits in areas such as frequency, schedule, inflight amenities, or brand image to support premium pricing. The nonprice approach may be difficult to sustain in respect of the most price-sensitive segments in some markets.

In practice, the management time spent on pricing has often been much less than that spent on other marketing mix variables. This is partly because the airline industry has a long history of setting prices in a non-competitive commercial environment which allowed costs to be passed on to consumers relatively freely. It is also because much of the information which economists' models like to assume is available for plugging into pricing decisions is, in reality, hard to come by and of dubious efficacy. But, perhaps more fundamentally, it is very difficult for any airline to assess in monetary terms the benefits and sacrifices embedded in the products being offered to each of its various markets.

It is nonetheless true that in many parts of the world price is becoming a more sensitive element in the service industry marketing mix than has sometimes been the case in the past. This is attributable largely to the greater availability of information to customers, as well as to the intensified competition spurred by deregulation. It is a trend which has taken hold in the airline industry over recent years and spread rapidly to a growing number of important markets.

Network carriers operating in liberalized markets not only have the challenge of using differential pricing and ticket conditionality as a competitive weapon with which to tap different demand elasticities and requirements for travel flexibility on individual flight sectors, but they must also try to maximize revenue to the network as a whole by ensuring that where a choice exists they sell space to passengers with the most revenue-rich itineraries. Selling space to high-yielding local passengers on a short-haul route might not be optimal from a network perspective if the sale were to displace demand from a customer (even a lower yielding customer) wanting to connect onto a long-haul flight. O and D revenue management systems have become available in recent years to help airlines with sufficient resources solve this problem; it is a particularly important problem for many international network carriers because - as mentioned earlier - business travellers connecting over their hubs account in general for a significant proportion of total revenues.

The conditions attached to fares - technically part of an airline's 'tariffs' - are sometimes looked upon as product attributes, as we saw in the last section of the chapter. Thus, the fewer the purchase and usage conditions, the more valuable this aspect of a carrier's service-price offer will be. Delta Express, for example, inaugurated service with a three-tier tariff structure in each of its markets, comprising 21-day and 7-day advance purchase fares and a walk-up fare; because (like ValuJet) it chose to make walk-up fares payable on booking and non-refundable, Delta Express was offering less value in this respect than Southwest - whose walk-up fares were not subject to these conditions.

More generally, tactical pricing decisions require knowledge of demand curves, segment elasticities, and likely competitor reactions.[42] This is knowledge to which relatively few carriers yet have adequate access. Availability of the accurate historical and forecast data necessary to make better-informed pricing decisions and the skills required to transform this data into knowledge are rapidly becoming critical success factors - certainly for full-service network carriers; such data is also a source of considerable organizational learning advantages and economies of scale.

Managing marketing communications [43]

The first issue is to identify the target audience. This might fall into one of four broad categories: customers, intermediaries, employees, and other stakeholders.

1   Customers: marketing communications can be used to influence the attitudes and behaviours of three types of customer. **Potential customers** are informed, persuaded, and reminded about the benefits specifically targeted at them and the merits of these benefits relative to what competitors are offering. This might involve single-benefit positioning (e.g. Cathay Pacific: 'Arrive in Better Shape'; KLM: 'The Reliable Airline'), double-benefit positioning (e.g. Thai : 'Centuries-old Tradition, State-of-the-Art Technology'), or even multiple-benefit positioning; but as more benefits are pushed, the scope for disbelief or confusion widens. The broader an airline's service mix, the more different types of customer it has to target, and the more important it becomes to ensure that each message gets through to the right people. Attracting customers to a service-price offer from the wrong segments can cause a mismatch between experience and expectations, both for them and for customers actually targeted, leading to dissatisfaction amongst both groups.

   It can nonetheless be difficult to prevent segments receiving messages aimed at other segments. Thus, promotional pricing intended for the leisure segment might aggravate passengers travelling in the same class on full fares, whilst messages trumpeting quality improvements targeted primarily at business class travellers will probably come to the attention of those in the 'main cabin' and might raise their expectations. Compounding the problem is the fact that most people who travel on business are also leisure travellers at some time each year.

A second purpose for communicating with potential customers is to reduce the risk they perceive arising from their inability to experience service before actually purchasing it. More generally, marketing communications is used to create and reinforce images, and to build in customers a sense that their association with a particular airline is akin to membership of a 'club'.[44]

Marketing communications have to be balanced between the strategic generation of awareness and building of a master-brand image on the one hand and tactical, shorter-term revenue stimulation on the other. Tactical communications tend to be oriented towards specific products (including destinations) and sub-brands. For example, early Delta Express advertising tended to be more market-specific and lighter in tone than advertising for the corporate master-brand; key objectives were to inform target customers about specific service-price offers in their markets, and to differentiate the low-cost operation from its mainline parent.

As air transport markets are liberalized, their competitive environments are shaped to a considerable degree by the costs of communicating to potential customers rapidly changing information about prices, schedules, routes, service advantages, and seat availability. Communication costs are an important (although by no means the only) driver of airline consolidation, the growth of hub-and-spoke networks, the integration of feeder services into these networks, and of the evolving competitive significance of CRSs. The marketing economies of scale to which such strategies contribute reduce unit information costs for large airlines and increase the risk of market entry for smaller competitors.

As well as potential customers, marketing communications can also be addressed to **consumers already participating in the service delivery system.** Individual service encounters communicate messages about the airline. Routine encounters can be scripted, perhaps subject to as much latitude as the nature of a particular type of encounter allows; non-routine encounters will in many cases be unscripted with, in an increasing number (but still a minority) of cases, staff empowered to act within defined parameters. Service environments also convey messages, as we will see in chapter 7. Encounters and environments are as much a part of the marketing communications effort as, say, advertising or public relations - they are simply oriented more towards generating repeat business.

A third category of customer to be communicated with is comprised of **consumers who have already been through the service delivery system.** Whether or not they become consumers again (assuming the existence of a future need to travel and the availability of a choice between alternative airlines) will depend in part upon how perceptions of their experiences measure up to prior expectations. Prior expectations will have been shaped by any earlier experiences with the airline, by the activities of its competitors, and - perhaps most importantly - by the airline's own marketing communications. Marketing communications are a significant benchmark against which consumers make postpurchase evaluations of the service experience. There is clearly a natural tension between, on the one hand, the use of marketing communications to stimulate demand and, on the other, the need to moderate the message in order to restrain expectations and so create a higher probability of consumer satisfaction.

In essence, the purpose of communicating with customers as a whole is to raise the percentages of people in each targeted segment who are aware of the airline's service-price offer, have tried it, have repeated the purchase, and are willing to do so again. For airlines emerging from regulatory protection and facing intensified competition, achieving this is not a simple challenge.

2   Intermediaries: because the airline industry still relies so heavily on retail intermediaries to distribute information about its services, and because these intermediaries can have a significant effect on customers' choice of carrier in some segments, communicating with travel agents and freight forwarders is an important (and expensive) part of any marketing communications function.

3   Employees: the marketing communications to which they are exposed affect the perceptions employees hold of their airline, and can influence how they see their role in the service delivery subsystem. Whilst this can and should be motivational, it may in fact be demotivating for staff to observe being marketed a level of service they know cannot be delivered.

4   Other stakeholders: any of the stakeholder categories discussed in Volume One, chapter 2 might be sufficiently important to warrant specifically targeted communications. Even where this is not the case, airlines emerging into less protected competitive environments than they have been used to must be increasingly sensitive to the agendas of a growing range of stakeholder groups when framing their general, image-building messages.

The message, medium, and marketing communications mix Marketing communications is a process of deciding who is to say what, to whom, how, and to what effect. After identifying the target audience and the communication objective, the message and the media have to be decided upon. This requires decisions about the communications mix, which will generally include advertising, public relations, personal selling (particularly to intermediaries and corporate accounts), and sales promotion.[45] Advertising, for example, might be segment-specific and benefits-oriented, route-specific, or more widely targeted at corporate image enhancement.[46] Larger airlines in particular rely heavily on public relations to maintain and improve their images; British Airways at one time had over 30 full-time public relations staff scattered around the world, working with approximately 50 agencies. As is true of the service conceptualization process discussed above, marketing communications should be responsive to changes in the competitive environment and to the requirements of different stages in both economic cycles and product life cycles. Finally, whenever an element of the service-price offer to a particular segment is being changed, an effort must be made to communicate the (presumably enhanced) value being offered.

A communications medium of growing importance is the World Wide Web. Airlines already display schedules, special offers, details of their frequent flyer programmes, and general interest information in their home pages, and some are now using them to preview product innovations; British Airways did this when it relaunched its service concept for first class in 1996, for example. A few carriers, however, have not been exercising the same level of control over their web sites as is applied to marketing communications employing more traditional media, with the result that several early efforts have been of poor quality - something that is doubtless just a 'teething' problem'.

One still largely untapped attraction of the Internet is the prospect it offers for two-way dialogues to be established between an airline and at least some of its customers. Communications from customers could be of a general nature, their primary merit from the airline's perspective being to build brand loyalty (although not all communications will achieve this, of course, any more than more traditional forms of communication are invariably successful); in addition, customers could be given opportunities to provide feedback on existing service-price offers or make suggestions for product innovations. Marketing communications would in cases such as these no longer be simply a question of 'broadcasting' messages, but could instead be extended to 'narrowcasting' as a means for some of the world's larger and/or more innovative carriers to build brand equity.

Because service-price offers are now changing more frequently and competition is intensifying in many markets, clarity in communications becomes both more important and more difficult. A good example of this challenge was the launch of Virgin's Mid-Class in the early 1990s. Targeting passengers travelling at the full economy class fare and therefore feeling entitled to a better range of benefits than those on discounted fares, the service concept was built around separate check-in facilities and more onboard space. This - rather than enhanced meal service, for example - was what research showed the segment to want. The task was to communicate the positioning of Mid-Class (the name of which was subsequently changed to Premium Economy) between the economy and business class offers and, in particular, to avoid any misconception that it was a business class service - which would have raised expectations and courted dissatisfaction.

The proliferation of code-sharing can make it especially difficult for marketing communications to intermediate successfully between expectations and perceptions of service. Delta, endeavouring to legitimize its extensive code-sharing arrangements, launched advertisements in the mid-1990s claiming that 'We put you on the best flight even if it isn't ours'. In respect of one or two of Delta's international code-sharing partners, this is not a claim that at the time looked particularly robust under detailed scrutiny.

As the industry globalizes, marketing communications is becoming a field of intense competition. The battle is not just one of messages, but one of economics. A start-up launching a small number of point-to-point routes will be able to focus its marketing communications expenditure and - as Morris Air did at Salt Lake City in the early 1990s - rely substantially on public relations and word-of-mouth rather than paid advertising at its home base. Aspiring network carriers face greater difficulties, however; the larger the network a new entrant tries to establish at the outset, the larger and/or more thinly spread its marketing communications expenditures will be. Ultimately, of course, a difficult-to-determine network size threshold will be crossed and information economies of scale will kick-in - provided the carrier survives sufficiently long. The wider a network, the more opportunities there are to exploit marketing economies of scale. The more potential customers who are aware of an airline's market presence - or whose general awareness of the carrier's size leads them to assume that it will be present in the markets where they want to travel, causing them to curtail their search for information about alternatives - the higher are the barriers to entry facing a challenger.

Alliances can help this process, as illustrated by the appearance of KLM's name and logo in Northwest's US domestic service environments and media advertising. Furthermore, with the exchange of net fares, alliance partners are able to use their salesforces to sell each other's products. Instead of selling single-airline volume, alliance field and telephone salesforces will increasingly find themselves expected to push what is optimal for complex, multi-unit networks.

Some of the world's larger airlines with sufficient resources have begun to build customer databases including, in addition to biographical data, information on interests, media exposure, and purchase history. These can be used for targeted promotions and other 'segment of one' micro-marketing purposes. Reversing the process, such promotions might be a useful aid to database segmentation; the segmentation variable in this case would be propensity to respond to promotions by altering travel behaviour. This is a simple form of the interactive marketing - with markets segmented in this case by actual behaviour and the marketing mix precisely tailored - which is growing in importance amongst some larger North American and European airlines but is still very much in its infancy across the industry as a whole.

> New data warehousing software and associated smart systems allow carriers to exploit customer databases from different sources within their own organisations and from alliance partners, and to marry profiles and purchasing and travelling habits to elements in their product databases. These systems allow a real-time capability to package for an individual customer a destination, a budgeted price, and product components such as flight, car hire, hotel bed and entertainment. Customer management could accelerate disintermediation, threatening the tour operator as well as the travel agent.[47]

Such database/direct marketing can help to target certain messages more precisely, something to which fragmentation of print and electronic media is also contributing in a number of countries. To be fully interactive, customers' responses then have to be stored and subsequently used as a basis for more precisely targeted future messages. But care is required in respect of the accuracy and integrity of the data, for legal reasons where there are data protection laws and, more generally, to ensure that efforts create neither a yawn nor a backlash amongst potential customers.

Managing distribution

An airline's distribution channels for passenger products have traditionally included:

- its own offices, telephone reservations numbers, and airport counters;
- travel agencies, including general sales agencies (GSAs), which in many countries have come to rely heavily on CRSs;
- consolidators and seat brokers;
- independent and affiliated tour operators;
- other airlines; and,
- rarely and only in the case of large carriers in a very few countries, staff implants into the travel departments of major corporate customers.

Direct customer access via computer into airline seat inventories is becoming available in a small number of countries, notably in the United States and Europe. The primary distribution channels in freight markets are various types of forwarder, other airlines, and direct sales to shippers moving significant volumes. Each channel presents different costs, benefits, and management challenges, but the principal issues as markets liberalize and competition intensifies are whether those selected are appropriate to the airline's competitive strategy and whether intermediaries will sell effectively on the airline's behalf.

In many countries, especially in North America and Europe, the travel trade is not a monolithic channel. In addition to chains and single-unit outlets serving the broad market, there can be specialization amongst business travel agencies, agencies serving ethnic markets, consolidators, and seat brokers, for example. Online travel agencies, transacting business through sites on the World Wide Web, are also a small but rapidly growing element supplying distribution services to some segments of the market. When the trade is fragmented in this way, airlines can use specific types of intermediary to target particular segments.

Travel agencies have benefitted from the proliferation and frequent changes in service-price offers since liberalization started, because knowledge of the variables enables them to tighten their hold on the retail distribution system. In regulated competitive environments travel agents are primarily vendors of tickets, whilst in deregulated and liberalized environments they become suppliers of information which customers have neither the time nor resources to acquire directly for themselves. The spread of CRSs has helped agencies do this job effectively.

As noted in chapters 7 and 9 of Volume One, airlines have been using various methods to assert greater control over distribution channels and reduce distribution costs. The situation differs widely between markets, however. In the United States, most leading airlines acted in 1994 to cap commissions as part of broader efforts to restructure their cost bases, and commission reductions began to be introduced in Europe during 1997; overrides are nonetheless still common. Elsewhere, overrides, other incentives, and high standard commissions remain important tools for carriers wanting to influence agents in favour of 'pushing' their services. But this can be an expensive and unsustainable way to build market share, and some airlines now prefer to invest in generating consumer loyalty in order to have customers 'pull' their services out of distribution channels; product differentiation, branding, frequent flyer programmes, and a commitment to establishing a benchmark for customer value and then meeting or exceeding the expectations created are increasingly important techniques for achieving this. We will be looking at them in Part Three of this volume.

Although airlines clearly need travel agencies, and in some markets GSAs, to represent them in the numerous locations where they cannot possibly afford to represent themselves, and also to explain their service-price offers (particularly to infrequent travellers), these intermediaries are expensive. Technology, in the form of online access by customers to information on service-price offers and seat inventories, and reengineered business processes - including automated ticketing and also ticketless systems - can together be expected in some countries to make gradual inroads over the next few years into the percentages of their business that airlines book through intermediaries. A small number of airlines -

particularly low-cost start-ups - will contribute to the trend towards disintermediation by selling only through direct channels, primarily the telephone. On the other hand, carriers without a well-established and widely communicated presence in particular markets will continue to rely on local agencies to push their services, and encouraging them to do this will be expensive in terms of both commissions and salesforce expenditures.

Integrating the marketing mix

Freedom to manage the product and price elements of the '4Ps' can be either constrained or irrelevant in regulated or non-competitive markets. The challenge confronting a growing number of airlines as markets are liberalized and become more competitive is to gain the skills not only to manage each marketing mix variable but to integrate all of them into a coherent proposition which customers in targeted market segments, intermediaries in distribution channels, employees, and other stakeholders understand, and which is both compatible with distinctive capabilities and consistent with the nature of the competitive advantage being sought. This can be complicated, because service-price offers are not so much discrete, clearly separable alternatives as points on a continuum of almost infinite possibilities.

One thing that is apparent is that as markets liberalize, costs associated with the nonprice marketing mix elements - particularly marketing communications and distribution - tend to rise rapidly. Airlines are in the early stages of a major push to bring these costs under better control - a push that is likely to result in significant reengineering of traditional channels and an enhanced role for new communications and distribution technologies.

Conclusion

Managing service-price offers is largely a question of deciding what type of value is to be offered to customers and how it is to be delivered. Historically, 'what' has been the responsibility of the marketing function, and 'how' has been subsumed into operations. As was first noted at the beginning of Volume One, this distinction is no longer clear. The positioning, design, pricing, promotion, and distribution of airline services now need to be seen as being intimately linked to the manner in which they are delivered. It is to service delivery that we turn next.

Notes

1   Rayport, J.F. (1994), 'Managing in the Marketspace', *Harvard Business Review*, November-December.

2   Strategic implementation costs money, frequently requiring heavy capital as well as current expenditures. The availability of resources to support chosen strategies is clearly a major issue, and the use of financial analysis to select investment alternatives in the context of both the chosen strategic thrust and scarcity of resources is a significant part of strategic management. It is not covered in this book, partly for reasons of space but largely because there are already several excellent specialized texts available. A good starting point for readers wanting further insights would be: Brealey, R.A., Myers, S.C., and Marcus, A.J. (1995), *Fundamentals of Corporate Finance* (International Edition), McGraw-Hill. The guiding principal, of course, should be not to invest in any asset or programme of expenditure unless confident of an acceptable return on the investment. This is a principal with which many airlines have had difficulty over the years.

3   The distinction between intended and emergent strategies is fully explained in Volume One, chapter 1.

4   Zeithaml, V.A., Parasuraman, A., and Berry, L. (1985), 'Problems and Strategies in Services Marketing', *Journal of Marketing,* Vol. 49. It should be noted that some authors identify other distinguishing features in addition, but these four are the most important. It is also worth noting that a lot of recent literature no longer sees tangible goods and intangible services as an 'either/or' distinction, but as offers situated somewhere on a product continuum stretching from almost entirely tangible (little or no service element in addition to the good(s)offered) to almost entirely intangible (few tangible good(s) in addition to the service offered). Finally, there is a growing body of literature emphasizing that services offered by different industries are not all the same in their degrees of intangibility, inseparability, homogeneity, and perishability.

5   Wright, L.K. (1995), 'Avoiding Services Marketing Myopia', in Glynn, W.J. and Barnes, J.G. (Eds.), *Understanding Services Management,* Wiley.

6   For a brief history of the evocative 'moment of truth' concept, see: Normann, R. (1991), *Service Management* (2nd edition), John Wiley & Sons, p. 16.

7   Zeithaml et al., op. cit.

8   The discussion in chapter 2 established several reasons why in this book 'price differentiation' and 'service differentiation' are recognized as two related but distinct forms of differentiation. Service attributes and price are intimately linked, and both should be used in conjunction to differentiate service-price offers and so influence buying behaviour. It needs to be repeated, however, that this perspective does not reflect the majority view in the literature, where pricing is not widely looked upon as a form of differentiation.

9   Koch, R. (1995), *Guide To Strategy,* FT Pitman Publishing, p. 238.

10   By 'price' we mean here 'monetary cost to customers'. It can be argued that also embodied in 'price' are nonmonetary costs measured in terms of time or convenience, for example. As noted earlier, high nonmonetary costs are better treated as low-quality service attributes: thus, a multistop or connecting service costs more time than a nonstop service and so compares unfavourably in terms of this particular attribute.

11   Nyathi, M., Hooper, P., and Hensher, D. (1993), 'Compass Airlines: 1 December 1990 to 20 December 1991, What Went Wrong? - Part 2', *Transport Reviews,* Vol. 13, No. 3.

12   A related point worth making is that in selling these packages under its own corporate brand name an airline is placing its image and reputation in the hands of external service providers more directly than is true of many other forms of outsourcing.

13   'Bundling' is the selling of separable products to buyers only as a package or bundle. The concept is so well-established in many industries that it is often not noticed. Attempts to unbundle airline services by making passengers pay for attributes such as baggage handling and inflight meals were a common strategy amongst the first wave of post-deregulation US start-ups, but success was short-lived. More recently, many carriers operating US domestic flights lasting under 2-2$^{1}/2$ hours removed meal service from their service-price offers, although this is not strictly 'unbundling' insofar as the option to purchase the missing attribute is generally unavailable.

The primary advantage of bundling is the opportunity it provides to differentiate. On the other hand, few such differentiations cannot be replicated and so price premiums to cover their costs are frequently unsustainable. The problem with unbundling (or, at least, being the first competitor to unbundle) is that unless it is accompanied by compensating price differentiation in respect of the core service, passengers will perceive a deterioration in value and be tempted to switch to any remaining 'full-service' offers.

14   Cited in: Lovelock, C.H. (1996), *Services Marketing* (3rd edition), Prentice Hall, p. 337.

15   The *OAG Business Travel Lifestyle Survey 1997* (cited in *Airline Business*, July 1997, p. 67) revealed the following rank orderings.
      - **Importance of factors influencing carrier choice (index out of 10):** schedule (8.27); safety (8.03); punctuality (7.22); comfort and legroom (6.84); efficient check-in (6.79); frequent flyer scheme (6.59); cabin staff (6.38); advance seat selection (6.33); cheapest available fare (5.54); lounge access (5.45); onboard food/drink (5.28).
      - **Most important inflight features (per cent):** legroom (91); angle of seat recline (72); food on demand (28); individual video (21); pillows and blankets (20); inflight beds (12); telephones (8); business facilities, e.g. PC/fax (5).
      'Data based on the views of 5,250 business travellers worldwide. Their countries of residence are USA 17%, UK 14%, Australia 12%, Italy 12%, France 10%, Germany 10%, Japan 9%, Hong Kong 8%, and Singapore 8%.' (Ibid.)

16   This is not to say that specific aspects of safety and security processes have themselves necessarily been commoditized. The effectiveness and efficiency of pre-flight screening vary greatly at different airports, although this is often not under the direct control of airlines. What is under their direct control, for example, is variables such as the quality of pre-flight safety announcements, attention to the placement of carry-on baggage, and ensuring ease of access to emergency exits; the level of attention to safety-related processes such as these can vary widely between airlines. Certainly, the public may be 'spooked' by media coverage of newsworthy events in the industry; this has happened in recent years in the United States with respect to regional carriers, low-cost airlines, and certain categories of foreign carrier. Nonetheless, in the absence of specific, publicized issues concerning one airline, a category of carriers, or a particular country, travellers on the majority of the world's airlines tend to see safety and security as matters for generalized concern rather than major inputs into their purchase decisions.

17   Boeing (1997), *Current Market Outlook*. A problem confronting some airlines as the industry restructures is that they have substantial investments sunk into fleets that are inappropriately sized to provide the higher frequencies demanded in liberalized competitive environments.

18   It is nonetheless true that brand loyalty and membership in a competitor's frequent flyer programme can, under certain circumstances, counterbalance the importance of frequency in the purchase decisions of some consumers.

19   This does, of course, depend to some extent upon whether the station concerned is a net generator or attractor of day-return traffic.

20   See: Holloway, S. (1997), *Straight and Level: Practical Airline Economics*, Ashgate, chapter 4.

21   The significance of image as a corporate resource is discussed in Volume One, chapter 15.

22   An alternative might be to require payment at the time of reservation and apply a no-refund policy in respect of passengers who fail either to cancel or to show for a flight. Those who cancel might be permitted to rebook, but would not get a refund and may have to pay an administration charge. Several low-fare carriers in the United States and Europe have applied policies such as this.

23   Service recovery is discussed at greater length in chapter 9.

24 Evidence as to the effect of passengers' experiences at airport terminals on carrier choice is sparse, but it appears to point to a relatively low-order impact compared to other considerations. See, for example: Etherington, L.D. and Var, T. (1984), 'Establishing a Measure of Airline Preference for Business and Non-business Travellers', *Journal of Travel Research,* Spring. Intuitively, however, it seems likely that terminals are a stronger consideration when a choice of alternative hubs is available over which to make a connection, or when an airline is - or is perceived to be - in control of a particular facility.

25 Whereas many older types, such as the DC-9, use only fresh, external air in their cabins, newer and larger types are more likely to use recirculated cabin air. Environmental control units on most modern aircraft can be operated at a reduced rate or, alternatively, one of the packs can be entirely shut down. The purpose is to save fuel expended on engine bleed air. In the United States, the FAA took a step in the right direction when in 1996 it passed rules enforcing lower carbon dioxide levels in aircraft certified under FAR Part 25.

26 It is to some observers quite remarkable that airlines get away with marketing long-haul first and business class services on the strength of their calm and peaceful atmosphere, fit for work or relaxation, and then sell space (often at substantial discounts) to children. It is difficult to believe that child-free cabins or zones on long-haul flights would not generate far more in revenue and goodwill than they would lose. Noise pollutes aircraft cabins as readily as cigarette smoke.

27 One of the most commonly recurring demands in airline consumer surveys is for greater seat pitch, particularly in economy/coach class. The dilemma carriers confront in this respect is that whilst they know that taking seats out will cost them forgone revenue on peak departures which anyway leave full, it is difficult to know whether the extra leg-room will generate incremental revenue during off-peak periods when the loss of capacity is not such an issue for the airline. Particularly in short-haul markets, there is a widespread view amongst airline managers that notwithstanding the undoubted attractions of additional space, purchase decisions are still more likely to be driven by schedule convenience, price, FFP awards, and service style; the feeling is that few people would wait around, say, 30 or 45 minutes beyond their preferred departure times in order to avail themselves of an additional couple of inches of seat pitch. In long-haul markets the argument is less clear-cut.

28 Some airlines programme regular washroom inspections (e.g. Lauda Air every 20 minutes), but many still do not.

29 Window escutcheons might need to be replaced regularly, but the removal and milling of windows themselves has until recently been a task reserved for heavy maintenance checks. Quick and cheap processes for sanding and polishing windows in situ are now available.

30 New galley technologies are helping airlines in the battle to offer higher standards of food and beverage service to premium passengers in particular. Examples include 'specialty coffee makers, constant pressure steam ovens and rapid wine chillers': Proctor, P. (1996), 'Going Gourmet', *Aviation Week & Space Technology,* October 7.

31 OECD (1997), *The Future of International Air Transport Policy: Responding to Global Change,* p. 36.

32 For a more detailed treatment of the cargo product, see: Shaw, S. (1993), *Effective Air Freight Marketing,* Pitman.

33 Boeing, *World Air Cargo Forecast 1994.*

34 ICAO (1996), *Manual on the Regulation of International Air Transport,* Doc. 9626, p. 4.6-2.

35 There is in fact a growing body of literature questioning the appropriateness of the 4Ps to services marketing - partly because (as we will see in chapter 7) there are several other important variables such as service providers, service environments, service delivery processes, and the customer herself which the concept ignores. Another criticism has been that the concept takes little or no account of customer loyalty. The first point is valid, but the second is debatable. The 4Ps nonetheless

retain a strong hold over practitioners and, without denying that the concept has its shortcomings, they do provide a useful framework within which to analyze important aspects of service-price management.

36   For a commentary on the reasons why US domestic full-fare passengers are generally unhappy with service standards, see: Donoghue, J.A. (1997), 'Ignorance & Bliss', *Air Transport World*, July. Donoghue notes that many US majors have spent too much time focusing on each other and convincing themselves that FFPs are adequate compensation for pared service, and not enough time listening to their customers.

37   See, for example: Shaw, S. (1990), *Airline Marketing and Management* (3rd edition), Pitman.

38   Hulbert, J.M. and Pitt, L. (1996), 'Exit Stage Left? The Future of Functional Marketing', *European Management Journal*, Vol. 14, No. 1.

39   Although not specifically oriented towards service industries, there is a useful discussion of marketing strategies at different life cycle stages in: Kotler, P. (1991), *Marketing Management* (7th edition), Prentice-Hall, chapter 13.

40   For a more complete discussion of price, yield, and yield management see: Holloway, op. cit., chapters 12, 13, and 14.

41   A value-based approach to pricing is oriented towards the buyer's perception of what she is getting for her money rather than towards the seller's costs. A major part of this perception is formulated as a result of management manipulating product design and other marketing mix variables to build value in the customer's mind. There is a little-used method of price setting which utilizes *conjoint measurement (or analysis)* to ascribe utility to each aspect of a product's features (such as frequency, departure times, and various aspects of inflight service, for example). These features are first identified, and customer utilities are then derived for each relative to price. The approach, which relies on polling consumers about their service preferences and willingness to pay for specific bundles of attributes, with all that this implies for cost and reliability, is subjective. Nonetheless, a large carrier's frequent flyer database might be sufficient to generate useful information on the perceived value, and therefore potential profitability, of either new products or enhancements to existing offers. See: Kucher, E. and Hilleke, K. (1993), 'Value Pricing Through Conjoint Measurement: A Practical Approach', *European Management Journal*, Volume 11, No. 3, September. An example drawn from the airline industry is illustrated in: Daudel, S. and Vialle, G. (1994), *Yield Management*, ITA, p. 12.

42   For an interesting description of 'the first known effort to estimate the impact of airline yield management in competitive markets, taking into account the YM capabilities of competing carriers', see: Belobaba, P.P. and Wilson, J.L. (1997), 'Cleaning Up on Yields', *Airline Business*, April.

43   For a full discussion of this topic, see: Fill, C. (1995), *Marketing Communications*, Prentice-Hall. This and similar specialized texts rightly recognize the possible participation of a greater number of players in any buying process than the single word 'customer' implies.

44   Normann, R., op. cit., p. 111.

45   Sales promotion includes point-of-sale displays, promotional literature, and direct mailings. Traditionally it has been taken to include short-term promotional pricing and money-saving 'special offers', but this is more properly considered part of the pricing variable in an airline's marketing mix. Patronage award schemes are also promotional tools; frequent flyer programmes are dealt with in chapter 10 in the context of customer loyalty.

46   An interesting break with traditional practice in the industry was launched by United in 1997. One of its principal corporate advertising messages was no longer to project an ideal travel experience as epitomized by the 30-year 'Friendly Skies' theme (which was dropped), but would instead recognize flaws in the experience identified by consumer research and communicate what United intended doing to rectify them.

47   Guillebaud, D. and Bond, R. (1997), 'Surviving the Customer', *Airline Business*, March, p. 57.

7 Service delivery as an interactive experience

The absence of a truly unique competitive strategy within a particular 'strategic group' of competing airlines sometimes means that real differentiation boils down to implementation - specifically, to the effectiveness and efficiency with which services are delivered. However competitive an airline's service-price offers might be, the services designed and the prices charged imply work in two areas:

- work on unit revenues: the focus here is on delivering products that can support the positioning and pricing chosen for them; and
- work on unit costs: attention in this area is on delivering products at a profit.

Any service delivery subsystem is part of an overall service management system which also embodies the service concept. Service delivery subsystems are comprised of component elements and processes. We will look first at components, the most important of which are consumers themselves, the service environment (including equipment and technology used), and service providers.[1] Figure 7.1 illustrates the relationships between these components. Later in the chapter we will look at service delivery processes. The focus throughout is largely on the delivery of passenger transport services, although many of the observations made are also relevant to the delivery of other types of service which airlines might supply.

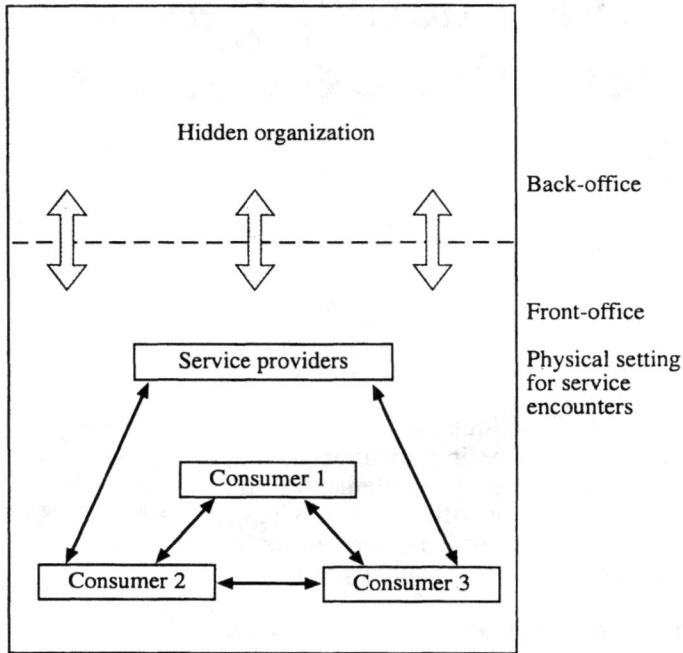

Figure 7.1 : Components in a service delivery subsystem

Consumers

Consumers as part of the service delivery subsystem

Bateson has proposed a three-stage model of consumer behaviour in respect of services.[2]

1   The prepurchase stage: Why do customers buy?
    • What are the needs and wants they are trying to satisfy?
    • How do they search for information about alternative means for satisfying these needs and wants - for alternative benefits?
    • How do they arrive at a shortlist of potential brand alternatives (i.e. 'the evoked set')?
    • How do they make their final choice?

It is answers to these and similar questions to which management of the marketing mix should respond.

2   The consumption stage: How do consumers react to the service delivery experience?
    • In particular, which aspects of service delivery have the most impact on the 'postchoice' evaluation process (an early and important part of 'postpurchase' evaluation)?

It is this stage with which we are here primarily concerned.

3   The postpurchase evaluation: To what extent do consumers perceive that the service rendered has matched expectations? In other words, how satisfied or dissatisfied are they with the service outcome?
    • What drives expectations?
    • What drives perceptions of service quality?
    • Is the consumer going to be a positive or negative participant, through word-of-mouth comments, in the airline's future marketing efforts?

We will return to this topic when looking at service quality and service recovery in chapter 9.

Consumers as actors in the delivery of air transport services

Consumer involvement in service delivery is an important consideration in delivery process design for a number of reasons.

1   Customer involvement is the source of the **experiences** that surround delivery of both the core transportation benefit and many of the supplementary benefits being purchased.

2   It provides an opportunity for an airline to add 'tangible' attributes to an essentially intangible offer.

3   Consumers of services are likely to experience directly any change in the configuration of one or more of the processes comprising a service delivery subsystem, particularly if they are physically present at the point(s) in the process being changed.

4   Consumers are affected by the presence of other consumers, some of whom might be from different market segments and therefore have different benefit requirements. We will return to this last point shortly.

Consumers' involvement in service delivery can be both physical and emotional.

1   Physical involvement is often active, but much of the time it is passive:

- in the case of active physical involvement, the consumer is in reality a 'co-producer'; this happens, for example, at check-in (especially if it is automated), on boarding, and during disembarkation and subsequent baggage reclaim;
- passive physical involvement occurs whilst waiting at various times during service delivery. The flight itself is commonly the longest period of passive involvement, although new interactive cabin technologies are beginning to reduce passivity.

2   Emotional involvement in the service delivery process often stems from the effects on a consumer's self-image of the image of the airline she carries with her into the service delivery subsystem. It is then further shaped by the effect of actual delivery experiences on that image. The same is true in respect of the use of a particular sub-brand, such as first or business class.

Consumers looking for confirmation of decisions

Consumers, therefore, are important participants in many service delivery processes. But, as explained at the beginning of this section, they are also decision-makers. In respect of a service delivery process in which they are involved, most consciously or subconsciously search for tangible 'clues' reinforcing the initial view that their decision to purchase this intangible and as yet unexperienced service was correct. This is part of the postchoice evaluation to which reference has already been made.

It was also mentioned above that service delivery processes give airlines opportunities to add tangibility to their service concepts. Two of the most important sources of tangibility are, first, the service environment and, second, the service providers. It is to these two components of the service delivery subsystem that we turn next.

The service environment

This includes not only the physical settings within which services are delivered, but also the equipment and techniques used to deliver them. It shapes consumers' perceptions through its visual impact, through the nature of the social interactions to which it gives rise, and through its impact on the effectiveness and efficiency of service delivery. Decor, lighting, background noise, signage, symbols, quality of materials, and spatial configuration (sometimes together referred to as 'atmospherics') all provide clues which make more tangible the essentially intangible service that has been purchased and which - during delivery - is being evaluated against expectations by consumers. These are strong image-carriers for employees as well as consumers, and they inevitably influence employee motivation, productivity, and satisfaction.

The problem faced by a lot of airlines is that they have limited control over many of the environments within which their services are delivered, notably the common-user areas of airports. This is one reason why, wherever possible, airlines offering highly differentiated first and business class brands in particular try to create their own spaces - check-in areas and lounges being primary examples - within which they have some measure of control over the image projected to consumers by the environment. Cabin decor and configuration have already been mentioned in the context of service conceptualization.

Bitner evocatively describes the physical or 'built' environments within which consumers and employees interact, within which service encounters take place, as 'servicescapes'.[3] She notes the power of the servicescape to affect the behaviour and perceptions of both categories of individual. Whereas back-office settings - the 'hidden organization' - should be designed to maximize process efficiency and employee satisfaction, front-office settings - or servicescapes - must also be designed with reference to their effect on consumers' perceptions.

Bitner argues that the role of a servicescape is:

- 'to provide a visual metaphor for an organization's total offering'.[4] It communicates image, utility, and quality in much the same way as the external packaging of a tangible good;
- to differentiate the organization, positioning it visually within its chosen market segment(s); and
- to facilitate consumers and service providers in the playing of their respective roles in the service delivery process, at the same time shaping social interactions within and between the two groups.

Modern technologies, notably virtual reality, offer the prospect of airline managers being able to bring alternative servicescapes to life during the design phase, before resources are committed to implementation, and also being able to simulate the performance of alternative service environments under different demand loading conditions.

Service providers

The focus here is on front-line personnel, although the fact is that everybody in an airline should be considered the provider of some sort of service - whether to internal or external consumers. Service providers are clearly a major potential source of differentiation in a high-contact industry such as the airline business. However, two types of stress can prevent them fulfilling their potential: role stress and interpersonal stress.

Role stress [5]

Service providers play a boundary-spanning role in each service encounter, interfacing between consumers and the airline. This role requires them to deliver a substantial part of the benefits package being offered by an airline to satisfy consumers' needs and wants. Ideally it should also involve them in the receipt and processing of information from consumers that can be fed back to shape future service conceptualization and delivery subsystem reconfiguration. This type of boundary-spanning can create in service providers a conflict between the demands and expectations of consumers on the one hand, and any restraints imposed either by service design or by configuration of the delivery subsystem on the other.

Traditionally, a fair number of airlines have responded to role stress by rigidly scripting their service encounters, and sometimes by allowing service providers to minimize consumer contact or - in the worst cases - actively hide from consumers whenever possible. These devices are still far from unknown today, although heightened competition is making them less tenable. There are, however, two alternatives that are being adopted by a small but growing band of carriers.

1   Actively involving front-line staff in the design of service concepts and the configuration of the processes through which they will be expected to deliver the benefits inherent in those concepts. This can be important where the structure and tenor of service encounters have an impact on employee motivation, performance, and satisfaction; in cases such as these, it may be particularly advisable to design service encounters with employees' as well as consumers' requirements in mind.

2   'Empowering' staff. Empowerment is a tricky concept, particularly in an organization such as an airline where strict adherence to procedures is often necessary to keep what is a highly complex system functioning smoothly and, in many cases, also to ensure safety. As the next subsections of the chapter explain, empowerment has its uses but in its most 'full-blooded' forms is not necessarily right for every organization despite current popularity amongst writers and consultants.

What is empowerment? Empowerment is not an 'either/or' choice, but the generic name for a wide range of alternative approaches to control which can be located along a continuum of possibilities. Bowen and Lawler have proposed a three-part typology.[6]

1   Suggestion involvement: staff actively contribute ideas, but management remains the final arbiter.

2   Job involvement: staff, possibly organized in teams, are given some latitude in the performance of their tasks but not necessarily an opportunity to redesign these tasks.

3   High involvement: the rarest of the three, staff are in this case able to participate in fundamental decisions affecting the design of their tasks and even the strategies of the company.[7]

They also note that higher forms of empowerment require senior management to share with front-line employees:

* information about the performance of the organization and its competitors;
* performance-linked rewards (the linkage of empowerment and performance-related compensation sometimes being referred to in the literature as 'enfranchisement');
* knowledge and skills sufficient to allow employees to understand and contribute to corporate performance; and
* power to make decisions which influence strategies and performance.

On a practical level, the essence of empowerment is that front-line staff become willing to fix problems if possible at the first point of contact, rather than instinctively hiding from that contact, reaching for the 'rule-book', or passing 'the buck' up the chain of command. Relatively few airlines have yet made serious moves in this direction, although the subject is now being fairly widely discussed.

Why empower? Thompson has suggested three reasons.

1   To sensitize companies to their external environments.

2   To save money through delayering, as British Airways has done by reducing from nine to five the number of management layers between the chief executive and customer contact staff.

3   To stimulate collaboration and teamwork.

There is, in addition, growing research evidence - none yet from the airline industry - that employee discretion (if used, which is not inevitable) has the potential to enhance consumer satisfaction.[8] In the mid-90s, both British Airways and Air France initiated major product relaunches in their premium cabins that shared the common theme of treating consumers as individuals and maximizing spontaneous, unscripted interactions with staff.
According to Carlzon:[9]

To free someone from vigorous control by instructions, policies and orders, and to give that person freedom to take responsibility for his ideas, decisions, and actions is to release hidden resources that would otherwise remain inaccessible to both the individual and the organization.

Fundamentally, use of empowerment assumes that given appropriate socialization, training, information, and motivation, service providers are capable of adding dimensions to service encounters that more rigorous procedural control mechanisms preclude. Much of the value added to any service experience in a high-contact delivery subsystem arises from direct encounters between service providers and consumers. Of course, there is an argument that although many of these human interactions can be scripted to a greater or lesser extent, they are anyway very difficult to control - thus making some degree of empowerment almost essential; nonetheless, there are several deep-seated objections to the concept.

Is empowerment for everybody? Not necessarily, because:

- the logic of empowerment requires managers to share information and coach rather than direct staff, neither of which are feasible in some cultural settings. This raises interesting issues in respect of cross-border alliances spanning different continents;

- to be effective, empowerment presupposes that an airline has available in its labour pool, and is willing to recruit and adequately compensate, high-quality people who are prepared and able to respond positively to the opportunities empowerment presents for them to improve customer service; and

- empowerment in the front-office can lead to inconsistent service, which might be considered to pose problems for heavily branded carriers that are selling, amongst other things, service consistency.

At the very least, empowerment needs the framework of well-understood corporate vision, mission, and objectives and the presence of functioning mechanisms for retention of overall control in the hands of senior management. Whether or not an empowering framework of this type can be fashioned from the procedural 'cages' within which most airlines have traditionally operated depends in part on the willingness of managements to set about changing values in order to create the types of corporate culture required to underpin such a transition. Willingness is spreading, but relatively slowly in what remains a predominantly hierarchical industry.

Interpersonal stress

This second type of stress common to service providers can arise as a result of consumers' attitudes and behaviours, a poor understanding of consumers' wants and needs on the part of service providers, or shortcomings in staff attitudes, accessibility, knowledge, or appearance as perceived by consumers. It can also arise when staff willing to deliver the expected benefits are unable to do so because of an inadequately configured service delivery subsystem. In the latter case, delivery process reengineering might be required. Fixes for other sources of interpersonal stress are more likely to be found in the areas of recruitment, training, and motivation - although a surprising number of airlines still seem to look upon the training of customer contact staff as a current expenditure ripe for pruning rather than a long-term investment in consistently high standards of customer service and in consistently low levels of (potentially expensive) suboptimal performance.

A few carriers now promote the view that if employees are not satisfied it is highly unlikely that they will be motivated to ensure that consumers are satisfied. This is reflected in the sequencing of the FedEx philosophy: 'people, service, profits'. Richard Branson's opinion on the importance of staff to customer satisfaction and shareholder value has already been quoted in chapter 3. Enlightened human resource policies are increasingly seen by some airline managements as an important source of workforce satisfaction, and therefore an integral part of any corporate culture oriented strongly towards high levels of customer satisfaction.

Of course, few managements would admit to being anything other than customer service oriented. As competition intensifies, however, so do pressures to back lip-service with action. Over a decade ago British Airways set about monitoring congruence between the values of its managers and those espoused by its transformational 'Managing People First' programme. It did this by using appraisal forms split into 12 domains and 85 criteria which to a large extent reflected the philosophies underlying that programme's approach to motivation and change. This type of initiative is not appropriate to every airline for reasons of history, culture, and resource availability. Nonetheless, it is now clear that how service providers feel about themselves and their airline affects the way they serve customers, and is therefore an important competitive variable and potential source of competitive advantage that should not be ignored in liberalized markets.

Particularly in the United States, overattention to quarterly results appears on occasion to have led to pursuit of unfocused and poorly rationalized labour cost reductions, cutting through the fat to the bone and giving insufficient prior consideration to the threat to product integrity posed by poor staff morale. Other threats arise from several different sources amongst the staffing trends currently evident in some countries: one, for example, is the growing tendency to hire part-time and temporary staff, who may be difficult to acculturate to a particular airline's service ethos and who may not identify their own long-term interests with those of their employers; another is the outsourcing of customer service processes to organizations which might pay little attention to the impact of staff morale on the airlines they service unless closely monitored under the terms of a tightly-drafted, performance-driven contract.

Service delivery processes

So far in this chapter we have considered consumers, the service environment, and service providers as components in the interactive experiences which occur within service delivery subsystems. Next we will consider the role of processes within such subsystems in the shaping of these experiences.[10] These are important because they affect both the consumer's perception and the reality of service quality; from an airline consumer's standpoint, there is often no material difference between 'service' and 'service delivery process'. This is why marketing and operations functions are being recognized by a growing number of airlines as fundamentally symbiotic.

Typologies of organizational processes

There are several typologies available to describe organizational processes. One that is widely used distinguishes between management, business, and work processes.

1   Management processes are those through which decisions are made and communications are effected between different levels of the hierarchy; they can be powerful carriers of an organization's culture and 'style'.

2   Business processes are company-wide flows of work, paper, information, tangible goods, people or whatever else it takes to transform system inputs into system outputs; they are frequently cross-functional, and it is here that many reengineering initiatives have been introduced.

3   Finally, work processes are the detailed operational activities which, together, underlie broader business processes; since the industrial revolution, such emphasis has been placed on the importance of breaking down these activities into their most basic elements that it can be a major challenge to reconfigure them around reengineered business processes in order to focus more coherently on delivering value to end-customers.

It is usually possible to identify a small number of **core processes**. Examples could include: designing and launching new products; communicating value to targeted markets and segments; managing brands; ensuring that services are delivered as scheduled; and ensuring that delivered services match or exceed customers' expectations. Mattson has suggested a four-stage typology of core strategic processes in service operations.

- Defining the customer: segmentation and design of appropriate service concepts and processes are the key tasks at this stage.
- Attracting the customer: the emphasis here is on attracting customers who have matching mental models of the structure of the service process, and on managing customers' expectations.
- Involving the customer: this process is one of motivating and rewarding the types of interaction between service providers and customers envisaged in the service concept and delivery strategy.
- Satisfying the customer: here the focus is on closing the experience gaps (e.g. between customers' expectations and perceptions of service received) to be discussed in Part Three of the present volume.[11]

Core processes are not necessarily easy to identify, but a useful starting point can be corporate purpose - the vision and mission which provide a context for the value proposition being offered to key stakeholders, particularly customers. Given this context, it should be possible to identify which processes have to be performed exceptionally well to deliver on the proposition. It is in core processes that competitive advantage is likely to be found. Other processes are not necessarily unimportant, but they are not 'core' and could be candidates for outsourcing. From time to time, core processes will need reconfiguring. This need might stem from the loss of a competitive advantage, unacceptable decline in process performance, and/or a pronounced market shift. Many airlines are facing one or more of these challenges at the present time.

When we talk about 'service delivery processes' in this chapter, it is primarily business processes in which customers are involved that are being referred to. Customer involvement in important processes is, as we have seen, one of the defining features of many service industries. The expression therefore casts a particularly wide net over the activities of an organization as contact-intensive as an airline.

Operational activities and service performance

Chase and Hayes have argued the need for a framework that relates operational activities to overall service performance.[12] They cite the usefulness of such a framework in the strategy development process, as well as its potential contribution to the positioning of a firm's operations relative to competitors. Furthermore, it can offer both a current perspective and a vision of the future to a firm's members. The classification they have proposed is illustrated in Table 7.1. Inevitably, no single airline is likely to fit into just one category in respect of each horizontal dimension, and neither is it likely that a carrier can move monolithically from being in every respect 'available for service' to being in every respect 'world class'; whilst skipping stages is difficult, transition times through each stage can be rapid - as several airlines have proven and others are endeavouring to prove; finally, slippage to the left can happen and needs to be guarded against. In increasingly competitive markets, particularly dense international markets, airlines are having to move from the 'available for service', state-owned flag carrier paradigm towards 'world class' delivery - although change is faster coming in some areas than others.

Many of the concepts already introduced in earlier chapters can be seen in this model. What links them here is the operations 'function'. Changes in operations, in service delivery processes, have the potential to affect the benefits package embodied in an airline's service concept; conversely, changes in the benefits package very often will involve operational reconfigurations of some sort. This underlines once again the intensely symbiotic nature of marketing and operations in a service environment because, as already mentioned, the interactive elements of service delivery processes are very much part of any service concept. In fact, some authors consider service delivery processes (and also service environments and service providers) to be integral parts of the marketing mix along with the traditional '4Ps'.[13] Others concentrate on the role of quality as an integrator of production and marketing orientations;[14] in chapter 9 we will see that strategic management is, as much as anything else, about the management of service quality. Bounds et al have proposed a model which highlights the centrality of quality concerns in process design; this is illustrated in Figure 7.2.

Stage	1. Available for Service	2. Journeyman	3. Distinctive Competence Achieved	4. World Class Service Delivery
	Customers patronize service firm for reasons other than performance.	Customers neither seek out nor avoid the firm.	Customers seek out the firm based upon its sustained reputation for meeting customer expectations.	The company's name is synonymous with service excellence. Its service doesn't just satisfy customers, it delights them, and thereby expands customer expectations to levels its competitors are unable to fulfill.
Operations	Operations is reactive, at best.	Operations functions in a mediocre, uninspired fashion.	Operations continually excels, reinforced by personnel management and systems that support an intense customer focus.	Operations is a quick learner and fast innovator; it masters every step of the service delivery process and provides capabilities that are superior to competitors'.
Service Quality	Is subsidiary to cost, highly variable.	Meets some customer expectations, consistent on one or two key dimensions.	Exceeds customer expectations, consistent on multiple dimensions.	Raises customer expectations and seeks challenges, improves continuously.
Back Office	Counting room.	Contributes to service, plays an important role in the total service, is given attention, but is still a separate role.	Is equally valued with front office, plays integral role.	Is proactive, develops its own capabilities, and generates opportunities.
Customer	Unspecified, to be satisfied at minimum cost.	A market segment whose basic needs are understood.	A collection of individuals whose variation in needs is understood.	A source of stimulation, ideas and opportunities.
Introduction of New Technology	When necessary for survival, under duress.	When justified by cost savings.	When promises to enhance service.	Source of first-mover advantages, creating ability to do things your competitors can't do.
Workforce	Negative constraint.	Efficient resource, disciplined, follows procedures.	Permitted to select among alternative procedures.	Innovative, creates procedures.
First-Line Management	Controls workers.	Controls the process.	Listens to customers, coaches and facilitates workers.	Is listened to by top management as a source of new ideas. Mentors workers to enhance their career growth.

Table 7.1: Four stages of service firm competitiveness

Reprinted from 'Beefing up operations in service firms', Chase, R.B. and Hayes, R.M., *Sloan Management Review*, Fall 1991 by Sloan Management Review Association. All rights reserved.

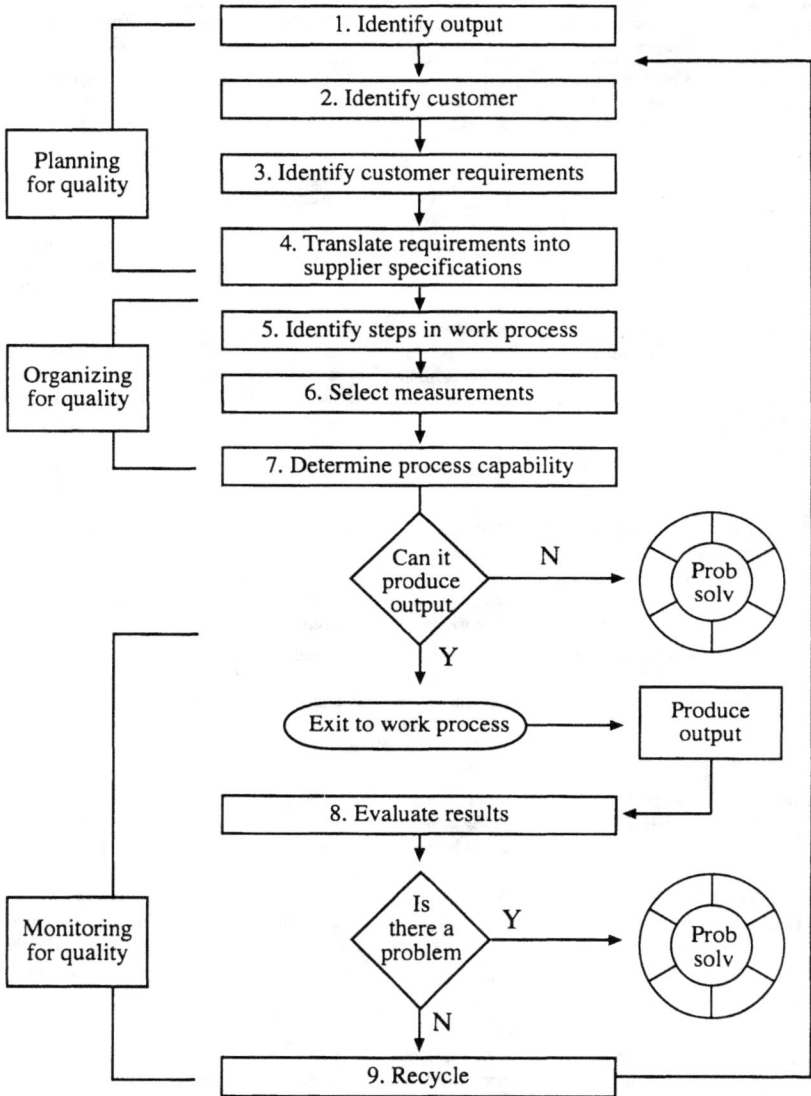

Figure 7.2 : Quality improvement process (QIP)

Source : Bounds, G., Yorks, L., Adams, M., and Ranney, G.,
Beyond Total Quality Management, McGraw-Hill, 1994, p.714.
Reproduced with permission of The McGraw-Hill Companies

Activity cycles

Opportunities to improve service quality arise at various points in consumers' activity cycles. The following is an example of a typical passenger activity cycle for an international flight involving one change of plane (although the possible distinction between customers - who purchase tickets - and consumers - who are the ones actually travelling - needs to be borne in mind).

1	Information search.	2	Evaluation of alternatives.
3	Enquiry re seat availability.	4	Reservation.
5	Ticketing (payment, followed by receipt of a ticket or a confirmation number).	6	Journey to the airport.
7	Check-in (queue and and encounter).	8	Security check (queue and encounter).
9	Passport control (queue and encounter).	10	Wait (lounge and/or gate).
11	Queue at gate.	12	Have boarding pass checked.
13	Queue in airbridge or coach.	14	Be welcomed aboard.
15	Find seat (assigned or not).	16	Store carry-on baggage and take seat.
17	Inflight experiences, routine and non-routine.	18	Recover carry-on baggage.
19	Queue to disembark.	20	Be bid good-bye.
21	Wait for the connecting flight (possibly preceded by check-in at a transfer desk and a security check before entering the transit/departure lounge).	22 - 32	Repeat activities 10 to 20.
33	Immigration (queue and encounter).	34	Wait for checked baggage.
35	Reclaim baggage.	36	Customs (queue and encounter).
37	Journey to final destination.	38	Reconfirmation of onward or return flights.
39	Solution with the airline of any problems that have arisen.		
40	Conscious and subconscious evaluation of experiences. This will in turn impact upon the first, information search, activity next time the cycle is repeated.		

Waiting for service Given that waiting is clearly a significant part of an air travel consumer's activity cycle, it is surprising how few airlines have adopted active wait management techniques outside the aircraft cabin (or even inside it in many cases) - let alone developed them into a science, as the Disney Corporation has done for example. Waiting can involve a scheduled wait (e.g. between connecting flights), a queue (e.g. at check-in), or an unscheduled wait (e.g. a delayed departure), and it can occur preflight (e.g. during ticketing, check-in or boarding), inflight (much of which is a scheduled wait for arrival at the destination) or post-flight (e.g. immigration, baggage reclaim, and the solution of any problems that may have arisen during the journey). Inevitably, waiting can have a negative impact on consumers' perceptions of service quality. It can be managed in two ways.

1   Through management of operational processes, such as 'Fast-Track' security and immigration channels for first and business class passengers or the better integration of connections over a hub.

2   Through the management of perceptions. Research has shown that the negative causality between waiting and service evaluation can be ameliorated by the use of moderators such as activities (e.g. entertainment) or service information (including, perhaps, progress of the flight or descriptions of the destination) to fill time; information about the attribution and duration of any wait, particularly if unscheduled or longer than anticipated, can be important in this regard.[15]

Encouraging more consumer encounters Also noteworthy is the number of points in the typical activity cycle at which positive human interfacing can be used to differentiate an airline's service from that of its competitors. Yet many carriers still have staff who prefer to minimize consumer contact because consumers are 'a nuisance', a potential source of conflict, or evidence of a fundamental power imbalance in the service encounter. Conversely, airlines confident of their service quality, confident of their people's abilities to enhance consumers' perceptions of service quality at each encounter, will set about building more encounters into their products. British Airways has done this in relaunching its Club World and Club Europe service concepts, for example.

Interestingly, this points to a source of paradox. Process automation to take the 'hassle' out of ticketing and check-in eliminates queues, reduces waiting, and smoothes the journey, but it also deprives airlines of an opportunity to use the forgone service encounters to add value to consumers' emotional experiences. Airlines appear to be judging, in most cases correctly, that at these particular points in the activity cycle there is more consumer satisfaction to be generated from rapid processing than to be lost from forgone service encounters.[16]

Early and positive encounters at each major stage of the activity cycle can nonetheless set the tone for consumers' perceptions of the entire service experience. In the airline industry, however, this can be difficult to achieve: looking again at the customer/consumer activity cycle, it can be seen that a lot of these activities might conceivably be outside the direct control of the carrier - being instead the responsibility of travel agents, airport authorities, government agencies, or passenger handling agents.

At outstations it is in fact quite conceivable that the first encounter between a consumer and the airline whose ticket she has bought will be at the aircraft door - unless, of course, it is a code-shared flight in which case there might never be any contact at all!

Flow-charting and horizontal processes

Processes can be analyzed by 'flow-charting' them. Alternative names in use include:[17]

- **service mapping**: the description of an existing service; and
- **service blueprinting**: the detailed planning of a new or revised process.[18]

Flow-charting is not simply an artistic exercise; it is an explicit specification of customer service levels. It should therefore reflect an airline's chosen strategic position. A low-cost/no-frills carrier will have a service flow-chart which differs in many important respects from that of a full-service network airline, for example. Nonetheless, the technique is only just beginning to make inroads into the airline industry and is not yet in widespread use as a service management tool.

Flow-charting links naturally to the idea of horizontal, cross-functional, customer-serving processes, which have already been referred to earlier in the book and will be looked at again in chapter 8. It addresses questions such as:

- What is each process in the service delivery subsystem supposed to do?
- What must happen if these objectives are to be achieved?
- What could happen to prevent them being achieved? In other words, what are the potential fail-points?
- How much leeway is there before service quality will start deteriorating below specifications?
- What tools, techniques, and practices are available to ensure as far as possible conformance to the specifications laid down during service conceptualization?

Flow-charting is, of course, just one step towards ensuring effective and efficient service delivery. Equally important, and often considerably more difficult, is the task of getting employees to 'buy into' what has been mapped-out. This is why the soft variables discussed at length in Part Two of Volume One - notably corporate culture and values - are vital to truly customer-focused service delivery.

Effectiveness and efficiency Flow-charting can help identify opportunities to improve the effectiveness/efficiency trade-off arrived at in process design. In this way it can be used to design-in value for both consumer and airline. Processes involve linked activities, which can be performed at a level somewhere along a continuum stretching from maximum effectiveness at one end to maximum efficiency at the other, with an ill-defined jumble of effectiveness/efficiency trade-off points in between. More helpfully, what processes should be achieving is minimum cost given a target level of effectiveness - that target having been dictated both by the markets an airline chooses (or is constrained) to serve and by where it decides to position itself within those markets.

Efficiency and effectiveness do not inevitably require a trade-off. Indeed, advocates of the 'quality is free' school of total quality management (TQM) broadly argue that a trade-off is never involved. The argument is that quality assurance programmes often save far more by avoiding service failure and recovery costs than they require in initial or ongoing investment. Whilst this can undoubtedly be true, it is not inevitably so; processes can usually be made more effective by devoting additional resources to them, but this might not necessarily be efficient.

Some service concepts permit considerable efficiency in their delivery - for example, inclusive tour charters operated with high seating densities, load factors, and aircraft utilization, and low seat accessibility and marketing costs. This efficiency can be reflected in low prices, leading to a balanced and effective service-price offer. Other service concepts carry much higher production costs because they do not permit as much efficiency in delivery processes - for example, high-frequency short-haul flights serving business segments with relatively small aircraft, high seat accessibility and marketing costs, and lower seating densities, load factors, and aircraft utilization. Again, these costs can be reflected in prices - higher in this case, but still allowing a balanced and effective service-price offer to be made. In the latter case, of course, increased competition in some liberalized markets puts pressure on the extent to which costs can be passed through to consumers, and this is one reason why airlines operating in such markets have to be as efficient as they can be at achieving target levels of service effectiveness.

If an airline's management has correctly identified needs and wants in the competitive environment, established objectives that must be fulfilled to meet them, and if these objectives are being met as a result of pursuing chosen competitive strategies, the airline is functioning 'effectively'. If competitive strategies are pursued and objectives reached at least cost, it is functioning 'efficiently'; this is the realm of cost management strategies - with use of the word 'management' here intended to convey an orientation towards value and the positioning of service-price offers which words such as 'control' or 'containment' do not always convey.[19] Effectiveness and efficiency are not always compatible. For example, hub-and-spoke networks are effective traffic gatherers and distributors, but they are not necessarily efficient in terms of resource utilization. As the demand for hub-bypass service grows, such networks inevitably also become less effective because they are not meeting that demand. Nonstop service will be effective, but as long as demand remains relatively thin the aircraft needed to serve it will be smaller - and therefore in all probability less efficient - than could be supported were traffic channelled over less direct routes. Once again, the close link between operations and marketing is clear.

Nonetheless, more efficient processes can sometimes both reduce costs and improve service effectiveness. Pursuit of this type of gain is the objective of organizational learning, which includes currently popular techniques such as benchmarking, continuous improvement and, more dramatically, process reengineering.

Benchmarking, continuous improvement, and reengineering It is not difficult to **benchmark** service outcomes against what key competitors are achieving, and neither is benchmarking against customers' expectations particularly challenging - provided the correct questions are asked. More difficult is the benchmarking of internal processes against industry standards; in many cases it is anyway better to benchmark against best practice outside the industry, at least in respect of processes that are not unique to airlines. Relatively few carriers yet do this. Benchmarking - like innovation - requires an open, searching, external orientation that has been slow in coming to many parts of the industry, although this is now changing.

Process improvements can be the result of a single innovative leap, a calculated reengineering initiative (see below), or continuous, incremental change. **Continuous improvement** is not a particularly new concept, either in the literature or in practice. What is new is the spreading recognition that the organizational learning which underpins it is not a prerogative of senior management alone, but something which takes place at all levels as people adapt to what they find out from the act of 'doing'. Figures 7.3 and 7.4 illustrate the use of 'fishbone analysis', a popular continuous improvement tool also known as an 'Ishikawa' or 'cause and effect' diagram.

Whereas benchmarking asks how effective and efficient an existing process is relative to what is being achieved by others, and continuous improvement looks for incremental gains in process efficiency and effectiveness, **reengineering** goes a stage further. It addresses not only how well something is being done, but why it is being done at all, by whom it could better be done if indeed it is necessary, and whether more could be achieved by throwing out the old rules and finding new ways of obtaining the desired outcome. Being 'world class' at something that is not necessary is no achievement. Using the typology introduced earlier, reconfiguration can be targeted at management, business, or work processes. In the latter area, for example, Delta reengineered technical operations as part of its Leadership 7.5 programme in the mid-90s by delayering and by cross-utilizing previously discrete and isolated skills within multifunctional teams focused around individual maintenance bays.

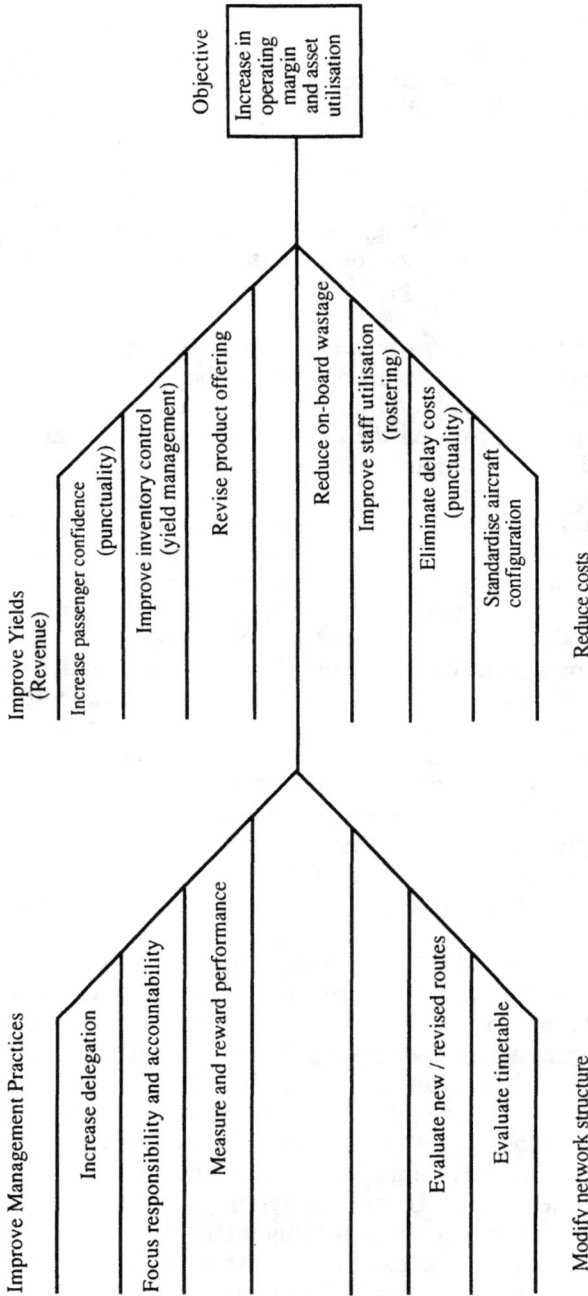

Figure 7.3: Application of fishbone analysis to an airline

Source : Morrow, M., *Activity-based Management*, Woodhead-Faulkner, 1992, p.138

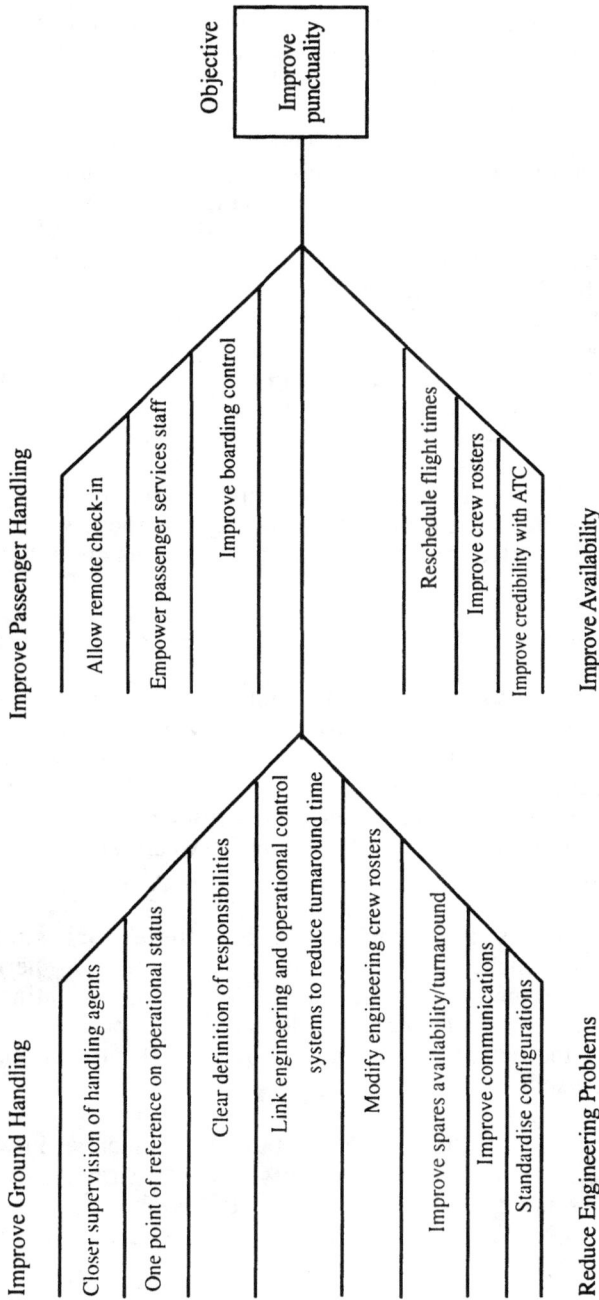

Figure 7.4: Applying Ishikawa to improving punctuality

Source : Morrow, M., *Activity-based Management* , Woodhead-Faulkner, 1992, p.139

Prototyped by one team and then diffused throughout the division, the initiative resulted in higher productivity and reductions in both staff numbers and costs.

Whereas benchmarking asks how effective and efficient an existing process is relative to what is being achieved by others, and continuous improvement looks for incremental gains in process efficiency and effectiveness, **reengineering** goes a stage further. It addresses not only how well something is being done, but why it is being done at all, by whom it could better be done if indeed it is necessary, and whether more could be achieved by throwing out the old rules and finding new ways of obtaining the desired outcome. Being 'world class' at something that is not necessary is no achievement. Using the typology introduced earlier, reconfiguration can be targeted at management, business, or work processes. In the latter area, for example, Delta reengineered technical operations as part of its Leadership 7.5 programme in the mid-90s by delayering and by cross-utilizing previously discrete and isolated skills within multifunctional teams focused around individual maintenance bays. Prototyped by one team and then diffused throughout the division, the initiative resulted in higher productivity and reductions in both staff numbers and costs.

Management of process costs [20]

The task of operations management is to understand what value the airline wants to deliver to targeted consumers, to separate those processes which add most to the value proposition from those which contribute little or nothing, and to control within the context of that value proposition whatever drives the costs of the contributing processes. Shank and Govindarajan have highlighted the distinction between 'structural' and 'executional' cost drivers.[21]

1   Structural cost drivers: these can be traced to the explicit strategic choices an airline makes in respect of such variables as network design, market segments targeted, methods of differentiating the service-price offer, product range complexity, and scope and scale of operations (e.g. the extent of vertical and horizontal integration, and the degree of outsourcing).

2   Executional cost drivers: these are attributable to the manner in which it is decided to combine resources in pursuit of the strategies which flow from 'structural' decisions. The next section looks at some of the ways in which technology is being used to reduce airlines' executional costs.

The use of technology to reduce executional costs   Sometimes the requirement is for pure number-crunching muscle, as in the larger sales and reservations systems; sometimes it is for scheduling abilities, as provided by software now available to allocate resources to each of the many tasks involved in moving passengers, cargo, and aircraft through the system; and sometimes it is for technology to help smooth and monitor the progress of passengers, cargo, and aircraft. Technology can be used to simulate the effect of process design alternatives before implementation, and either to replace or to augment human inputs into existing processes. In either case, the introduction of automation should be seen not just as an opportunity to save time and money over manual processes, but as a chance to reexamine those processes with a view to competing more effectively as well as efficiently and possibly even to redefining the scope of competition. Improved process control can provide a platform from which to build competitive advantage, but achieving this may require changes in attitudes and behaviour amongst service providers.

Realistically, process automation may not necessarily be a high priority for small carriers with low traffic volumes and labour costs - particularly where capital and foreign exchange are scarce. On the other hand, even the smallest carriers do now have access to off-the-shelf solutions for automating airline-specific processes as well as routine business transactions common to any commercial enterprise. For the airlines which develop and sell these solutions, technology can become a source of revenues and, possibly, profits.

Productivity-enhancing changes in back-stage processes might not be noticed by consumers. However, some back-stage and all front-stage changes inevitably affect consumers' experiences during service delivery; in these cases, the beneficial impact of such changes on airline productivity has to be weighed against whatever consequences are implied for service quality. Sometimes the outcome is 'win-win'. An example is the use of technology by FedEx and several other express carriers to manage every activity from booking, to truck despatch, ground and flight operations, through to delivery and billing, and also to simulate system performance under emerging scenarios and formulate contingency plans to cope with weather or technical problems; the purpose of the technology is not just to improve resource productivity by integrating separate processes into a smoothly functioning, holistic system, but also to enhance service quality and consistency.[22] Where a 'win-win' situation is less clear-cut, management might be faced with potentially difficult trade-offs to evaluate.

The following paragraphs outline some of the processes within key airline-specific functional areas which are continuing to benefit from the application of technology (excluding airframe and engine technologies, which were addressed in chapter 7 of Volume One). The list is a sample and, evidently, is not intended to be comprehensive. It is also worth bearing in mind that a key source of process enhancement for the future is the use of IS/IT as enablers to link these functional 'silos'.

1   **Scheduling** of flights and both physical and human resources.

Example: American Airlines estimated in the early 1990s that crew optimization models were saving around $80 million a year, and that decision support software to assist fleet assignment was generating incremental revenues in excess of $100 million per annum by matching aircraft types as closely as possible to evolving demand across a particular schedule integration; Delta's Coldstart fleet assignment model has been estimated to save several hundred million dollars each year;[23] on a more comprehensive level, larger airlines have in recent years been introducing highly automated and centralized operations centres to coordinate equipment and crew control, flight-following, meteorology, and maintenance control functions for the purposes of enhancing both routine operational planning and tactical responses to non-routine system disruptions (e.g. the Operations Control Center inaugurated by Delta in 1996); 'Systems Operations Advisor', a real-time decision support system introduced by United at its operations centre in Chicago is estimated to have made significant savings by minimizing flight delays.[24]

2   **Passenger reservations and processing:**
   • fare quotes and yield management;
   • reservations/inventory control;
   • ticketing;
   • check-in;
   • customer services;
   • boarding, baggage tracking etc.

Examples: 'palmtop' computers linked to central databases to facilitate the checking-in of passengers away from counters (a system that has met with both marketing and technical objections from some carriers[25]); electronic ticketing/ticketless travel and automated check-in procedures; the use of personalized smart cards incorporating a memory capability and a radio frequency identification device (RFID - a microchip capable of being interrogated by a radio) could change the way frequent travellers are processed through several of the stages in their activity cycles which currently require active physical involvement.[26]

3   **Ground operations:**
   • ramp control;
   • gate allocation and management;
   • departure control.

4   **Flight operations:**
   • crew rostering (referred to under scheduling above);
   • FANS (see Volume One, chapter 8);
   • flight planning;
   • training.

Example: flight planning software is available which can make trade-offs between the cost of additional fuel-burn required to meet a schedule under adverse prevailing weather conditions and any commercial costs of failing to meet that schedule (e.g. rerouteing or accommodating passengers who will miss connections).

5   **Cargo reservations and processing:**
- space control and reservations;
- terminal control;
- shipment data capture;
- shipment tracking;
- interfaces with forwarders, consumers, airport authorities, and agencies such as customs.

Examples: integrated carriers place hardware and software at customers' sites which turn consumers into co-producers by facilitating calls for pick-up, the weighing of shipments, cost calculations, customer invoicing, the printing of shipment labels, the charging of cost back to the consigning department (if a separate shipping department is used), initiation of electronic funds transfer in response to the invoice, and provision of answers in real-time to shippers' tracking enquiries; mobile communications systems such as DHL's SmartData and FedEx's COSMOS were installed to allow the real-time tracking of every shipment in their networks - considered a high-value benefit by many customers, and also a tool for the carriers to monitor their performances against service commitments; automated cargo systems are available (but not yet widely used) which manage yield (allowing informed decisions to be taken, for example, on whether or not to accept a 'spot-priced' shipment), monitor rejected-demand levels, and trigger sales calls if bookings from key customers decline; technology is being used to advise details to the carrying airline as soon as a shipment is collected by a forwarder from the consignor, rather than leaving the airline in the dark as to what is going to arrive for carriage until it actually arrives.[27]

6   **Maintenance and engineering:**
- maintenance planning (including time and cycle tracking, log-book monitoring, requirements planning, and repair turntime estimation);
- purchasing;
- inventory control (ideally sensitive to variable seasonal requirements);
- reliability tracking/performance monitoring;
- compliance monitoring;
- manpower allocation.[28]

Examples: aircraft performance can be monitored at an engineering base either real-time or via the transmission of data downloaded after every flight, so that maintenance controllers with access to complete records and manuals can troubleshoot or simply plan more efficiently; moving maintenance manuals from paper and microfilm onto CD-ROM can save hundreds of thousands of dollars on 'look-up' time each year at a large airline's maintenance base; it has been estimated that introduction of a distributed systems architecture for handling maintenance data, originally developed by the US Defense Department, is capable of reducing United's maintenance downtime by an amount equivalent to the annual utilization of as many as five aircraft; small airlines unable to justify the costs of establishing direct EDI linkages with airframe manufacturers' parts databases are able to use Web sites - such as the one inaugurated by Boeing in 1996 - to enquire about availability and lead times, place orders, and monitor shipment status; automated maintenance planning can:

i   boost maintenance programme yield by ensuring that aircraft are brought in for heavy checks with as little time as possible remaining before these checks are due - the potential saving of one such check over the life of an aircraft being possible by using automated rather than manual planning methods;
ii   schedule resource utilization more efficiently, either reducing the need for staff and facilities or freeing them for third-party work;
iii   improve the productivity of maintenance schedulers; and
iv   enhance planning flexibility in response to unforeseen airworthiness directives, aircraft utilization changes, or alterations in fleet composition.

7   Catering:

Example: robots are increasingly being used to assist in meal preparation and tray setting, such that an Australian-designed system first used by SATS in Singapore needs just four staff to pre-set 340 economy class trays in under 25 minutes.

8   Finance and general:
   • revenue accounting (passenger and cargo);
   • cost accounting;
   • general ledger and other financial systems.

The automation of processes needs to be closely aligned with the management of information, because information must flow into processes to make them work and then back out again to confirm their proper functioning or to stimulate a change in either their objectives or their configuration. The sharing of information with external parties - suppliers, handling agents, airport and ATC authorities, for example - is gradually being automated by larger airlines alongside the internal sharing of information.

Conclusion on process efficiency and effectiveness

Inevitably, there are hurdles to overcome in arriving at any required effectiveness/efficiency trade-off.

1   The true value-adding potential of intermediate processes (and even end-attributes) can be very difficult to determine.

2   The same is true of the structure and behaviour of costs associated with individual value-adding activities. Furthermore, with the exception of a few airlines that have pioneered activity-based costing and management - British Airways being an early example - accounting systems tend to be oriented towards 'static' structures such as cost centres and functional units rather than 'dynamic' processes and their constituent activities, which often transcend internal boundaries.

3   Attainment of a balance between effectiveness and efficiency is complicated in a service industry by the fact that the consumer is an active participant in many important service delivery processes, with the result that any visible or experienced trade-offs which fall below expectations will damage perceptions of service quality. This could happen, for example, if having fewer check-in counters leads to longer queueing times, or if reducing cabin crew numbers on a particular type is responsible for slower service responses.

Nonetheless, in general terms there is a requirement to pitch appropriately tailored service-price offers into each target segment, and then adjust production processes both to the economics of the network and the expectations of targeted consumers. In other words, a certain value proposition is embodied in an airline's service-price offers to targeted segments, and both process input costs and productivity must be managed to ensure that this value can be delivered profitably. After that the challenge is to improve continuously on cost and productivity performance without lowering, and ideally whilst raising, service standards.

Even this level of analytical simplicity is not without its caveats, however. Effectiveness/efficiency trade-offs will differ between target segments, assuming a carrier chooses to serve multiple segments; yet many airline service delivery processes are common across the range of passenger market segments. This commonality matters little if at all in respect of back-office processes, and can even be a source of efficiency when economies of scale or scope are available to be exploited. But in the front office it may hinder the effectiveness of service delivery into top-end segments.

Offering multiple services can be a source of ineffectiveness whenever consumers in different segments having separate benefits expectations are present in essentially the same service delivery system. There is some segregation - at check-in, in airport lounges, and in aircraft - between consumers who have responded to different service-price offers, but many stages of the customer/consumer activity cycle are experienced in common. Complicating matters further is the fact that even within each category sharing a segregated facility, such as a lounge or an aircraft cabin, are consumers from different market segments likely to be looking for different benefits. Thus, in a business class lounge or cabin individuals travelling for work-related reasons on the full business class fare will often be mixed with families that have paid discounted business class excursion fares (or perhaps even the full fare as well) to get home on vacation. By using essentially the same delivery processes to serve these different segments - possibly distinguishing between them only through a price/ticket-conditionality trade-off - the airline inevitably risks failing to deliver promised benefits and therefore failing to satisfy or exceed the expectations of at least one group.

Furthermore, within any one segment there will be people who each have very different expectations of service delivery processes. Some business travellers, for example, want largely to be left alone so they can work, whilst others will expect recognition and pampering during what they consider to be an 'off-duty' period. This is why - as mentioned in the last chapter - individuality, individual choice, and the customization of some aspects of service delivery in response to what is learned over time about individual customers are becoming a part of the service concept in some major airlines' premium cabins.

One issue which the foregoing discussion underlines is a fundamental challenge inherent in airline market segmentation exercises first referred to in chapter 10 of Volume One: **customers** (i.e. purchasers of services) can be **segmented** in all sorts of imaginative ways, but the realities of the industry's service environments - primarily airports and aircraft - mean that the opportunities for **consumers** (i.e. users of services) to be **segregated** along the same lines during service delivery are much more limited.

Conclusion on service conceptualization and delivery

Whilst the 'Where to compete?' question addressed by corporate strategies is answered in product and geographical market terms, the 'How to compete?' question at the centre of competitive strategy is answered by reference to service-price offers and to the processes used to manage and deliver them. The two are nonetheless closely linked because the 'Where?' must be informed by the 'How?' This view of competition as being 'capabilities-based' is consistent with the opinions of some observers -

discussed in Volume One, chapter 15 - that it is processes as much as products and markets which underpin competitive advantage.[29]

But to translate capabilities into competitive advantage it is necessary to stake out a strategic position which embodies mutually consistent choices in respect of service conceptualization and delivery. What mutually consistent choices can lead to is a distinctive 'activity system' that helps set an airline apart from its competitors; this concept was also introduced in chapter 15 of Volume One. Figure 7.6 outlines Southwest's activity system. It is taken from the work of Porter, who uses activity system maps to 'show how a company's strategic position is contained in a set of tailored activities designed to deliver it. In companies with a clear strategic position, a number of higher-order strategic themes [in the dark circles] can be identified and implemented through clusters of tightly linked activities [in the light circles].'[30]

For example, the facts that Southwest's service concept does not include meal service, interline baggage transfers or seat assignment, that its network product is largely oriented towards point-to-point routes of a broadly similar length into and out of relatively uncongested airports, and that it operates a single-type fleet of B737s, all interact to contribute to fast gate turnarounds and high aircraft utilization;[31] this, in turn, helps underpin the low fares that differentiate the airline's service-price offer - an offer which includes high-frequency service but provides no benefits in respect of meal service, interline baggage transfer, seat assignments, and so on.[32]

Porter takes this classic example of systems thinking one step further by identifying three types of fit (which are not mutually exclusive).

1   First order fit: activities are consistent.

2   Second order fit: activities are self-reinforcing.

3   Third order fit: efforts are optimized through cross-functional coordination and exchanges of information. It is at this level of system integration that fit between service concept and operational processes can be translated into a strategic position that is both sustainable and difficult for competitors to decode and imitate, irrespective of how readily the individual components in the system might themselves be isolated and replicated.

Activity systems relevant to changing industry conditions can often be easier for start-ups to establish from the ground up than for long-established airlines to redesign and reengineer from inherited positions. Several incumbents have risen to the challenge, but many traditional 'flag carriers' have yet to take their first substantial steps along what can undoubtedly be a difficult path.

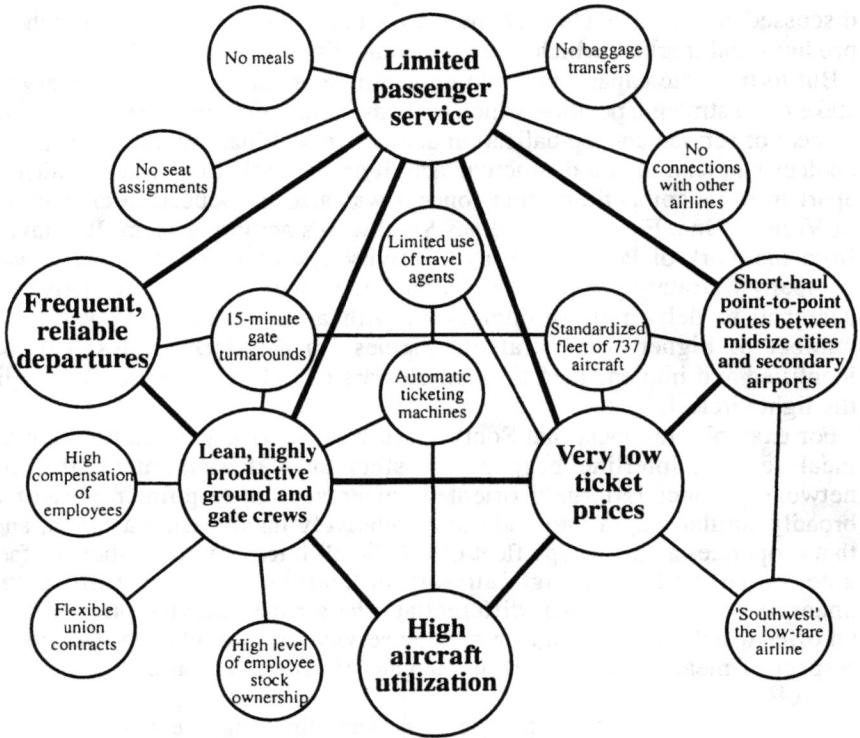

Figure 7.5: Southwest Airlines' activity system

When strategy is thought of in terms of optimized activity systems, it becomes abundantly clear that airlines wanting to follow this route to competitive advantage need to be thinking carefully about the design of their corporate infrastructure. It is to the topics of organizational architecture, coordination, and control that we turn in the next chapter.

Notes

1   Albrecht and Zemke made an important early contribution in this field with a model of customer service which recognized service strategy, systems, and people as component elements: Albrecht, K. and Zemke, R. (1985), *Service America: Doing Business in the New Economy,* Dow Jones Irwin. Eiglier and Langeard define as a servuction system 'the systematic and coherent organization of all the physical and human elements of the customer-company interface needed to provide a service whose commercial features and quality standards have been determined'. This term

has come into widespread use in the literature: Eiglier, P. and Langeard, E. (1987), *Servuction, le marketing des services*, McGraw-Hill (quoted in Daudel, S. and Vialle, G. (1994), *Yield Management*, ITA, Paris). However, the notion of a service management system embodying service concept and service delivery owes much to the pioneering work of Richard Normann. See, for example: Normann, R. (1991), *Service Management* (2nd edition), John Wiley & Sons.

2   Bateson, J.E.G. (1995), *Managing Services Marketing* (3rd edition), Dryden, chapter 2.

3   Bitner, M.J. (1992), 'Servicescapes: The Impact of Physical Surroundings on Customers and Employees', *Journal of Marketing*, Vol. 56, April.
    A 'service encounter', as the term is widely used in the literature, is in fact any interaction between a service organization and its customers - whether taking place face-to-face, by mail, over the telephone, or electronically. Each encounter contributes to the forming of an impression about the organization by the customer. In this chapter, usage of the term largely describes direct interpersonal contact - because these contacts are potentially very high in impact and, more particularly, because it is in these cases that the simultaneity of service production and consumption taking place within a service delivery subsystem is at its clearest.

4   Ibid., p. 67.

5   For a full discussion of role stress, see: Bateson, op. cit., chapter 4.

6   Bowen, D.E. and Lawler, E.E. (1992), 'The Empowerment of Service Workers: What, Why, How, and When?', *Sloan Management Review*, Spring.

7   In an interesting article, Eccles notes that these categories bear striking resemblance to well-established concepts that have been around for a long time (suggestion schemes, job enrichment, and worker participation respectively). He also voices skepticism about some of the more radical claims advanced by proponents of empowerment. (Eccles, T. (1993), 'The Deceptive Allure of Empowerment', *Long Range Planning*, Vol. 26, No. 6.)

8   Thompson, J.L. (1993), *Strategic Management* (2nd edition), Chapman & Hall, p. 626. For a full treatment of the potential impact of employee discretion on consumers, see: Kelley, S.W. (1993), 'Discretion and the Service Employee', *Journal of Retailing*, Vol. 69, No. 1, Spring.

9   Carlzon, J. (1987), *Moments of Truth*, Ballinger, chapter 1.

10   The literature commonly distinguishes between 'service operations' and 'service delivery'; this equates to the distinction first drawn in chapter 3 between back-office (or back-stage) and front-office (or front-stage) operational tasks. Because the distinction is not germane to the present discussion, use of the expression 'service delivery' in this chapter embodies both types of operations.

11   Mattson, J. (1994), 'Improving Service Quality in Person-to-Person Encounters: Integrating Findings from a Multi-disciplinary Review', *The Service Industries Journal*, Vol. 14, No. 1.

12   Chase, R.B. and Hayes, R.H. (1991), 'Beefing Up Operations in Service Firms', *Sloan Management Review*, Fall.

13   See, for example: Payne, A. (1993), *The Essence of Services Marketing*, Prentice Hall.

14   See, for example: Ballantyne, D. (1991), 'Coming to Grips with Service Intangibles Using Quality Management Techniques', *Marketing Intelligence & Planning*, 8, 6.

15   Taylor, S. (1994), 'Waiting for Service: The Relationship Between Delays and Evaluation of Service', *Journal of Marketing*, April. This article focuses on pre-process delays.

16   An interesting comment on the trade-off between technology and human contact in the context of service encounters has come from the CEO of Brazilian carrier TAM. Reflecting on the introduction of a new check-in system which radically reduced the time required to greet and process each passenger he observed, 'The guidelines I gave my people concerning the development of this system are that it should be quick enough to eliminate queues but slow enough so people didn't lose contact...This is

vital for companies that provide services. Because we deal with people and people do have emotions, feelings, heart. They are eager to be treated with smiles and eye contact.' (Quotation from Rolim Adolfo Amaro, cited in: Lima, E.P. (1997), 'Out of the Niche', *Air Transport World,* July, p. 175.)

17 Lovelock, C.H. (1996), *Services Marketing* (3rd edition), Prentice Hall, p. 61.

18 Blueprinting is closely associated with the work of Shostack, notably: Shostack, G.L. (1987), 'Service Positioning Through Structural Change', *Journal of Marketing,* Vol. 51, January.

19 Effectiveness is 'doing the right things'; efficiency is 'doing things right'; excellence is 'doing the right things right'. The key imperative in much of the management literature since the early 1990s has been to find ways to do 'more of the right things right with less'.

20 For a more complete description of current airline cost management strategies, see: Holloway, S. (1997), *Straight and Level: Practical Airline Economics,* Ashgate, chapter 7.

21 Shank, J.K. and Govindarajan, V. (1992), 'Strategic Cost Analysis and Technological Investments', *Sloan Management Review,* Fall.

22 In contrast, a study by IT vendor Unisys has found that 'traditional' combination carriers and forwarders together have been slow to reengineer their processes. In respect of these carriers and forwarders:
  • international cargo shipments average around six days from consignor to consignee - a figure which has changed little since an IATA study of the issue was undertaken in the early 1970s; and
  • the shipment activity cycle involves 41 events, compared to just 11 in most integrators' activity cycles.
  (Cited in: Odell, M. (1997), 'Freight Frighteners', *Airline Business,* March.)

23 Subramanian, R., Scheff, R.P. Jr., Quillinan, J.D., Wiper, D.S., and Marsten, R.E. (1994), 'Coldstart: Fleet Assignment at Delta Air Lines', *Interfaces,* 24:1.

24 Rakshit, A., Krishnamurthy, N., and Yu, G. (1996), 'Systems Operations Advisor: A Real-time Decision Support System for Managing Airline Operations at United Airlines', *Interfaces,* 26:2. For an interesting overview of the potential offered by new-generation operations centres, see: Nordwall, B. (1997), 'Operations Centers Are Airline Money-Makers', *Aviation Week & Space Technology,* June 16.

25 See, for example, objections raised by Delta and cited in: Henderson, D.K. (1996), 'On the Bar-code Road', *Air Transport World,* September, p. 89. Separately, Swissair enables passengers to reconfirm their North American reservations on the carrier's Web site, and Singapore Airlines' passengers travelling in First or Raffles (business) Class are able to check-in be e-mail when outbound from Singapore. (Whitaker, R. (1997), 'Web Fever', *Airline Business,* February.)

26 For a brief account of current developments in passenger and aircraft facilitation, see: ICAO (1996), *The World of Civil Aviation 1995-98,* Circular 265-AT/109, pp. 60, 61.

27 Nonetheless, '...forwarders and carriers are concerned with ground delays that neither can control but that impact equally on their overall operations and their relationships with shippers. Despite technological advancements in ground handling, an estimated 91% of the time in shipment is spent on the ground, being handled 36 times on average, and requiring 16 individual documents to complete transshipment. Much of it is government bureaucracy, which only will get worse if proposed security procedures are implemented without adequate input from the air-cargo industry'. (Nelms, D.W. (1997), 'At the Crossroads', *Air Transport World,* January, p. 58.)

28 An interesting account of the use of a decision support system to allocate maintenance manpower and track the efficiency and effectiveness of an airline maintenance department can be found in: Dijkstra, M.C., Kroon, L.G., Saloman, M., Van Nunen, J.A.E.E., and Van Wassenhove, L.N. (1994), 'Planning the Size and Organization of KLM's Aircraft Maintenance Personnel', *Interfaces,* 24:6.

29 See, for example: Stalk, G., Evans, P., and Shulman, L.E. (1992), 'Competing on Capabilities: The New Rules of Corporate Strategy', *Harvard Business Review*, March-April.

30 Porter, M.E. (1996), 'What Is Strategy?', *Harvard Business Review*, November-December.

31 Starting with flights from its growing Nashville 'hub' to the West Coast in 1997, Southwest has begun introducing some longer stage lengths into its traditionally - and still predominantly - short-haul network. This change in operating strategy might have adverse effects on its activity system if passengers' catering expectations on flights of up to five hours rise higher than beverages and peanuts, and if the carrier's legendary 15-minute turnarounds are compromised. On the other hand, unit costs should benefit from the network's longer average stage lengths (for reasons explained in Holloway, op. cit.).

32 Porter, op. cit. It should be noted that Porter's work does not refer to 'price differentiation' in the sense that the expression is used here. (The merit of viewing price as a variable subject to 'differentiation' in conjunction with service differentiation was discussed at length in chapter 2.) An example of activity systems amongst European charter airlines can be derived by reading between the lines of the following article: McMullan, K. (1995), 'Europe's New Wave: The Global Paradox', *The Avmark Aviation Economist*, December.

8   Corporate infrastructure

In this chapter we will be looking at changes taking place in the corporate architectures through which airline strategies are being implemented. The structures and processes to which these give rise are, in principle, designed both to effect and to control the implementation of strategies. In practice, there are several reasons why reality is not quite so straightforward.

1   Structures and processes put in place to implement and control the current strategy influence future choice of strategy; internal politics make this inevitable.

2   Structures and processes rarely keep pace with incremental changes in strategy, either because of inertia or because of practical difficulties.

3   The particular nature of some of the technologies deployed by airlines, especially aircraft and information technologies, has tended in the past to militate against structural or processual flexibility.

These problems have perhaps been less acute for small, flexible airlines, those with strong and charismatic leaders, and those embarking on a strategic 'great leap forward'. In future, more flexibility is going to be required of all carriers if structures and processes are to be effective both in the control of fast-moving 'intended' strategies and in the nurturing of 'emergent' strategies.[1]

Structure

Since the early 1960s, the view has been widely held that structure should follow strategy, although in practice - as just noted - organizational structures frequently lag strategic change and sometimes never respond to it at all. More recently there has been recognition that structure - because of its effect on information flows and decision-making - can itself strongly influence the choice of strategies as well as their manner of implementation; indeed, it is not impossible for the causality to be reversed such that structure drives strategy. Finally, because the details of implementation may not be perfectly foreseeable at the time a strategy is formulated, they might have to be worked out through action; action often leads to changes in the course of strategy - this being, as was observed in chapter 1 of Volume One, why realized strategies do not necessarily reflect what was originally intended.[2] At the very least, the strategy-structure linkage should be characterized as 'interactive'.

In this part of the chapter we will look first at external and then at internal architecture. Several issues raised earlier in the book will be revisited, in order to consider the changing relationship between structure and competitive advantage.

Structure as a source of competitive advantage

The strategy-structure linkage - how an airline organizes itself and its 'constellation' of relationships with external partners such as suppliers and distributors - can be a source of competitive advantage, as noted in chapter 17 of Volume One. The key variable here is the manner in which - given a choice - airline managers choose to mix vertical, partnership, and market relationships when structuring the creation and delivery of services. It is a variable that clearly has implications for coordination and control processes because to the extent that some of the world's airlines are restructuring their architectures, they are also having to learn novel skills to help manage new types of relationships with suppliers and alliance partners; neither the rules of traditional bureaucracies nor the guidance of the price mechanism necessarily suffice.[3] This fact was touched upon in chapter 8 of Volume One and in chapter 5 of the present volume, when discussing suppliers and alliances respectively.

Perhaps somewhat unhelpfully, it is impossible to reach a simple, prescriptive conclusion in respect of whether externalization can in itself be a source of competitive advantage for airlines prepared to think in these terms. There is no 'one best way' forward. Much depends upon the specific circumstances of each carrier - the situation in which it finds itself, the vision of the future that has been articulated, and the perceptions held by its senior managers, employees, and other key stakeholders. What can be done is to draw a distinction between two extremes on a conceptual continuum.

1   At one extreme might be the traditional flag carrier - vertically integrated, dealing with suppliers on a largely transactional basis, and moving hesitantly if at all towards whole-hearted adoption of one or more of the partnership, outsourcing, and alliance techniques discussed in chapter 8 of Volume One, and in chapters 1 and 5 of the present volume.

2   At the other extreme might be an airline which sees processes (and accompanying skills) falling into one of two distinct categories:

- core processes that should be retained inhouse: these could include strategic positioning, service conceptualization, network management, brand management (including marketing communications and certain other aspects of the marketing mix), quality assurance, and management of ongoing customer relationships (through frequent flyer programmes and customer information systems, for example); and
- processes that might be externalized: these could include capacity provision in certain markets, many back-office processes, and (subject to tightly-drawn performance criteria) even some front-office processes.

Taken to its extreme, the hierarchical structuring still typical in the industry would give way to small teams of 'knowledge workers' responsible for orchestrating a network of suppliers and partners. Extreme, but far from implausible; this could, for example, be a template for global airlines that some observers think likely to emerge from the alliances currently being formed - a template for organizations that must think globally yet act locally, integrating the whole yet allowing sufficient flexibility for its components to be locally managed. What has still to be established beyond reasonable doubt is just what does in fact constitute the core of an airline. Looked at from the reverse angle, whilst an *economic* case has presumably been made by the growing number of airlines choosing to outsource noncore processes and to grow by using alliance mechanisms, a generally accepted *strategic* case remains elusive - particularly as far as outsourcing is concerned.

Wherever an airline lands on this continuum, structure is unlikely to be a unique and sustainable source of competitive advantage in itself. It is as part of an overall 'configuration' uniting vision, mission, objectives, culture, strategic position, structures, and processes that structure can make a significant contribution.

The heart of distinctive competence and competitive advantage may lie not in the possession of specific organizational resources and skills; these can usually be imitated or purchased by others. Rather, competitive advantage may reside in the orchestrating theme and integrative mechanisms that ensure complementarity among a firm's various aspects: its market domain, its skills, resources and routines, its technologies, its departments, and its decision-making processes. Indeed, organizations may be viewed as systems of interdependency among these components, all of which must be coordinated to compete in the marketplace. It is the complexity and ambiguity of these relationships that give some organizations unique capacities that are all but impossible to copy. Configuration, in short, is likely to be a far greater source of competitive advantage than any single aspect of strategy.[4]

It is as a result of these 'complementarities among strategy, structure, and systems' that 'distinctive competencies emerge and strategic implementation is facilitated'.[5] There is clear linkage here to the 'activity systems' highlighted at the end of chapter 7. One of the symptomatic facets of the global airline industry's current transition is that a growing number of carriers are now confronted by a need to seek the protection of an inimitable 'configuration' as a substitute for the rapidly disappearing umbrella of regulatory protection, yet at the same time intensifying environmental instability and complexity argue in favour of a 'loose coupling' to ensure maximum flexibility. New 'architectural skills' are clearly required of airline managers - skills which are only gradually becoming widely available.

Approaches to internal architecture

Turning more specifically to internal architecture, Lynch has identified the following major approaches to airline organization.[6]

1   Centralized entrepreneurial/autocratic: frequently found in smaller carriers and characterized by a chief executive, often a founder, who is unwilling to relax the close control maintained over all activities. This approach can be inappropriate to large airlines if it hampers balance between the need for strong strategic direction on the one hand, and for the delegation required in order to implement strategies on the other.

2   Centralized functional/operations bias: this emphasizes the production functions, such as flight operations and engineering, and tends to be relatively insensitive to the marketplace and to external environments in general (except, perhaps, the technological environment).[7]

3   Centralized functional/marketing bias: this integrates the traditional 'sales' function with 'traffic' functions such as ground handling, customer services and other areas directly affecting elements of the marketing mix.

4   Decentralized by region: each region has a cluster of functional departments, but it is the region itself that is the primary organizational unit. Common amongst some large North American

and European carriers, this structure has been superseded in a number of cases by decentralized product-based or matrix approaches.

5   Decentralized by product: generally this is an early form of matrix management, because the product groups into which the structure can be broken down are seldom permitted to have their own functional departments.

6   Matrix or grid: this approach attempts to integrate a geographical or product structure (or possibly even both) with a functional structure. 'Product' could be defined by reference to specific routes or route-groups under the control of route managers, and/or to service concepts such as first or business class. It is not impossible for a matrix approach to be in operation in an airline notwithstanding that its organization chart does not make it apparent that this is so.

There has been a widespread historical tendency for airlines to be structured as highly centralized single-unit enterprises, often functionally oriented. This is not inappropriate for small carriers, or even for larger airlines operating in relatively stable competitive environments. As markets are liberalized and environmental turbulence intensifies, it risks becoming anachronistic. The result has been that decision-making authority and the accountabilities which should go with it have in some airlines been increasingly pushed out of the corporate centre and down into geographical or product-oriented units closer to the marketplace. Nonetheless, quite a few of the world's larger airlines remain unusually centralized in comparison with companies of similar size (as measured by revenues and asset bases).

One way of looking at the impact of the industry's current transition on an individual airline's organizational structure is to consider the following five questions.

Is the airline a 'unit' or a holding company?

In the cases of larger carriers engaged in a variety of activities in addition to transporting passengers and freight, there has been a tendency for the airline to act as a holding company (in substance if not always in legal form), with other activities housed in divisions or possibly subsidiaries. Some carriers have moved in recent years to separate airline operations more clearly from engineering, catering, and other non-air transport activities and place each into a true holding company structure. The airline usually remains by far the most significant element in terms of revenue - although certainly not always in terms of profits.

Such reorganizations can be beneficial if they clarify the cost and revenue performances of each unit and lead to the creation of more entrepreneurial cultures, supportive of initiative, responsibility, and accountability. For example, when Swissair reorganized in the mid-90s, the airline core was separated into a standalone division; this focused attention on its lack of consistent profitability relative to several other divisions which, for a number of years, had been masking the weak performance of air transport operations.[8]

Is the network actively managed as a single system, or divided into geographical fiefdoms?

Network management is an evolving discipline that in its fully developed form integrates service conceptualization, route and production planning, pricing, distribution, loyalty programmes, and service delivery. For example, as large international airlines move towards managing costs and revenues over their entire networks, it makes less sense to organize passenger sales geographically; managers and sales personnel in one region will increasingly be required to make decisions which might primarily benefit another region.

There are clearly some knotty political issues involved in any attempt to move from a geographical focus towards fully integrated network management. Many carriers are nonetheless recognizing the need to give a network orientation to processes that have traditionally been housed within functional and/or geographic 'silos'; cross-functional teams are one possible first step towards a more integrated approach, and the evolution of inter-airline alliances - a primary motivation for which is often to exploit network synergies - provides added impetus and a sense of urgency.

Is the hierarchy tall or flat?

An airline's history and the culture of its home country strongly influence organizational structure and the nature of authority relations. Sometimes, however, structural change lags wider societal shifts. Many airlines, particularly in North America and Europe, have been slow to reflect societal change by moving away from the hierarchical, vertical 'command and control' model towards leaner and more participative structures operating with wider spans of control.

The trend towards delayering - the preference for flatter structures - has recently accelerated, albeit somewhat unevenly. One motivation is to save costs by stripping out middle management; another is to accelerate response times by bringing front-line staff into closer contact with top management, and in achieving this perhaps also to make corporate culture more customer-oriented. Organizations are better able to 'learn' when managers are hierarchically close to the customer, to the action, and to the fail-points at which service needs to be improved.

A new perspective on hierarchy The traditional view of decision-making in airlines for years owed much to a quasi-military model, with the 'troops' in the front-line being given little room to manoeuvre around the orders passed down the chain of command. This is gradually changing. In a small number of cases the change is more than gradual. FedEx, for example, claims that (at least at a perceptual level) the organizational pyramid has been 'inverted' to place customers at the top, served by front-line staff who are supported and coached rather than directed by middle managers, who in turn are supported by top management. Each layer is looked upon as a 'supplier' of services to the layer above.

The practical point in this colourful imagery is that the airline is being driven by customers' needs and wants rather than by internally oriented, functional frames of reference inherited from the past. No longer does, say, the desire to have a great flight operations set-up or a smoothly functioning sales organization predominate to the exclusion of wider considerations.

Are decision-making and accountability for performance centralized, or have they been decentralized out into and down the structure?

Whilst IS/IT offer scope for central decision-makers to loosen the reins without losing sight of what is happening in distant corners of their global empires, technology also has the potential to centralize decisions that in the past have been made locally. An example could materialize in time from the changes currently underway in airline distribution; as carriers deploy technologies that will help them gain greater control over distribution channels, one result could be that power over this aspect of the marketing mix will become increasingly centralized.

When discussing decentralization, a distinction needs to be drawn between decentralization of operating authority and decentralization of strategy-making. The former is much more common than the latter, yet it is the latter which is more likely to give rise to the emergent strategies first discussed in the opening chapter of Volume One.

Operating authority As far as operating authority is concerned, it is now broadly accepted - if not always acted upon - that turbulent liberalized markets require decision-making close to the 'customer-face', because there is too little time for decisions to wind there way through bloated corporate bureaucracies. For example, Delta - not historically renowned for fleetness of foot - gave unprecedented autonomy to its London-based European regional managers in the mid-1990s to deal with the worsening internal and external situations facing the Atlantic network acquired from Pan Am.

Strategy formulation Decentralized strategy-making has also been spreading recently, with a trend - embraced even by several state-owned

European flag carriers - towards smaller decision-making units. Some of the issues raised were discussed in chapter 1 of the present volume. The decentralization of strategic management processes to discrete business units is relatively straightforward when these units operate in ancillary industries, such as engineering and maintenance, avionics, catering or ground handling. Devolution of responsibility for core airline operations to 'route centres' or similar units can be more difficult - both philosophically and practically. Again, if a unit is relatively self-contained in terms of its fleet and route network, the problems are surmountable; responsibility for marketing strategy, operations, local hiring, and outsourcing can fairly easily be devolved. Certainly there is a strong argument for keeping the salary structures, working practices, and training regimens of self-contained regional (i.e. commuter) operations fully separate from those of the parent carrier.

On the other hand, the fact that airlines operate networks of interdependent routes and interchange aircraft around these networks leaves devolution of full profit responsibility to geographical regions potentially hostage to the peculiarities of internal accounting methodologies. In the case of large carriers, unless an internal market for the leasing of aircraft between regions is to be established somebody somewhere has to be making centralized asset allocation decisions for the benefit of the network as a whole. Some airlines are nonetheless committed to decentralization of profit responsibility across their networks. Even Air France briefly made this a central plank of its recovery strategy in the mid-1990s.

The same issue raises interesting questions about the extent to which potential synergies between alliance partners such as British Airways and Qantas can be *fully* exploited without some form of central control. Thinking globally and producing locally is not without its challenges.

> The successful megacarriers will be the ones whose senior managers sort out their priorities, and establish the correct boundaries between what is properly a central decision and what ought to be left to local managers. Equally, they will establish ways of dealing with the complexities and conflicts which are inevitable as global groupings come together.[9]

As markets become more complex and volatile, the relationship between senior managers and front-line personnel needs to change. Senior management should communicate a vision of the airline and its future and, as far as possible, ensure consistency within the current activity system; but, particularly in larger airlines, it also needs to be prepared to delegate more than has historically been the case in a majority of carriers in order to allow quicker, more flexible responses to marketplace dynamics. Adjusting to this change is a challenge not just for senior managements, of course. Where a corporate culture encourages blame avoidance and the use of committees or other bureaucratic devices to delay decision-making and diffuse responsibility - something that is still not uncommon at state-owned flag carriers - a time-consuming and possibly wrenching programme of culture change will first be necessary before authority and accountability can be delegated down into the organization.

Is the airline's structure organized around the flow of customer-serving processes?

Functional and, in the case of some larger airlines, regional orientations continue to prevail in the industry, but just a few carriers have started delegating authority and responsibility in respect of the whole-company, horizontal processes which flow across functional boundaries. This section takes a look at the characteristics of 'horizontal organizations', which some observers believe will in future be a structure seen more commonly amongst the world's airlines. A number have already begun to restructure around the customer. British Airways, for example, was reoriented in this way early in its corporate transformation, so that departments having direct customer contact all reported to the head of marketing. One advantage of this approach is that customers, their needs, and how to satisfy them become the central focus. Marketing is not looked at in this case as a purely functional activity focused largely on the 4Ps of the marketing mix, but embraces as well the human, servicescape, and operational aspects of actual service delivery that were discussed in the last chapter.[10] We referred to this type of perspective at the end of chapter 3, where Lovelock's concept of the 'service management trinity' (marketing, operations, and human resources) was also mentioned.[11]

The systems approach The systems approach sees every organization as a unified complex of processes, each defined by a flow of materials, intermediate goods, people, and/or information. Any one process is likely to be comprised of tasks or operations which, in many cases, will be performed by employees housed in different specialist departments. The processes are integrated, in principle, by a common purpose. Those most aligned with each other can be separated into categories called subsystems, which are interdependent and together comprise a system. Their interdependence means that any event or change in one subsystem will have repercussions elsewhere in the system.

   Although Ishikawa and several other writers treat systems and processes as synonymous, it is more helpful to think in terms of systems being comprised of many different processes. People certainly speak about 'strategic planning systems' or 'financial systems', but for analytical purposes it is preferable to refer to them as processes. Each process involves a distinct flow of information, customers, or some tangible input such as food or aircraft parts, and the airline as a whole is a single system encompassing subsystems of linked processes.

Processes are dynamic, whereas organization charts are frequently static and do not reflect either system objectives or the reality of the flows actually running through the system they are supposed to describe. The structure mapped by an organization chart will not necessarily mirror the subsystems functioning within any particular airline.

Subsystems of linked processes should themselves be closely related in practice. The theme which draws them together is value: the airline's capability to design, produce and deliver benefits at a chosen level of quality, and the sacrifices demanded of customers in return. This is what is being strategically managed within and between the subsystems. This is what integrates them.

Horizontal organization Horizontal organization, whether an alternative or an adjunct to a vertical hierarchy, centres around a small number of core processes which cross functional boundaries and ultimately link through to the satisfaction of customers' needs, wants, and expectations. Quite a few companies in the aerospace industry have recently moved in this direction, but only a small number of airlines have taken tentative steps along the same path. Ostroff and Smith have distilled ten principles which they consider 'lie at the heart of horizontal organizations':[12]

1 Organize around processes not tasks.
2 Flatten hierarchy by minimizing the subdivision of workflows and eliminating non-value-added activities.
3 Assign ownership of processes and process performance.
4 Link performance objectives and evaluation to customer satisfaction.
5 Make teams, not individuals, the principal building blocks of organization performance and design.
6 Combine managerial and non-managerial activities as often as possible.
7 Treat multiple competencies as the rule, not the exception.
8 Inform and train people on a 'just-in-time-to-perform' basis, not on a 'need to know basis'.
9 Maximize supplier and customer contact.
10 Reward individual skill development and team performance, not just individual performance.

Most large airlines have traditionally been organized hierarchically along lines based on professional functions (i.e. sales, personnel, finance etc.), geographical areas (i.e. Europe-Middle East, Latin America etc.), products (i.e. first class, cargo, tours etc.), or some combination of these. The result has been that work is divided into narrowly defined tasks, allocated to specialized units, and then reintegrated by locating each unit within a vertical hierarchy.

This task orientation tends to promote a perspective which is inward-looking rather than focused outwards onto the role that each particular unit is performing within the end-to-end, cross-functional, horizontal processes that deliver customer value. Orientations like this can be a powerful, and negative, driver of organizational culture. There tends to be a narrow focus on control to the exclusion of cross-functional communication about, and responsibility for, value-adding processes as a whole. Organizations frequently become fragmented, complex, and unfocused. Best at channelling information upwards and control downwards, hierarchical structures often fail to promote horizontal information flows.

Orientation towards horizontal, customer-serving processes promotes a different type of focus. The focus on value-building widens from 'what is done' to incorporate 'how things are done', from 'what benefits are being offered to customers' to 'how these benefits are being offered' and 'how it is being made easier and more attractive for customers to do business with the airline concerned'.

Some form of hierarchy is always going to be required for control purposes and because of economic efficiencies offered by the division of labour. Furthermore, in technologically complex enterprises such as airlines there will inevitably be important pockets of highly skilled professionals whose tendency is to concentrate thought and effort on their own areas of expertise rather than the customer-satisfying purpose of the overall system. The danger lurking behind this inevitability is the inward-looking, power-oriented culture such pockets foster unless they are consciously integrated into the horizontal processes of which they are each just one component.

Complex organizations have to be sliced one way or another and responsibility given to somebody for what happens in each slice. But doing this only vertically, relying entirely on hierarchical structures, creates barriers to the integrated design and delivery of customer value. The systems approach, as we saw at the end of the last chapter, offers a better alternative.

The power of the systems approach comes from viewing airlines as a whole rather than as a jigsaw of parts, and orientating this overview towards the horizontal processes which serve customers rather than the vertical processes which primarily serve top management's need to feel in control. Cross-functional activities can be better integrated. This holistic view of the airline promotes a customer rather than a departmental focus and opens minds to the possibility that the entire horizontal flow, rather than just isolated functional parts of it, could be better managed.

Better management in this context means improved value for the customer: more perceived benefits in return for the same sacrifices, or the same perceived benefits for less sacrifice. In short, the systems approach is more likely to be value-driven and to promote continuous improvement than a tall, hierarchical structure. Cross-functional learning is better suited to the design, production, and delivery of customer-perceived value than are traditional hierarchical processes. Figure 8.1 illustrates these points.

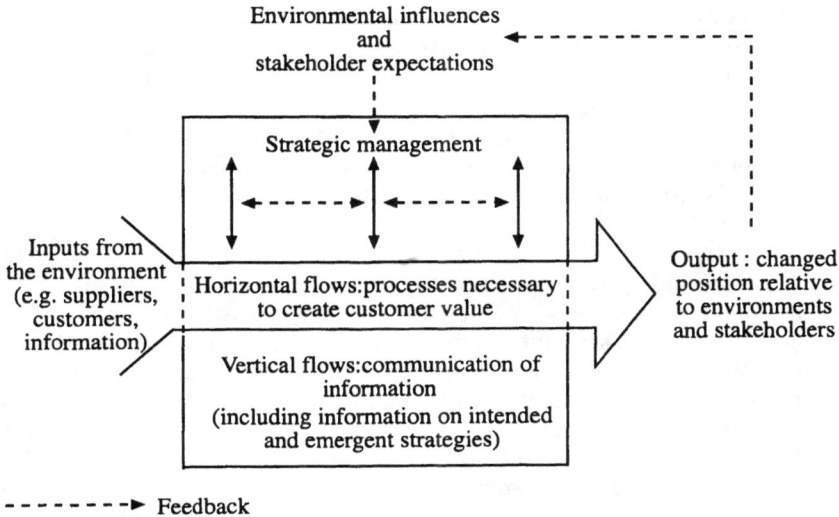

Figure 8.1 : The centrality of horizontal, cross-functional flows in a systems environment

'Lean organizations', of which we have been hearing a considerable amount since the early 1990s, are those which minimize the number of people required to work on horizontal processes and yet still produce the desired customer value, thereby raising productivity; 'delayering' removes unnecessary layers of middle management separating horizontal processes from strategic leaders. Flattening the hierarchy, made possible by massive improvements in the cost-effectiveness of information technologies, enables senior management to be more rapidly aware, and directly supportive, of events as they emerge in the horizontal, customer-serving processes.

Clearly, there is a role for vertical structures even within the systems approach. There is no 'one best way', every company's choice being contingent on its particular situation. In a handful of airlines, however, the primary focus has indeed moved towards cross-functional, value-adding horizontal processes and vertical lines of communication have been shortened. FedEx for example, a company of close to 100,000 people, has just seven vertical layers encompassing everybody from front-line employees to the CEO.

There is a lot of literature discussing how a systems approach can in practice be wrung from a hierarchical structure. Bounds et al have suggested a useful integrative framework to give it all some degree of coherence. They identify two fundamental approaches.[13]

1   The construction of horizontal linkages to patch together an existing hierarchy. Techniques in this category include ad hoc teams, committees, and development of the 'internal customer' concept which treats the next stage in every process (even if internal to the system and not directly involving a final customer) as a client to be served and provided with value. Functional units still exist, but are now seen as pools from which resources can be drawn rather than as centres of control.[14]

2   The second group of approaches goes further by realigning managerial roles and responsibilities to mirror, rather than just accommodate, horizontal processes. The key point is that specific managers are given ownership of a process, implying responsibility for its performance and improvement. This eliminates the scope for buck-passing which exists when any process is subdivided into discrete functional units. The early prototype, matrix management, has since been augmented by a variety of cross-functional, product-focused, or customer-focused techniques.

For those companies needing to make the transition from a 'vertical' to a 'horizontal' corporation, Byrne has itemized the following steps.[15]

- **Identify** strategic objectives.
- **Analyze** key competitive advantages to fulfill objectives.
- **Define** core processes, focusing on what's essential to accomplish your goals.
- **Organize** around processes, not functions. Each process should link related tasks to yield a product or service to a customer.
- **Eliminate** all activities that fail to add value.
- **Cut** function and staff departments to a minimum, preserving key expertise.
- **Appoint** a manager or team as the "owner" of each core process.
- **Create** multi-disciplinary teams to run each process.
- **Set** specific performance objectives for each process.
- **Empower** employees with authority and information to achieve goals.
- **Revamp** training, appraisal, pay, and budgetary systems to support the new structure and link it to customer satisfaction.

The systems approach is not simply a trendy concept. It is an application which, although still not widely used in the airline business, is practical and offers various methodologies for improving the value-creating processes that lie at the heart of strategic management. More efficient value creation is an art which carriers in increasingly competitive markets are going to have to learn as the industry's current transition runs its course.

Whatever form is chosen, the essential point about organizational architecture is that it should be designed for both effectiveness and efficiency. What this means is that it must both promote and control for the attainment of corporate objectives, and it must do this whilst at the same time contributing to the minimization of costs incurred in reaching them.

Coordination and control processes

> What will be the biggest managerial challenge faced by airline chiefs in years to come? There are many candidates: marketing in a deregulated environment; cost cutting; attracting new business; finding new markets; alliances; managing union relationships. But the biggest challenge will probably be controlling the enterprise.[16]

Closely linked to an airline's choice of structure are the coordination and control processes which, in many cases, influence structure in the first place. *Coordination* processes are concerned with flows of information to facilitate consistent decision-making throughout an organization; '*control* is a management process which provides assurance that activities are contributing towards goals as planned and which enables the correction of deviations'.[17] Structure differentiates an airline into organizational units, and integration pulls it all together again ensuring coordination and control. The more complex an organization's structural differentiation (not to be confused with product differentiation), the more complex are likely to be the coordination and control processes required to facilitate strategy implementation. This is a challenge which global alliances will certainly not escape.

As was explained in chapter 1 of Volume One, strategic management is an iterative process. When environments become more complex and turbulent, the iterations need to be almost continuous.[18] Feedback is the essential catalyst for each new iteration, and this can be viewed in one of two ways.

1   The classical perspective, exemplified by the thermostat metaphor, sees feedback as being essentially negative: strategies are monitored against pre-established performance criteria, and deviations are then identified and corrected. Rectification might require one or both of changed objectives or a new approach to implementation.

2   The alternative view rejects the notion that organizations are essentially systems operating in stable equilibrium, and that stability

can be restored by simple cause and effect adjustments to objectives and strategies. Instead, feedback is characterized as being complex, nonlinear, and positive - with cause and effect submerged in far too many action-reaction loops to be isolated for the purpose of fine-tuning an outcome. Organizations are fundamentally unpredictable systems, and the best that can be achieved is effective management of their unstable boundaries - certainly not control over specifically planned futures. This unpredictability and instability is the seed-bed for emergent strategies.

'Control' and 'change' can therefore be considered two sides of the same coin. Whilst progress with intended strategies has to be monitored, tight control within the context of increasingly turbulent environments can be counterproductive if it stifles change and the emergence of new strategies from the experience of implementation. Emergent strategies come to the fore in conditions of uncertainty. For airlines this can present a problem: whilst the nature of the industry requires detailed operational planning, the nature of its environments now requires rapid learning and sufficient flexibility to accommodate what emerges from the implementation of intended strategies.[19]

Coordination in pursuit of mission, objectives, and operating goals

Particularly for large airlines, there is a balance to be struck, perhaps a paradox to be resolved, between on the one hand the requirement for network integration and the comprehensive overview needed to exploit economies of scope, density, and (where they exist) scale and, on the other hand, the need to allow decentralized decision-making close to the marketplace. For example, if systemwide load factors are low, is that the fault of inadequate fleet planning, scheduling, yield management, or selling? Is there a problem with the service concept or service delivery? Where in the network does the fault occur? Who is responsible for integrating capacity, pricing, and promotional decisions across the network?

In large airlines the decision environment is becoming too complex for single individuals to master, and the answer is increasingly going to be to use IT to enable decentralized decision-making within the context of improved knowledge at the centre about what is happening throughout the organization as a whole. In a lot of cases this change is taking time to materialize, with the result that those airlines that have been investing heavily in IT are building a substantial lead over others in the manipulation of data into information and knowledge. This capability is becoming a critical success factor (CSF) in the most competitive markets.

Another coordination mechanism that has been adopted by some large carriers is the use of cross-functional teams. British Airways is a keen exponent of the merit of teams for bringing different functional points of view to bear on issues and problems confronting the airline as a whole.[20] United has shown enthusiasm for issue-oriented task teams, creating over 50 in the first year after its employee buyout. A number of carriers also use teams within functional areas; the use of flexible, self-directed work teams has become increasingly common at European maintenance centres, for example.

Control

If a 350-seat aircraft flies 4,000 kilometres with 300 passengers on board, 1.4 million ASKs of output will have been produced and 1.2 million RPKs will have been sold. These output and traffic figures will be recorded irrespective of whether the plane arrived on time or several hours late. But in terms of outcome - particularly in terms of customer satisfaction and loyalty - the difference between the two circumstances could be profound.

All airlines have control systems in place, but most are oriented towards quantitative outputs, primarily system ASKs/ATKs and RPKs/RTKs and, of course, financial targets. Very few have control systems oriented to outcomes, particularly customer satisfaction, progress towards qualitative strategic milestones such as the successful building of brand loyalty and an appropriate corporate image (i.e. strategic as opposed to purely financial controls), and changes in the attitudes of stakeholders other than customers. Few monitor whether the capabilities likely to be required to succeed in the future are being actively nurtured; even though the future is unknowable in detail, the type of demands it might reasonably be expected to place on an organization's capabilities nonetheless need to be assessed. It is here that effective and efficient control can actually become a source of competitive advantage. The problem is that the necessary data is often not readily available. Sir Colin Marshall recognized this soon after his arrival at British Airways, and so established mechanisms to create it.

Control, which needs to be oriented towards mission, objectives and CSFs, and should be externally-focused on customers, competitors and the marketplace as well as internally focused on productivity, can take one of two forms: hard or soft.

Hard controls These are characterized by the imposition of rules and procedures and by the monitoring of objective measures of performance against plans and budgets. They are increasingly running up against environmental turbulence (which can kill an intended strategy and give birth to an emergent strategy), and they can also be inconsistent with the need perceived by some managements to empower front-line staff in order to create competitive advantage out of service encounters. Another problem is that most traditional cost and management accounting systems are not oriented towards the cost and quality of activities and horizontal processes or to the measurement of customer satisfaction, all of which are becoming increasingly important targets for management attention.

Timeliness of information is also an issue. Top management should in principle have access to profit information the instant doors are closed on each flight - although this is clearly easier for a small, point-to-point operator to achieve than for a large network carrier. Certainly, comprehensive data should be available immediately at the end of every month; competitive markets move too quickly to allow waiting around for several weeks before finding out what is working and what is not.

Finally, very few airlines go as far as British Airways, which established a marketplace performance unit as long ago as 1983; this unit tracks over 300 measures of performance, most of which are oriented to customers' perceptions of what the airline is achieving rather than to a purely operational or financial perspective. Such customer advocacy - which British Airways also pursues through its brand management and customer relations organizations - is still a rarity in the airline business, even amongst large and well-resourced carriers.

Soft controls Here we are talking about management style, communications, reward and motivation, and corporate culture. Shared values and a corporate culture relevant to mission and objectives, image, service concept, and service delivery processes are particularly important in a high-contact, geographically dispersed service business such as an airline. The provision of value to consumers is, at least on the passenger side, an outcome of service delivery processes which themselves are at the same time both strongly technological in orientation and yet marked by complex social interactions. Corporate culture helps shape - albeit never entirely control - these interactions, and (as several aircraft accident investigations have revealed in the last few years) it also has much to do with how technology is handled. As was noted in chapter 14 of Volume One, however, culture is not monolithic. For example, the British Airways culture espousing excellence in operations and in customer service harboured a subculture capable of propagating the 'dirty tricks' campaign against Virgin Atlantic.

An important tool in the building of corporate culture is communications. This is briefly discussed in the next section.

Communications

The slowness with which staff at some major US and European airlines absorbed the new competitive realities overtaking the industry in the early 1990s speaks either of willful myopia on a grand scale or a failure of managements adequately to grasp and communicate the nature, extent, and implications of what was - and still is - happening.

> In a decentralized, customer-driven company a good leader spends more time communicating than doing anything else. He must communicate with the employees to keep them all working towards the same goals, and he must communicate with his customers to keep them abreast of the company's new activities and services.[21]

Open and clear intra-organizational communications are vital in any effort to gain commitment to a shared vision and to help provide a common frame of reference as an aid to decision-making. In addition to its importance to the attainment of 'hard-side' targets, the impact of open, morale-boosting communications on 'soft-side' variables cannot be underestimated. For example, an early contributor to Kenya Airways' turnaround prior to the sale of a minority stake in the company to KLM in the mid-90s was a face-to-face communication programme ('Building Pride Together') managed by Time International - the organization responsible for British Airways' 'Putting People First' culture change programme a decade earlier.

The majority of airlines have some sort of communications programme, although few can rival FedEx's live television network - FXTV - which, as well as serving other communications needs, airs a programme every morning to review worldwide operations the previous night. In 1996, British Airways' top management announced plans to launch a daily 15-minute inhouse television news programme to be aired globally. The purpose of this £2-3 million initiative was to inform and motivate staff and also to impose greater accountability on managers by putting them in front of the cameras. Pilots and cabin crew were to have access at their hotels overseas. This last point highlights the inherent difficulty of communicating with staff scattered around an extensive network; the response from a small number of airlines has been to establish internal information systems (or 'intranets') using sites on the World Wide Web. Most carriers use more prosaic media, such as training sessions, meetings, and newsletters.

Communicate what? The answer here is vision, mission, objectives, operating goals, what it is the airline has set out to achieve, and a sense of each individual's role in the corporate and competitive strategies adopted to achieve it. Communications need to encapsulate what an airline is doing in its markets, what value it is adding, and why it would be missed were it not in business. There is little empirical evidence that this sort of communication is yet widespread in the industry.

Why communicate? There are many possible answers, but amongst the most important are:

- to help build consensus about how to achieve shared objectives, and to integrate efforts in pursuit of chosen strategies;

- to motivate;
- to imbue people with a better understanding of the need for continuous change, whether this involves managing costs, improving service, accepting greater responsibility or perhaps even devolving some responsibility down the line. Frank and reasoned communication can be particularly vital when outsourcing and downsizing create job insecurity and lower morale;[22]
- to elicit commitment to, and involvement in, the corporate purpose; or
- to explain and build commitment to a move away from a functional orientation towards a focus on processes.

Given the number of people likely to be involved - their personalities, different cultural backgrounds, dispersed locations, varying levels of education, and personal circumstances - these are inevitably unattainable across the board in any sizeable carrier. Nonetheless, even partial success can generate corporate momentum.

What is the role of 'internal marketing'? [23] There are two primary definitions of internal marketing.

1   The first, which we have already met, embodies a recognition that even employees and departments not having direct contact with external customers are still suppliers of something which adds value for internal customers, and thus indirectly for external customers as well.

2   In addition to being a tool for integrating back-office with front-office activities, internal marketing is also sometimes defined as the use of traditional marketing techniques as communications devices to involve and motivate employees and gain their commitment to the corporate purpose. This relates back to the importance of employee satisfaction as a prerequisite to customer satisfaction, mentioned in Volume One, chapter 16 and in chapter 7 of the present volume. 'In other words, satisfying the needs of internal customers upgrades the capability to satisfy the needs of external customers.'[24]

A common factor shared by both definitions is the breaking down of organizational barriers, making everybody aware of their interlinking roles in serving the external customer. In practice, the literature reveals few formal internal marketing programmes other than the widely reported efforts of SAS and British Airways in the 1980s, although the essence of such programmes is sometimes captured in the 'quality circles' that a small number of airlines have established (frequently now under a different name).

Information as a change agent Turning from the communication of broad corporate purposes to the communication of detailed operational information, several airlines have recognized that the widespread distribution of information is a potentially powerful tool for overcoming resistance to change and enabling the decentralization of decision-making. Authority and accountability can be pushed down the hierarchy, and a move away from top-down models of control towards the empowerment model introduced in the last chapter can be encouraged. British Airways has been using information quite deliberately in this way for several years as, beginning more recently, has Lufthansa.

Structure, processes, and strategic positioning

This and the preceding chapter have together made a case for the adoption of approaches to service delivery, organizational architecture, and coordination and control processes that are flexible, responsive, and empowering. Nonetheless, whilst it is certainly true that structural changes in the industry and the external environments within which it operates are creating pressure for these new approaches, there are still plenty of examples of carriers that are successful despite practising more traditional methods.

Bowen and Lawler have drawn a distinction between what they call 'the control model' and 'the involvement model': the control model is a traditional form, based on the belief that productivity and service quality are best secured through a hierarchy of tightly-drawn vertical relationships; the alternative model involves all employees, rather than managers alone, in coordination and control - relying 'much more on self-control and self-management, as supported by participatory management and training'.[25] Endeavouring to determine the better route to success, Bowen and Lawler make the following observations.

Turning to the question of service via the production line or empowerment, it is also difficult to pick a winner. Just look at the following test cases:

- In 1990, Federal Express became the first service organisation to win the highly coveted Malcom Baldridge National Quality Award. The company's motto is "people, service, profits". Behind its brightly coloured blue, white, and red planes and uniforms, there are self-managing work teams, gain-sharing plans, and empowered employees seemingly consumed with providing quality service to their customers - whose individual needs for pick-up time and locations, and destinations, are flexibly and creatively serviced.

- At UPS, referred to as "Big Brown" by its employees, the company's philosophy was clearly stated by Jim Casey when he founded the company: "Best Service at Low Rates". Here, too, we find turned-on people and profits. But we do not find empowerment: instead we find controls, rules, a detailed union contract and carefully studied work methods. Nor do we find a promise to do all things for customers, such as handling off-schedule pick-ups and handling packages that don't fit size and weight limitations. In fact, rigid operational guidelines help guarantee the customer reliable, low-cost service.

Federal Express and UPS present two very different "faces" to the customer and behind these faces are two different management philosophies and organisational cultures. Federal Express is a high-involvement, horizontally coordinated organisation which responds to customers with empowered employees who are encouraged to use their judgement above and beyond the rule-book. UPS is a top-down, traditionally controlled organisation, in which employees face customers directed by policies and procedures that are based on industrial engineering studies of how all aspects of service delivery should be carried out and how long they should take (although, lately UPS has shown signs of becoming more flexible and less bureaucratic).[26]

Bowen and Lawler's conclusion is that despite the widening clamour for involvement and empowerment, the case in terms of performance outcome is mixed.[27] They nonetheless believe that, looking at service industries as a whole, it 'would seem to be that more service organisations currently operate on the control end of our continuum than is called for by the business situation they face and the strategies they have adopted'.[28]

One reason for the slowness with which some service industries have moved towards a high-involvement approach is that they have until recently been confronted with less pressure to change than have many manufacturing industries. This has prolonged a lingering attachment to the hierarchical control model dispensed with over the last two decades by a lot of manufacturing companies. Pressure to change, as we have seen throughout both volumes of this book, is now affecting most parts of the air transport industry. Whilst the express package business might, because of its nature, continue to lend itself to alternative approaches, it is intuitively appealing to believe that growing customer expectations in a high-contact business such as the passenger side of the airline industry will increasingly call for involvement, empowerment, spontaneity, and responsiveness - at the very least in the front office. This belief permeates Part Two of the present volume, and it reflects one of the more important symptoms of the transition through which the industry is currently passing.

Conclusion

One of the primary organizational challenges facing airlines today can be traced to the fact that, as first noted in the Preface, increasingly dynamic competitive environments are creating friction between the need for flexibility in marketing and stability in operations. Complicating matters further is the point, already made at several places in chapters 6 and 7, that the distinction between marketing and operations - between service conceptualization and service delivery - is not one that is always readily apparent to customers.

What is called for is a structure which adapts to rapidly shifting external environments whilst still facilitating day-to-day operational stability. Drawing on and extending seminal work on organization structures by Mintzberg,[29] Bowman and Carter have modelled what they call the 'machine adhocracy'.[30] This conceptual structure contains four groups of processes which, in both design and capability, embody many of the requirements being imposed on the real organizational structures of airlines emerging from the relative stability of regulated environments into highly dynamic, liberalized environments. Bowman and Carter's groupings are: the strategic apex, the operating core, the technostructure, and the university.

1 **The strategic apex.** Responsible for the 'efficient management of the current mission of the firm' and 'for the strategic development of the business', the strategic apex is required to make industrial, vertical, product, and geographical scope decisions, fund the airline, establish its culture and value system, and coordinate interfaces both within the company and between the carrier and external stakeholders such as 'suppliers, alliance partners, customers, [and] distribution channels'.[31] Over-involvement in the day-to-day running of the business is to be avoided.

2 **The operating core.** Charged with 'producing high quality services (in terms of conformance quality) at lowest costs', people in the operating core - 'the heart of the business' - 'need to understand what it is the customer values, and they need to organise in ways that can most effectively deliver value'.

   The operating core consists of a series of linked activities, and it should only undertake those activities in which it can demonstrate competence relative to competitors, or potential suppliers...If there is no strategic advantage in the firm carrying out the activity itself, then it should be subcontracted.

   In order to cope with an unpredictable and changing task environment, operations in the core will need to demonstrate flexibility, either through individuals maintaining a wider set of skills (feasible where the tasks are relatively straightforward), or through teams of specialists forming and reforming into teams to tackle varying task requirements.[32]

3   **The technostructure.** Responsible 'for the efficient delivery of high conformance quality', the technostructure will be involved in a variety of processes including but not limited to quality assurance and various human resource management tasks.[33]

4   **The university.** Much more than a traditional staff function but no less vulnerable to cost-cutting initiatives, the university as conceived by Bowman and Carter is responsible for: 'research into new products, or new processes; helping staff develop new skills and knowledge; providing valuable information on customers, competitors etc....Whereas the operating core and the technostructure concern themselves primarily with the efficient delivery of the current set of ...services, the university is focused on change and development. Its role is to stimulate the continual transformation of activities in the operating core'.[34] One of its key functions is to build the firm's competencies by developing inimitable new know-how to replace established know-how that is susceptible to systematization and so, over time, to degradation into common practice. It was noted at several points in Part Two of Volume One that tacit knowledge - ways of thinking and doing that are unique to the airline concerned - is sometimes one of the few substantial resources differentiating firms within any strategic group. It is also a powerful driver of the unique 'activity systems' discussed in the last chapter.

There is no implication here that airline organization charts will shortly become home to a profusion of strategic apexes, operating cores, technostructures, and universities. Furthermore, Bowman and Carter themselves recognize that even as a concept their 'machine adhocracy' is vying for relevance with other evolving models, such as 'virtual organisations, alliance networks and forms of learning organisation'.[35] They have nonetheless suggested a concept which clearly incorporates many of the key macro-level concerns that airline organization structures must accommodate as the industry's more complex and commercially dynamic future unfolds.

In the final analysis, each carrier must look to its own circumstances and strategic position to determine what is and what is not an appropriate structure. Karlöff, citing Prahalad and Doz, suggests a four-point analysis of the appropriateness of organizational structure.[36]

1   Which essential functions ought to be kept together from the standpoint of overall strategy?

2 Which functions call for local adaptability and closeness to the customer?

3 Where do the advantages of large-scale operation lie, and what is the position with regard to economies of scale and the Experience Curve?

4 How is the motivation of leaders and other people affected?

Karlöff adds the cautionary note that the entrepreneurialism associated with decentralized structures can be motivating and productivity-enhancing during cyclical economic upturns, but that stronger central coordination is frequently required in order to take the difficult decisions faced during downturns. Furthermore, there is always a danger that the revenue benefits attainable from decentralization will get eaten away by the higher costs to which, without careful attention, it often gives rise.

Airline performance in the new environments faced by the industry will be the result of many different factors, but two will be particularly important:

- the ability to establish a consistent strategic position (Part One of this volume) that is responsive to changes in external and internal circumstances (Volume One, Parts One and Two respectively); and
- the ability to create an activity system and an organizational infrastructure capable of implementing the strategies required by the chosen position (Part Two of this volume).

In the final part of the book we turn from implementation to outcome. Chapter 9 will look at service quality, failure, and recovery, and chapter 10 will consider customer loyalty and retention.

Notes

1   The distinctions between 'intended' and 'emergent' strategies are discussed in Volume One, chapter 1.
2   Genus, A. (1995), *Flexible Strategic Management,* Chapman & Hall, p. 99.
3   Ibid., p. 135.
4   Miller, D. (1996), 'Configurations Revisited', *Strategic Management Journal,* Vol. 17, pp. 509, 510.
5   Ibid., p. 510. However, it is worth noting that Miller cautions against 'too much configuration'. He notes that, 'Ultimately, there is a danger that such very highly configured firms will become too simple - too dominated by a single world view, too monolithic, too driven by one theme or function. This is especially likely to occur in powerful, successful organizations where managers are left to their own devices.'
6   Lynch, J.J. (1984), *Airline Organization in the 1980s,* Macmillan.
7   The different types of external environment - sociopolitical, economic, technological, and competitive - are discussed in Volume One, Part One.
8   The holding company at the head of the new structure is SAirGroup. Beneath it are:

- SAirLines: encompassing air transport operations (Swissair, Crossair, 49.5 per cent of Sabena, and several smaller holdings in other carriers), distribution (Traviswiss), and financial support (Airline Financial Support Services, based in Mumbai);
- SAirServices: incorporating MRO activities (SRTechnics), ground handling (Swissport), IT (atraxis), real estate (aviReal), and SAC Invest Ltd.;
- SAirLogistics: covering air cargo (Swisscargo - the Swissair cargo operation - together with a shareholding in Cargolux and the cargo operations of Crossair and Sabena), and cargo logistics (Cargologic, Jetlogistics, and Jacky Maeder); and
- SAirRelations: encompassing hotels (Swissôtel), catering (Gate Gourmet and Rail Gourmet), duty-free outlets (Nuance), restaurants (Restorama), and hospital catering (Restosana).

9   *Airline Business,* April 1993, p. 7.
10   The fact that in a service industry it is usually quite difficult to define precisely where 'marketing' ends and 'operations' begins can sometimes lead to overcentralization. Whilst it is certainly true that operational concerns such as safety and schedule integrity are core product attributes which greatly affect consumers' perceptions of service quality, not every airline would necessarily find it appropriate to go as far as British Airways did in integrating operations into marketing; at one point, approximately 75 per cent of the carrier's employees were reporting, directly or indirectly, to the marketing director.
11   Lovelock, C.H. (1996), *Services Marketing* (3rd edition), Prentice Hall, chapter 13.
12   Ostroff, F. and Smith, D. (1992), 'Redesigning the Corporation', *The McKinsey Quarterly,* No. 1.
13   Bounds, G., Yorks, L., Adams, M., and Ranney, G. (1994), *Beyond Total Quality Management,* McGraw-Hill International.
14   Payne, A. and Clark, M. (1995), 'Marketing Services to External Markets', in Glynn, W.J. and Barnes, J.G., *Understanding Services Marketing,* John Wiley & Sons.
15   Byrne, J.A. (1993), *Business Week,* December 20, reproduced in Lovelock, op. cit., p. 578.
16   *Airline Business,* October 1996, p. 7.
17   Band, D.C. and Scanlan, G. (1995), 'Strategic Control Through Core Competencies', *Long Range Planning,* Vol. 28, No. 2.
18   The concepts underlying environmental 'complexity' and 'turbulence' are discussed in Volume One, chapter 2.
19   As is explained in the first chapter of Volume One, 'emergent' strategies are strategies which emerge unplanned from day-to-day activities; they can be contrasted with 'intended' strategies, which are usually the product of a formal planning exercise. The 'environments' referred to in the text are discussed in Volume One, Part One.
20   An excellent summary of the simultaneous use of cross-functional teams and staff empowerment by British Airways can be found in: Bevan, D. (1997), 'The Passenger Reception System Project', presentation to the IATA *Information Management 97* conference, Atlanta, 4th-8th May. This presentation describes the use of cross-functional teams and front-line staff involvement in the design of a new check-in system at London Heathrow. The challenges successfully overcome were not simply technical, but also cultural insofar as resistance to change was entrenched amongst long-serving customer service agents who had the deepest understanding of the existing system.
21   Carlzon, J. (1987), *Moments of Truth,* Ballinger, p. 88.
22   Festa, P. (1997), 'Wheeling Out the Service', *Airline Business,* January.
23   The literature is inconsistent in its definitions of internal marketing. See, for example, the discussion in: Rafiq, M. and Ahmed, P.K. (1993), 'The Scope of Internal Marketing: Defining the Boundary Between Marketing and Human Resource Management', *Journal of Marketing,* 9.

24 Lewis, B.R. (1995), 'Customer Care in Services', in Glynn and Barnes, op. cit., p. 73.
25 Bowen, D.E. and Lawler, E.E. III (1995), 'Organising for Service: Empowerment or Production Line?', in Glynn and Barnes, op. cit.
26 Ibid., p. 275.
27 Ibid., p. 276.
28 Ibid., p. 292.
29 Mintzberg, H. (1979), *The Structuring of Organizations*, Prentice-Hall.
30 Bowman, C. and Carter, S. (1995), 'Organising for Competitive Advantage', *European Management Journal*, Vol. 13, No. 4.
31 Ibid., p. 429.
32 Ibid., pp. 429, 430.
33 Ibid., p. 430.
34 Ibid.
35 Ibid., p. 432.
36 Prahalad, C.K. and Doz, E.L. (1987), *The Multinational Mission*, The Free Press, cited in Karlöff, B. (1993), *Key Business Concepts*, Routledge, p. 70.

Part Three
Outcome

9 Service quality, failure, and recovery

A distinction was drawn in Part One of this volume between corporate strategies and competitive strategies; the former address the 'Where to compete?' question, whilst the latter deal with 'How to compete?' Ultimately, it is by making appropriate decisions on how to compete that the bills get paid and profits are made. As markets progressively liberalize and competition becomes more fierce, the need to satisfy consumers and retain them in a loyal customer base has become central to strategic management. And central to consumer satisfaction and retention are decisions taken about the quality, and therefore the customer value, inherent in an airline's service-price offers.

In liberalized and, particularly, deregulated markets it is quality of service, together with price, that positions a carrier in the strategic space carved out by its choice of competitive strategy.

Quality and value

The airline industry has been rife with 'customer service (or care) programmes' since the early 1980s and, in several cases, considerably earlier. But doubts have been expressed about how much some of these efforts have really achieved. They commonly focus on the extent to which service delivery processes conform to design specifications, rather than on customers' perceptions of whether their expectations have been met. For an integrated carrier such as FedEx, for example, quality is not simply a matter of getting shipments to their destinations on time and undamaged; quality is also about consumers' perceptions of each service encounter, from the initial call for pick-up to the final invoice. The same is true for a passenger airline, the quality of which will be judged in the marketplace by a lot more than its success in getting people and their baggage to where they are going. The essence of quality is what consumers get out of their activity cycles rather than what airlines put into them. Conformity to expectations is the key.

Extensive reference has been made to service-price offers. What is meant by this expression is 'service attributes of given perceived quality' and 'the price demanded for this bundle of attributes'. The offer is a value proposition which customers will compare against their perceptions of any competing value propositions available in the market(s) relevant to them. High perceived quality might support a price premium where pricing freedoms exist whilst lower perceived quality might not, but both high and low quality offers are capable of providing 'value' if their prices are appropriate to the quality levels concerned. 'Value is simply quality, however the *customer* defines it, offered at the right price.'[1]

Sources of service quality

In the course of a ground-breaking ten-year research programme investigating service quality, Parasuraman et al identified five dimensions within which customer service expectations are formed.

1   Reliability: the ability to perform the promised service dependably and accurately.

2   Tangibles: the appearance of physical facilities, equipment, personnel, and communications materials.

3   Responsiveness: the willingness to help customers and provide prompt service.

4   Assurance: the knowledge and courtesy of employees and their ability to convey trust and confidence.

5   Empathy: the caring, individualized attention provided to customers.[2]

Perceived service quality will, according to much recent research, be a function of how an airline performs in each of these dimensions - whether or not it meets or exceeds customers' expectations of what they **should** experience. From this perspective, quality is rooted not in traditional customer service programmes and lip-service to being customer-driven or customer-focused, but in a clear understanding of expectations and detailed attention to the specific implementation variables addressed in Part Two of this volume: the service concept; service delivery; and the corporate infrastructure.

The five dimensions of quality need to be kept under constant review from two perspectives:

- quality level: this reflects choices made when conceptualizing the service (chapter 6 of this volume) and designing the service delivery subsystem (chapter 7). Customer expectations should be designed into an airline's service concept and its delivery processes. 'Designing in' rather than 'inspecting in' is a leading mantra of quality converts, but the really tough nut to crack is the absorption of a quality consciousness into corporate culture; and
- quality consistency: whatever the quality level chosen for each targeted market or segment, airlines will want to strive for consistent delivery of services at the selected levels. Dependent upon many of the issues discussed in chapters 7 and 8, consistency is never going to be entirely possible to achieve in a high-contact service industry. It is nonetheless something that leading airlines are increasingly aiming for. Corporate culture is a key enabling variable.

These perspectives are no longer relevant just to individual airlines, or to different products and sub-brands offered by any single carrier. Management time is in future going to have to be devoted as well to the maintenance of compatible and consistent levels of quality within alliances. In the mid-90s, for example, service quality at Thai Airways International was openly admitted to be a matter of concern to alliance partners Lufthansa and United.[3] Issues such as this will inevitably grow in number and significance as airline managers refocus away from the formation of alliances and onto the active management of quality and customer value within each grouping.

Being served is a psychological experience, affected by time, location, external cues, and the moods and attitudes of those involved. Because they are intangible, heterogeneous, and experiential incidents involving a shifting cast of participants, no service encounter is ever going to be precisely the same as any other. Each passenger enplanement and each freight shipment involves a different provider-consumer interface, and this makes inevitable the frequent 'remixture' of service - that is, the delivery of a service in a manner not envisaged when it and its delivery processes were designed. Furthermore, the fact that services are produced and consumed simultaneously means that the delivery process itself is as much subject to consumer evaluation as is the outcome.

This is why corporate culture is such an important variable. Services can never be entirely standardized; there is an understandable search for consistent standards of service delivery in some airlines, particularly those trying to leverage their corporate names into brand identities, but the ultimate goal is impossible to reach. Corporate culture, however, can serve to narrow the parameters within which variations in consistency occur.

Measuring quality

It was noted in the last chapter that as long ago as 1983 British Airways established a marketplace performance section as one of five principal operating units in the company. Its remit was to ensure that the airline was achieving what it set out to achieve in terms of service. Singapore Airlines tracks its own performance by using survey and other data to produce a Quality/Productivity Index. Delta has a Quality Service Index which it uses to help price its service offers relative to those of competitors in specific markets.[4]

Service quality, of course, is an elusive construct, difficult to define and measure. Measurements of quality fall into two categories depending upon whether they are focused on the performance of airline systems - which require 'hard' measures - or the behaviour of staff, particularly as they interact with consumers - which require 'soft' measures.[5]

1   Hard measures: airlines are fortunate insofar as quite a lot of their activities can be subjected to statistical analysis. Punctuality, holding time on reservations lines and the number of failed calls, check-in queueing times, denied boardings, time to arrival in the baggage hall of the first and last bags off an incoming flight, and the baggage mishandling rate can readily be measured on the passenger side, for example; on the cargo side, document handling accuracy, 'flown as booked' and 'delivered as promised' rates, delivery queueing times, and claims handling are amongst the many variables that can be monitored. Often, these measurements reflect deliberate effectiveness/efficiency trade-offs in process design - as when check-in lines are reduced by manning more desks or cabin service response times and contact levels are increased by raising cabin staff numbers. On occasion, though, effectiveness can be maintained or improved at the same time as efficiency is boosted - as often happens when processes are reengineered and/or automated.

    A major challenge facing the management team that engineered the turnaround of Continental Airlines in the mid-90s was to change corporate culture. This they did by altering ways in which the airline measured success - the principle being that if what customers value is made the focus of rewards, it will become the focus of employee attention. Energies were shifted from cost reduction to *efficient* customer satisfaction, with ontime performance and various measures of service consistency taking precedence. Two years into the turnaround, Continental was earning a premium over average yields and revenues per ASM in the US industry.[6]

    An important point to bear in mind is that it is vital to understand what customers feel about the specific variables being measured, because some will inevitably matter more than others; thus, process improvement designed to shave two minutes off a check-in queue might matter more than two minutes off baggage delivery. American Airlines has been tracking elapsed times between gate arrivals and the opening of aircraft doors, for example, because research revealed that passengers' perceptions of ontime performance improve if doors are opened less than 25 seconds after 'brakes on'. The moral is to discover and monitor things that matter to the customer.

2   Soft measures: the best ontime performance in the business is highly commendable, but service encounters that fall short of consumers' expectations will erode whatever customer loyalty might otherwise have been engendered. Service encounters are difficult to control or measure objectively - hence the importance of a genuinely service-oriented corporate culture. This point relates back to the discussion of 'soft controls' in chapter 8, and to choices made between the production line/hierarchical control model of corporate organization and the involvement/empowerment model.

> Soft quality requires flexibility, quick response to market changes, decentralization, empowerment of people and creativity. People cannot create, that is find fresh approaches to situations, if they are blocked by rigid patterns and attitudes.[7]

Of course, exactly what 'service-oriented' should mean in practice will depend on the design of the service-price offer being made to the marketplace. After a literature search and in-depth passenger interviews, Lewis and Sinhapalin suggested the following list of variables that require consideration and measurement.[8] It clearly emphasizes the 'complex, multidimensional' nature of service quality.[9]

GENERAL SERVICE	INFLIGHT SERVICE
Readiness of employees	Interior decor of cabin
Willingness of employees	Cleanliness of cabin
Knowledge/skill of employees	Cleanliness of washrooms
Ease of contact	Comfort of seats
Politeness of employees	Amount of legroom
Performing right the first time	Helpfulness of crew
Understanding customer needs	Politeness of crew
Appearance of personnel	Knowledge of crew
Keeping customers informed	Appearance of crew
Credibility of the company	Sufficient crew
Security	Accessibility of crew
Availability of seats	Food alternatives
Convenience of schedules	Taste of food
Ontime departure	Availability of music
Wide range of products	Availability of movies
Modern technology	

GROUND SERVICE
Equipment used
Attitude of staff
Accessibility of staff
Knowledge of staff
Appearance of staff
Information/care during delay

One possible approach to the measurement of service quality is to develop simple performance measures for the attributes - such as those above - believed best to define that service.[10] An alternative approach that has been particularly influential since the mid-1980s is based on 'gap theory'. The focus of gap measurement is the difference between:

- consumers' expectations - what previous experience and/or other sources of information (such as word-of-mouth assessments or marketing communications) lead consumers to feel they *should* receive; and
- consumers' perceptions of what they have in fact received from a particular airline.[11]

We will be meeting gap theory again later in the chapter, when considering service failure and recovery.

Expectations are not static over time, of course:

- as levels of service performance increase, so generally do consumers' expectations;
- as customers' experience of an industry's service widens and knowledge of alternatives becoming available in liberalized or deregulated markets deepens, their tolerance of deviations from expectations tends to narrow; and
- as carriers make increasing efforts to differentiate themselves by offering more supplementary product attributes, expectations of the benefits that should be derived from these new attributes tend to become embedded and the relative importance of expectations in respect of established attributes might also change.

Market research and the monitoring of quality should go hand-in-hand. Airlines use a wide range of techniques, including: focus groups and advisory panels (comprised of frequent flyers and corporate travel managers, for example); interviews; mail, inflight, and airport surveys; complaints and compliments tracking; and staff surveys, both of competitors and the subject airline itself. Staff are in a good position to see problems developing before they affect customers' perceptions and are a valuable source of insight. Singapore Airlines, for example, requires staff to report on their service experience whenever they submit claims for travel expenses.

In 1992, Air Canada first tested hand-held electronic devices to obtain instant feedback on individual flights and overcome the 'collation lag' inherent in paper surveys. A few airlines have used PCs provided in their premium class lounges to similar effect. The availability of interactive IFE on long-haul flights might in future provide another opportunity to obtain real-time customer feedback.

Managing quality

Because quality hinges on people and their attitudes, top management commitment and employee involvement are vital. This is easy to write but difficult to achieve. Nonetheless, some airlines are taking it seriously. Lufthansa is one that has used external consultants to provide quality improvement training. Every KLM employee is engaged in a quality awareness programme. Several airlines have sent top managers through the Disney quality programme in Florida.

Initiatives of this type are complicated by the fact that quality means different things to different people depending, in part, on their functional backgrounds and, in part, on how much time they have available in their daily routine to think about the subject. Ishikawa has proposed the following.

> Narrowly interpreted, quality means quality of product. Broadly interpreted, quality means quality of work, quality of service, quality of information, quality of process, quality of division, quality of people, including workers, engineers, managers, and executives, quality of company, quality of objectives, etc.[12]

Nonetheless, ambiguity remains rife. According to some, quality cannot be touched or seen but it can be sensed. This is both true and largely unhelpful. Perhaps quality is not so much a 'What?' as a 'Why?' and a 'How?' 'Why do we satisfy customer expectations in this way?' 'How could we satisfy them better?' 'How can we anticipate future expectations and satisfy them?' It is possible that quality is nothing more than the will to ask, and to keep asking, these questions, and to learn from and act upon the answers. Without doubt quality is very much more than a traditional customer service training programme. Neither is it simply a question of the extra olive in a salad. It is an amalgam of product attributes, delivery processes, customer expectations, and consumer perceptions. As such, it is neither a technique nor a programme, but something which should permeate strategic management. A force shaping strategic perception and guiding strategic action. Lauda Air has taken the unusual step of actually creating an identifiable symbol of its commitment to high-quality service, which it calls the 'Service Angel'.

Although time-consuming to pursue, quality is not always as expensive as it might first appear. Quality is not necessarily something to be traded-off against costs but something which, if applied diligently throughout an airline, can reduce them. In the early 1990s Federal Express, an undisputed leader in the quality movement, estimated that it cost around $800 million a year to deal with delays and resolve errors - and this figure took no account of potential future revenue lost from some of the dissatisfied customers.[13] When Continental - as part of its mid-90s renewal strategy 'Go Forward' - started offering cash bonuses to employees keyed-off the airline's rating in monthly DOT ontime performance statistics, it found that the cost of what turned out to be a highly motivating and effective scheme was less than was being saved by having fewer passengers to reroute or accommodate as a result of missed connections. The lesson is that investments in improved quality may lead to reduced costs.

Because of its high-contact nature, investments in quality made by the airline industry encompass not just technology and processes but also the recruitment, training, and recurrent training of people who are capable of delivering service at the required level of quality on - as far as possible - a consistent basis. Service quality and airline productivity can be complementary - as is usually the case when new aircraft types are introduced, for example. On the other hand, when productivity improvements are sought without the aid of new technology there is a greater chance that quality and productivity will pull in opposite directions and require trade-offs to be made; as we have seen already, output and outcome, efficiency and effectiveness, are sometimes in conflict.[14] This is particularly likely in the front office, because processes here are invariably visible to, and experienced by, consumers.

> Marketing managers should be included in productivity improvement programs whenever these efforts are likely to have an impact on customers. And because customers are often involved in the service production process, marketers should keep their eyes open for opportunities to reshape customer behaviour in ways that may help the service firm to become more productive. Possibilities for cooperative behaviour include adopting self-service options, changing the timing of customer demand to less busy periods, and making use of third party suppliers of supplementary services.[15]

Quality yields an outcome - a satisfied customer (or better, according to a fashionable dictum originating several years ago from Toyota, a 'delighted' customer); an outcome rather than an output. Thus, in the final analysis quality can be defined as whatever the customer says it is. The customer's voice in competitive markets is heard through the medium of demand: 'quality may be thought of as any product attribute that increases demand for the product at a fixed price'.[16] In competitive markets it will become as much a part of the process of airline strategic management as any grand alliance, aircraft order, or entertainment technology. Indeed, these pillars of airline strategy should be subordinate to quality. Quality *is* what is being strategically managed, and alliances, fleet plans, and inflight products are just some of the operational tools available for delivering it.

A few airlines have joined the quality 'bandwagon' - gaining ISO9000 or similar accreditation for their quality management processes, for example, or even launching 'total quality' programmes; Emirates is just one example. Some have responded to the growing tendency of freight shippers in particular to insist on carrier accreditation under national or international quality standards. Many more, however, have not. For those facing heightened competition in liberalized competitive environments, quality is a strategic issue regardless of whether it is formally recognized as such.

'Quality' attaches to the 'service' part of the service-price offer every airline makes in such markets. Where there is meaningful differentiation between competitive offers and this differentiation is perceived as being high in quality, a price premium might be sustainable. On the other hand, where quality is perceived by customers to be essentially indistinguishable (perhaps because differentiation focuses on inconsequential attributes or insubstantial differences, or because customers lack adequate information on service quality variations) the spotlight will focus on price.

By locating itself in the matrix illustrated in Figure 9.1, an airline can use the level of service inherent in its offer to the marketplace, together with the price that can be commanded, to position itself in strategic space. Whatever service is offered - whether rich in supplementary attributes or more basic - the quality of what is in fact offered should be to the highest feasible standard. Customers might well buy into low- or no-frills service, but this does not mean that those service attributes that are still on offer from the carriers concerned will necessarily be acceptable irrespective of quality; safety is perhaps the attribute which most strongly demonstrates this point.

Earlier in this volume we referred to some carriers being 'stuck-in-the-middle' in terms of their geographical and/or product scope (chapter 1) or their competitive strategy (chapter 2). A key aspect of this problem as far as product scope and competitive strategy are concerned centres on quality. There appears in some markets to be a trend towards polarization of demand between low-service/low-price offers and high-service/premium-price offers. Once again, however, low levels of service in terms of the number of attributes on offer need not equate to low quality in respect of whatever is in fact being offered; corporate values, culture, and the service style they reinforce can be major factors here, as Southwest's success exemplifies.

High ┌──────────────┬──────────────┐
     │   │   │
     │   │   │
     │   │   │
SERVICE ├──────────────┼──────────────┤
     │   │   │
     │   │   │
     │   │   │
Low └──────────────┴──────────────┘
     Low   High
              PRICE

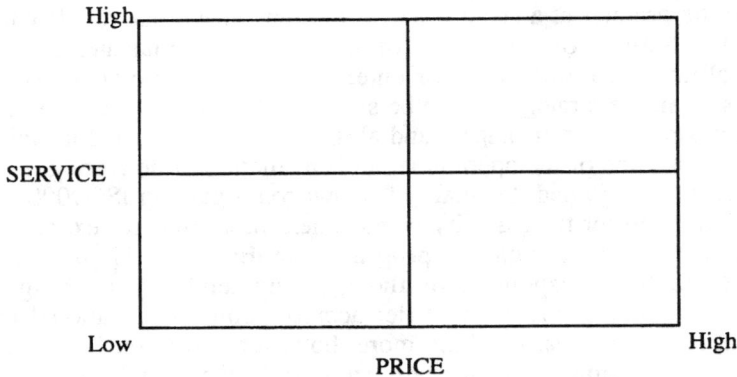

Figure 9.1 : A strategic space for the positioning of service-price offers

Service failure and service recovery

'Zero defects' - a concept at the heart of total quality management - is not a model that works particularly well in the service sector, where there are as many possible defects as customers in aggregate are able to perceive.[17] Nonetheless, a presentation by Air New Zealand delivered to the 1996 conference of the Worldwide Airline Customer Relations Association (WACRA) estimated that only 19 per cent of customers dissatisfied with the quality of a service would use it again given the choice.[18]

Service failures happen for reasons which may not be within the control of an airline or its employees. Sometimes they happen because of the behaviour of consumers themselves - seeking special treatment, for example, or making errors when playing their roles in participative service delivery processes. Two certainties are that:

- service failures will inevitably occur; and
- affected consumers will tell many more people about their experiences than they would have done had those experiences been positive.

Because of the complexity of the airline industry and the millions of service encounters in which even a moderately sized carrier engages every year, the number of potential fail-points is very large. Those involving human interactions are difficult to monitor, and even the more 'mechanical' aspects of service delivery might fail for some reason from a consumer's standpoint notwithstanding that they appear to the airline concerned to be performing in conformance with expectations.

Service gaps

The research into service quality undertaken by Parasuraman et al since the early 1980s and referred to above has revealed four 'gaps', any one of which could lead to a fifth gap and become a source of service failure.[19]

Gap 1: between consumers' expectations and management's perceptions of consumers' expectations. This arises when management does not know what consumers want and need.[20]

Gap 2: between management's perceptions of consumers' expectations and the service quality specifications actually established. Even if management accurately perceives what it is that targeted consumers expect, the commitment and/or the resources required to deliver it might be lacking.

Gap 3: between service quality specifications and the service actually delivered. The correct specifications have in this case been established, but delivery processes fail to meet them.

Gap 4: between the service actually delivered and the promises communicated to consumers with respect to that service. Consumers' expectations can be raised by marketing communications to levels above what they would otherwise have been and, possibly, above what a particular airline is able to deliver. In other words, this gap is created by 'overpromising'.

These four gaps are internal failings within the airline. Each can lead to a service failure as perceived by consumers.

Gap 5: between consumers' expectations and perceptions. Service failure happens not just when delivery falls short of some specification standard, but when consumers perceive it to fall short of what they had expected.

  Any failure superficially attributable to one of these gaps will invariably have a 'root cause' which needs to be addressed. For example, Gap 3 might be created by poor punctuality, the root cause of which could be airport or airway congestion, an ageing and mechanically unreliable fleet, tight timetabling, or inefficient turnaround procedures. This would be an example of a **process failure**. Worse would be a **capability failure**, where the airline concerned simply does not have the capability - the skills and/or resources - to deliver what is required to serve a particular targeted market or segment. Another major source of service failure in any contact-intensive service industry is **encounter failure**, which happens when a service encounter fails to meet expectations.

  Flow-charting, a concept introduced during the discussion of service delivery processes in chapter 7, can be a useful tool to help identify potential fail-points in both back-office and front-office processes.[21]

Useful, perhaps, for closing gaps 3 or 4, this is not necessarily a technique that will close gaps 1 or 2. For the latter purpose, airlines will have to undertake research into the congruence between consumers' expectations and managers' perceptions; anecdotal evidence suggests that relatively few yet do this.

But the gap which ultimately must be managed is gap 5. United recognized this explicitly when in 1997 it launched a $400 million customer satisfaction programme designed to upgrade both hard and soft service attributes, focusing primarily on customers' expectations and perceptions rather than - as in the past - on competitors' activities. The initiative, which was built around a core Customer Satisfaction Philosophy, was targeted in particular at the business segment, in response to extensive survey evidence revealing widespread dissatisfaction amongst business travellers with the standards of service offered by airlines in the United States.

Quality information systems

The achievement and maintenance of targeted quality standards - whatever these might be - require, amongst other things, a willingness on the part of managers to listen both to customers and to front-line staff.[22] In highly competitive markets, there is a growing case in favour of formalizing the 'listening process'.

> Companies need to install an ongoing service research process that provides timely, relevant trend data...Companies need to build a service quality information system, not just do a study. Conducting a service quality study is analogous to taking a snapshot. Deeper insight and a sense for the pattern of change come from a continuing series of snapshots taken from many angles.[23]

Complaints are a valuable source of information on service failure and a potentially invaluable learning experience. They should be facilitated; research shows that the majority of dissatisfied consumers never complain, preferring instead simply to take their business elsewhere - assuming this to be possible, which it is in a growing number of air transport markets. On the other hand, complaints that are dealt with in a timely, positive (i.e. not defensive), and responsive manner tend in the majority of cases not to lead to customer defections.

Some airlines still hide from this potentially valuable source of feedback, making it difficult to complain and frequently using their internal procedures to turn dissatisfied consumers into transgressors. It remains relatively rare to find on ticket wallets or on tickets themselves the invitations to comment about the product that are found on the packaging of consumer goods in many countries. On the other hand, a growing number of airlines do now have systematized procedures for logging, coding, responding to, and learning from complaints.

> Southwest Airlines is a great believer in using customer complaint, compliment, and suggestion letters to monitor airline performance and stimulate internal research and self-analysis. About 1,000 customers write to the airline every week and a staff of several dozen people in two departments is kept busy researching problems and responding to customers.[24]

Some carriers have invested significant sums of money in the effort; British Airways, for example, spent well over £4 million on 'Caress' (Customer Analysis and Retention System). For the future, sites on the Internet offer an additional medium through which to receive complaints, comments, and compliments. It is nonetheless tempting to believe that not enough is yet being done by airlines as a whole to tap this important source of information.

Service recovery

Whilst a service failure cannot be recalled to the factory, recovery is nonetheless often possible. Indeed, because production and consumption of the air transport product are simultaneous, it is sometimes feasible to identify failures as they develop and initiate service recovery immediately. Although unsatisfactory service is inherently more difficult to 'replace' than a bad product, if correctly handled a service failure need not lead inevitably to a dissatisfied customer. Conversely, research has shown that between one third and a half of unsatisfactory service encounters can be attributed to the inability or unwillingness of employees to respond appropriately to service failure - what is called 'double deviation' from customer expectations.[25] There is also evidence that expectations of successful service recovery grow with the quality of the service-price offer that has been 'bought into', with the reputation of the airline, and with the loyalty that a particular consumer feels she gives to the carrier concerned.

Because the air transport service is comprised of a core attribute and numerous supplementary attributes, it is quite possible for failure in respect of just one attribute to negatively affect consumers' perceptions of the entire experience. Indeed, failure in a supplementary attribute can tarnish the effect of successful delivery of the safe, timely locational transformation service that lies at the core of each airline's offer to its markets. A passenger who has had to queue for what is considered an excessive time in order to check-in, for example, will quite probably board the aircraft with a very different attitude compared with what would have been the case had the check-in process been smoother. This attitude could affect perceptions of inflight service - particularly if the flight is relatively short, so providing less time to forget the ground experience; it may also reduce satisfaction gained from ontime arrival or other successfully delivered benefits.

Cost cutting in one subsystem or process, as opposed to cost management with the likely impact on customers' perceptions kept clearly in mind, can easily lead to a service failure that reflects badly on the entire airline. Hence the value of systems thinking, which was discussed in chapter 8 of this volume and permeates much of the book.

Appropriate levels of service recovery How far an airline should go in its recovery efforts ought to reflect:

- the importance of the affected customer in terms of current and potential business; and
- the severity of the error in terms of its future impact on the relationship.[26]

Service recovery efforts should to a considerable extent be guided by the nature of the failure and the estimated lifetime value of the customer concerned.[27] For example, a serious service failure involving a high-value customer must be prioritized for recovery and follow-up. Similarly, whereas a relatively trivial failure affecting a low-value customer might not warrant recovery efforts beyond the norm, the same failure involving a high-value customer could justify more focused service recovery and follow-up.

What makes this prescription difficult to operationalize for most airlines is their inability to put a monetary value on customer relationships. A few carriers are now beginning to build databases - often keyed-off frequent flyer programme or executive club memberships - capable of capturing information that allows them to:

- arrive at approximate valuations of customer relationships (about which there will be more to say in the next chapter); and
- detect drop-offs in service usage over time, which might be indicative of either or both specific, unreported service failures or a general decline in the airline's competitiveness.

Structured approaches to service recovery Many airlines are now addressing a wider range of potential service failures than in the past, when how to deal with delays was often the primary focus. Some have responded to their more competitive circumstances by initiating structured approaches to service recovery. The particular nature of the express package business, for example, makes it possible to build a service recovery capability into the organizational structure. FedEx has a three-tier recovery system comprised of customer service representatives, trace agents, and the company's executive services group. Each is empowered, up to varying levels of expenditure authority, to deal with service failures.

On the passenger side of the industry, an interesting issue is the compatibility of recovery responses within alliances. Where these are incompatible, however justified the reasons, customer dissatisfaction in the event of service failure might be heightened by a recovery response that falls short of expectations. For example, a carrier which operates regional services under a franchised British Airways sub-brand identity might be constrained by virtue of some of the locations it serves from feeding and accommodating weather-delayed passengers, whereas British Airways itself has a policy of doing so.[28]

There are two important challenges when adopting a structured approach to service failure and recovery.

1   The first is to have in place the people and processes necessary to recover from specific failures at identified potential fail-points. Value chain analysis and flow-charting can help here, but perhaps the most important step is to train employees to recognize and recover from service failures. 'Service recovery strategies should be flexible, and integral to this is the role of front-line employees and the extent to which they have been *empowered* to respond to the customer.'[29]

2   The second is to learn from these specific failures and, as far as possible, avoid repeating them.

Figure 9.2 illustrates use of the Ishikawa/fishbone/cause-and-effect technique, first introduced in chapter 7, to assist with the learning process. Developing Ishikawa's work, Lovelock has proposed that factors which might cause a specific problem should be identified (e.g. in brainstorming sessions) and categorized into one of eight groupings: facilities and equipment; materials and supplies; front-stage personnel; back-stage personnel; procedures; information; customers; and other causes.[30]

In the final analysis, 'quality failures weaken brand loyalty'.[31] Conversely, '[s]uccessful service recovery has economic benefits in terms of customer retention and loyalty'.[32] It is to customer retention and loyalty that we turn in the next chapter.

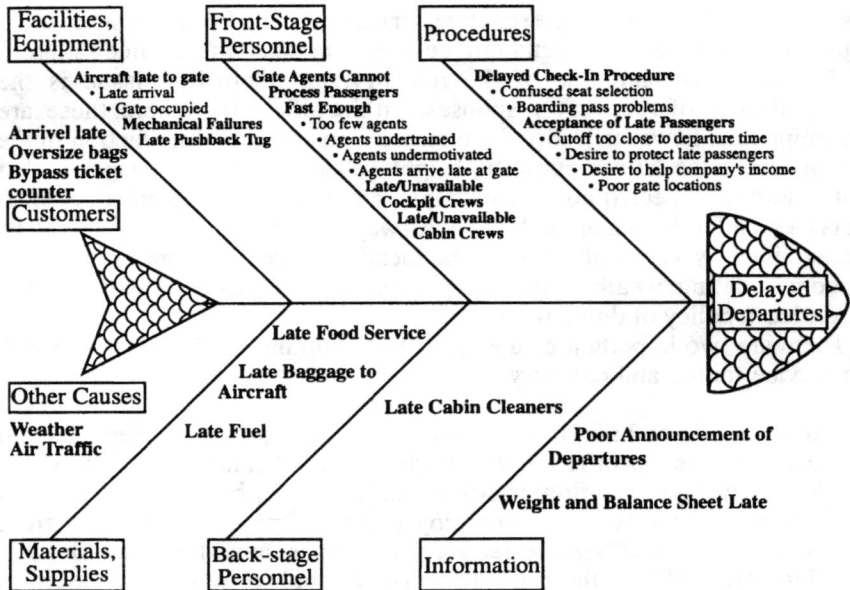

Figure 9.2: Cause-and-effect chart for airline departure delays
Source : Chistopher Lovelock, *Product Plus*, McGraw Hill, 1994, p. 218. Reproduced
with permission of The McGraw-Hill Companies

Notes

1   Gale, B.T. (1994), *Managing Customer Value*, The Free Press.
2   Parasuraman, A., Zeithaml, V.A., and Berry, L.L. (1991), 'Understanding
    Customer Expectations of Service', *Sloan Management Review*, Spring.
3   Muqbil, I. (1996), 'Thai Tight Rope', *Airline Business*, September. Aside from
    service quality, Thai's partners were also reported to be concerned about government
    delays in building a new airport to serve Bangkok - something considered vital to
    fulfill the city's long-term potential as an attractive hub. (Ballantyne, T. (1997),
    'Military Thai Down Options', *Airline Business*, February.)
    (It should be noted that some of Thai's partners subsequently denied being unduly
    concerned about the carrier's service quality. See, for example: Odell, M. (1997),
    'Reid All About It', *Airline Business*, November.)
4   For an excellent description of how FedEx measures its quality performance, see:
    Bounds, G., Yorks, L., Adams, M., and Ranney, G. (1994), *Beyond Total Quality
    Management*, McGraw-Hill, pp. 524-530.
5   This is an approach adopted by British Airways in its handbook 'Quality in Customer
    Service'. For an interesting general discussion of quality measurement and its
    techniques, see: Band, W.A. (1991), *Creating Value for Customers*, John Wiley &
    Sons, chapter 4.
6   Flint, P. (1997), 'Speed Racer', *Air Transport World*, April.
7   Lima, E.P. (1995), 'The Human Element', *Air Transport World*, February.
8   Lewis, B.R. and Sinhapalin, D. (1991), 'Service Quality: An Empirical Study of
    Thai Airways', *Proceedings of the European Institute for Advanced Studies in
    Management*, Brussels, May, p. 365.

9 Devlin, S.J. and Dong, H.K. (1994), 'Service Quality from the Customer's Perspective', *Marketing Research,* Vol. 6, No. 1.

10 See, for example: Cronin, J.J. Jr. and Taylor, S.A. (1992), 'Measuring Service Quality: A Reexamination and Extension', *Journal of Marketing,* Vol. 56, July.

11 Gap theory is closely associated with the work of Parasuraman, Zeithaml, and Berry referred to earlier in the chapter. An important outcome of this work was the development and refinement of an instrument - SERVQUAL - designed to measure service quality. SERVQUAL operationalizes the service quality construct as 'the difference between two 7-point rating scales - one to measure customers' expectations about companies in general within the service sector or category being investigated, and the other to measure customers' perceptions about a particular company whose service quality was to be assessed'. For a review of the development of SERVQUAL, a description of how to use the instrument, responses to concerns raised in subsequent critiques, and a comprehensive listing of references to the work of Parasuraman et al. over the decade it took to research the subject, see: Parasuraman, A. (1995), 'Measuring and Monitoring Service Quality,' in Glynn, W.J. and Barnes, J.G. (Eds.), *Understanding Services Management,* John Wiley & Sons; the foregoing quotation was taken from p. 148 of that work. Another comprehensive treatment of the topic can be found in: Buttle, F. (1996), 'SERVQUAL: Review, Critique, Research Agenda', *European Journal of Marketing,* Vol. 30, No. 1.

12 Ishikawa, K. (1985), *What is Total Quality Control? The Japanese Way,* Prentice Hall, p. 45, quoted in Bounds et al., op. cit., p. 80.

13 Barksdale, J.L., Chief Operating Officer, Federal Express Corporation, quoted in Bounds et al., op. cit., p. 537.

14 See: Lovelock, C.H. (1996), *Services Marketing* (3rd edition), Prentice Hall, chapter 11.

15 Ibid., p. 488.

16 Besanko, D., Dranove, D., and Shanley, M. (1996), *Economics of Strategy,* John Wiley & Sons, p. 382.

17 This is probably why consumer satisfaction guarantees are relatively rare in service industries as a whole, and practically unheard of in the airline business (other than in respect of the integrated carriers on the cargo side, of course). British Airways has run a number of guaranteed satisfaction programmes providing frequent flyer miles in compensation for legitimate complaints, but these have to date been limited in duration and restricted to members of the airline's Executive Club flying in premium cabins on specified routes.

18 Lima, E.P. (1997), 'Hurdling Service Problems', *Air Transport World,* January.

19 Parasuraman, A., Zeithaml, V., and Berry, L.L. (1985), 'A Conceptual Model of Service Quality and its Implications for Future Research', *Journal of Marketing,* 49, Fall.

20 This gap has been the subject of several studies. See, for example: (i) Gourdin, K.N. and Kloppenburg, T.J. (1991), 'Identifying Service Gaps in Commercial Air Travel: The First Step Towards Quality Improvement', *Transportation Journal,* Fall; (ii) Lewis, B.R. and Sinhapalin, D., op. cit. It should not be forgotten that gaps can result from **over**provision of services - that is, being **over**effective by giving passengers attributes they do not want or too much of those that they do want - although this problem will probably not be a source of service failure.

21 Lovelock, op. cit.

22 Ibid.

23 Berry, L.L., Parasuraman, A., and Zeithaml, V.A. (1994), 'Improving Service Quality in America: Lessons Learned', *Academy of Management Executive,* Vol. 8, No. 2.

24 Lovelock, op. cit., pp. 475, 476.

25 Bitner, M.J., Booms, B.M., and Tetreault, M.S. (1990), 'The Service Encounter: Diagnosing Favourable and Unfavourable Incidents', *Journal of Marketing,* January.

26   Barnes, J.G. and Cumby, J.A. (1995), 'The Cost of Service Quality: Extending the Boundaries of Accounting Systems to Enhance Customer Value', in Glynn and Barnes, op. cit.
27   Lifetime value is discussed in chapter 10.
28   Comment made by the Managing Director of CityFlyer Express at an *Airline Business* conference in June 1994.
29   Lewis, B.R. (1995), 'Customer Care in Services', in Glynn and Barnes, op. cit., p. 81.
30   Lovelock, op. cit., pp. 478, 479.
31   Ibid., p. 480.
32   Lewis (1995), op. cit., p. 81.

10 Customer retention

Customer loyalty and relationship marketing

Customer loyalty

Customers who are satisfied are more likely to be loyal than those who are not - although satisfaction is certainly not, in itself, sufficient to ensure retention. A key objective of any airline should be to attract and retain targeted customers - those for whom a service-price offer has been designed and who, presumably, should value it the most. There is an argument that market share *quality* (i.e....'the proportion of a company's business represented by loyal customers registering repeat sales'[1]) should be given as much attention as market share itself. The issue in this case is no longer simply how to sell services, but how to retain customers - particularly high-value customers.

The potential value of loyal customers can be considerable. It has been pointed out that a $1,500 per month FedEx account could be worth up to $360,000, assuming a ten-year customer relationship and referral of one new ten-year account.[2] The following calculations, put forward by a former President of Canadian Airlines International, provide ample evidence of the same phenomenon in the scheduled passenger business.[3]

1   Business Travel: President's Club Gold Canadian Plus Frequent Flyer.
      Average transaction: $600.
      Average number of annual transactions: x 30.
      Average annual duty-free purchase: $300.
      Average annual asset value: $18,300.
      Number of years of travel: x 10.
      Asset value: $183,000.
      Customers gained through word of mouth: x 5.
      Revenue value of a satisfied customer: $183,000 + $915,000.

2   Leisure Travel: family of four.
      Average transaction: $200 per person.

Average number of annual transactions: x 4.
Average annual duty-free purchase: $90.
Average annual asset value: $890.
Number of years of travel: x 20.
Asset value: $17,800.
Customers (families of four) gained through word of mouth: x 5.
Revenue value of a satisfied customer: $17,800 + $89,000.

Estimates of lifetime value can be useful guides to the development of relationship marketing programmes and, as noted in the last chapter, tools to assist in managing service recovery.

Developing a lifetime value forecast for each customer is accomplished by a combination of data mining [in customer data warehouses] and algorithms designed to suit [a] particular airline. Typically they involve frequency, recency and some financial component such as revenue or net profit. When this value is developed, service personnel can make far better decisions on how to react and reduce the impact of travel incidents [i.e. service failures]. Ideally [what is wanted is] to spend as little as possible - [whilst doing] as much as is necessary to make the customer delighted, to maintain their loyalty and hopefully to increase their lifetime value.[4]

Customer loyalty, a prerequisite for customer retention in truly competitive markets, does not just happen; it is something that has to be worked at systematically. In this context, 'working at' customer loyalty means making superior value propositions to targeted customers, and being perceived to deliver consistently on these propositions in a way that at least matches customer expectations.

Relationship marketing

A number of airlines are now directing greater efforts than in the past to customer retention, aiming to satisfy the most important of their existing customers and build longer term relationships with them. Customer retention is in fact closely linked to relationship marketing, which we met in chapter 3 of the present volume.

Relationship marketing is the union of customer service, quality, and marketing. Relationship marketing emphasizes the importance of customer retention, product benefits, establishing long-term relationships with customers, customer service, increased commitment to the customer, increased levels of customer contact, and a concern for quality that transcends departmental boundaries and is the responsibility of everyone throughout the organization.[5]

Ongoing customer relationships are assets; they do not appear on an airline's balance sheet, but in highly competitive markets they can be as important to earning power as any tangible resource.[6] They have been aptly likened to the opening of an emotional bank account, from which withdrawals in the form of tolerance can be made in the event of service failure and into which deposits are placed in the form of customer satisfaction with each successful transaction or recovery.[7] In the business travel segment, corporate downsizing has made customer loyalty more important than ever as fewer people do more of the travelling in affected companies.

It is generally believed to be cheaper to market to existing satisfied customers, particularly those that can be identified on a database, than to mass market for new customers. The important word is 'satisfied'. A satisfying service experience is often taken as a good predictor of future satisfaction, which is important for a service industry unable to offer pre-experience trials. It can also be cheaper to deliver services to existing customers because they are familiar with the practices and procedures of the airline concerned - that is, with its 'script'; they therefore tend to require less special handling than would an infrequent traveller buying the same class of service.

Customer defections

The primary purpose of any retention effort is to limit customer defections. Five possible reasons to defect can be identified.[8]

1   Price.

2   Preference for a competitor's newly available alternative product, which is perceived to offer superior value.

3   Poor service, which could stem from failure of the core attribute, a supplementary attribute, a service encounter, or service recovery.

4   Exit of the defector from the market.

5   Switching to an alternative technology offered by a competing industry.

The key skills in 'defection management' are to know how many customers are being lost, to understand why, to find out where they are going, and to remedy the situation. This is not as easy to achieve in the airline business as in some other service industries, because airlines are network operations serving (in many cases) multitudes of discrete geographical markets and customers who are to a considerable extent anonymous. Nonetheless, those investing in extensive customer

information systems (discussed in Volume One, chapter 10) will be
increasingly able to monitor changes in tracked usage patterns and rates
amongst their more important customers; as we saw in chapter 6 of the
present volume, they will also be able to integrate product creation and
tailored distribution into 'segment of one' marketing efforts.

It was observed in the last chapter that complaints can in themselves be a
useful source of information. Although a particular complaint might not
lead to loss of the complainant's business, uncounted silent defections could
be attributable to the same problem were it to be systemic. Just as when
investigating service gaps, it is necessary to dig beneath superficial reasons
for defections to identify their **root causes**: long lines at check-in
counters, for example, could result from inadequate staffing, inefficient
employees, poor systems support, unreliable baggage belts, or space
constraints inhibiting provision of sufficient service points. If the problem
is staff inefficiency, the root cause might be found in recruitment,
training, motivation, or overall morale.

Switching costs

Airlines need to be building loyalty amongst both their end-users and
intermediaries such as travel agents and freight forwarders. Close attention
has long been paid to intermediaries, who are - despite recent assaults by
some airlines on their distribution costs - still commonly plied with
incentives in addition to 'standard' commissions. One source of loyalty in
either case is the imposition of switching costs; airlines have used
commission overrides to impose these on travel agencies, for example,
whilst express package companies have used proprietary hardware and
software placed in shippers' offices to the same effect. The imposition of
switching costs on the vast number of passengers present in competitive air
transport markets is less easy, but over the last few years more airlines
have been trying. Three of the most important techniques used are
frequent flyer programmes, corporate rebates, and product branding. The
latter is purely emotional in appeal, whilst the former can of course
involve real switching costs. The next three sections of the chapter will
look at each of these in turn.

Frequent flyer programmes

Around 30 per cent of British Airways' passengers generate 70 per cent of
its revenue - remarkably close to the 80/20 'Pareto Rule'.[9] It has been
estimated that 'frequent flyers' in the United States, classified using the
common twelve or more trips per annum criterion, account for some 40
per cent of airline revenues.[10] According to Pavaux:

Frequency of travel being closely linked to profession and social category, some passengers travel much more often than others. So we find air travel heavily concentrated in this category of frequent travellers. Thus, in the United States, in 1992:

- 8 per cent of travellers made ten or more return trips in the year, representing 27 per cent of all trips taken,

- 72 per cent of travellers made only three trips or less than three each, representing in all just under 40 per cent of all trips taken.

In a country like France, the distribution is even more unbalanced. In 1993, 85 per cent of air travellers made only three or less than three return trips in the year whilst just 4 per cent of travellers made ten or more trips. But these latter made more than 30 per cent of all trips taken by the whole French population. The attention that airlines give to their frequent flyers is easily understandable, since, while they may be few in number, they contribute much more than the others to their turnover. These frequent flyers are often people travelling chiefly for business reasons. And we also know, from a recent survey carried out by *Business Travel News* among 94 firms, that business class on board aircraft is the one most used by those making international business trips. Nearly half (49 per cent) of these travellers choose business class, 26 per cent opt for economy class, 16 per cent travel on excursion fares and only 9 per cent elect to travel in first class. Thus more than half of all business trips (58 per cent) are made in first or business class. These trips therefore contribute a great deal to carrier income.[11]

Clearly, generating loyalty amongst hard-core travellers - now colloquially referred to in some circles as 'road warriors' - is important both in revenue terms and, particularly, to the establishment of any serious relationship marketing effort. Survey data generated by OAG rates the following as the most important FFP benefits sought by business travellers.[12]

Rank	Benefit	Index (1 to 5)
1	Wait-list priority	4.5
2	Mileage points	4.4
3	Upgrade possibilities	4.1
4	Recognised status	3.9
5	Lounges	3.9
6	Partner privileges	3.1
7	Special offers	2.9
8	Points for leisure pursuits	2.4
9	Magazines/newsletters	2.3

A number of airlines had executive clubs for several years. These offered various travel-related and other benefits to high-yield passengers able to clear what were in many cases fairly stiff qualification hurdles, but free flights were seldom on offer. In some cases these clubs still exist on a paid subscription basis, but many have been folded into frequent flyer programmes (FFPs) by basing membership on mileage or points earned during a given period. Frequent flyer programmes emerged out of the specific market circumstances of the early post-deregulation years in the United States, when established carriers were looking for ways both to fend off low-cost new entrants and to entice travellers to accept circuitous routeings over their rapidly expanding hubs. Free trips and/or upgrades awarded in return for loyalty, as evidenced by accumulated trip mileage, soon became a popular marketing tool because they allowed large incumbents to leverage the mileage-generating power and appealing award destinations available on their networks but unavailable to small competitors.

US and non-US programmes

Frequent flyer programmes remained a primarily US phenomenon until the early 1990s, when the growth of the three strongest US majors - particularly United and American - into international markets vacated by Pan Am and TWA stimulated European, Asian, and Latin American carriers into a response. Some international airlines have preferred to remain aloof, relying on service quality and/or occasional 2-for-1 ticket offers and similar promotions, but a growing number have succumbed. Most low-cost carriers have also shunned FFPs because of their expense relative to perceived benefits given the nature and structure of these airlines' operations, although several do offer more basic loyalty schemes to reward frequent usage.

There are still distinctions to be drawn between US FFPs on the one hand and most non-US programmes on the other, although the linkages between different programmes - especially those of alliance partners - may ultimately lead to elimination of many of the differences. One distinction between US and many non-US programmes is that the latter are often less generous. Perhaps the most fundamental distinction is that the US FFPs tend to be open access, whilst outside the United States airlines generally focus more precisely on high-yield business travellers (many of these, together with their families, also being leisure travellers on their own time, of course); some non-US carriers still impose membership qualifications. The result is that the US programmes have many more members, a high proportion of whom are not individually significant in revenue terms. To deal with this, some US airlines have in recent years begun offering tiered memberships, with nonlinear awards and benefits other than mileage - such as priority wait-listing, excess baggage allowances, or lounge access - available to members qualifying (by virtue of a high product usage rate) for the upper tiers.

Such tiered membership programmes are not limited to the United States. British Airways' Executive Club is an example of a programme that awards 'miles' which can be redeemed over a number of years in the form of air travel, and 'points' which are accumulated to attain annually renewable silver- and gold-tier status entitling members to bonus mileage awards dependent upon class of travel and to certain ground service privileges irrespective of class of travel. The objective behind awarding points and having members requalify each year is to consolidate brand loyalty by limiting the incentive for high-value customers to accumulate mileage awards in competing FFPs. What FFPs do not tell airlines is how frequently their customers use competitors; tiered membership schemes and nonlinear award structures are designed to give high-value customers a strong reason to avoid 'defecting' whenever the airline concerned is offering service in a market where these customers want to travel.

Advantages of frequent flyer programmes

Frequent flyer programmes were originally created to induce brand loyalty and, by influencing customers' choice of airline, to boost market share and revenue. More recently, they have also become useful tools for cementing loyalty to marketing alliances by permitting members of one partner's programme to accumulate mileage whilst travelling on another partner's flights. Whenever well-developed FFPs are in competition, and particularly in mature, slow-growing markets, the issue is now not so much what will be gained from launching an FFP as what would be lost by abandoning one.

Although there might still be some opportunities for differentiation and market share gain where competitors do not offer similar programmes, the real value of FFPs in the marketing mix arguably lies elsewhere. Relatively untapped though it remains in many cases, the source of this value is the customer information available from FFP databases; the demographic and lifestyle data provided on enrollment, the ability to track product usage over time, and the potential for mapping behaviour in response to variations in the service-price offer - and particularly in response to targeted promotions - can be the foundation of customer retention through customized relationship marketing. As noted in chapter 10 of Volume One, this data can be a particularly valuable input into the customer information systems which several airlines are now building. Such benefits may also compensate carriers for the fact that in some markets over 85 per cent of their passengers book through travel agencies which, accordingly, are in a position to know more about consumers than the airlines carrying them.

Frequent flyer programmes can be useful demand management tools. In an industry as prone to peaking as the airline business, the granting of bonus awards to direct demand towards off-peak periods and lightly loaded flights, and the use of variable redemption terms or redemption black-outs, can be helpful in the ongoing battle to bring demand and capacity into better balance. Furthermore, by analyzing frequent flyer patronage on specific flights it is possible to estimate the percentage of passengers travelling on business; this, in turn, can contribute to more accurate price elasticity estimates and so improve revenue management. Finally, FFPs can generate incremental revenues - and possibly attract new customers - for carriers selling 'miles' to other producers of goods and services wanting to offer them as awards in their own loyalty schemes.

Disadvantages of frequent flyer programmes

Frequent flyer programmes are not without their disadvantages. They are expensive, in terms of hardware, software, and manpower, both to establish and to administer. As programmes mature, however, their primary purpose is not simply to build a customer base but to retain it - and retaining customers is generally considered to be cheaper than adding to them. Use of the information on an FFP database is capable of being more cost-effective than are expensive, broadly targeted mass marketing campaigns. To the extent that FFP costs result in both the generation of incremental revenue from retained customers and also more effective marketing communications expenditures they can, in fact, represent good value. British Airways is believed to spend up to 40 per cent of its marketing communications budget on frequent flyer promotions, with much of this attributable to direct mail shots aimed at specific segments of its Executive Club database.

On the other hand, there are hidden costs. That many US airlines are prepared to tolerate earning less than 5 per cent of their passenger revenues from first class cabins which hold around 10 per cent of their seats and occupy approximately 15 per cent of aircraft floorspace says much about the attraction of upgrades as a form of FFP redemption. The more that load factors in the economy/coach cabin exceed approximately 70 per cent, the greater is the opportunity cost involved in 'giving away' the space allotted to first class cabins.

Another concern has been the potential for revenue displacement (i.e. the taking of seats from revenue passengers by FFP members redeeming their awards) and revenue dilution (i.e. the use of awards to contribute towards the cost of trips that would otherwise have been paid for in cash). These were very real problems in the early years of FFP development, but the combination of sophisticated yield management techniques to limit or completely black-out award travel on high-demand flights, together with sometimes onerous redemption conditions, has greatly reduced the impact of revenue displacement. Furthermore, the award non-redemption rate is believed to be very high, with possibly as much as 70 per cent wastage of entitlements in the United States. The latter point has also reduced concerns amongst accountants and financial analysts about the contingent liabilities inherent in overhangs of unredeemed entitlements.

There are, however, ethical criticisms that have been levelled at FFPs. The potential for large incumbents to use the reward and redemption opportunities provided by their extensive networks to erect barriers to the market entry of smaller challengers has been a source of concern for competition authorities in both Europe and the United States. In practice, small airlines have been able to overcome this disadvantage by banding together with other relatively small carriers to form a common FFP (e.g. LatinPass and Passages), by joining one or more larger airlines' FFPs, or by doing both.[13] These are certainly not cost-free options, but that in itself is hardly prima facie evidence of anticompetitive behaviour by the megacarriers.[14]

An ethical issue less readily dealt with is the fact that existence of FFPs might encourage business travellers to fly more often, on more circuitous routeings, and at higher fares than they would otherwise do. Whilst there is research evidence to suggest that this happens, it can in principle be argued that employers should be capable of policing such abuses for themselves. More difficult is the related question of whether it is appropriate to reward an individual for purchases made with his or her employer's money. Where the purchaser pays for a ticket, the effect of an FFP award is similar to a price rebate in return for 'bulk buying'; where company funds are used but the individuals making the purchase decisions themselves benefit from ensuing awards, airlines are interceding in agent-principal relationships. Few boards of directors would be impressed were their companies' equipment expenditures dictated by which supplier was offering Hawaiian vacations to staff making the purchase decisions, so it is difficult to understand the relative equanimity with which many accept the personal accumulation of FFP awards. Of course, a large proportion of the senior corporate managers who respond with such equanimity are probably themselves FFP members. Some companies do in fact now insist that FFP benefits are not made proprietary to individual members of staff, and several airlines have helped in this regard by offering corporate FFPs.[15]

Perhaps the most important criticisms of FFPs are that they are becoming so widespread they no longer provide much differentiation, that their deliberately opaque terms and conditions mask a slow but discernible coalescense towards a general norm (at least in the high-yielding segments), and that the US market in particular has reached such saturation with its multiple memberships that loyalty is no longer assured. There are three possible ripostes to this.

1   Logically, a passenger enrolled in several programmes should concentrate patronage on just one whenever travelling in a market where the airline concerned is present - otherwise it will take longer

to reach an award target, by which time the rules might have changed or earlier unused earnings will have become time-expired.[16]

2   When a passenger is based in a country or city whose air transport markets are dominated by a single carrier (which it is assumed here has established an FFP), her best method for accumulating mileage or award points rapidly will generally be to use that carrier - unless a significant number of the other airlines which each individually serve only a few of the markets out of that country or city choose to link their FFPs in some way. Thus, despite apparent similarity, FFPs can offer very different propositions to customers depending upon where they are based and the nature of their travel patterns.

3   Far more important, the real value of FFPs to airlines will increasingly lie in the use of their databases for fine-tuning the marketing mix and initiating carefully targeted direct marketing efforts within the context of a comprehensive customer retention and relationship marketing programme. This can be achieved either independently or, subject to adequate safeguards, in cooperation with alliance partners. Initiatives could include the selling of non-airline goods and services to what in many cases is a consumer group with well above-average purchasing power.

Corporate rebates

Large airlines with extensive network coverage are in a strong position to offer corporate rebates to significant customers. Rebates could include one or more of price breaks, free upgrades, or the waiving of conditions normally applied to discounted fares (which itself amounts to a form of price break).

Like commission overrides used by airlines to buy travel agencies' loyalty, rebates are generally nonlinear, driven by thresholds applied either to absolute levels of expenditure or to the number of journeys made on a specific group of routes or over the network as a whole in a given time period. As each threshold is crossed, the rebate earned becomes significantly more attractive. Airlines with large networks emanating from a dominated hub or national market (perhaps augmented by relationships with alliance partners) clearly have more to offer local companies, because any one competitor is likely to be strong - if at all - in only a small number of those markets and so unable to offer the scope of coverage probably required by a corporation generating trips to a wide range of destinations. To the extent that corporate rebates are indeed discontinuous rather than linear - being triggered by attainment of agreed volume thresholds - they offer discounts which are not based on volume economics, and so could be anticompetitive in the sense that they are designed to bind customers to the supplying airline rather than to pass on cost savings.

Branding

A brand is an amalgam of name, symbol, signage or design which identifies and differentiates the services of one particular airline or group of airlines. It embodies the service experience by communicating a 'personality' redolent of how the airline behaves, the tone of its corporate culture, and the values that drive its actions. The Virgin brand identity, for example, is widely seen as individualistic, innovative, and nonconformist; it stands for fun, flair, value for money, and competitiveness. A brand encapsulates many of the implementation variables discussed in Part Two of this volume, operationalizes the strategic choices discussed in Part One, and describes the quality variable discussed in chapter 9.

But a strong brand name is not simply a statement of identity. It is a prompt used to trigger associations with a particular type of service encounter and service environment, and with a certain type of service experience. Brands can be used to build emotional bonds between customer and airline, filling the void left by commoditization of the industry's hardware and the gradual erosion of loyalty to airlines as 'national champions'.[17]

A brand name can be vocalized (e.g. British Airways), but a brand mark can only be described (e.g. the British Airways 'Speedmarque' logo and the KLM crown). A 'strong' brand comes readily to the minds of customers thinking about a particular product class, it conjures vivid and positive images, and it is considered dependable - its story is believable. This applies whether the story being told is of intercontinental luxury - such as British Airways First - or 'cheap-and-cheerful' short-haul functionality - such as Southwest; both have strong identities which powerfully convey their own distinct messages to targeted segments. A brand is an intangible asset. Like every other asset it has a job to do, the task in this case being to communicate with and build loyalty amongst a target group of customers. A strong brand is a unique source of competitive advantage because it is an essentially inimitable resource; other brands - perhaps strong in their own separate ways - can compete with it, but they cannot clone its distinct personality.

Attitudes to airline branding

Since the early 1990s, and particularly since Philip Morris slashed the price of its leading cigarette brand on 'Marlboro Friday', the real worth of brands has come under the microscope. Opinions in the airline industry are polarized. Some see airline products as essentially so similar that brands are at best a substitute for language, a name rather than a distinct offer, and at worst a source of confusion in increasingly crowded marketplaces.[18] Certainly, it is true that relatively few strong sub-brand identities have yet been developed and that many airlines have not been able even to establish sufficient service consistency to allow them to make the transition from corporate name to corporate master-brand. Quite a few airline managers doubt the wisdom of spending on brand-related 'frills', and a significant number question the sub-branding of price-driven, non-premium products.

The contrary opinion is that brands do indeed have a valuable, if still underdeveloped, role to play in the industry and that brand management skills are becoming a critical success factor in highly competitive liberalized markets. This more positive perspective can be summarized in the following points.

1   A brand carries information. It is an important part of the marketing communications mix; in fact, it encapsulates the messages embodied in that mix. A brand conveys information about:
    • tangible product attributes;
    • the corporate culture that underlies service delivery, and so shapes the service delivery experience;
    • the type of value to be expected; and
    • psychological benefits available to consumers.

2   The information conveyed by a brand image creates expectations, which are themselves elements in the customer satisfaction and quality 'equations' discussed in earlier chapters. The existence of expectations reduces consumers' search time and perceived risks. Air travel is in essence a 'credence good'; in other words, quality and standards of service are important but are impossible to assess before consumption. Branding is intended to make assessment easier.

3   Branding makes an emotional appeal in respect of product benefits, supplementing purely rational attempts at persuasion that might get lost in the noise of competing claims and counterclaims being generated in increasingly competitive markets. Metaphor and symbol sometimes carry stronger messages than bald facts.[19]

4   Sub-brands can be used as vehicles for targeting service-price offers into distinct segments. If a service has been effectively branded it will develop a 'franchise' in the minds of customers in its target segments so that whenever they want a product in a particular market (e.g. business class out of Singapore) they will think first of that specific brand (e.g. Raffles Class). This is one of the essential goals of branding - generation of loyalty and a relationship such that customers will buy even if, say, the schedule offered is not the most convenient or the fares charged are not the cheapest.

5   Branding therefore supports 'pull marketing', where customers are motivated to 'pull' products out of the distribution system rather than intermediaries being relied upon (and incentivized) to 'push' them out. This can shift somewhat the balance of power between producers (i.e. airlines) and intermediaries (i.e. travel agencies).

6   An effectively branded service might sell at a premium over similar competing services. For example, it has been established by research carried out on routes between the United Kingdom and Europe that the British Airways brand name generates a 3 per cent price premium.[20] There is an argument that what separates a brand on the one hand from a product name or 'label' on the other is nothing more than the ability to sell a branded product for more than a functionally equivalent competitor.[21] This is debatable; price, particularly in a yield-managed network industry, is too volatile a criterion by which to judge the distinction between a name and a brand. That distinction is probably best judged by reference to the level of service consistency on offer, with a brand implying greater consistency than a simple name or label. This is very subjective ground, however, and perhaps the most that can be said is that 'effective branding' is like 'high quality' - you know it when you see it.

7   A well-established brand can smooth entry into new geographical or product markets. British Airways, for example, began in the mid-90s using its brand as a source of leverage in a programme intended to transform the company from an airline into a 'world travel business'.

8   Finally, in a small number of cases a strong brand has been known to preserve the independence of an affiliate from a potentially dominant shareholder. Crossair benefitted in this respect for many years, although other factors were also at work. Franchisees can play this game as well. A full participant in The Delta Connection, Comair has nonetheless preserved a clear sub-brand identity in its markets and the same is true of several other US regionals.

Branding is in the front-line of the battle against commoditization of airline seats. Commoditization is a situation in which differences between products are either not recognized or not valued by customers and price alone, rather than the source of supply, drives purchase decisions. In the most price-sensitive segments of many markets airline seats do indeed appear to have become a commodity, and it is now fashionable to argue that commoditization of the entire industry is inevitable. The money being spent on branding by some of the industry's more sophisticated management teams suggests that there is a strong body of opinion which thinks otherwise.

What can be branded?

The corporate master-brand It was observed above that one possible distinction between a brand and a simple name or label is the fact that a brand evokes expectations of service consistency. Earlier in the book it was argued that an important foundation of service consistency is corporate culture. Core values that shape corporate cultures are the framework for any branding strategy. A master-brand is imbued with these values; if sub-brands exist, the same values should also permeate the portfolio to ensure it functions as a consistent whole. Thus, values associated with the British Airways master-brand must, in a manner relevant to the segments each serves, also be associated with sub-brands such as Club World and World Traveller.

Air transport services: passenger sub-brands[22] Although there are alternative approaches, we will here distinguish between three types of sub-branding: product-oriented, route-oriented, and distribution-oriented sub-branding. As many of the examples below clearly illustrate, the three are not mutually exclusive.[23]

1   **Product-oriented sub-branding.** Many airlines sub-brand their premium services - Virgin Atlantic's Upper Class, Singapore Airlines' Raffles Class, or United's Connoisseur Class, for example. This is particularly true on long-haul routes, but there are also examples in short-haul markets - such as British Midland's Diamond Class and British Airways' Club Europe. A surprising number of the airlines offering long-haul first class service do not clearly sub-brand it, even when strenuous efforts are being made to create a distinct business class sub-brand. Relatively few carriers have made serious attempts to sub-brand their economy class products. (Where single class service is all that is on offer, this might not matter of course.) TWA upgraded long-haul economy and sub-branded it Comfort Class in 1993. In the same year, Cyprus Airways upgraded its inflight product and introduced the Apollo and Aphrodite sub-brands for business and economy classes respectively. By far the leading exponent of product sub-branding to date has been British Airways, which has separately branded the following (in addition to its low-cost intra-European subsidiary).
    • Intercontinental products: Concorde, First, Club World (business class), and World Traveller (economy class).[24]
    • Intra-European products: Club Europe and Euro Traveller.
    • UK trunk: SuperShuttle.
    • Regional: British Airways Express.

      [E]ach has a key brand proposition and a set of clearly stated product specifications for preflight, inflight, and on-arrival service. To provide additional focus on product, pricing, and marketing communications, responsibility for managing and developing each brand is assigned to a brand management team. Through internal training and external communication, staff and passengers alike are kept informed of the characteristics of each brand.[25]

When an airline with a high-quality image wants to discount or to offer something less than its full-service product to a particular target segment, care is required to ensure that the perception of value that has been nurtured in the minds of other customers or users of other products is not diluted. Sub-branding can sometimes help. Shuttle by United, for example, was separately sub-branded to distinguish its value proposition from that offered by the mainline carrier: the initial purposes were to lure customers away from Southwest with an offer clearly distinguishable from one they had already rejected from mainline United, to prepare a defense against future incursions into United's network by low-cost challengers, and also to create in the minds of mainline customers a distinction between what they were buying and what Shuttle customers were buying. This initiative was one of a number of 'low-cost' airline-within-an-airline ventures that appeared in the United States in the early and mid-1990s, aimed in most cases at serving price-sensitive segments without eroding the consumer franchise expressly built around hub-based, full-service systems.

The dangers inherent in sub-branding products which diverge markedly from the image of the master-brand but are nonetheless closely associated with it include:

- failure to make a distinct service-price offer, instead selling simply a detuned version of the full-service product at deeply discounted prices;
- cannibalization of the mainline client base; and
- failure to create a clear sub-brand identity for the new venture, so risking confusion and alienation amongst customers and staff, as happened in the case of Continental Lite. Both the United Shuttle and Delta Express endeavoured to learn from Continental's mistakes. Attaching the benefits offered by an established master-brand - benefits such as safety and reliability, for example - to a sub-brand offering a radically different value proposition is nonetheless always going to require deft brand management if dilution of other master-brand psychological attributes is to be avoided. The transformation of EuroBelgian into Virgin Express in 1996 raised issues regarding use of the high-quality Virgin master-brand in conjunction with a low-cost/low-frills sub-brand. Despite the potential for confusion in customers' minds as a result of their very different positioning, it was felt that common use of the Virgin

name was justified by shared characteristics such as value for money and a propensity both to take considered commercial gambles and 'tweak' the establishment. On the other hand, Virgin did at that time terminate its franchise agreement with short-haul Irish airline CityJet because it saw a potential conflict between that carrier's full-service product and the no-frills Virgin Express identity.

2   **Route-oriented sub-branding.** There are two broad types:
- some airlines separately sub-brand certain categories of route (variously defined by reference to traffic density and/or length of haul and/or the nature of demand), often using affiliates or franchisees. This is particularly common on thin regional routes, where the 'Express', 'Eagle', 'Connection' and similar sub-brand identities created by US majors were early examples. The approach has since been copied widely in Europe by operations bearing 'Commuter', 'CityLine', 'Express' and similarly evocative names. Further up the scale of traffic densities, Singapore Airlines uses SilkAir on relatively thin intra-Asian routes, and several airlines use affiliates to fly some of their leisure routes (e.g. KLM uses Martinair, Japan Airlines uses Japan Air Charter (JAZ), and Lufthansa uses Condor). British Airways has also attempted to create sub-brand images for short-haul jet services operated out of London Gatwick and larger British provincial centres;
- individual routes or limited route-groups (as opposed to general categories of route) are very occasionally given specific brands. This has been done in respect of shuttles in the United Kingdom, Canada, Brazil, Scandinavia, France, and the northeastern United States, for example.[26] In 1994, Japan Airlines turned its Hawaiian services over to low-cost affiliate JAZ and at the same time branded the routes 'Super Resort Express', regaling aircraft with tropical imagery and introducing inflight service to match. Linked by ownership, Aéromexico, Mexicana, and AéroPeru have co-branded flights from the United States through Mexico to South America as 'Alas de America'.

3   **Distribution-oriented sub-branding.** As well as sub-branding products and/or routes, a very small number of carriers have taken to sub-branding the direct release of surplus seats into the retail market (rather than through consolidators or other wholesalers). British Airways, for example, has sub-branded as 'World Offers' the periodic release of surplus seat inventory. Not only does this limit image dilution, but these two words in themselves help convey three marketing messages: global network coverage ('World'), low cost ('Offers'), and good value (inherent in the positioning of the British Airways master-brand).[27] In the mid-1990s, Delta began sub-branding as Escape Plan '96 (then '97 etc.) the release to FFP members of

deeply discounted, late-availability weekend space out of its Atlanta and Cincinnati hubs.

Air transport services: cargo sub-brands The majority of combination carriers have been left behind by the branding exploits of integrators such as FedEx, UPS, and DHL in the express package business. Even in express and regular heavy freight markets there are very few airlines that have successfully established brand preference amongst significant shippers. When airlines do make the attempt to brand cargo products, it is not uncommon for much of their volume anyway to be sold through forwarders on a commissionable basis - forwarders who in some cases are unenthusiastic about retailing branded products.[28] Serious efforts have been made to turn British Airways World Cargo into an effective sub-brand, and a small number of other sub-brands (e.g. KLM Cargo and Lufthansa Cargo) and corporate master-brands (e.g. Cargolux) have also been successfully established.[29] In general, however, this is not a field of endeavour in which branding has yet made much headway.

Other services: sub-brands or independent master-brands? Many airlines now have affiliates that are actually or potentially substantial players in their own markets for services other than air transport. Some are clearly sub-brands trading off their places in hierarchies each topped by an established master-brand (e.g. Lufthansa Technik), whilst others are or are becoming separate master-brands in their own right (e.g. Sabre and Gate Gourmet). The distinction is arguably semantic, but the importance of successfully branding such ventures - particularly those participating in increasingly crowded markets - is not. Interestingly, when Swissair corporatized its IT division in 1996 the decision was taken to cut it adrift from the master-brand by naming it 'atraxis'.[30]

Brand management

This is a skill that is still very much under development in most of the airline industry. Its essence is to understand and use the 'brand platform' - that is, the elements and attributes of the brand which make it unique - in order to manage and satisfy customers' expectations, and to maximize opportunities for earning incremental revenue through brand extension. In an industry able to offer relatively few qualitative functional differences between equivalent products, a distinct brand - or possibly in the case of larger airlines, a hierarchy of sub-brands below a corporate master-brand - is increasingly being seen as an important tool for influencing the purchasing behaviour of customers - customers who are being given ever more degrees of freedom in their choice of products.

Brand equity At the beginning of this section, a 'brand' was identified as an intangible asset. The value of this asset will depend upon how powerful it is - whether a particular brand simply provokes awareness, or whether it enjoys brand preference or, better still, brand loyalty. The following four variables are sometimes used to diagnose the power of a brand.

- **Weight.** The influence of a particular brand on its market. This measure is more than mere market share.
- **Length.** The success of the brand to reach across the market or several market places, or its potential to do so.
- **Breadth.** The variety of ages, consumer types and countries in which the brand is recognised.
- **Depth.** The degree of commitment to the brand, including the intimacy consumers feel with the brand.[31]

Effective management of a powerful brand creates what is widely referred to as 'brand equity'. Aaker has succinctly defined this as '...a set of assets and liabilities linked to a brand's name and symbol that add to or subtract from the value provided by a product or service...'[32] He goes on to identify the components of brand equity, all of which need to be actively managed:

- perceived quality;
- brand awareness;
- brand identity (i.e. the personality and character associated with the brand); and
- brand loyalty (i.e. resistance to switching where an alternative exists - resistance that might be based on preference, habit, or unacceptable switching costs).

Brand equity can erect barriers to market entry which potential competitors will find expensive and time-consuming to surmount. It can be leveraged through 'brand extension'. Leveraging brand equity to support a launch - or a relaunch - is likely to be much less expensive than launching a 'brand new' product; the proviso is, of course, that the brand equity being leveraged has something relevant to say about the particular new product.

Strong brand equity provides room to manoeuvre as an airline changes its value proposition over time in response to evolving market circumstances. Such changes might be for better or for worse from the customers' point of view, although these days the belief is widely propagated that only improvements to customer value can be contemplated. Were a change to be particularly marked, the airline concerned would in effect be repositioning its brand. (Repositioning can also happen independently of changes to the service-price offer, as when a brand's image shifts without the reality of the offer changing.)

Brand and product life cycles It was explained in chapter 15 of Volume One that brands have life cycles. If properly managed, these can be long. The emotional appeal of any particular brand needs to be kept in tune with shifts in consumer values - shifts such as those distinguishing the values widespread in developed economies in the 1990s from those of the previous decade, for example. In 1996, Southwest started promoting itself as 'Southwest Airlines: A Symbol of Freedom', highlighting one of the principal benefits being offered to its customers; whilst remaining consistent with the company's previous theme of being 'the' low-fare airline, this subtle shift in emphasis moved the focus of what was being offered away from low price as an attribute in itself and towards the benefit - the individual empowerment to travel - derived from that attribute. The shift was consistent with the growing importance of individual differences and personal choice to which reference was made during the discussion of service conceptualization in chapter 6 of this volume.

At a more functional level, brands frequently outlive the individual service concepts offered under their name. Thus, Cathay Pacific's Marco Polo business class has been around since the early 1980s (and the trade name even longer than that), but the underlying product it describes has been reformulated and relaunched on several occasions. British Airways' long-haul business class was relaunched as Super Club and then Club World in 1984 and 1988 respectively, and Club World itself was relaunched in 1993 and 1996. Super Club offered a wider seat than its predecessor, but other than that was largely a rebranding effort; the initial launch of Club World was both a rebranding and an attempt to redesign and sub-brand the entire travel experience in line with customers' needs and perceptions at that time; the relaunched Club World in 1993 retained its sub-brand identity but enhanced the service concept described by that identity, introducing new seats and videos to the inflight experience, ground amenities such as Fast-Track and arrivals lounges at some airports, and an advertising message promoting refuge from the daily pressures of business.

Product life cycles are becoming shorter in the airline business, as in other industries. A 'refresh rate' of once every three to five years is now considered desirable by some leading exponents of airline product sub-branding. British Airways regularly relaunches the service concepts underlying its sub-brands. Such proactive management of service concepts and sub-brands requires almost continuous market research and product investment - something which relatively few competitors have the resources to match. In 1996, for example, the British carrier began a £500 million customer service investment programme with a £115 million relaunch of First and Club World. American Airlines announced that year that it would be spending $400 million on improvements to its international business class product. Air France was at the same time taking the relatively unusual step of upgrading both its first and business class products under the shared L'Espace sub-brand, differentiating between them on the basis of the number of degrees of seat recline available in each: L'Espace 180 and L'Espace 127 respectively. In 1997, Delta launched a $100 million programme to upgrade its international business class.

Alliance branding An emerging challenge, noted in chapter 5, is the management of brand equity across networks of allied entities that could include a core airline, special-purpose units or subsidiaries, franchisees, and code-sharing partners. Although developments are still at an early stage, several broad approaches to the alliance branding conundrum can be identified.

1   The merging of brand identities and the delivery of common, largely indistinguishable products. The earliest exponents of this approach were KLM and Northwest, and its risks in the absence of a complete corporate merger were highlighted when theses two carriers started a wrangle over governance issues in 1995.

2   The subsuming of other brand identities into a dominant partner's master-brand, with the smaller 'partners' operating perhaps in geographical and/or product niches as sub-branded entities. The clearest manifestation of this at the present time is in the field of franchising. If this trend is to spread, master-brands will need to be managed in such a way that they have 'sufficient global appeal to allow franchisees to distribute [them] worldwide'.[33]

3   The maintenance of separate, regionally strong master-brand identities alongside the master-brand of a dominant (or, at least, influential) shareholder. Leveraging the brand equity created by both British Airways and Qantas, for example, into something beneficial to both - and doing so against the background of an agreement, reflected in the Australian carrier's articles of association, that stipulates retention of the Qantas brand name - will stretch even the undoubted brand management skills of British Airways. What is likely is that common sub-brands will ultimately be used to bridge the gap created by separate master-brands - but this is speculation, and it begs all sorts of questions in respect of corporate culture that no alliance has yet begun to tackle seriously.

    Because of its relatively strong recognition in France, the Air Liberté brand was retained by British Airways when it acquired the carrier and merged it with existing French subsidiary TAT. In due course, however, franchising - or at the very least introduction of some closer linkage between Air Liberté and the British Airways master-brand - seems a likely development.

4 The 'lite branding' of a code-sharing partner's presence on a route operated by another carrier, through signage, announcements, the presence of uniformed staff on the ground and in the air, and possibly also superficial changes to items of decor such as cabin panels (as Continental and Alitalia have done, for instance). Naked (as opposed to common-product) code-sharing raises particularly difficult issues with regard to the possible dilution of brand equity. This is as true in the case of highly publicized, comprehensive, 'global' alliances as in more focused, market-specific arrangements. The problem can be complicated where the code-sharing partner has a significantly weaker brand identity than the operating partner - a good example being the operation of several intra-European trunk routes out of Brussels by Virgin Express on behalf of Sabena.

5 The branding of the alliance itself. Delta, Singapore Airlines, and Swissair were amongst the first to form a global alliance, and they did so under the name 'Global Excellence'. Delta then went on to form the 'Atlantic Excellence' partnership with Swissair, Sabena, and Austrian. In 1997, Air Canada, Lufthansa, SAS, Thai, and United announced that their cooperation in areas such as sales, frequent flyer programmes, recognition of high-value customers, lounge access, code-sharing, and network management generally would henceforth be branded under the name 'Star'; the arrangement was to be joined later by Varig and several others. None of these initiatives has to date resulted in establishment of clearly identifiable brands and, although some efforts to create consistent levels of service amongst partners have been made, common products have yet to materialize. Nonetheless, whilst skeptics abound, others see such developments as incipient signs of the emergence of truly global megacarriers.[34]

Whatever the approach taken, when large, heavily branded airlines - whose interests may perhaps encompass subsidiaries, affiliates, and alliance partners - purport to offer a 'seamless' travel experience, a key challenge is to ensure service consistency. Total assurance is impossible, of course. Nonetheless, to attain acceptably high standards of consistency, heavy investments in staff training and also close attention to corporate culture are required.

Conclusions on branding Branding is now seen by a growing number of airlines as a discipline on which they have to catch up. Successfully changing a brand image - or, alternatively, creating a brand out of what starts as little more than a simple identity - is not easy, but it can be done. Continental achieved reasonable success in the mid-90s, building its Business First brand and rebuilding its overall corporate reputation on the rubble of what, in marketing terms, had been a shambolic decade. Around the same time, Air France set about creating a clearly-defined and internationally appealing brand personality out of its 'Frenchness' - an attribute that had previously been little more than a corporate identity tag.

The preferences which drive brand loyalty come from many different sources, but at their heart will often lie a service concept relevant to the segment in question, clear marketing communications, effective service delivery, and a perception of good value in the minds of consumers. Large incumbents usually have sufficient resources - although not always appropriate skills - to build brand equity, and once built it can be a barrier preventing entrants from eroding market share without incurring high costs.[35]

What can be achieved is dictated to a large extent by available skills and resources, but also by strategic intent - the will to 'stretch'.[36] Nonetheless, even when it has been successfully built, brand equity can be fragile if mismanaged - as Pan Am proved.[37]

> ...whenever brand names are neglected, what is known as 'the commodity slide' begins. This is because the physical characteristics of products are becoming increasingly difficult to differentiate and easy to emulate. In situations like these, one finds that purchasing decisions tend to be made on the basis of price or availability...the process of decay from brand to commodity [takes place as] the distinctive values of the brand are eroded over time...[38]

Conclusion

Figure 10.1 illustrates a model of a service-profit chain proposed by Heskett et al. It relates several of the factors discussed in this and earlier chapters to employee satisfaction, customer loyalty, and profitability.

Customer loyalty is now commonly linked in the literature to employee loyalty. Heskett has expressed the linkage in the following way.

> Market share quality often results directly from efforts to build the satisfaction and loyalty of service workers who are in direct contact with customers. Employee satisfaction results from initiatives to match attitudes and skills with jobs, train and recognise people, rethink work, and provide technological support to increase the capability to deliver results to customers. It clearly requires attention to both operating and human resource management issues, once again a bridging of functions.[39]

Operating Strategy and Service Delivery System

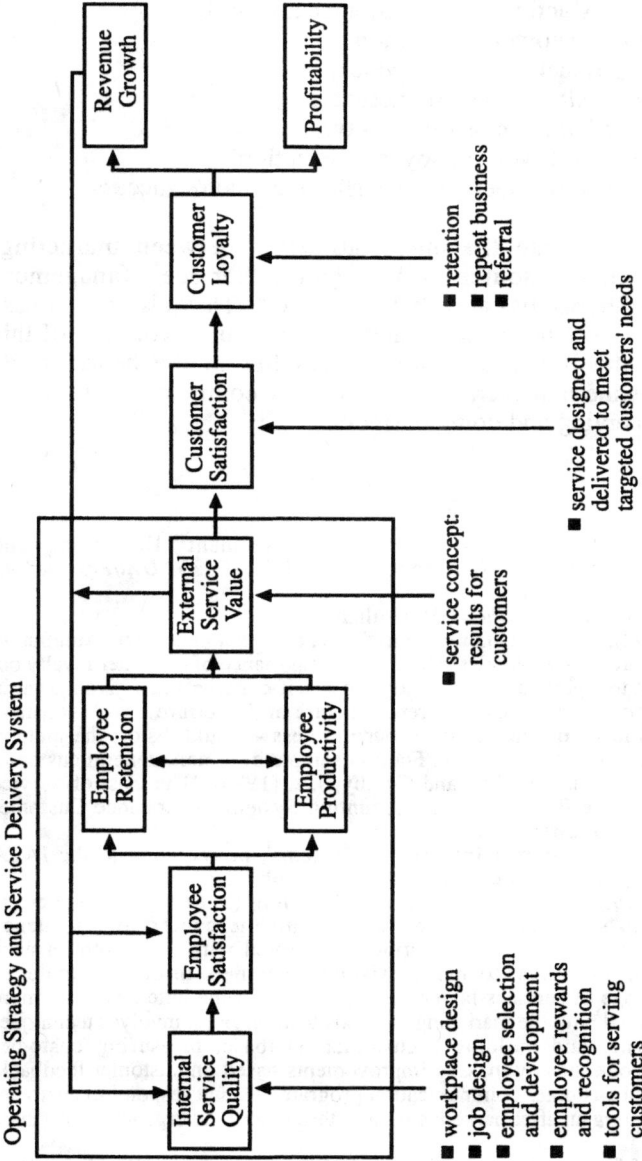

Figure 10.1 : The links in the service-profit chain
Reprinted by permission of *Harvard Business Review*. From "Putting the service-profit chain to work", by Heskett. J.L., Jones, T.O., Loveman G.W., Sasser, W.E. Jr., and Schlesinger, L.A., March - April 1994. Copyright © 1994 by the President and Fellows of Harvard College; all rights reserved.

Extending this relationship, Heskett et al have summarized the causal links in their 'service-profit' chain.[40]

1. Customer loyalty drives profitability and growth.
2. Customer satisfaction drives customer loyalty.
3. Value drives customer satisfaction.
4. Employee productivity drives value.
5. Employee loyalty drives productivity.
6. Employee satisfaction drives loyalty.
7. Internal quality drives employee satisfaction.
8. Top management leadership underlies the chain's success.

These points encapsulate the interrelationship between marketing, operations, and human resources - Lovelock's 'Service Management Trinity', to which reference has already been made.[41] They also encompass many of the most important themes running through both volumes of this book. Mastery of the linkages between them lies at the heart of the challenge facing airline managers as their industry continues its transition to new ways of perceiving and doing business.

Notes

1   Heskett, J.L. (1995), 'Strategic Services Management: Examining and Understanding It', in Glynn, W.J. and Barnes, J.G. (Eds.), *Understanding Services,* John Wiley & Sons, p. 453.
2   Peters, T. (1988), *Thriving on Chaos,* Macmillan.
3   Jenkins, K.J. (1992), 'Service Quality in the Skies', *Business Quarterly,* Autumn, p. 13. These figures are a valuable illustration of the importance of customer loyalty but they do apply just to a particular airline serving specific markets at a given point in time. In Europe, for example, the different structure of the leisure travel industry - notably the importance of the inclusive tour business - would distort the picture, although not necessarily the principle. For an example of a more general customer valuation model, see: Barnes, J.G. and Cumby, J.A. (1995), 'The Cost of Service Quality: Extending the Boundaries of Accounting Systems to Enhance Customer Value', in Glynn and Barnes, op. cit.
4   Thornett, B. (1997), 'Customer Information Systems', presentation to the IATA *Information Management 97* conference, Atlanta, 4th-8th May.
5   Bateson, J.E.G. (1995), *Managing Services Marketing* (3rd edition), Dryden, p. 457. Bateson also sets relationship marketing into the context of 'frequency marketing' and 'aftermarketing'. The former, concerned with the 'depth' of each customer relationship, aims 'to make existing customers more profitable by broadening the range of services bought...' (ibid., p. 456); the latter, hitherto more commonly associated with the marketing of goods than services, involves techniques such as 'identifying and building a customer database, measuring customer satisfaction, and continuously making improvements based on customer feedback, establishing formal customer communication programmes that respond to customer feedback, and creating an aftermarketing culture throughout the organization'. (Ibid., p. 457.)
6   For an account of how 'customer equity' might be measured, see: Blattberg, R.C. and Deighton, J. (1996), *Harvard Business Review,* July-August.
7   Band, W.A. (1991), *Creating Value for Customers,* John Wiley & Sons, p. 119.

8   DeSouza, G. (1992), 'Designing a Customer-retention Plan', *The Journal of Business Strategy*, March/April.
9   CAA (1994), *Airline Competition on European Long-Haul Routes*, CAP639.
10   Stephenson, F. and Fox, R. (1987), 'Corporate Attitudes Toward Frequent-flyer Programs', *Transportation Journal*, Vol. 27, No. 1.
11   Pavaux, J. (1995), 'What the Demand Will Be Like', in Pavaux, J. (Ed.), *Air Transport Horizon 2020*, ITA, pp. 57-59.
12   *OAG Business Travel Lifestyle Survey 1997*, cited in *Airline Business*, July 1997, p. 67. 'Data are based on the views of 5,250 business travellers worldwide. Their countries of residence are USA 17 per cent, UK 14 per cent, Australia 12 per cent, Italy 12 per cent, France 10 per cent, Germany 10 per cent, Japan 9 per cent, Hong Kong 8 per cent, and Singapore 8 per cent.' (Ibid.)
13   LatinPass is a joint FFP launched by several Latin American carriers in 1995. (See: Nuutinen, H. (1995), 'A New Continent of Privatized Airlines', *The Avmark Aviation Economist*, December.) Passages is a joint programme established by a number of East and Southeast Asian airlines (some of which are not, in fact, particularly 'small' in output terms). Joint or shared programmes may have disadvantages, however; one of the most obvious is the potential accessibility of proprietary customer information, and another is the question of maintaining a carrier's specific brand identity and corporate image in dealings with members. The first is generally surmountable (e.g. through use of a fulfillment house for mailings), whereas the second can be more troublesome.
14   In the early days of the FFP phenomenon it was in fact common for the largest airlines themselves, including United and American, to affiliate foreign carriers to their FFPs in order to gain access to markets and to attractive award destinations beyond their own, still primarily domestic, networks. More recently in Europe, the European Commission has on several occasions made approval of a merger or marketing alliance conditional on, inter alia, the dominant carrier accepting affected competitors into its FFP.
15   Tax authorities might ultimately have a voice in the attractiveness of individual awards. Although taxing FFP benefits has been widely discussed for over a decade, little has yet happened. However, Sweden's announcement of its intention to do just that from 1997 may prove to have been a harbinger of things to come.
16   Whether this is a factor, or whether in the event of competing memberships the airline choice criterion reverts to product attributes (such as convenient departures, frequencies and so on) is an interesting question.
17   It nonetheless needs to be kept in mind that, 'Brands don't create wealth; customers do. Despite the fashionable concern with brand power, few would dispute that highly visible brands are just one instrument among many with which to build customer equity; they are a magnet to attract new customers and an anchor to hold existing customers. Brands are never more important than the customers they reach.' (Blattberg and Deighton, op. cit., p. 143.)
18   Van Mesdag, M. (1991), 'What Needs Changing in Brand Strategies?', *Marketing Intelligence & Planning*, Vol. 9, No. 7. For example, one of several reasons why Lufthansa terminated its reduced-service 'Express' brand on domestic routes in the early 1990s was reported to have been the confusion created amongst customers who failed to distinguish between the 'mainline' and 'Express' service concepts.
19   Lannon, J. (1991), 'Developing Brand Strategies Across Borders', *Marketing and Research Today*, August. Evidence of the emotional appeal that brands are capable of exerting can be seen in luggage tags displayed on bags and briefcases to signal use of what is perceived to be a high-quality product.
20   Cronshaw, M. and Thompson, D.J. (1991), *Sources of Rent and Airline Deregulation in Europe*, Centre for Business Strategy Working Paper, London Business School.
21   See, for example: Kay, J. (1995), *Foundations of Corporate Success*, Oxford University Press, p. 251.

22   For most small airlines and quite a few large ones as well, the question of sub-brands is moot. If a brand exists at all, it is in these cases the corporate master-brand alone. Nonetheless, smaller airlines can certainly build a high-quality corporate brand without going to the expense of developing sub-brands; this was true of Emirates in its early days, for example.

23   The discussion of geographical and product scope in chapter 1 made it apparent that there is often considerable overlap between these two dimensions in particular. Nonetheless, for analytical purposes it can still be useful to think in terms of products and routes as separate, even if very closely linked, identities.

24   In fact, the very expression 'economy class' was believed by British Airways to have been part of the problem that sub-branding needed to address. Market research in the late 1980s showed that a large proportion of the increasingly important leisure market had an unclear picture of the carrier's products, felt it to be largely a businessman's airline that was too expensive and unapproachable, and in particular resented being classed as 'economy' passengers. This led in 1990 to the £70 million relaunch of economy class as Euro Traveller and World Traveller, the purpose being to generate loyalty and firmer yields in (what was henceforth to be referred to as) 'the main cabin' by making the airline's core values more appealing to this segment of passengers. The primary product label for tour products became 'Leisure Traveller', replacing separately marketed and distributed City Breaks, Poundstretcher and Speedbird Holidays. Progress in establishing some of the brand identities appears to have been slower than anticipated: the word 'economy' was originally intended to have been eliminated from signage within 18 months, for example, but several years later it was still clearly in evidence at check-in counters - presumably to avoid confusion amongst infrequent travellers unaware that they had become 'Euro' or 'World' travellers.

25   Lovelock, C.H. (1996), *Services Marketing* (3rd edition), Prentice Hall, p. 323.

26   Not all are true shuttles insofar as seats on some are not guaranteed without a reservation. For example, La Navette services introduced by Air France in the mid-90s between Paris Orly on the one hand and Marseilles, Nice, and Toulouse on the other have no back-up crews or aircraft on standby to fly extra sectors in the event of unaccommodated demand (although back-ups are available in case of a need to replace unavailable aircraft or crews). Quite aside from the additional costs of the back-ups that would be necessary to support a guaranteed seat policy, there is the question of slot availability for unscheduled extra flights at peak times.

27   In 1996, British Airways started trial use of its World Wide Web site as a supplementary channel through which to distribute 'World Offers' seats.

28   Shaw, S. (1993), *Effective Air Freight Marketing,* Pitman, p. 95.

29   British Airways World Cargo had a spotty record for consistent service delivery in some markets up until the mid-90s. London Heathrow operations were particularly troublesome prior to the opening of the carrier's new cargo centre. A major turnaround effort is in progress at the time of writing.

30   The future of atraxis came under close scrutiny in 1997, with IT outsourcing by Swissair a serious possibility.

31   Interbrand Group, cited in: Moules, J. (1997), 'Brand Warfare', *Information Strategy,* April, p. 28.

32   Aaker, D.A. (1995), *Strategic Market Management* (4th edition), John Wiley & Sons, p. 207. The same author has produced an interesting article describing how brand equity might be measured in practice: Aaker, D.A. (1996), 'Measuring Brand Equity Across Products and Markets', *California Management Review,* Vol. 38, No. 3.

33   Jones, L. (1996), 'Keeping Up Appearances', *Airline Business,* October.
     An interesting early example of cross-border brand extension taking place at the time of writing is provided by TAM-Mercosur. Originally the Paraguayan flag carrier Lapsa, the airline was privatized in 1995 and the following year (after a spell under the management of a consortium led by Ecuadorean carrier Saeta) brought under the direct and indirect control of interests associated with Brazilian group TAM. It then

became one of several airlines operating under the umbrella of the TAM master-brand, notably:

- Transportes Aéreos Regional - TAM Regional: a primarily short-haul carrier lying at the heart of a group which takes the acronym 'TAM' from one of its earliest operations - Táxi Aéreo Marilia;
- Transportes Aéreos Meridionais - TAM Meridional: a Brazilian subsidiary established to operate domestic trunk routes and services to the United States; and
- Transportes Aéreos de Mercosur - TAM Mercosur: formerly Lapsa.

34 As noted in chapter 5, the future of Global Excellence is at the time of writing in doubt because of Singapore Airlines' withdrawal and linkage with Star member Lufthansa.

All Nippon and Cathay Pacific have been separately linked to Lufthansa and United respectively, but the talks at this time are being described as bilateral in nature rather than precursors to the two carriers joining Star. (All Nippon anyway has existing links with Delta and with Delta's Atlantic Excellence partner, Austrian; the Japanese carrier currently appears to prefer an ad hoc, rather than a more comprehensive and all-embracing, approach to alliance relationships - although this may eventually change.) Whilst one reason for the 'looseness' of the Star Alliance as described at its launch was doubtless to avoid the scrutiny by competition authorities that the much more closely integrated American Airlines/British Airways proposal was then undergoing, it would be premature at this stage to interpret what appears to be primarily an effort in systematized cooperation as a nascent megacarrier with its own distinct brand.

35 Holloway, S. (1997), *Straight and Level: Practical Airline Economics*, Ashgate, chapter 2.

36 These concepts are explained in Volume One, chapter 15.

37 The residual strength of the Pan Am brand was, however, a major factor in the launch of the low-cost/full-service start-up which began operations under that name out of New York in 1996. (See: Walker, K. (1997), 'It's All In The Name', *Airline Business*, March.)

38 McDonald, M.H.B. (1989), *Marketing Plans* (2nd edition), Butterworth-Heinemann, p. 83.

39 Heskett (1995), op. cit., p. 453.

40 Heskett, J.L., Jones, T.O., Loveman, G.W., Sasser, W.E. Jr., and Schlesinger, L.A. (1994), 'Putting the Service-Profit Chain to Work', *Harvard Business Review*, March-April, quoted in Lovelock, op. cit., p. 510.

41 Lovelock, op. cit., chapter 13.

11 Conclusion

Painful though it is likely to be for some airlines and their workforces, the transition which the two volumes of this book have been examining is in fact a restructuring of the industry which - if allowed to run its course - will lead eventually to a marked change in the composition of firms supplying the world's output of air transport services. Market forces, left unconstrained in their pursuit of efficiency, have the potential to alter both the number and geographical dimensions of these firms. That institutional rigidity will in fact slow the transition was made clear in chapter 3 of Volume One. Nonetheless, powerful pressures for change are emerging from all four of the environments identified in the first volume. Examples of these pressures include:

- sociopolitical environment: the growing momentum of regulatory reform, which is materializing in parallel with a widening perception amongst stakeholders that airlines should be profitable commercial enterprises rather than just tools of public policy;
- economic environment: the shifting global balance of economic power, which is taking place within a context of simultaneous globalization and regionalization;
- technological environment: the constant development and rapid diffusion of new production and marketing technologies; and
- competitive environment: the changing relationships between many airlines and their suppliers and distributors, the worsening of infrastructural constraints at key points in the global air transport system, the enfranchisement of increasingly demanding and knowledgeable customers with greater choice, and the intensification of competition for the loyalty of those customers.

These and other changes are confronting airlines with new challenges, requiring in particular more operational and commercial flexibility in order to accommodate the structural adjustment being mandated by evolving demand, supply, and institutional circumstances. Many of those circumstances represent marked discontinuities in historic trends, so inhibiting the use of simple extrapolation as a tool for forecasting the future of what are anyway becoming more complex and turbulent environments. The structural adjustment in the way business is done in air transport and supplier markets - the 'transition' from which this book draws its title - is proving painful for some industry participants because of their different starting points in terms of efficiency, adaptability, institutional support, and infrastructural or geographical advantage. It is also complicated by the fact that some of the environments which are giving rise to changes necessitating adjustment are, at the same time, in other ways inhibiting adjustment. Two prime examples of this dialectic can be found in the sociopolitical environment:

- aeropolitics: bilateral relationships in a number of key air transport markets have been or are being liberalized, yet liberalization is uneven and its encouragement of restructuring in pursuit of greater economic efficiency on the supply side of the industry is weakened by restrictions on cross-border ownership of airlines, as well as by the distorting effects of public subsidies still being given to some state-owned carriers;
- competition laws: a growing number of air transport markets are becoming less subject to industry-specific commercial regulation and increasingly subject to general competition laws from which they have previously been fully or partially exempted, but the application of these laws is sometimes slow, less than fully transparent, and prone to invite jurisdictional conflict whenever there is a significant international dimension involved.

In Volume One we discussed many of the environmental changes - external and internal - which are promoting structural adjustment within the airline industry. Because this transition is uneven as a result of the variable environmental circumstances and different starting positions facing individual airlines, some of the alternative strategies discussed in Part One of Volume Two are not yet open - or, perhaps, not yet relevant - to every carrier. As the transition unfolds, these strategies - together with the new ways of looking at their implementation and outcome discussed in Parts Two and Three of the second volume - will become increasingly relevant. The art of flexible, customer-focused strategic management - the lens through which the two volumes have examined the industry's current transition - will also become increasingly relevant.

For Product Safety Concerns and Information please contact our EU
representative GPSR@taylorandfrancis.com
Taylor & Francis Verlag GmbH, Kaufingerstraße 24, 80331 München, Germany